Running Randomized Evaluations

D0706272

Running Randomized Evaluations

A PRACTICAL GUIDE

RACHEL GLENNERSTER *and* KUDZAI TAKAVARASHA

PRINCETON UNIVERSITY PRESS

Princeton and Oxford

Published by Princeton University Press, 41 William Street, Princeton, New Jersey 08540
In the United Kingdom: Princeton University Press, 6 Oxford Street, Woodstock, Oxfordshire
OX20 1TW

press.princeton.edu

Cover design by Leah E. Horgan

Library of Congress Cataloging-in-Publication Data

Glennerster, Rachel.
Running randomized evaluations : a practical guide / Rachel Glennerster
and Kudzai Takavarasha.
      pages   cm
   Includes bibliographical references and index.
   ISBN 978-0-691-15924-9 (hardcover : alk. paper) — ISBN 978-0-691-15927-0
(pbk. : alk. paper)
   1. Evaluation research (Social action programs)   2. Social sciences—Research.
I. Takavarasha, Kudzai, 1973–   II. Title.
H61.G5544 2013
001.4′34—dc23
                                                            2013014882

British Library Cataloging-in-Publication Data is available

This book has been composed in Minion Pro with ITC Franklin Gothic Display by
Princeton Editorial Associates Inc., Scottsdale, Arizona

10 9 8 7 6 5 4 3 2 1

CONTENTS

PREFACE

Over the past 10 years, there has been a dramatic increase in the quantity and quality of rigorous impact evaluations that have tested the effectiveness of specific approaches to reducing poverty from Britain to Burkina Faso. Randomized impact evaluations have enjoyed a particularly dramatic increase in popularity. Twenty years ago, few randomized evaluations were carried out by governments (outside the United States), international agencies, or nongovernmental organizations—except as a way to test the effectiveness of medicines or vaccines. Today hundreds of randomized evaluations are being undertaken by all sorts of different organizations and on virtually every subject of importance to policy, including education, health, governance, the environment, and empowerment.

These randomized impact evaluations are improving our understanding of the fundamental processes that underlie the persistence of poverty and the pathways out of it. Each evaluation answers some questions and raises new ones, the next building on the last, successively adding to our knowledge of what works, knowledge we need to design better programs and more effectively fight poverty.

We have written this book for those who want to help generate a rigorous evidence base on ways to reduce poverty wherever it exists in the world by running (or taking part in) rigorous impact evaluations. Running a randomized evaluation requires making hundreds of practical decisions and constant trade-offs, especially in resource-poor settings where the best-laid plans can be quickly overtaken by events. Much of this book draws on the practical experience of the Abdul Latif Jameel Poverty Action Lab (J-PAL), a research network based at the Massachusetts Institute of Technology with affiliated research centers and researchers at universities around the world.

The camaraderie within J-PAL means that every publication, conference, or talk has many contributors, including those who never attract the limelight. So many people have provided input and advice on this book that it is almost disingenuous to isolate just two authors. Pascaline Dupas and Michael Kremer have answered hundreds of our questions and commented on numerous drafts over the several years it has taken to write this book. They are also responsible for getting us into the randomization business in the first place. Marc Shotland gave valuable input and advice on virtually every chapter and is the creator of the online tools that accompany this book. Alison Cappellieri created the appendix, glossary, and bibliography and copyedited the entire book. Claire Walsh fact checked all mentions of existing studies. Leah Horgan designed the figures and the cover, and John Floretta gave detailed input on Chapter 5. Ben Feigenberg and Ben Marx checked the technical precision of our nontechnical language, especially in Chapters 4, 6, and 8, and Ben Marx generated all the power graphs. Catlin Tulloch and Anna Yalouris helped with the examples on cost-effectiveness. Michael Kremer and Ben Olken patiently helped us work through some of the tougher econometric issues. We are deeply grateful for the detailed comments of many anonymous referees and are particularly grateful to Guido Imbens and Jörn-Steffen Pischke for their very thorough and thoughtful reviews, which led to a much improved book. Finally, without Mary Ann Bates this book would never have seen the light of day. Her fresh eyes, good judgment, creative rewrites, and merciless blue pencil whipped the book into shape.

None of the work described in this book would have been possible without the dedication of all the implementing organizations that opened their programs up to evaluation. They spent countless hours discussing what should be tested and how, figuring out how to bring an element of randomization into their programs, and advising on how different outcomes could be measured. They also demonstrated considerable courage, knowing that an evaluation might find that their programs did not work. The nongovernmental organizations and their leaders who were among the pioneers of this work in developing countries deserve special mention: Chip Bury at International Child Support Africa, Neelima Khetan at Seva Mandir, and Madav Chavan and Rukmini Banerji at Pratham.

ABBREVIATIONS AND ACRONYMS

3ie	International Initiative for Impact Evaluation
AHTS	Agricultural Household Tracking Survey
BMI	body mass index
CCT	conditional cash transfer
CDD	community-driven development
CDF	cumulative distribution function
DIME	Development Impact Evaluation
ETP	Extra Teacher Program
FICA	Federal Insurance Contributions Act
FMB	First Macro Bank
FWER	family-wise error rate
IAT	implicit association test
ICS	International Child Support
IID	independent and identically distributed
IRB	institutional review board
ITN	insecticide-treated (bed) net
ITT	intention-to-treat
J-PAL	Abdul Latif Jameel Poverty Action Lab
LLIN	long-lasting insecticide-treated net
MDE	minimum detectable effect
MFI	microfinance institutions
MIT	Massachusetts Institute of Technology
NERICA	New Rice for Africa
NGO	nongovernmental organization
NONIE	Network of Networks on Impact Evaluation

PACES	Programa de Ampliación de Cobertura de la Educación Secundaria
PAP	pre-analysis plan
PPP	purchasing power parity
PTA	parent–teacher association
RDD	regression discontinuity design
SBM	School-Based Management
SCA	structured community activity
SD	standard deviation
STI	sexually transmitted infection
SURE	seemingly unrelated regression estimation
TDA	tax deferred account
UP	Uttar Pradesh
VDC	village development committee
VEC	village education committee
WDR	World Development Report
WHO	World Health Organization

Running Randomized Evaluations

1 The Experimental Approach

This chapter provides an example of how a randomized evaluation can lead to large-scale change and provides a road map for an evaluation and for the rest of the book. The modules in this chapter are as follows:

MODULE 1.1: The Power of Randomized Evaluations
MODULE 1.2: A Randomized Evaluation from Start to Finish

MODULE 1.1 The Power of Randomized Evaluations

This module provides an example of how a small nongovernmental organization, by subjecting its program to rigorous evaluation, can generate evidence that can change the lives of millions of people.

In 1994 I went with Michael Kremer to visit the family he had lived with for a year in rural Kenya.[1] We met up with many of Michael's old friends, including Paul Lipeyah, who told us of the work he was doing with International Child Support (ICS) Africa, a nongovernmental organization (NGO) helping government schools in Busia, a neighboring district in Kenya's Western Province. Paul asked us what advice we might offer for improving the effectiveness of ICS programs. Could Michael help evaluate what they were doing? Michael suggested randomized evaluation: if ICS wanted to understand the impact of their programs, they could randomly choose the schools in which they worked and the order in which they phased in new programs.

---

1. The first-person reflections in this chapter are those of Rachel Glennerster.

Over the following years, ICS randomly evaluated many approaches to improving education outcomes, including providing additional inputs (classrooms, textbooks, teachers); reducing the cost of going to school (providing free school uniforms and school meals); and offering performance incentives (merit scholarships for girls, bonuses for teachers who attended school regularly). Sometimes the programs had the expected impact, and sometimes they did not. But ICS, in partnership with a growing number of researchers, kept innovating and testing in the areas of education, agriculture, women's empowerment, clean water, and health. Their knowledge of how to improve lives and how to evaluate programs kept growing.[2]

In 1997, ICS (in line with World Health Organization recommendations) phased in a program of treating children en masse for intestinal worms (such as hookworm and schistosomiasis). The results were astonishing. Deworming reduced the absenteeism of children in local schools by 25 percent, making it the most cost-effective program for increasing schooling that ICS had tried. Long-term results showed that women who had been dewormed as girls received more education and were more likely to grow cash crops, whereas men who had been dewormed worked 3.5 hours longer per week and were more likely to hold manufacturing jobs and earn higher wages.[3]

On the strength of the evidence, in 2009 Prime Minister Raila Odinga announced a program to deworm 3 million of Kenya's most at-risk children. In 2012 the program was expanded to include pre-school children, in part on the basis of further evidence of cogitative gains for young children from deworming.[4] In 2013, programs to deworm 40 million children are being implemented in Kenya and around the world. ICS could never have hoped to reach so many children with their own programs, and yet through the influence of their evaluation they have helped millions of children in Kenya—and around the world.

Since 1994 we have learned a lot about which programs work and which do not and also about how to run randomized evaluations.

2. The evaluation team at ICS eventually split off from ICS and became Innovations for Poverty Action, Kenya.

3. Studies of this program by Sarah Baird, Joan Hamory Hicks, Michael Kremer, and Edward Miguel are summarized as Evaluation 1 in the appendix.

4. Owen Ozier, "Exploiting Externalities to Estimate the Long-Term Effects of Early Childhood Deworming," working paper, University of California, Berkeley, 2001.

Until that point, most randomized evaluations of social programs were performed in rich countries in partnership with governments and at very high cost. But the experience of partnerships between researchers and organizations such as ICS showed that it was possible to conduct high-quality randomized evaluations with small organizations on limited budgets and in very poor settings. Although many government programs are being evaluated with randomized evaluations, NGOs have also proved to be flexible and innovative partners in this effort to learn. The challenge of working with new partners on new questions and on modest budgets has spurred innovation in randomized evaluation methodology.

We have learned how to introduce randomization into programs in creative ways, account for and measure spillovers, reliably measure difficult-to-measure outcomes like corruption and empowerment, get the maximum statistical power from a very limited budget, minimize attrition, and design evaluations that answer fundamental questions about why humans behave the way they do and how to motivate changes in behavior.

In this book we have gathered many of the practical innovations from this large body of work. Our goal is to enable more people and organizations to undertake and commission high-quality randomized impact evaluations and thus to build a wider and deeper evidence base on how best to combat poverty. Our hope is that we will see the generation and application of rigorous evidence grow even faster than in the past two decades. By innovating and testing and by feeding the evidence back into even more innovation, evaluators and practitioners can improve the effectiveness of policies and programs and make a real difference in people's lives.

MODULE 1.2 A Randomized Evaluation from Start to Finish

In this module we provide an overview of the steps in planning and running an evaluation and indicate where these topics are covered in the rest of this book. We tell the story of a randomized evaluation of an education program in India that I experienced firsthand from inception through implementation and analysis to scale-up.[5]

---

5. Abhijit Banerjee, Rukmini Banerji, Esther Duflo, Rachel Glennerster, and Stuti Khemani, "Pitfalls of Participatory Programs: Evidence from a Randomized Evaluation in Education in India," *American Economic Journal: Economic Policy* 2 (2010): 1–30.

Starting right: Choosing the right question to test

Ten years after my trip to Kenya described in Module 1.1 , I was working with a group of researchers at the Massachusetts Institute of Technology (MIT) planning our next evaluation. We had recently started what is now the Abdul Latif Jameel Poverty Action Lab (J-PAL) with the objective of promoting the use of randomized evaluations and helping ensure that the results are used to influence policy. Although randomized evaluations (and most of the lessons in this book) are valuable across many disciplines and many regions of the world, our main expertise was in development economics. In prioritizing our work, therefore, we wanted to start by understanding the areas in which rigorous evaluation could be most valuable in informing the debate about poverty in developing countries. Which innovations showed promise but were untested? Which programs were popular with governments and NGOs but had little rigorous evidence to support them?

Community accountability programs were a priority that repeatedly emerged in the conversations we had with organizations working in developing countries as well as in our review of the literature. The enthusiasm for this approach was well articulated in *World Development Report 2004: Making Services Work for Poor People.*[6] The report documented the low quality of services and the lack of accountability, including the chronically high absenteeism of service providers. It argued that community accountability is one of the best ways to improve failing services. The poor who suffered the brunt of the failures were not just more motivated to get services working than were bureaucrats; they were also better positioned because they were right there, at the point of delivery, to monitor the providers. If they were empowered to apply their motivation and monitoring advantages, they would hold providers accountable and services would improve.

In practice, this empowerment took the form of establishing community oversight bodies for schools and clinics and providing communities with information about their rights and the services they should expect. International agencies, NGOs, and governments were all looking to integrate the approach into their work.

There were reasons to think that community accountability would work in practice. Advocates pointed to correlations between active

6. World Bank, *World Development Report 2004: Making Services Work for Poor People* (Washington, DC: World Bank, 2003).

participation of citizens in school and clinic oversight and high-quality services, and cases in which increases in participation were associated with improved services. A popular example was documented in a study from Uganda, in which the government had started disbursing grants directly to schools. A survey found that only 25 percent of these grants were reported as reaching the schools. In response, the government started informing communities of how much money had been allocated to each school, and a few years later, 82 percent of the grants were reported to be reaching the schools.[7]

It was unclear, however, whether the correlation between community involvement and high-quality service outcomes meant that community involvement caused these high-quality outcomes. Communities with high levels of citizen involvement tend to be different from those with low levels of involvement in a number of ways. For example, the town of Brookline, Massachusetts, where I live, has very good public schools and an unusual form of governance in which

CHAPTER 2 explains why it is hard to distinguish the impact of a program from other factors. We discuss alternative approaches the evaluator can use for estimating impact and show how randomized evaluations can help him or her to isolate the causal impact of the program.

citizens take responsibilities typically given to full-time town employees. But Brookline also has an unusual concentration of people with high levels of education. People move from miles away and pay high taxes so that their children can attend Brookline's public schools. It is hard to know to what extent the school outcomes are due to the citizen oversight and to what extent they are due to the emphasis on education among local families. More important, it is not clear whether another town encouraged (or mandated) to take up the Brookline model of citizen involvement would achieve the same outcomes.

What about the Uganda example, in which services improved when the information given to local people was increased? Even there it was unclear how big a role empowering communities with information played in the observed changes. Some people believed that the accuracy with which money transfers to schools were recorded had been low during the first year and improved over time. In addition, information on how few of the grant funds made it to the schools was also reported

7. Ritva Reinikka and Jakob Svensson, "The Power of Information in Public Services: Evidence from Education in Uganda," *Journal of Public Economics* 95 (2011): 956–966.

to the Ministry of Education and to donors, and that caused quite a stir. Was it providing information to the ministry and the donors or providing it to the community that caused the change?[8] It's hard to tell.

Because the approach of empowering communities to hold service providers to account was popular and there was little rigorous evidence of its impact, we decided to prioritize this as one of the questions we wanted to test using a randomized evaluation.

Finding a specific context in which to test the question

Among those keen to both develop and test a community accountability program was Pratham. Pratham is the largest organization, apart from the government, working on education in India. Was India the right context? Was Pratham the right partner?

The education sector in India was plagued by poor public services. The absence rate among primary school teachers was 25 percent,[9] and only 45 percent of teachers present were in the classroom teaching.[10] Pratham had found in other work that even many children who attended school regularly could not read or do simple math by grades 3 and 4.[11] Services were bad and highly centralized; there was scope, therefore, for community accountability to make a difference. The researchers decided that India was a relevant context in which to test a community accountability program.

Pratham was, in fact, an ideal evaluation partner. They knew a lot about education in India, and they wanted to test a community mobilization program. Pratham had previously worked with another J-PAL team, including Abhijit Banerjee and Esther Duflo, to evaluate a remedial education program that trained local young women and placed

8. There is evidence that those schools in closer proximity to a newspaper outlet saw larger improvements in recorded flows of funds, which the authors attribute to greater access to information about the mismatch of funds. However, having a principal and parents with greater access to a newspaper is likely to be correlated with other factors that might lead to greater improvement in recorded flows.

9. World Bank, *World Development Report 2004: Making Services Work for Poor People* (Washington, DC: World Bank, 2003; Nazmul Chaudhury, Jeffrey Hammer, Michael Kremer, Karthik Muralidharan, and F. Halsey Rogers, "Missing in Action: Teacher and Health Worker Absence in Developing Countries," *Journal of Economic Perspectives*, 20 (2006): 91–116.

10. Michael Kremer, Nazmul Chaudhury, F. Halsey Rogers, Karthik Muralidharan, and Jeffrey Hammer, "Teacher Absence in India: A Snapshot," *Journal of the European Economic Association* 3 (2005): 658–667.

11. This study by Abhijit Banerjee, Shawn Cole, Esther Duflo, and Leigh Linden is summarized as Evaluation 2 in the appendix.

them in local schools as tutors for children who had fallen behind. The evaluation had found the program highly effective in helping these children catch up in reading and arithmetic. Pratham wanted to adapt this model to a rural setting and reduce costs by relying on volunteers rather than paid tutors. Successful as their program had been, Pratham also believed that improving the education of children in India required improving the quality of education in the government schools on which most children relied. They had a vision of citizens coming together to ensure that India's children had a better future both by exerting pressure to improve public education and by taking direct action to improve learning. Further, Pratham understood why randomized evaluations were useful, they were in the early design phase of a new program allowing the joint development of the research and project design, and they had the ability to bring a successful program to scale. The research team also recruited Stuti Khemani at the World Bank to bring to the project the expertise and perspective of the World Bank on community accountability programs.

Together, Pratham and the research team decided that Uttar Pradesh (UP) would be a good location for the program and its evaluation. UP is one of India's largest states, with 20 million primary school–aged children. But school quality there was very low: the survey we conducted at the start of the evaluation (our baseline) showed that only 42 percent of 7- to 14-year-olds could read and understand a simple story. Because it would not be feasible to introduce community oversight boards with legal backing to some (randomly selected) schools and not others, we needed a context in which such an oversight board existed but was not very active. UP had legislation mandating that VECs oversee all public schools in a village, but most did not function. Laws existed that gave communities a number of paths to influence the quality of their schools: communities could complain to their members of parliament, local village councils could request funding to hire local assistant teachers, and the village councils had discretionary funds they could use to improve local services. Within UP we chose to pilot and evaluate the program in Jaunpur District, which was close to the state average in terms of literacy and was one of the districts where Pratham was not already working at the time.[12]

12. Some of our qualitative work was done in Gauriganj (Amethi) in the constituency of MP Rahul Gandhi, the son of former Indian prime minister Rajiv Gandhi. However, we became concerned that attempts to put pressure on the education system

CHAPTER 3 discusses how to prioritize questions for an impact evaluation, when nonrandomized methods are sufficient, why understanding the local context is critical in designing an evaluation, and how to choose the right location and partner for undertaking an evaluation.

Given our chosen context, we refined our general community accountability question to this: is there a way to mobilize communities to effectively use existing accountability systems in UP to improve educational quality?

The groundwork: How did we arrive at the final three interventions?

Over the period of a year, the researchers and Pratham worked together to design the program and the evaluation. Their objective was a program that represented best practices in the area of community mobilization to enhance service accountability and was tailored to the local environment but was replicable. We also had to select which of several alternative versions of the program to rigorously test against each other in the study. Finally, we had to determine how to measure the impact of the program.

Honing the design of the program

Both Pratham and the researchers wanted to design and test a program that would be replicable at large scale. In other words, it needed to be relatively inexpensive and not rely on highly trained or educated staff. Scalability concerns also limited the resources Pratham would put into any single village mobilization effort.

We needed to check whether the theory behind the intervention made sense in Jaunpur District. Was the level of learning low? Was there room to improve education (for example, was the rate of teacher absenteeism high)? Did communities have mechanisms they could use to improve education quality? What were the roles and responsibilities of the VECs? If a village wanted an additional assistant teacher or wanted to fire an existing one, how exactly could they do that? How much money did the village council have that could be directed to education? Was there a gap in knowledge that a potential intervention could fill? Did the community know how poor learning levels were? Did everyone know the roles and responsibilities of the VEC? Was

to reform might create more response in such a high-profile district than would be typical, and so we moved to Jaunpur.

there relevant information that the village head knew but was not sharing widely (in which case pressing the village head to share that information might be a good strategy)? We spent time in government offices in the state capital of Lucknow finding out exactly what laws were on the books and talked to village heads, teachers, VEC members, students, community members, and national and state education activists.

We found that learning was very poor in Jaunpur, but most people overestimated the level of learning in their community and were shocked when they realized how little their children knew. According to the law, communities had a number of ways they could press for change, most of which ran through the VECs; yet there was very little knowledge of the VECs, what their powers were, how much money they had, or even who was on them. Although village heads tended to know about VECs and could produce a list of the names of the committee members, the committees were usually inactive. In several cases even those whose names were on the lists of committee members did not know of the existence of the committees, let alone that they were on them.

Both Pratham and the researchers wanted to incorporate best practices from other states and countries. The results would be most useful if the evaluation tested a program that the rest of the world would consider a good example of a program designed to mobilize communities to demand quality services. To that end, we studied the *World Bank Participation Sourcebook* as a guide to community participation programs and sought to include all aspects of the guidelines into the program.[13]

The program also needed to work on the ground. So the team spent months going village to village figuring out how best to convey information about both the poor quality of education in the communities and the mechanisms communities had to press for change. How best could one stir up interest in pressing for change? Was it best to have many small discussions or one large meeting that the teacher and the village head attended? How could Pratham best steer the conversation on education away from the perennial topic of the food rations for children attending school and back to the subject of whether children were learning and how to improve that learning?

13. Bhuvan Bhatnagar, James Kearns, and Debra Sequeira, *The World Bank Participation Sourcebook* (Washington, DC: World Bank, 1996).

Choosing which iterations of the program to test

The researchers and Pratham had many questions about the relative merits of different ways to design a program for community mobilization for accountability, but we knew we had the money and statistical power to compare only a few alternatives against each other. The qualitative work helped us choose which alternatives to focus on.

For example, we had planned to test a very inexpensive intervention that simply provided information on learning levels in the community, the resources available for education, and the mechanisms for generating change on posters distributed throughout the village. But when we put up posters in a community and showed up the next day, we found that most of the posters were gone. This experience did not prove that posters would not work: we had tried using them in just one village. But based on this experience, we thought the chances that this strategy would work were low enough that it was not worth rigorously testing a poster-based intervention. We opted for testing a more interactive approach relying heavily on community meetings to promote information sharing.

One hypothesis to emerge from our qualitative work was that the more actively involved communities were in discovering the inadequate learning levels in their community, the more likely they were to take action to remedy them. Two alternative versions of the program that were ultimately evaluated were designed to test this hypothesis. Pratham developed a testing tool simple enough to be used by community members to determine how many of their children could recognize letters or words and read simple paragraphs or stories. In one arm of the study, communities themselves would generate the information on children's learning and present it at a community meeting at which attendees would go on to discuss what action to take.

We also decided to use the opportunity to test the new version of Pratham's remedial education program (Read India) designed for rural settings. Pratham saw the community mobilization program and the Read India program as natural complements: community mobilization around education and an understanding of levels of reading in the community would be necessary to recruit volunteers to teach children in remedial reading camps after school. From a research perspective, testing community mobilization with and without Read India would help us unpack reasons for the success or failure of community mobilization. For example, if people did not take action through the public system but did take the opportunity for direct action provided by Read India, it would suggest that the problem was not lack of interest in education or a lack of willingness to take action but rather a lack of faith in the responsiveness of the public system. Similarly, one concern people have about efforts outside the public system is that they undermine motivation to take action within the public system. We would be able to see if action to reform the public system was stronger, weaker, or the same when an option to improve education outside the public system was offered.

The interventions tested

All three interventions Pratham finally implemented adopted the same basic structure to share information on education and on the resources available to villagers to improve the quality of education.

1. Providing information on improving education services with VECs

Pratham spent two days initiating small discussions about education throughout the community, culminating in a large communitywide meeting at which teachers and the village head were prompted to provide information about the resources available to improve education in the village, the composition of the VEC, and what resources it receives. Pratham facilitators provided fact sheets and filled in any gaps in information. They also met with every member of the VEC to inform them of their roles and responsibilities.

2. Creating village-based scorecards on reading skills

The second intervention built on the first, adding the use of a simple tool that Pratham staff taught community members to use to assess the reading outcomes of their own children and the village as a whole. Community members used the tool to generate a village "reading report card" that was then shared with other community members at the village meeting.

3. Demonstrating volunteer-run Read India afterschool camps

The third intervention supplemented the first and second interventions by providing a way for a motivated citizen to directly improve education levels. Pratham asked for local volunteers to hold afterschool reading camps and trained them over the course of four days in a simple pedagogical technique for teaching reading. The volunteers held after-school camps for children who wanted to attend for two to three months, with an average of seven support visits from Pratham staff during that time.

Piloting the interventions

In addition to the qualitative work Pratham and our research team did to develop the interventions, we also conducted a formal pilot of the interventions in several villages. The pilot had several purposes: it was a final check to see whether the program as designed was feasible and had a reasonable chance of success; it helped us understand in greater detail some of the pathways by which the program might change education, enabling us to refine our intermediate and final outcome measures; it allowed us to test our baseline data collection instruments; and it generated data that we used to decide what sample size we needed for the full-scale evaluation.

The pilot was quite promising. People in the villages were enthusiastic during the small-group discussions and at the large community meetings. There was a high level of attendance and participation in the conversations. Parents tested their children on basic literacy, and people became very engaged. Pratham ran the pilot, and the researchers performed a qualitative analysis of it. Observing the steps that communities took in response to the intervention led to new questions in our survey designed to pick up actions along these lines that other communities might take.

Random assignment

The evaluation was conducted in 280 villages in Jaunpur District in the state of UP. Districts in India are divided into administrative blocs. In each bloc, on average, there are about 100 villages. Four of these blocs were randomly selected to participate in the study, and the study villages were then randomly selected within each bloc. The study is thus representative of Jaunpur District (and its population of 3.9 million) as a whole.

Because the VECs were seen as key targets of the program and there was only one VEC per village, it was not possible to randomize individual households in and out of the program. An entire village needed to either receive the program (be a treatment village) or be a comparison village. In other words, we needed to randomize at the village level. We worried that the existence of the program in one village might benefit neighboring villages. For example, one village might complain about school quality to their MP and the MP might then press for changes in all the schools in her constituency. If this happened, it would lead us to underestimate the impact of the program. We thought this type of action was unlikely, but we nevertheless decided to track how many complaints were made to MPs. In randomizing villages into different treatment groups and a comparison group we used a technique called stratification. This meant that we were sure to have equal numbers of villages in each treatment group from each block and that the level of reading scores at baseline would be the same for all the different treatment groups and the comparison group. We made the random assignments using a computer-based random number generator to assign each of the 280 villages in our study to one of the four groups described in Table 1.1.

CHAPTER 4 discusses how to randomize, including whether to randomize at the individual or the group level, how to deal with potential spillovers at the design stage, and whether and how to stratify. It also covers the mechanics of randomization.

TABLE 1.1 Random assignment of treatment groups for community accountability evaluation

	Intervention		
Group	Participants provided information on how to improve education	Participants create village-based scorecards	Volunteers run Read India camps
Comparison group (85 villages)	—	—	—
Treatment Group 1 (65 villages)	X	—	—
Treatment Group 2 (65 villages)	X	X	—
Treatment Group 3 (65 villages)	X	X	X

Note: An X in a cell indicates that the group receives a given treatment; a dash indicates that the group does not receive that treatment.

Data collection plan

To plan our data collection we started by mapping exactly how each of the alternative programs being tested could lead to changes in learning levels. Underlying each program alternative was an assumption that people had too little information about the quality of education and that education quality would improve if they participated more in the oversight of schools. The second program variant assumed that being involved in creating information (through the creation of report cards) helps reduce the information gap more efficiently and motivates more action. The Read India program variant assumed that people need a way to respond to poor education quality without going through the government bureaucracy. Figure 1.1 shows a very simplified version of the theory of change for the project.

For each step in the theory of change we developed an indicator. For example, to confirm low schooling quality we measured teacher absenteeism. This involved making surprise visits to schools to see whether teachers were present and teaching.

To test knowledge of learning levels we asked parents how well they thought their children could read and then tested their children. This required that a household survey be administered to a random sample of households in the village. At the same time, we asked about parental involvement in their children's education. (Which schools did their children attend? When did they last visit their children's schools? Did they speak at the village meeting about education? Did they check whether their children attended school or did homework?) We wanted to check whether parents, on hearing about poor learning levels, would take action outside the formal government system—for example, by monitoring homework or sending their children to private schools.

To measure gaps in knowledge of how to influence education quality, we asked parents, village leaders, and members of the VECs if they had heard of the VECs and whether they knew the committees' roles and responsibilities. This required a village leader and VEC member survey. We asked these questions again at the end of the project, which allowed us to understand whether the program was successful in reducing knowledge gaps.

CHAPTER 5 covers how to use a theory of change to develop a comprehensive data collection plan and how to ensure that the chosen indicators reflect real changes on the ground.

Need	Input	Output	Outcome	Impact
Poor school quality - low levels of learning - high rates of teacher absenteeism				**Sustained improved learning**
Lack of awareness of - learning outcomes - village education committees (VECs) - village funds for education	**Information provided on** - testing tools - role of VECs - village funds	**VECs function** **Requests for assistant teachers** **Monitoring visits of schools**	**Reduced knowledge gap** **More assistant teachers** **Reduced teacher absenteeism** **Additional expenditure on schools**	
Lack of participation - by parents in their children's education - by village councils through failure to discuss education at meetings	**Motivation** - discussions and meetings - encouragement of action	**Parents more involved** - get extra tutoring - visit schools, talk to teachers - switch to private schools	**Students spend more time on** - homework - reading **More students go to private schools**	
Lack of tools to act	**Training held for** - Read India program	**Classes held** - students turn up	**Children complete** - classes	

FIGURE 1.1 Simplified theory of change

To measure inputs, the research team (independent of Pratham) carefully monitored implementation of the program, checking that village meetings were held, volunteers trained, and reading camps held.

Our final measure of impact was child learning. At the end of the program we retested the same sample of children on basic literacy and numeracy.

All data collection was carried out by an independent survey company with close monitoring by the research team. A team of monitors, hired directly by the research team, redid a random sample of surveys to check the accuracy of the survey company's work.

Power analysis

We decided on the number of villages in each treatment group and the comparison group by conducting a power analysis. Because we randomized entire villages in or out of the program, one of the most important determinants of statistical power was the number of villages allocated to each version of the program. However, we also needed to decide how many households to interview per village. We realized that we needed only about 10 households per village to get a reasonably accurate picture of what people knew about the VEC. However, to be able to pick up changes in learning levels we would need data on many more children. We therefore tested all the children in the 10 households we interviewed and also tested children in a further 20 randomly selected households where we did not ask questions of the parents.

We had a strict budget limit that covered both the program and the evaluation. We wanted to test six different versions of the program, but our analysis suggested that we had sufficient statistical power to test only three alternative treatments and a comparison group. We also decided to have more of a sample in our comparison group than in any of our treatment groups. This would enable us to very precisely test the average impact across all the community mobilization approaches compared to the comparison group.

We had to decide how small a difference in learning levels we wanted to be able to detect. We used the results of the previous study on Pratham's urban remedial education program as a guide to what the "success" of the program might look like. The rural program was much less expensive than the urban one because it relied on volunteers. In addition, unlike in the urban program, in the rural program children could choose to go to extra classes after school, so attendance at the remedial sessions was likely to be much lower, reducing our statistical power. For these reasons we wanted to be able to detect an impact that was smaller than that achieved in Pratham's urban program. We also wanted to be able to separately estimate the impact of the program on children with different initial learning levels—particularly those who started off with very poor reading levels. We therefore did a survey before the program started to be able to identify those children.

CHAPTER 6 explains how to use power analysis to choose the sample size, the number of treatment arms, and the minimum detectable effect an evaluation wants to detect.

The final sample consisted of 2,800 households, 316 schools, 17,533 children (ages 7–14) tested in reading and math, and 1,029 VEC members who were interviewed (including village heads) from the 280 villages.

Implementing the program (and monitoring that it was implemented well)

The three interventions were implemented between September 2005 and December 2005. A full-time research team monitored activities in Jaunpur to ensure that the randomization protocol was followed and document how well the program was implemented. The risk that those in the comparison group would benefit from the program was minimized by randomizing at the level of the legal village unit so that individuals in the treatment and comparison groups were geographically separated. Monitoring data suggested not only that the program was properly implemented but also that people responded by attending and speaking up at meetings. All treated villages held at least one meeting, and some held more than one. The meetings were well attended, with good representation and participation from different hamlets, castes, and genders.

In 55 of the 65 villages in Treatment Group 3 (i.e., 84 percent of the total), volunteers started reading camps serving a total of 7,453 children in the villages (135 per village on average). In our random sample of surveyed children, 8 percent had attended the camps in the Treatment Group 3 communities.

The *final (or endline) survey* took place in March and April 2006, three months after the treatment arms had been implemented. Enumerators were urged to make every effort to find the same households

CHAPTER 7 explains how to minimize the risk of things going wrong with the evaluation, such as people in the comparison group gaining access to the program or people dropping out of the study.

and the same children they had interviewed the previous year. In total, the endline survey included 17,419 children, which included all but 716 of the children in the baseline survey.

Analyzing the data

Once the surveys were complete, the survey company entered all the data into a database in two separate rounds and reconciled any discrepancies between the two versions.

The actual analysis was fairly straightforward for this evaluation. We simply compared the level of knowledge, action, and learning in villages in each treatment group with those in the comparison group, adjusting for the fact that we had randomized at the village level by clustering our standard errors. The difference represented the effect of the program.

The large number of outcomes that could have been affected by the interventions created a danger of "cherry picking" results or "data mining." In other words, there was a danger of consciously or subconsciously highlighting results that showed large effects and ignoring others. To avoid this risk, we created groups, or "families," of related variables based on our theory of change and tested them as a group. For example, we grouped all outcomes related to parents' knowledge of children's learning levels into one outcome and all outcomes related to parents' involvement with schools into another. For each family of outcomes we calculated the average effect. Our main outcomes were these average effects across many outcome variables.

Although the community mobilization program worked at a community level, the Read India afterschool camps were attended by some children but not others. In addition to looking at the average effect of each intervention, therefore, we also estimated the impact of the Read India program on those children who attended the camps. Rather than looking at outcomes for specific children who attended (which would not be random), we used a technique called "instrumen-

CHAPTER 8 discusses data analysis, including adjusting for how randomization was carried out and for low take-up of the program. It also discusses analysis with multiple outcome variables and the pros and cons of committing in advance to how the data will be analyzed.

tal variables" by which average treatment effects are adjusted by average take-up rates.

Our start-to-finish timeline was as follows:

2004	Discussion of which questions were the most important, focusing on community involvement for improving government service delivery
July 2004	Ongoing discussions with Pratham about partnering on a large-scale randomized evaluation of community accountability and their flagship Read India program
July 2004–July 2005	Qualitative fieldwork
March 2005	Selection of villages
March–April 2005	Conduct of census
April 2005	Conduct of baseline survey
April 2005–July 2005	Running of pilot program
September 2005– February 2006	Implementation of the three treatment arms immediately following election of new village leaders
March–May 2006	Conduct of follow-up endline survey
June 2006	Beginning of data analysis and writing up of results
2007 onward	Dissemination of results through discussions with Pratham and Indian policymakers and, more broadly, presentations at the World Bank and academic conferences
2007	Pratham's receipt of a $9.1 million grant from the William and Flora Hewlett Foundation and the Bill and Melinda Gates Foundation to help them scale up the Read India program in more than 300 of the 600 districts in India
2010	Publication of academic paper

What the results of this study mean for policy

Days before the baseline survey was launched, the research and Pratham teams gathered in Jaunpur to train the enumerators from the survey company on how to administer Pratham's reading test as part of the survey. Rukmini Banerji, at the time Pratham's head of research and head of the northeastern region, took this moment to speak to the Pratham team. She recounted how they had spent many months developing the new program, field testing it, and learning all the nuances of how to engage the community in conversations and how to get parents invested in their children's learning levels. Now these economists from MIT were going to help evaluate it. "And of course," she said, "they may find that it doesn't work. But if it does not work, we need to know that. We owe it to ourselves and the communities we work with not to waste their and our time and resources on a program that does not help children learn. If we find that this program isn't working, we will go and develop something that will."[14]

Rukmini's words were a reflection of the courage Pratham and many other implementers showed in putting their programs on the line and admitting that they might not work. But her words also summed up the rationale for evaluation.

The results of the evaluation

Neither providing information on the channels for improving education nor helping citizens gather information on the status of education in their villages led to greater involvement of parents, VEC members, or teachers in the school system. Nor did these interventions lead to private responses such as extra tutoring or moving children to private schools. Given these results, it is not surprising that there was no impact on learning from the first two interventions. The program helped narrow the knowledge gap (on levels of learning and VEC roles) but only modestly, despite the widespread and enthusiastic participation in community meetings.

In contrast, where Pratham conducted the Read India intervention, not only did volunteers teach almost 7,500 children in after-school camps but literacy rates also improved. The average improvements were modest: a 1.7 percent increase in those who could recognize letters, for example. But the program was designed to help those who could not yet read. Among this group we saw much more impressive effects. Children who could not recognize letters before the program started were 7.9 percent more likely to be able to recognize letters at the end of the program in Treatment Group 3 villages. And once we adjusted for the

14. This quote reflects my memory of Rukmini's speech.

fact that only 13 percent of children who could not recognize letters attended reading camps, we calculated that the camps led to a 60 percent increase in the ability to recognize letters among those who could not recognize letters at baseline. Twenty-six percent of those who could not recognize letters but attended camps could read fluently as a result of the camps.

What did the results imply?

We had two challenges in interpreting the results. We had to understand what had happened in the specific program in UP, why some interventions had worked and others had not. But we also wanted to figure out what this told us about community accountability programs in general. For this we would need to put our results in the context of those from other emerging studies.

In our academic paper we concluded, "In the UP context, providing information on the status of education and the institutions of participation alone is not sufficient to encourage beneficiary involvement in public schools. . . . [However,] information combined with the offer of a direct channel of action can result in collective action and improve outcomes. . . . In the UP context there seemed to be a greater willingness of individuals to help improve the situation for other individuals (via volunteer teaching) rather than collective action to improve institutions and systems." We noted, "This may be specific to the Indian schooling bureaucracy. Parents may be too pessimistic about their ability to influence the system even if they are willing to take an active role, or parents may not be able to coordinate to exercise enough pressure to influence the system. Nevertheless, the results do suggest that some caution is warranted when recommending standard beneficiary control approaches."[15]

Pratham responded to the results of the evaluation in a number of ways. Although they did not give up on their objective of changing Indian public schools for the better, they put much less faith in doing it through village councils and VECs. The simple testing tool that was developed in UP is now used to test children throughout India in the Annual State of Education Report. The district and state report cards

---

15. Abhijit Banerjee, Rukmini Banerji, Esther Duflo, Rachel Glennerster, and Stuti Khemani, "Pitfalls of Participatory Programs: Evidence from a Randomized Evaluation in Education in India," *American Economic Journal: Economic Policy 2* (2010): 1–30, quote on p. 5.

that come out of this testing generate considerable media attention and are intended to put pressure on state and district officials to improve education quality and focus on learning (as opposed to school attendance or school meals). The evaluation results showing the success of Read India helped Pratham win significant additional funding and led to an expansion of Read India to more than 23 million children across India. But Pratham was concerned that although their camps worked for those who attended, only a modest proportion of those who needed help went to the camps. Pratham's long-term goal is to take their pedagogical techniques into India's public school system. They have therefore continued to innovate and evaluate, increasingly working with state governments. Some of their innovations have proved successful, others less so, and continuing to test and evaluate has helped them differentiate between the two outcomes.

At the international level, too, researchers and practitioners have continued to innovate and evaluate how to improve the quality of public services for the poor. A number of studies emerged around the same time as ours. The most similar was a study of a community mobilization program in Uganda that rejuvenated the community oversight committees of local clinics, provided information about the poor quality of services (such as high rates of health worker absenteeism), and worked with communities and health workers to devise ways to improve service quality. The result was reduced absenteeism and improved health.[16] In some ways the results seem in stark contrast to our own, but in other ways there were similarities. In both cases, community participation structures existed prior to the program but were nonfunctional. Arguably, providing communities with very direct actions they could take was a feature of the successful elements of both studies. Since then we have learned that providing information about the quality of schools in Pakistani communities with competition between public and private schools helped improve test scores; empowering school committees in Kenya had no effect,[17] but giving those committees resources to hire

16. Martina Bjorkman and Jakob Svensson, "Power to the People: Evidence from a Randomized Field Experiment on Community-Based Monitoring in Uganda," *Quarterly Journal of Economics* 124 (2009): 735–769.

17. Banerjee et al., "Pitfalls of Participatory Programs"; Christel Versmeerch and Michael Kremer, "School Meals, Educational Achievement and School Competition: Evidence from a Randomized Evaluation," World Bank Policy Research Working Paper 3523, World Bank, Washington, DC, 2004. http://ssrn.com/abstract=667881 or http://dx.doi.org/10.2139/ssrn.667881.

local teachers resulted in higher test scores, and training those committees in their monitoring role enhanced this effect.[18] We also learned that community monitoring of local road projects in Indonesia was less effective than outside audits in reducing corruption.[19]

What can we conclude from all this evidence? We have found that community oversight can improve service quality in the right situations, but it is hard to make it work. There is no single simple answer to the question of whether beneficiary participation works. I was taught in my very first economics lecture that the answer to many economic questions is "It depends," and in this case the answer seems to depend in complex ways on the details of the program and the institutional setting. But we now understand a lot better than we did in 2004 what success is likely to depend on. The accumulated evidence has led to a much more nuanced and informed discussion about community accountability programs and provided considerable food for thought for those designing these programs.

> CHAPTER 9 discusses how evidence from randomized evaluations can provide insights for policy, including how to decide when results are likely to generalize and how to make cost-effectiveness comparisons.

And this is the nature of our journey. We innovate and test. The results move us forward but also generate more questions, which again need to be answered through testing. But over time we learn. We understand more about what is working where and why, and this helps us develop better programs that lead to better lives.

In this book we seek to give practical advice to those who want to be part of this journey by contributing to the growing base of evidence from randomized evaluations on how to improve the lives of the poor.

---

18. This study by Esther Duflo, Pascaline Dupas, and Michael Kremer is summarized as Evaluation 3 in the appendix.

19. Benjamin A. Olken, "Monitoring Corruption: Evidence from a Field Experiment in Indonesia," *Journal of Political Economy* 115 (2007): 200–249.

2 Why Randomize?

This chapter explains why randomized evaluation can help determine what impacts were caused by a program. The modules in this chapter are as follows:

MODULE 2.1: Why It Is Difficult to Measure Causal Impact
MODULE 2.2: Advantages and Limitations of Nonexperimental and Quasiexperimental Evaluation Methods
MODULE 2.3: How Randomization Can Help Infer Cause
MODULE 2.4: Advantages and Limitations of the Experimental Approach

---

MODULE 2.1 Why It Is Difficult to Measure Causal Impact

Measuring causal impact requires us to compare what happened with the program with what would have happened without the program. This module discusses the fundamental problem of causal inference, namely that we can never observe the same people at the same time both with and without the program: we never directly observe the counterfactual.

What is causal impact?

Causal impact is the difference in outcomes that is *caused by* the program. In other words, to estimate the impact of a program, we need to examine how the people who participated in the program fared compared to how they would have fared if they had not participated in the program. This hypothetical condition is called the *counterfactual*. However, we never observe the counterfactual directly. We observe only what happens with the program, not what would have happened in the absence of the program, and so we have to make an inference about the counterfactual. This is the fundamental problem of causal inference. Often we infer the counterfactual from what happened to other people or what happened to the participants of the program before the start of the program. But when we make these inferences, we have to make assumptions: for example, that the people who did and did not participate in the program would have had the same outcomes in the absence of the program. The validity of our estimate depends on the validity of those assumptions.

Example: Did a school uniforms intervention improve learning?

Imagine that we would like to improve educational attainment for children in an area where many children are officially enrolled in school but do not attend regularly and learning levels are quite low. Every two years there is a national survey of the reading and math skills of primary school children. The latest survey finds that half the 8-year-olds in the district we are examining cannot read a simple first-grade paragraph.

We are working with an NGO in the area that wants to help improve educational outcomes and wants to evaluate the impact of giving students school uniforms.[1] In this area, uniforms are not formally required, but there is strong social pressure to wear one, and some children say they are too embarrassed to attend school regularly if they lack a uniform. We think that giving each child a free uniform may help them attend school more regularly and, ultimately, learn more.

The NGO has enough resources to give away 200 uniforms and does so. After two years, the NGO wants to know whether the program worked. Did giving children uniforms help them attend more regularly and learn more? The survey of learning is conducted again, and the reading scores of the children who got the uniforms are higher than they were before the program started. It seems that the program has made a difference. But before we expand the intervention to other schools, we want to know for sure whether the change in reading scores can be attributed to the uniforms intervention, or whether something else caused reading scores to rise. How can we go about finding

---

1. This example is inspired by a study by Esther Duflo, Pascaline Dupas, and Michael Kremer and is summarized as Evaluation 4 in the appendix.

out? Is the before-and-after comparison the right comparison for assessing the program?

Many factors (other than a program) can influence changes over time

In the two years between the two learning tests, many factors will have influenced the learning levels of the children who received uniforms. Some are internal to the children in the program: they grow and mature week by week. Even if they never set foot inside a school or open a textbook, children may still learn basic arithmetic from selling trinkets on the street or learn to recognize letters from observing their siblings reading from billboards and labels around them. Program children are also exposed to external events: teachers and parents may change the amount of time and resources they invest in teaching, or the central government may implement a school feeding program in our program schools, which encourages more children to go to school.

All of these events could affect the school attendance and reading scores of the children we are following, and they would do so even if these children were not given uniforms by our program. If we simply measure attendance and reading scores before and after the program, we have no way of telling whether any changes are due to the uniform program or whether some or all of them are due to the many other things that changed and influenced the school attendance and learning of the children in our program during the same time.

Selection matters: Those who sign up for or are chosen for a program are different from those who do not

Instead of comparing reading scores before and after giving children uniforms, we could also compare the reading levels of those children who received free school uniforms to those who did not participate in the program. However, those who receive a program are often different from those who don't. Perhaps we announced our uniforms program and asked parents to sign up. We then gave uniforms to the first 200 children whose parents signed up with the NGO. It's quite possible that the parents who signed up early are more organized or better connected and care more about education than those who did not sign up early.

In other words, these parents differed in ways that would be difficult to observe or measure, and these unobservable differences in parents may also affect how they are able to support their children in attending school and learning to read. The more motivated parents may also have the skills and means to send their children to school each day and support their learning by helping them with their homework or by having newspapers around the house. If we compare the scores of those students who got uniforms to the scores of those who did not, we might find that their scores are higher. But this may be due to differences in the motivation of parents, not to our uniforms program.

Alternatively, our program may have targeted the poorest students, who were most in need of uniforms. But the neediest children likely also face other barriers to attending school. In this case, when we compare those who did and did not receive free uniforms, those with uniforms may have lower attendance rates and test scores. Does this mean that our uniforms program kept children from attending school and reduced their scores? There's no good way to tell. It could simply be that children who received uniforms were behind to begin with, and the uniforms were of no help. Or the uniforms may have helped children attend more regularly, but not often enough to catch up with their better-off peers.

We call the tendency for those who receive a program to be different from those who do not get a program selection. Selection can be caused by different people's self-selecting into the program or by the program administrators' allocating the program to particular types of people. If we fail to account for selection in our impact evaluation, we can introduce *selection bias* into our estimate of impact. In other words, we risk attributing differences in outcomes to the program when they are actually caused by preexisting differences in those who self-selected or are selected for the program.

The fundamental problem of causal inference: Finding a valid counterfactual

In the preceding example, after our program was implemented, we would have liked to compare the outcomes of the children who received uniforms with the outcomes of exact clones of these children who did not receive uniforms. In the real world, of course, we can't observe the same group of people both with and without our program at the same time, and there is no way to find exact clones of the people in our program. We can never know what would have happened in the absence of the program. As we said earlier, we never directly observe the counterfactual.

In Modules 2.2 and 2.3 we discuss how we use different evaluation techniques in an attempt to mimic the counterfactual. All these approaches, however, have to address the fundamental issue that we can never see any one person or any group of people in two conditions at the same time. We therefore end up comparing different groups of people, one group that receives the program (the *treatment group*) and one group that does not receive the program (the *comparison group*). Although there is no exact replica of any specific treatment individual in the comparison group, overall we aim to have similar average group characteristics.

For example, in our uniforms program we are worried that the extent to which parents care about education may affect our outcomes (attendance and test scores) and also be correlated with whether a parent signs up for the program. Every parent is unique, and it will be hard to find two students with parents with exactly the same income levels and degrees of interest in their children's education. Even within families, parental interest may vary between, say, first and later-born children. But if we have many children in the treatment group and in the comparison group, we can find groupings in which the level of income and parental interest in their children's education is the same *on average* between the two groups. All quantitative impact evaluation methodologies have the same aim—to identify treatment and comparison groups that, on average, have similar characteristics—but the methodologies differ in exactly how they identify these different groups.

MODULE 2.2 Advantages and Limitations of Nonexperimental and Quasiexperimental Evaluation Methods

An impact evaluation is only as good as the comparison group it uses to mimic the counterfactual. In other words, the comparison group should mimic what would have happened in the absence of the program. A bad comparison group ruins an evaluation and makes the impact estimate invalid. We discuss a number of different methods of finding a comparison group (the counterfactual) in this module.

Below we discuss the advantages and limitations of some of the most common impact evaluation methods other than randomized evaluations. Randomized evaluations are not the only valid way to conduct impact evaluations. The methods discussed below can be effective—if the specific conditions exist that are needed for that method's assumptions to hold. They have the advantage that they can be used retrospectively; in other words, we can go back in time and study the impact of a program that took place years or even decades ago, thus potentially allowing us to measure long-run outcomes even though we have only just started our evaluation. However, the conditions needed for a nonexperimental or quasiexperimental approach to be valid do not always apply. We discuss the assumption required for each evaluation approach below. We focus mainly on quantitative methods of impact evaluation, because these methods are the ones with which we have the greatest expertise, but we start with a short discussion of qualitative methods.

Qualitative impact evaluations

Perhaps the most obvious approach to understanding how a program or policy has changed people's lives is to talk directly to those affected. Qualitative researchers have a wide range of tools for eliciting from participants the impact of a program or policy on their lives. Direct observation can document how individual actions and group dynamics change over time. Open-ended interviews have the advantage of allowing issues to be raised by participants that evaluators might never have thought of and thus might not ask about in closed-ended survey questions. Focus group discussions allow for a pooling of knowledge and experience from a range of community members who may have had different experiences of a policy or program. This interaction between participants can generate insights that no one individual may have. Many qualitative techniques have been developed to help evaluators investigate issues that are painful for individuals to discuss or difficult for them to confront directly, such as experiences of war, corruption, and sexual harassment. For example, participants may be asked to tell a story, draw a picture, or use a physical representation of their experiences or beliefs.

The advantage of the approach

The great benefit of qualitative approaches is the richness of the information collected. For example, rather than just collecting data on the number of days a week a child goes to school, a qualitative analysis can capture the child's level of enthusiasm about school. Qualitative approaches can also document in considerable detail potential mechanisms through which a program may work. Quantitative approaches require that this richness be boiled down into a few numbers. This translation into numbers is necessary in order to apply statistical techniques—for example, to say whether the difference between the experiences of two groups is statistically different. But there is no doubt that something is lost in the translation. Even most quantitative evaluators will rely on qualitative techniques at some point. In particular, they are likely to use focus groups and open-ended discussions with participants to generate hypotheses that are then tested using qualitative techniques. When interpreting the findings of a study, quantitative evaluators will often provide quotes from participants or describe in detail the experiences of some individuals. In other words, they will combine quantitative and qualitative evidence. Quantitative evaluators are also increasingly drawing on qualitative techniques to develop quantitative nonsurvey measures of outcomes (we catalog the most popular of these in Module 5.4).

Who is in the comparison group?

Many qualitative studies do not attempt to draw conclusions about the impact of a program or policy. They simply describe a situation. However, qualitative impact studies use a range of approaches to create a comparison group. Often the comparison group is implicit rather than explicit. For example, when participants discuss how the program has changed their lives, the implicit comparison group is the same individuals before the program. Hybrid approaches, however, are emerging whereby qualitative techniques are used to compare treatment and comparison groups (including randomized treatment and comparison groups).

Required data

The difference between qualitative and quantitative approaches is that the latter do not attempt to boil experiences down to data, although most qualitative evaluators will include some data in their assessments.

Required assumptions

If we are to use qualitative approaches to attempt to judge the impact of a program, we must make a number of assumptions. First we must assume that either the evaluator or the participant must have a good understanding of the counterfactual—that is, they must know what would have happened in the absence of the program. When we ask participants how a program changed their lives, we are asking them to disentangle all the many changes that were going on in society from those that were driven by the program. This is a hard task, and to some extent we rely on the evaluators to help the participants sort out which of the changes that they associate with the program are in fact general trends and which are program impacts. This, however, assumes that the evaluators know the counterfactual.

The second assumption is either that participants are not influenced by what they think we want to hear or by their own expectations or preferences or that we can see through any biases they may have. There is substantial evidence that people see what they expect to see or want to see. For example, if people expect women to perform poorly, this influences their assessments. Studies have found that the number of women selected for elite orchestras is much lower when auditions are done face to face (and gender is observed) than when those auditioning are behind a curtain (and gender is hidden).[2] Qualitative researchers are trained in techniques that attempt to address these biases. These biases are also an issue for quantitative researchers, and we discuss some solutions in Chapter 5.

Finally, we have to trust that the evaluators have summarized the information in an unbiased way. There are set rules about how to summarize data: we take averages, we look at the level of variation in one group versus another, we measure the level of inequality, and so forth. There is more room for judgment when qualitative evaluators draw conclusions about the impact of a program from the information they have collected. We have to assume that this process is not influenced by the expectations or preferences of the researchers.

Simple before-and-after (pre/post) comparisons

Before-and-after comparisons measure how program participants improved (or changed) over time. The outcomes of the participants are recorded before the program is implemented (baseline outcomes), and these are then compared to the outcomes of these same individuals after the program ends (endline outcomes).

Who is in the comparison group?

Program participants themselves, before participating in the program, serve as the counterfactual.

2. Claudia Goldin and Cecilia Rouse, "Orchestrating Impartiality: The Impact of 'Blind' Auditions on Female Musicians," *American Economic Review* 90 (2000): 715–741.

Required data

We must collect data on the outcomes of program participants before and after the program is implemented.

Required assumptions

When we use the preprogram outcomes as the counterfactual, we assume that the treatment group's outcomes would have remained the same without the program. We assume that the program was the only factor influencing any changes in the measured outcome over time.

There are many reasons why these assumptions would not hold. As we discuss in the school uniforms example in Module 2.1, many factors other than the program we are evaluating can change the outcomes of program participants over time. These factors include the following:

1. *Concurrent changes in the external environment* Imagine that at the same time that the free uniform program is implemented there is widespread flooding. The harvest is bad, and children do not have enough to eat. The floods leave a lot of stagnant water, enabling mosquitoes to breed, so children suffer from more malaria, and this affects their ability to go to school and learn. If we compare test scores at the beginning and the end of the year, we will underestimate the impact of the program; we might even conclude that it had a negative impact. If, on the other hand, there is a good harvest or the government introduces a school feeding program that improves school attendance, we would overestimate impact by assuming that all the improvements were due to our program.

2. *Concurrent individual changes: Maturation* Sometimes it is individuals who change rather than their external environment. These natural changes can lead to changes in outcomes. In our uniforms example, over the year the children will grow older, and as they mature, their cognitive abilities will increase. This maturation can increase their performance on a learning test even if they did not go to school. A before-and-after comparison attributes all changes in learning to the program, thereby overestimating its impact.

3. *Rebounding (regression to the mean)* Quack doctors around the world have long relied on the fact that most people who are sick get better on their own. If you give them some innocuous potion, you can claim the credit for their recovery. A similar rebounding effect is

found in communities suffering from war or drought or in individuals suffering from unemployment. Because programs are often conducted in places and with individuals that have been hit by adversity, there is a risk of taking inappropriate credit for natural improvement just as a quack doctor does. A before-and-after comparison attributes any rebound to the program.

Participant–nonparticipant or cross-section comparison

A *cross-section comparison* measures the difference between program participants and nonparticipants after a program is completed.

Who is in the comparison group?

Individuals who didn't participate in the program (for any reason) but on whom data were collected after the program make up the comparison group.

Required data

We must collect data on the outcomes of program participants and nonparticipants after the program is implemented.

Required assumptions

We must assume that nonparticipants are identical to participants except for program participation and that they were equally likely to enter the program before it started (i.e., there is no selection effect).

Selection bias: The problem of preexisting differences

Participant–nonparticipant comparisons alleviate some of the problems of external environment, maturation, and rebounding discussed earlier. However, the people who choose to participate in a program (or who are chosen to benefit from a program) are often systematically different from those who do not. This is called the selection effect.

Let us return to our uniforms example and the case in which widespread floods, poor nutrition, and high malaria rates reduced test scores. Imagine there that are 210 schools in a district in which free school uniforms are distributed, and at the end of the evaluation we compare the outcomes of the schools in the treatment group to those of the schools in the comparison group. If the comparison group was subject to the same floods as the treatment group, the two groups would be comparable in terms of external environment.

But what if the treatment and comparison groups had different outcomes to start with? Perhaps we sent the free uniforms to the lowest-achieving schools or those in the poorest part of the district, and when we compare program schools to nonparticipating schools it appears that the program *lowered* scores. Or perhaps our program targeted the schools with the most students, but these larger schools also had more resources and a more engaged parent community, which means that their children's test scores were higher to begin with. Now when we compare the scores of participating schools to those of nonparticipating schools, these preexisting differences make it appear that our program *increased* scores.

Multivariate regression

Individuals who received the program are compared with those who did not, and other factors that might explain differences in the outcomes are "controlled" for. In other words, we run a regression of our outcome indicator against treatment status and other indicators that might explain our outcome variable.

Who is in the comparison group?

Individuals who didn't participate in the program (for any reason), but on whom data were collected make up the comparison group.

Required data

In this case we need data not only on indicators of the outcomes of participants and nonparticipants but also on other "explanatory" or "control" variables as well (e.g., age, income levels, education). The control variables need either to be collected at baseline or to be characteristics, like age, that do not change as a result of the program.

Advantage of the approach

Multivariate regression is designed to overcome some of the problems with the simple difference approach outlined above. In our uniforms example, if we are concerned that children in our treatment schools come from slightly poorer households than those in our comparison schools, we can estimate the relationship between income and test scores. We can then factor out any difference in test scores between treatment and comparison groups that is due to differences in income. We then assume that any remaining difference is due to the program.

We do this by running a regression of test scores on treatment status and on family income. For more details on analysis, including how to run a regression of outcome on treatment status, see Chapter 8.

Required assumptions

We must assume that the control variables we include in our regression include all the relevant ways in which our treatment and comparison groups differ. In particular, we must assume that there are no characteristics that were excluded from the regression (because they are unobservable and/or have been not been measured) that might be different between the two groups and that might affect the outcome variables.

Selection bias: Unobservable differences

The assumption above can be hard to justify. Programs that have some element of self-selection (programs in which people have to decide to participate) are particularly likely to have participants who are different than nonparticipants on traits that are hard to measure, such as motivation or confidence. Yet unobserved traits like motivation are likely to be correlated with many outcomes such as test scores and income. Even when there is no self-selection of who receives a program, we may worry that those deciding where a program should first be introduced had a reason for their decision and that this may lead to unmeasured differences in participants and nonparticipants. At a personal level, we may know the history of how the selection of the program area evolved and feel confident that there are unlikely to be unmeasured differences between participants and nonparticipants. But it can be hard to prove this claim. By their nature, unobservable differences are unobservable, so we cannot prove that there are no unobservable differences between groups with our data. An alternative approach, discussed below under regression discontinuity, is to explicitly exploit the decision rules for introducing a program to create a counterfactual.

Statistical matching

One particular form of multivariate regression is *statistical matching*. Program participants are compared to a group of nonparticipants that is constructed by finding people whose observable characteristics (age, income, education, and so on) are similar to those of the people in the treatment group.

Who is in the comparison group?

The comparison group can be formed in two ways:

> *Exact matching.* Each participant is matched with at least one non-participant who is identical on selected observable characteristics—for example, they have the same gender, age, and occupation.
>
> *Propensity score matching.* Characteristics such as age and income are used to predict who will participate. Every participant and nonparticipant is given a probability or propensity to participate. Each participant is matched with a nonparticipant with the same propensity to participate.

For example, we may find that age, income, education, and past voting habits are correlated with whether or not a person votes. Similarly, educated and wealthier women are more likely to take up microfinance, as are married women. We can calculate the probability that any given woman would take up microfinance if it were made available to her. We can then match a woman who, according to her characteristics and our calculations, had a 60 percent chance of taking up microfinance and did take it up with another woman who also had a 60 percent chance of taking up microfinance but did not take it up.

Why, if these women had the same probability of taking up microfinance, did one take it up and the other not? There are two slightly different approaches to propensity score matching that give slightly different answers to this question. One approach matches those who had access to the program with those who did not have access to the program but had a similar probability of taking it up if they had access. For example, if microfinance is available in some areas but not in others, we match women with a high probability of taking up microfinance in areas with access to microfinance with other women with similar probabilities in an area that does not have access to microfinance.

The other approach to propensity score matching is to find comparators within the group who have access to the program. As discussed below, this approach assumes that the difference in actual take-up is due to chance.

Required data

We need data on outcomes as well as "variables for matching" for both participants and nonparticipants. If we want to match people on many different characteristics, we are likely to need large sample sizes and data on lots of variables for matching.

Advantages of the approach

Propensity score matching is a version of multivariate regression. Its advantage is that it puts the most weight on those in the comparison group who are most like those in the treatment group (on observable measures) and who are predicted (based on these characteristics) to be most likely to take up the program. The disadvantage is that it imposes more assumptions than a standard multivariate regression, as we discuss below.

Required assumptions

For this approach to create a valid counterfactual, the set of factors on which we match people must be sufficiently comprehensive that there are no remaining differences between the treatment and comparison groups that might be correlated with our outcome of interest (except for participation in the program). As in the general case of multivariate regression, unobservable factors like motivation are a major concern. We have to assume that we have matched people on enough other characteristics that are correlated with unobservable characteristics that there is no difference left.

Whenever we make this assumption, however, we need to ask ourselves, "If the nonparticipants are just as likely as the participants to take up the program, why didn't they?" Two different approaches to matching answer this question in different ways and require slightly different assumptions. Both of these approaches can be used for exact matching or propensity score matching.

By matching across those with and without access, we find which characteristics predict take-up among those who have access to the program and then find people with those characteristics in an area that does not have access to the program. We compare people with equal probability of take-up in access areas and nonaccess areas. For this comparison to give us an unbiased estimate of the impact of the program, we have to assume that there is nothing that is correlated with access that also has an effect on our outcomes. For example, if microfinance is available in some districts and not in others, we may worry that the districts with access to microfinance are systematically different in some unmeasured way from those that do not have access. Maybe the microfinance organization chose to enter districts because they perceived that they had a greater potential for growth. This potential for growth may not be picked up by any of the variables on which we are matching.

When we match between participants and nonparticipants within program areas, everyone in our study is eligible for the program. Thus we worry less about shocks that will affect one group but not the other. But now we are left with the puzzle of why, given that the non-participants have the same observable characteristics as the participants, they did not take up the program. The only assumption that will make our evaluation valid is that it was entirely due to chance that some people took up the program while others didn't. Our matching variables are so good that we have explained every difference that could be explained, and chance is the only remaining factor. For example, two women had an equal probability of participating in microfinance, but one happened to pass the microfinance office on her way to visit a friend, whereas the nonparticipant had a friend in the other direction.

Difference-in-difference comparisons

This approach combines a before-and-after comparison with a participant–nonparticipant comparison. It measures changes in outcomes over time of program participants relative to the changes in outcomes of nonparticipants.

Who is in the comparison group?

This group is made up of individuals who didn't participate in the program but on whom data were collected.

Required data

We need data on the outcomes of program participants and non-participants both before and after the program is implemented.

Advantages of the approach

This approach deals with the problem of unobservable differences between treatment and comparison groups, as long as those differences have the same effect on outcomes across time. For example, in our school uniforms case we would compare the improvement in test scores for those who did and did not get uniforms. To the extent that those parents who signed up early for the uniforms were also more diligent in helping their children with their homework, their test scores were likely to be higher both before the program starts (as measured in a baseline survey) and in our final or endline survey. As long as the effect of having more motivated parents is constant over time, the difference in parental motivation between treatment and comparison groups will not affect the change in test scores. As a result, the comparison of changes in test scores between treatment and comparison groups will be a valid estimate of the impact of the program.

Required assumptions

We must assume that if the program hadn't existed, the two groups would have had identical trajectories over this period. In other words, we have to assume that any differences in characteristics between the treatment and comparison groups do not have more or less of an effect on people's outcomes over time. In our uniforms example, if our treatment group has more motivated and educated parents and if having more motivated and educated parents is more helpful as children get older and their work gets harder, our assumption is invalid. Sometimes we can look at past trajectories of our treatment and comparison groups and check whether these were similar before the program started. This will require several rounds of data collection before the program starts. However, even with this added data it can be hard to convince skeptics that because trajectories in the treatment and comparison groups were similar in the past, their future trajectories would have been similar if not for the program.

Many difference-in-difference designs also require that there be no mismeasurement at the baseline. For example, imagine that we provide a remedial education program to children with low test scores at baseline. If in fact all children have exactly the same level of knowledge but some happen to have received low test scores at baseline because of bad measurement, the scores of these children will automatically bounce back to the average at the endline even if the program does not work. We will incorrectly conclude that the program worked.

Regression discontinuity design (RDD)

This approach is used to evaluate programs that have eligibility cutoffs. For example, children whose parents fall below an income threshold have access to free school meals or those with test scores higher than a certain value get into an elite school. Participants who are just above the cutoff are compared to nonparticipants who narrowly missed the cutoff.

Who is in the comparison group?

The comparison group is made up of individuals who are close to the cutoff but fall on the "wrong" side of that cutoff and therefore do not receive the program.

Required data

We need information on exactly how program participation is decided (i.e., where the cutoff is), data on the variables that are used to determine the cutoff (such as income or test scores) for the entire sample, and outcome data. Because we typically use only those participants just above and below the cutoff rather than all participants, RDD works best in evaluating programs with large numbers of participants and nonparticipants.

Advantage of the approach

In other nonexperimental methodologies we have to make assumptions about why people or areas were chosen for the program and hope that there was not some element of this process that introduced unobserved differences between participants and nonparticipants. The advantage of RDD is that if we know exactly what the rules for program allocation are, we can test whether or not they were adhered to, and thus we are less concerned that there is some factor in the allocation that we are not accounting for.

Required assumptions

This approach can answer only questions in cases for which we happen to have a good cutoff that is suitable for the RDD approach. The program rules must introduce a bright discontinuity between those who are eligible and those who are not, and we must be confident that the official criteria for the cutoff were actually followed in practice. (For example, we must be confident the politically powerful or wealthy were not able to game the system and receive the program despite having missed the cutoff.)

We must assume that the cutoff rule was not engineered to produce a certain result (for example, to get a politically favored person or area to just meet the cutoff) and that narrowly meeting or missing the cutoff is the only important difference between individuals directly below and directly above the cutoff score. To say this more precisely, we know that those just above the cutoff will be marginally different at the start of the program according to whatever criterion is used for the cutoff, but we must assume that the effect of this marginal difference has only a marginal impact on outcomes.

For example, if we want to evaluate the impact of going to an elite secondary school in Boston or Kenya on future income and we know that admission is based strictly on test scores, we can compare the outcomes of children who just reached the test score cutoff to attend the elite schools and those who just missed the cutoff.[3] Not all those above the cutoff will end up going to the elite schools, but their probability of going jumps up sharply at the test score cutoff. We know that test scores are correlated with future income, but all we need to assume for this approach to be valid is that the relationship between test scores and income would not change sharply exactly at the cutoff in the absence of elite secondary schools. So if we find a sharp jump in the relationship between test scores and future income precisely at the elite school cutoff, we can assume that most of this jump is due to the increased probability of going to an elite school.

One drawback of the approach is that it tests the impact of the program only for those close to the cutoff. In the Boston and Kenyan school examples, we might imagine that the effect of going to an elite school might be different for those who just scraped in and therefore were always toward the bottom of their class compared to those who were average or at the top of their class at the elite school. If we are thinking of expanding a program, the impact on those at the cutoff may be exactly the policy-relevant question.

Instrumental variables

This approach can be used when participation in a program can be predicted by an incidental factor, or "instrumental" variable, that is

3. Adrienne M. Lucas and Isaac Mbiti, "Effects of Attending Selective Secondary Schools on Student Achievement: Discontinuity Evidence from Kenya," working paper, accessed June 1, 2013, http://siteresources.worldbank.org/INTDEVIMPEVAINI/Resources/3998199-1286435433106/7460013-1313679274012/Paper-Lucas_Mbiti_Secondary_201101.pdf; Atila Abdulkadiroglu, Joshua D. Angrist, and Parag A. Pathak, "The Elite Illusion: Achievement Effects at Boston and New York Exam Schools," NBER Working Paper 17264, National Bureau of Educational Research, Cambridge, MA, 2011.

uncorrelated with the outcome (other than by predicting participation and, through participation, the outcome).

Geographic features can sometimes make good instruments. For example, imagine a remote valley in Indonesia that is separated from a less remote, more densely populated area by a high ridge of mountains.[4] In some parts of the valley, the population can get TV reception designed for the more populated area on the other side of the mountain ridge, and in other parts of the valley the reception is blocked by a particularly high peak on the ridge. Nobody actually crosses the ridge when they want to visit the nearest town; it is much easier to take a different route down the valley and around the ridge. Whether a given community receives TV reception, therefore, is uncorrelated with remoteness or land quality. The height of the nearby ridge affects the population only through its effect on their ability to receive a TV signal. We can then use the height of the ridge to assess the impact of TV on outcomes such as social capital or attitudes toward women.

Who is in the comparison group?

In this case, individuals who are less likely to participate in or benefit from a program or policy because of a nearly random factor are in the comparison group.

Required data

We need data on outcomes, the "instrument," and other control variables.

Advantage of the approach

The advantage of the instrumental variables approach is that it allows us to estimate the causal impact of something that suffers from selection bias by finding an instrument that predicts take-up but is not subject to selection bias. So in our TV example, owning a TV is a choice, and thus comparing people with and without TVs is not a good way to find the causal impact of TV: those who choose to own one are very different from those who choose not to or cannot afford one. But if having a working TV is predicted by something that is not

---

4. This example is inspired by Benjamin A. Olken's paper "Do Television and Radio Destroy Social Capital? Evidence from Indonesian Villages," *American Economic Journal: Applied Economics* 1 (2009): 1–33.

a choice, such as the height of the nearest mountain, we can use this to learn about the effect of TV.

Required assumptions

Instrumental variables require a very strong assumption that the instrument affects the outcome only through one specific channel. In our example, the assumption is that the height of the mountain affects social capital or attitudes toward women only through its effect on TV reception. If the height of the nearest mountain affected how long it took to get to the nearest town, it would not be a valid instrument. Nor would it be valid if the height of the nearest mountain affected how much rain the community received, the depth of the river, or the quality of the agricultural land.

It is worth noting that instrumental variables allow us to estimate the effect of a program, policy, or technology only for a very specific group of people. In our TV case, we learn about the impact of TV on those who live in areas where TV reception is dependent on nearby geographic features. We do not learn about the effect of TV in densely populated areas with their own broadcast mast.

Module 2.2 summary

- Qualitative impact evaluations assume that researchers' priorities do not influence the way information is summarized and that beneficiaries and/or the researchers can tell what the counterfactual would have been.
- Before-and-after comparisons assume that any change over time is due to the program.
- Cross-section comparisons assume that any difference between participants and nonparticipants is due to the program and that there is no selection bias (i.e., no systematic differences) between those in the program and those not in the program.
- Multivariate regressions assume that any difference between participants and nonparticipants can be controlled for in a regression. To control for differences, we must be able to measure them.
- Difference-in-difference comparisons correct for differences in starting levels between participants and nonparticipants and compares changes over time between the two groups. We must assume that in the absence of the program there would be no

difference in the changes over time between participants and nonparticipants.

- Statistical matching sometimes matches those with access to a program with those who do not have access. In this case, matching assumes that there is nothing systematically different between those who do not have access to the program and those who do once we have done our matching. In other words, there was no important reason why some had access to the program and others did not.

- Statistical matching among those with access to the program assumes that (among those who are matched) whether or not someone takes up the program is a matter of random chance.

- Regression discontinuity can be used only when a program has clear rules for eligibility that produce a bright-line cutoff between participants and nonparticipants. It compares those just below and just above the cutoff and assumes that the participation rate is the only thing to jump sharply at the cutoff.

- Instrumental variables require that there be a factor that is not subject to selection bias and predicts participation but affects outcomes only because it predicts participation. The instrumental variable cannot affect anything else of importance through any other channel.

MODULE 2.3 How Randomization Can Help Infer Cause

Randomized evaluations are a type of evaluation that can help us measure causal relationships. This module explains how random assignment helps us create a comparison group that is a valid counterfactual because it is, on average, the same as our group that receives an intervention.

The key feature of a randomized evaluation is that the people who have access to the program or benefit from the policy are selected randomly. This ensures that there are no systematic differences between those who receive the program and those who serve as the comparison group. This is called *random assignment* and differs from *random sampling*, in which people are randomly selected to be surveyed (see Box 2.1). It is this random assignment that gives randomized evaluations an advantage in measuring what impacts were caused by the program.

BOX 2.1 *Random assignment is not random sampling*

In both random assignment and random sampling we use a random process to select units (individuals, households, schools, etc.). But there is a crucial difference. In random sampling we take a population and use a random process to select units to create a group that is representative of the entire population. We can then measure characteristics of this group and infer from them the characteristics of the entire population. (Most surveys use this approach.) In random assignment we take a study population—a pool of eligible units—and use a random process to assign units to different groups, such as treatment and comparison groups (i.e., we use it to determine access to a program).

All randomized evaluations use random assignment, but most also use random sampling. For example, if we are testing the impact of a program that provides free school uniforms to children in a school, we randomize which school receives the program (random assignment). But we may need to interview only some of the children in each school to get a good picture of impact. (Chapter 6 explains how to determine how many children to interview.) We therefore pick a random sample of children to interview in both treatment and comparison schools (random sampling), and this gives us a good indication of the outcomes of all the children

We may also use random sampling to decide where to perform the evaluation in the first place so that our results will be representative of a wider population (just as a survey is representative of a wider population). This approach is discussed in Chapter 4.

The process of random assignment typically follows a number of steps (illustrated in Figure 2.1):

Define the people who could be eligible for the program. First we define the sample of people from which we will later select the treatment group. It could be that all households in a village are eligible for support. Or our program may be open only to households that fall below a certain poverty threshold. We must have a complete list of all those units (individuals, schools, or clinics) that are going to be in our evaluation before we start the randomization process. In many contexts, this may mean that we need to start by conducting a census of the people in the village or of the schools in the district, because the relevant administrative data may not exist or may be of poor quality.

Randomly assign which units are in the treatment and the comparison groups. From this pool of eligible units, we assign units to

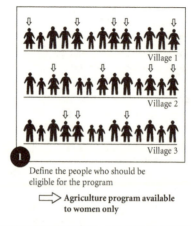

1. Define the people who should be eligible for the program

⟹ Agriculture program available to women only

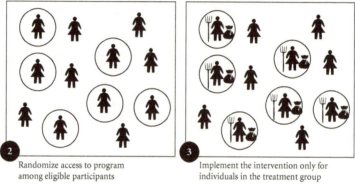

2. Randomize access to program among eligible participants

3. Implement the intervention only for individuals in the treatment group

FIGURE 2.1 Steps in the randomization process

different groups by a random process such as a toss of a coin, use of a random number generator, or a lottery. These different groups will then be given access to different types of programs (the treatment groups) or not given access to a program (the comparison group). Chapter 4 provides more details on the pros and cons of different ways of randomizing. The important point is that assignment is purely by chance, so allocation into either the treatment or the comparison groups is completely unrelated to any characteristic that could affect the outcomes. As long as we are working with a large enough number of units, the two groups will be statistically identical. Both will have roughly the same mix of people who are motivated to run businesses or are not; more advanced students and those who are less prepared for school; the socially connected and the socially ostracized.

A key advantage of the randomized approach is that in addition to *observable* characteristics (such as income and test scores), *unobservable* characteristics that we don't have a measure of (such as motivation or talent) will also be balanced between the groups. This means that, on average, the treatment and comparison groups will be comparable at the onset of the program, and their trajectory would be the same in the absence of the program.

Implement the intervention only for individuals in the treatment group. After randomization we provide access to the program or the intervention only to individuals, villages, or schools in the treatment group. (For more details on the level of randomization, see Module 4.2.)

Although most people are familiar with the use of randomized evaluations to test the effectiveness of medicines, randomized evaluations also have a long history in agriculture (Box 2.2). We cannot (and should not) force people to comply with our research protocol. We can only offer the program, and people have every right to refuse for whatever reason. Some will take us up on our offer, and some will not; some in our comparison group will find a way to participate in the program. As we will discuss in greater detail in Chapters 4 and 6, our ability to measure impact will be much stronger if the actual take-up of the program matches our assignment perfectly. However, as long as the proportion of people who actually receive the intervention is higher in the treatment group than in the comparison group, we still have a valid way to measure the impact of the program. (See Chapter 7, which explains ways to help ensure take-up matches assignment as closely as possible.)

MODULE 2.4 **Advantages and Limitations of the Experimental Approach**

Randomized evaluations answer specific questions in a transparent way without requiring a lot of assumptions. They are designed before a project starts, allowing new, tailored data to be collected. But these charac-

The concept of a control and experimental group was introduced in 1747 by James Lind when he demonstrated the benefits of citrus fruits in preventing scurvy using a scientific experiment.* As a result of his work, Lind is considered to be the father of clinical trials. The method of randomly assigning subjects to comparison and treatment groups, however, was not developed until later.

Randomization was introduced to scientific experimentation in the 1920s when Ronald A. Fisher conducted the first randomized agricultural experiments. Fisher's experimental fieldwork culminated with his landmark book *The Design of Experiments*, which was a key catalyst for the growth of randomized evaluations.

Randomized trials were introduced to government-sponsored social experiments in the 1960s. Rather than being small-scale experiments conducted on plants and animals, these new social experiments were significantly larger in scale and focused on people as the subjects of interest. The model of social experimentation was applied in both Europe and the United States to evaluate programs such as electricity pricing schemes, employment programs, welfare programs, and housing allowances. Since then, social experiments have been used across disciplines and in a variety of settings around the world to guide policy decisions.

*Duncan P. Thomas, "Sailors, Scurvy and Science," *Journal of the Royal Society of Medicine* 90 (1997): 238.

teristics also imply drawbacks: one study can answer only a few questions, and special data collection is expensive. This module describes how understanding these advantages and limitations can help us determine when to use randomized evaluations and when not to.

Tailoring the evaluation to answer a specific question

As we discussed in the previous module, randomizing the allocation of a program or part of a program allows us to determine the causal impact of what we randomize. The advantage of this is that we have precise control over what we randomize and thus what we study. We can randomize the allocation of an entire program, in which case we will learn the impact of the entire program. We can randomize different components of a program, in which case we will isolate the impact of the different parts of the program. We can design our evaluation to precisely test a theoretical concept that economists have worried about for years or to test a contentious policy question. In other words, we can tailor the evaluation to answer exactly the question we need to have answered.

In the United States, as in many other countries, the poor tend to live in concentrated geographic areas. Many people have speculated that these concentrations of poverty can perpetuate poverty: there tend to be fewer jobs in poor areas, schools may be underfunded and attract less qualified teachers, young people have few successful role models, and crime levels are often high. But it is hard to disentangle the effects of being poor from the effects of being surrounded by other poor people, because the poor who live in disadvantaged areas tend to be different from those who live in richer areas. Researchers worked with the US Department of Housing and Urban Development, which was planning to give housing vouchers to poor families eligible for government housing support, to do this.[5] Some of the families continued to be eligible to receive traditional housing support (access to subsidized housing units in their neighborhoods), while others were given one of two types of vouchers. The first was to subsidize private housing in a neighborhood with less than 10 percent poverty, while the second was to subsidize private housing in a new neighborhood but with no restriction on the poverty level. In other words, the researchers were able to introduce an element of randomization as to whether people lived in poor neighborhoods or not and thus disentangle the effect of poverty on health, employment, and child outcomes from the impact of living in a poor neighborhood on these same outcomes. In this case, the randomized evaluation enabled the researchers to design the evaluation to answer the precise question of interest in a way that would have been difficult to achieve with quasi-experimental approaches.

In Module 4.6 we review a number of examples of other actual randomized evaluations that demonstrate the flexibility of the technique. We show how it can be used to answer underlying questions of human behavior as well as more straightforward questions of whether a program works.

The specificity of the randomized methodology comes with a downside, though. With one treatment group and one comparison group we can answer only one question: what is the impact of the difference in experience we create between these two groups? If we have multiple treatment groups, we can answer more questions, but this greatly

5. This study by Jeffrey Kling, Jeffrey Liebman, and Lawrence Katz is summarized as Evaluation 5 in the appendix.

increases the cost of the study, and the number of questions we can answer is still very limited.

A contrasting approach is to collect very detailed data on a range of important topics from a representative sample of people across a country or state (examples include the Demographic and Household Surveys and Living Standard Measurement Surveys run by the World Bank, the Micro Sample of the Census or the Current Population Survey in the United States, and their equivalents in other developed economies). In a panel survey, the same individuals or households are interviewed over time: the Indonesia Family Life Survey, the Mexican Life Survey, the Townsend Thai Survey, and the National Longitudinal Study of Youth in the United States are good examples of this approach. These surveys tend to be very large scale and to cover a wide geographic area; often they are nationally representative. They play an important role in describing conditions and trends (which is critical to good program design, as discussed in Module 3.1), and although they are expensive, they have been used to answer many different questions by a wide variety of researchers.

Evaluators often take advantage of quasirandom shocks that have occurred between different waves of large-scale surveys to employ the techniques (discussed in Module 2.2) to evaluate particular policies and programs. For example, the Townsend Thai Survey was used to evaluate the impact of the government's Thai Million Baht Fund, which created locally run microfinance pools in villages across Thailand. Exactly which impact evaluation questions it will be possible to answer with these large, repeated surveys will depend on the shocks that occur, and these may not always be clear at the start. In other words, the advantages and limitations of this approach are the reverse of those of randomized evaluations.

Generalizability: Randomized evaluations answer a question in a specific context

The question of generalizability is often raised with regard to randomized evaluations, and this can take two forms. First, if the experiment is not conducted well, the results obtained may be influenced by the fact that people behave differently when in an experiment or because a different kind of person or organization than is found in the rest of the population agrees to participate in an experiment. We discuss how to design an experiment that minimizes evaluation effects in Module 7.4 and considerations in testing a replicable program in Module 3.3.

The second and most commonly cited concern about generalizability is whether and under what circumstances the results found in one context apply to other contexts. Unlike the very large national surveys discussed above, randomized evaluations tend to collect data on the specific area in which an evaluation is implemented, which may include a few hundred communities.

The broad question of whether and when results from one evaluation will hold in other contexts is an important one, and we discuss it in detail in Module 9.2. It is worth noting that the question of generalizability is an issue for all evaluations, whether randomized or not. If studying one time and place told us nothing about other times and places, there would be little reason to undertake any evaluation or research. What we need to understand (and can learn by comparing the results of different evaluations) is how and when results from one study help us understand what to do in another situation. As we discuss in Module 9.2, we can generalize only with the help of theory, but our theory can be informed by the evidence we acquire from randomized evaluations.

The need for few assumptions and the transparency of findings

Because we create random variation in exposure to a program or policy, we do not need to make as many assumptions when making causal statements based on a randomized evaluation as we do when we use other approaches to impact evaluation. We do not need to assume that those who did not sign up for a program are just as motivated as those who did sign up. We know that, at least on average, the treatment and comparison groups will be the same in all dimensions at the start of the evaluation.

When we use a simple randomized design, the results of a randomized evaluation can be relatively straightforward to interpret, making the results transparent. As we discuss in Module 8.1, the simplest designs can be analyzed by comparing the mean of our outcome measure in the treatment group with the mean in the comparison group.

The limited number of assumptions and the transparency of the results can provide credibility, which can be useful in convincing policymakers of their relevance. Arguments between researchers about how to interpret a study's results and the sensitivity of those results to different assumptions or different ways to analyze the data can easily turn off policymakers.

We do not want to overstate this advantage. Not all randomized evaluations are equally simple to analyze or present. We may test many different program variants against each other, which will complicate the analysis. If take-up of the program in the treatment group is low or we cannot find all those we interviewed at the start of the study after the end of the study, we may have to address this problem in the analysis, making it more complex and less transparent. We may also compare the impacts of the program on different types of participants (we discuss the different ways to analyze the results of randomized evaluations in Module 8.2). It is also increasingly common to combine the results from randomized evaluations with statistical modeling techniques. This combined approach allows us to answer more questions, but it does require us to make more assumptions.

For example, a study in Kenya examined the impact of protecting natural springs (encasing each spring in concrete and adding a pipe to bring the spring water to the surface without allowing it to become contaminated).[6] A random sample of springs in the area was chosen for protection. By comparing the health outcomes of those living near the protected springs to the outcomes of those living close to unprotected springs, it was possible to estimate the impact of the program on health. However, the researchers also examined the extent to which people who lived between a protected and an unprotected spring were willing to walk farther to collect their water from a protected spring. By making assumptions about the value of people's time, they estimated a "willingness to pay" for clean water. Using both the actual health benefits of clean water and the willingness to pay for clean water, they constructed an implicit value of a child's life. They also estimated that a private entrepreneur would not find it worthwhile to invest in protecting the springs because they would not be able to charge much for the clean water that was generated.

In other words, by adding a number of assumptions, it is possible to use the results of randomized evaluations to answer a wider range of questions, which has a number of benefits. But when we do this, we give up some of the benefits of simplicity and transparency of analysis.

The results of randomized evaluations can also be less than clear cut if there is debate about the quality of the study. It is certainly the

6. Michael Kremer, Jessico Leino, Edward Miguel, and Alix Peterson Zwane, "Spring Cleaning: Rural Water Impacts, Valuation, and Property Rights Institutions," *Quarterly Journal of Economics* 126 (2011): 145–205.

case that not all randomized evaluations are of equal quality. However, judging the quality of a randomized evaluation arguably takes less expertise than is needed for some other methodologies. We present criteria to use when assessing the quality of a randomized evaluation in Module 9.1.

Prospective evaluation

Randomized evaluations are nearly always prospective evaluations. In other words, they tend to be designed before the program they are evaluating starts (we discuss a few exceptions below). This generates both advantages and limitations.

Collecting targeted data

Like other forms of prospective evaluation, randomized evaluations allow us to collect detailed data that are tailored to the needs of the evaluation, including data collected before the start of the program (baseline data). Some nonexperimental designs rely on a change in policy as the strategy for identifying causal impact. Because the studies are often conceived after the policy change, the data needed to estimate the impact of the change in policy may not be available. The set of questions that can be answered is limited by the data that can be found (data collected in national surveys that happen to have been conducted at the time of the policy change, for example) or reconstructed ex post. For more discussion on the benefits of having baseline data, see Module 5.2.

Again, however, this benefit comes with a downside: in this case, cost. It is often argued that randomized evaluations are costly, and in many cases they are, with data collection nearly always representing the vast majority of any costs. As a result, the cost of a randomized evaluation will vary greatly depending on the particular data needs of a study. Recent randomized evaluations have ranged in cost from a few thousand to many millions of dollars depending on the length of time over which the study runs, the number of alternative approaches that are tested, whether individuals or whole communities are randomized (see Module 4.2), and the type of outcome measures that are collected.

For example, a study that randomized the price at which pregnant women were willing to purchase insecticide-treated bed nets was relatively cheap. Individual women were randomized to receive nets for different prices, which meant that the sample size for the study could be relatively small (see Module 6.2) and geographically concentrated. One of the main outcomes of the study was whether the women purchased the nets, which was observed immediately. Enumerators also went back to individuals' houses to see whether they hung the nets (and whether paying for the nets made purchasers more likely to hang the nets once they had them), but even data on this outcome were relatively easy to collect and were collected shortly after the study started.[7]

There are cases in which randomized evaluations have used data collected by others to assess impact. For example, researchers examining the impact of serving in the Vietnam War were able to use data from Social Security tax records to examine the impact of the draft lottery on earnings.[8] Researchers studying a program of the Colombian government that gave vouchers to attend private schools to randomly selected children were able to use government data on who took the university entrance exam (a good predictor of high school completion) to conduct a relatively inexpensive, long-term follow-up to the study.

Using data that are already being collected by others dramatically reduces the cost of an evaluation, but the downside is that only outcomes on which data happens to have already been collected can be examined. In general, it is rare for data to have been collected on exactly the right individuals and at exactly the right time to be useful as outcome measures for a randomized evaluation, except when the randomization is on a massive scale.

Collaborative design and evaluation

Systematic, creative experimentation, in the tradition of research and development, can lead to innovative solutions. This often requires that the policymaker and the social scientist breach the designer–evaluator distinction and collaborate on the design of the intervention. Because randomized evaluations are prospective and require close cooperation between the evaluator and the implementer, these types of long-

7. This study by Jessica Cohen and Pascaline Dupas is summarized as Evaluation 6 in the appendix.
8. Joshua Angrist, "Lifetime Earnings and the Vietnam Era Draft Lottery: Evidence from Social Security Administrative Records," *American Economic Review* 40 (1990): 313–336, and "Did Vietnam Veterans Get Sicker in the 1990s? The Complicated Effects of Military Service on Self-Reported Health," Working Paper 09-19, Center for Economic Studies, US Census Bureau, Washington, DC.

run, in-depth partnerships often develop. Such partnerships can foster the design of new interventions that draw on practical experience, theory, previous impact evaluation results, knowledge of local conditions, and feedback from the local population. By clearly delineating a project as a pilot, the implementing agency may be able to try out new ideas that are more adventurous than they would have been able to try if launching a larger-scale program.

For example, a sequential experiment in Kenya's Western Province examined the relative merits of free distribution and user fees for insecticide-treated (bed)nets (ITNs) in terms of the coverage and use of those nets, which prevent malaria. In the short term, free distribution increases coverage rapidly, but user fees could increase the psychological commitment to using the product. In the long term, free distribution could, in theory, reduce coverage by reducing willingness to buy ITNs. The first experiment examined the impact of price on short-run ITN demand and use, finding that as the price increases, demand falls precipitously and that—contrary to conventional wisdom —as the price increases, usage remains the same.[9] Are there ways to reduce this sensitivity to price, to make people more willing to pay more for ITNs? The second experiment piloted a number of marketing campaigns on the same poor population. None of them had an impact, suggesting that only price matters. But what are the implications of free distribution for long-run coverage? Will people get used to free ITNs and so be less willing to buy them? Or will people learn about the benefits of ITNs and so be more willing to buy them? The third experiment suggests that those who were offered nets for free were more likely to pay for them later, presumably because they had learned that they were useful. This approach of designing new studies that build on the previous ones in the same context is facilitated by being able to tailor the questions very precisely, as we can with prospective evaluations.

Long-term results emerge in the long run

A disadvantage of doing a prospective evaluation is that we have to wait for the program to be implemented, the impact to be felt, and the data to be collected and analyzed before we can assess its impact. How

---

9. This study by Jessica Cohen and Pascaline Dupas and subsequent follow-up studies by Pascaline Dupas are summarized as Evaluation 6 in the appendix.

long we have to wait depends on the question we are trying to answer. Some questions can be answered quickly. In other cases, changes in outcomes take a long time to appear (Module 5.2 discusses the timing of data collection).

For example, when researchers wanted to assess alternative approaches to fundraising, they sent fundraisers door to door to collect money for a charity, randomizing the scripts used to solicit the money. In some cases respondents were asked to buy a lottery ticket (with the proceeds going to a charity), in others they were told that their contribution would be matched, and in others they were simply asked for a contribution. The outcome was the amount of money donated, and thus was immediate.[10]

In contrast, an evaluation examining the impact of education and child marriage on health outcomes in Bangladesh randomized a subsidy to families with unmarried adolescent girls (designed to encourage delayed marriage) and educational support to help girls stay in school. The program was effective in delaying marriage and increasing education, but its long-term effects on fertility, complications in pregnancy, and the health of future children will become apparent only over the long term.[11]

Evaluation methodologies that can be used retrospectively (like those that exploit quasirandom shocks that have happened in the past, as discussed in Module 2.2) do not have this limitation. For example, an evaluation of the Rockefeller Foundation's deworming program, which was offered in the US South in the early 1900s, used the timing of program rollout and variations in worm density in different geographic areas to create a counterfactual. The evaluation was done in the early 2000s and was immediately able to look at the long-run impacts of the program.[12] In contrast, a randomized evaluation of deworming in Kenya had to wait 10 years in order to assess 10-year impacts.[13]

10. Craig E. Landry, Andreas Lange, John A. List, Michael K. Price, and Nicholas G. Rupp, "Toward an Understanding of the Economics of Charity: Evidence from a Field Experiment," *Quarterly Journal of Economics* 121 (2006): 747–782.

11. This study by Erica Field and Rachel Glennerster is summarized as Evaluation 7 in the appendix.

12. Hoyt Bleakley, "Disease and Development: Evidence from Hookworm Eradication in the American South," *Quarterly Journal of Economics* 122 (2007): 73–117, doi: 10.1162/qjec.121.1.73.

13. For more details, see the study by Sarah Baird, Joan Hamory Hicks, Michael Kremer, and Edward Miguel, summarized as Evaluation 1 in the appendix.

Randomized evaluations are not always appropriate or useful

There are many important questions that cannot or should not be answered by a randomized evaluation. In Module 2.2 we have already discussed a range of nonrandomized impact evaluation methodologies and the assumptions under which they are valid. If opportunities arise in which these assumptions hold and a nonrandomized approach will be faster and easier than a randomized evaluation, it makes sense to use these alternative approaches. Other questions can be answered without an impact evaluation at all, or in other cases a randomized evaluation is incapable of answering the question well.

When an impact evaluation is not needed

Many important questions do not require an impact evaluation of any kind. For example, if we find that in a textbook program the textbooks are not delivered or are not used, there is little point in measuring their impact. We cover many other cases in which evaluation approaches other than impact evaluation are sufficient in Module 3.1.

Randomized evaluations are not good at assessing macroeconomic policy

The comparative advantage of the experimental approach is that it can answer specific questions about causal impact. In order to answer them well, we need many units to randomize. But if the policy we want to assess can be introduced only at a national level and if take-up of that policy is immediate for everyone in the country, it will be almost impossible to conduct a randomized evaluation: we would need to randomize some countries to adopt the policy and others not to do so.

An example of such a policy is the adoption of a fixed exchange rate, because there is only one exchange rate for the whole country and everyone is affected by the exchange rate policy. When a policy is introduced nationally but not taken up everywhere, it is still possible to perform a randomized evaluation, as we discuss in Module 4.3. Most macroeconomic questions, however, fall in the category of policies it would be hard—if not impossible—to evaluate using a randomized evaluation.

Randomized evaluations are not good at capturing general equilibrium effects

When an outcome is the result of thousands or potentially millions of interactions by different people, we say that it is established through a general equilibrium. An example is the price of gas in Massachusetts. Millions of people in Massachusetts purchase gas in a given week, and thousands of different gas stations sell it. Many factors affect the price, including the world price of gas, local demand, transport costs, the exchange rate, taxes, and refinery capacity. Prices are set through a complex interaction of all these factors. Although prices at one gas station may not be exactly the same as those at another gas station in the same state, there will be a relationship between them. This means that if we shock one part of the system (for example, by randomly raising the price or cutting demand) we will change the whole system (even if only slightly). We will have created what is called a *general equilibrium effect*. Randomized evaluations are not good at capturing these general equilibrium effects because, by definition, the effect is one that is felt at an entire system level, and thus there is no comparison group (at least not within the system). The only way we can use randomized evaluations to look at general equilibrium effects is if we can randomize at the level of the system.

Most wages and prices are established by equilibrating demand and supply between many different purchasers and consumers, and thus any impact of a program on general wages and prices in the area will be hard to capture. This has two implications: first, our estimates from a randomized evaluation may not capture the effect of the program if it were scaled up to the entire population because we have ignored general equilibrium effects, and second, there are important questions that we cannot answer because they are explicitly about general equilibrium effects.

Let us take the example of education and its impact on earnings. We can subsidize the cost of going to school for a random sample of children (maybe by buying them a free school uniform or paying school fees). We can then follow the children we subsidize and those we don't. We may find that those we subsidized get three more years of schooling on average than those we did not subsidize, and they also earn higher incomes later in life. We can conclude that the schooling caused the higher incomes, and we can calculate the impact of schooling on earning. But what would happen if everyone in the country suddenly earned more? Would the wages of educated people fall because there were so many more of them? If so, our evaluation would overestimate the impact of education on earnings if the policy were scaled up. On the other hand, there might be general equilibrium effects that go in the other direction. Perhaps having a concentration of more educated people in the country attracts more foreign invest- ment or generates more innovation, which has positive effects on incomes. If this is the case, we will have underestimated the impact of education on earnings if the program were scaled up.

The second issue is that we may specifically be interested in general equilibrium effects themselves. We may want to know whether a large increase in the number of educated workers helps attract more foreign investment. The only way we can measure general equilibrium effects is if markets are segmented—in other words, if smaller local markets are at least partly influenced by local demand and supply. We can then ran- domize at this local level. For example, a project in France randomized the percentage of local youths that were given job training. They found that helping one young person get a job had a negative effect on the pros- pect of other young people in the area finding a job.[14] As this example makes clear, general equilibrium effects are a form of spillover—that is, a case in which the impact of the program spills over from those targeted by the program to others. We discuss spillovers and what to do about them in much more detail in Modules 4.2 and 7.3. When markets are somewhat separate from each other, the spillovers are confined to the local area. With a large-scale randomized evaluation we might be able to assess these spillovers, but it will be impossible to measure the effects that are truly general—that is, the ones that affect the entire economy.

The inability to pick up general equilibrium effects is probably one of the most serious drawbacks of randomized evaluations, but it is not unique to them. Anyone using an evaluation methodology that com- pares one group of people exposed to a program with another group that is not has to worry about general equilibrium issues. It is only when we can compare whole systems that have experienced different shocks that we can measure general equilibrium impacts. The alternative is to build a model of the entire system and make assumptions about how the different parts of the system interact. This is called a general equilib- rium model. These models, while relying on a lot of assumptions, are explicitly designed to estimate likely general equilibrium effects.

In the next chapter we discuss in more detail what types of ques- tions can be answered well with impact evaluations and randomized evaluations and which cannot or should not be answered by random- ized evaluations.

---

14. This study by Bruno Crépon, Esther Duflo, Marc Gurgand, Roland Rathelot, and Philippe Zamora is summarized as Evaluation 8 in the appendix.

Ethical considerations

All evaluation and research that involves human beings raises ethical issues. Randomized evaluations have both ethical advantages and limitations. We start by setting out principles for assessing the ethical implications of any research involving human subjects. It is worth noting that the principles set out here are explicitly for research rather than evaluation. Research is defined (for purposes of these principles) as systematic study that generates lessons that can be applied more widely than in a particular case. In most cases our objective in conducting an evaluation is to draw wider lessons, suggesting that at least for this purpose we can think of our evaluations as research.

Ethical guidelines for evaluation and research

Ethical guidelines exist for researchers working with humans as subjects of their research. Many research organizations have *institutional review boards* (IRBs) that must approve any research proposals involving human subjects before they can proceed (unless the research is deemed to involve minimal risk) and that evaluate proposals against ethical guidelines.

Most ethical guidelines for researchers follow similar principles to those set out in the Belmont Report, which came out of the US National Commission for the Protection of Human Subjects, and we briefly cover the main points here in order to discuss how and when randomized evaluations are compatible with these principles.[15] We strongly encourage all those undertaking research to familiarize themselves with the details of this report and with relevant local guidelines. The three principles in the Belmont Report are the following:

- *Respect for persons.* People's decisions need to be respected. In particular, participants in research must give informed consent to participate in the research. Some groups need to be especially protected because they may not fully understand the risks of participating in research (for example, children) or may find it difficult to refuse to participate (for example, prisoners).

15. The Commission was established in the United States following concerns about unethical research conducted during and after the Second World War. The report can be found at US Department of Health and Human Services, "The Belmont Report," accessed November 28, 2012, http://www.hhs.gov/ohrp/humansubjects/guidance/belmont.html.

- *Benefice.* Researchers should avoid knowingly doing harm—for example, by encouraging take-up of a program that they have reason to believe is harmful. However, avoiding all risk can be harmful to society in general if it prevents research that could have wide benefits to society as a whole. Thus the overall benefits to society of the research always need to be balanced against the risks. Researchers should seek to maximize possible benefits and minimize possible harm.

- *Justice.* The allocation of risks and benefits between different groups of people should be fair. It is important to avoid a situation in which one group bears all the risk and another stands to reap all the benefits. For example, it would be unjust if a potentially risky vaccine were tested on prisoners and, once approved, were made available only to the rich.

Informed consent

The respect-for-persons principle requires that we tell those whom we would like to take part in a study what the research is about and ask their permission to make them part of the study. This is usually done as part of the baseline survey. The experiment is explained, and participants are asked for their permission to continue. Depending on the level of risk, either oral or written consent is required. Oral consent can often be beneficial, because it allows the illiterate (who might otherwise be too intimidated to participate) to be included in the program and the study, but usually special permission is required from the illiterate. In some situations, if risks are minimal and getting informed consent would either be very difficult or undermine the validity of the experiment, the informed consent rules can be waived or participants can be given partial information. An example of this would be a study in which explaining that an experiment was looking at participants' levels of racial bias might change how people answered questions.

There can be some ambiguity over informed consent rules when only a subset of those who take up an evaluated program is surveyed for the study. This arises mainly when a whole community is randomized to gain access to the program. In some cases those not surveyed are not considered part of the study, and thus informed consent from them is not required. Usually, although access is open to the whole community, individuals still have a choice as to whether to participate, and the decision to take up the program can be considered informed consent (as long as the implementer carefully explains the program to those who decide to take it up). If, however, take-up is not voluntary (for example, if fluoride or chlorine are added to the municipal water source), it becomes particularly important for the entire community to be consulted and any risks explained. Even when take-up is voluntary, it is good practice to inform the entire community about the study and the program in cases in which the entire community is randomized to receive access to a program.

Evaluating questions of relevance to the population being studied

Usually social science research is designed to answer questions relevant to the population being studied. For example, we study job counseling for unemployed youths in France because we want to improve job prospects for youth in France. We study the take-up of bed nets for pregnant women in the Western Province of Kenya because we want to design policies for increasing the use of bed nets by pregnant women in that area. This enables us to comply with the justice principle.

Do evaluations deny access to a program?

But what about the benefice principle? Don't randomized evaluations do harm because they lead to people being denied access to a program from which they would otherwise have benefited? And don't they involve testing programs whose benefits and risks are unknown on the poor? Before addressing these questions it is worth pointing out that these two concerns are in direct opposition to each other. The concern that randomized evaluations deny access to a program makes the assumption that we know a program is beneficial. In most cases, however, we do not know the impact of the program—that is why we are evaluating it. The concern that we are testing an unknown program implies we should "deny" access to everyone in case the program has negative effects. The case that research, and in particular randomized evaluations, are ethical comes from the position that if we do not know whether a program is beneficial, society benefits if its impacts are tested before it is scaled up to more people. There may be some risk to those who experience the program first, but those risks need to be balanced against the potential benefits of better understanding its impacts; those risks are explained to participants, and they accept them voluntarily.

Usually conducting a randomized evaluation neither increases nor decreases the number of people who are likely to receive a program even in the short run; it simply changes the geographic spread of the program. Without the evaluation, the program might be delivered to all eligible people in one district, but with it the program may be delivered to half the people in two districts. Sometimes changing who receives the program may have ethical implications: for example, if a program is very carefully targeted to the neediest, evaluating it with a randomized evaluation may require finding a larger, less targeted pool. We discuss the ethical issues in this case and how to design an experiment that minimizes harm in more detail in Module 4.3, in which we consider a particular randomization design known as a treatment lottery around a cutoff.

Weighing the risks and benefits

It can even be ethical to perform a randomized evaluation if doing so reduces the number of people receiving a program in the short run (for example, because wide-scale rollout is delayed to allow a pilot to be evaluated). Again, we need to weigh the likely risks and benefits. We have to weigh the potential harm caused to those who would have received the program earlier had we not done the research against the potential benefit from having rigorous evidence on its impact. The benefits include being able to use evidence of a positive impact to raise more funding to expand the program in the long run if it is effective or being able to replace the program with something more effective if its impact is disappointing. The evaluation may avoid harm if we find that the program has unintended negative consequences and it is not scaled up as a result.

For example, a program run by ICS designed to strengthen local women's self-help groups by providing training and finance in Kenya's Western Province was evaluated through a randomized evaluation. The results showed that the treatment groups were more likely to be taken over by richer, more educated women, while the most vulnerable women ceased to be members.[16] The evaluation helped ICS avoid scaling up a program that everyone had thought would be beneficial to vulnerable women but that had arguably hurt the interests of some of those it was designed to help.

16. Mary Kay Gugerty and Michael Kremer, "Outside Funding and the Dynamics of Participation in Community Associations," *American Journal of Political Science* 52 (2008): 585–602.

In weighing costs and benefits, an important consideration is how much evidence we have on the likely benefits of the program. If we already have good reason to think that a program will be beneficial, this means the bar for the benefits of doing the research must necessarily be higher.

Finally, it is worth noting that it can be ethical for researchers to evaluate a program they may be concerned has harmful effects, although the criteria under which such studies are approved are tightly regulated and the potential benefits of these studies need to be high. Imagine that there is a program that is quite commonly implemented but that the researcher is concerned may have harmful effects. The researcher does not have enough evidence to convince those running the program that it is harmful and should be shut down. It might well be that the benefits of gathering evidence of harm through a research program would outweigh the potential risks to those who take part in the research. The key criteria for moving forward ethically in such a context would be that there is no hard evidence that the program is harmful (if there were, we could use that evidence to have the program shut down without the evaluation), that all those taking part in the study will be warned of the potential risks, and that the evidence generated is likely to be effective in reducing the prevalence of the program in the future if the results show it causes harm.

Cross-cultural views on what is ethical

The ethical guidelines briefly summarized above were formulated in the United States. If we are running a randomized evaluation in another country, it is important to take into account views of what is ethical in that country. Many countries outside the United States have their own ethical guidelines and review processes, either at the national level or within individual institutions, for research involving human subjects. These can help researchers take into account local cultural ethical standards. For the most part, the guidelines these institutions follow are similar to US guidelines, although in some cases they are more explicitly medical in nature and less appropriate to the needs of social scientists. In some countries IRBs for research involving human subjects cover only medical studies, and in others the coverage is unclear. Even if there is no local review board or no review board that covers social science evaluations, it is important to understand which approaches would be considered ethical locally and which would not.

In the places J-PAL researchers have worked, using randomization or a lottery to share scarce resources is in general seen as an appropriate and ethical approach. Indeed, in many cases beneficiaries see randomization or a lottery as fairer than their typical experience, which may include allocation based on political connections, the magnitude of a bribe, or some unexplained and seemingly arbitrary decision-making. However, it is important to make sure that randomization is done in an appropriate way. For example, it may be that randomly choosing some children in a class to receive a free lunch while not giving a free lunch to others in the same class may be considered inappropriate, while choosing some schools to receive a free lunch while not giving it to all schools is considered quite normal.

We discuss how ethical issues should be incorporated into the decision on whether to randomize at the group or the individual level in Module 4.2 and the particular ethical issues related to different forms for randomized evaluations in Module 4.3.[17]

17. For further reading on the ethics of randomized evaluations, see Rachel Glennerster and Shawn Powers, "Assessing Risk and Benefit: Ethical Considerations for Running Randomized Evaluations, Especially in Developing Countries," in *Handbook on Professional Economic Ethics* (Oxford, UK: Oxford University Press, forthcoming).

3 Asking the Right Questions

This chapter is about how to decide when to perform a randomized evaluation, which programs or issues should be given priority for testing using this methodology, and which questions can be answered using other methodologies. The chapter contains the following modules:

MODULE 3.1: Questions That Do Not Need an Impact Evaluation
MODULE 3.2: Questions That Need an Impact Evaluation
MODULE 3.3: How to Prioritize among Impact Evaluation Questions

MODULE 3.1 Questions That Do Not Need an Impact Evaluation

There are many different types of evaluations, including needs assessments, process evaluations, and impact evaluations. Each is designed to answer a different type of question. In this module we discuss what information gaps can be filled by doing an original evaluation of each type as well as what we can learn from existing evidence by doing literature reviews and cost-effectiveness projections.

In the previous chapter we saw that performing a randomized evaluation confers a number of advantages for generating the information that we need for evidence-based policy. But undertaking a good randomized evaluation is hard and can be expensive. We should undertake one only when the benefits from the lessons we learn are likely to outweigh the costs. We should not conduct a randomized evaluation every time we implement a program. Nor do we need a randomized evaluation every time we have a question about whether and how a program is working. Many important questions can be answered by other types of evaluations, such as needs assessments or process evaluations.

Different questions require different methodologies

In seeking to improve the effectiveness of policies and programs, we need to tackle a wide range of questions: strategic questions about objectives, descriptive questions about the problems and opportunities on the ground, process questions about how smoothly a program is functioning, and impact questions about whether a program is changing lives. And for all of these questions we would ideally like to know not just the answer for our own organization, context, and program but also what others have learned. How does our strategic focus overlap with or complement those of other organizations? How does the impact of our program compare to the impact of alternative approaches tested by others? Different evaluation methods are suited to these different types of questions.

We don't need a randomized evaluation to answer most of the questions discussed here. However, we do need to answer all these questions if we want to conduct a good randomized evaluation. In particular, we need to have good descriptive information on the participants and the context of the program, know the objectives of the program, and have good process indicators that will tell us whether the program we are evaluating was well implemented.

Strategic questions: What do we want to achieve?

What are our objectives? Where should we focus our attention? Are we trying to improve health or education? For whom? What particular outcomes do we care the most about? These are critical questions. They are not, however, the focus of this book, nor do we have particular expertise in helping organizations prioritize among high-level strategic objectives. We do not discuss strategic questions any further except to note that the first and critical step in good program design and evaluation is to be able to articulate program objectives with precision.

Descriptive questions: What are the needs?

To design a good program or policy, we must have a thorough understanding of the context. What is the reality on the ground? What problems and opportunities are the targeted people facing? How are they already dealing with these problems? How are they taking advantage of their opportunities? Answering these questions is critical to designing better programs and better evaluations. A good descriptive assessment can also raise questions about whether an existing program is appropriately designed or filling a real need.

Process questions: How well is the program being implemented?

How is the program functioning? Are the supplies getting where they need to go on time? Is the program reaching the right people? Process questions can be answered without an impact evaluation and can tell us a lot about whether a program is working.

Impact questions: Did it work?

Given that the program was implemented, did it change outcomes for those it targeted? We may want to know if the program as a whole worked. Or, if the program had many components, did the components work best alone or as a package? Which components were most critical to its effectiveness? We may also want to know about theories that inform the design of comparable programs. For example, some program designers create programs that charge for products and services in the belief that people who are willing to pay for them are more likely to use them appropriately. We may design a set of evaluations to find out if this assumption holds: does charging really improve targeting to those who need and value our product or service and would use it appropriately?

The needs assessment

We can learn a lot by carefully collecting descriptive information, both qualitative and quantitative. The types of questions *descriptive surveys* or needs assessments can answer include the following:

- What groups in the population should be targeted (for example, which have the greatest need or would benefit the most)?
- What problems and opportunities does the targeted group face?
- What are the possible reasons for the problems they face?
- What are people already doing to resolve these problems and meet the underlying need?
- What challenges remain unaddressed?

When are needs assessments most useful?

Descriptive methodologies can be very powerful. They are the basis of good program design. The understanding of context that they provide helps ensure that a program is designed to solve a problem that really exists in a specific context, matters to the targeted people, and fits their constraints and opportunities. Needs assessments can also help pinpoint weaknesses in existing programs. For example, they can tell us why targeting is poor or the rate of take-up is low. Focus groups may tell us that people find that a program is located too far away or operates at inconvenient times; absenteeism surveys can show us whether program staff are regularly absent; take-up surveys can assess what fraction of potentially eligible participants are actually using a service; and random supply checks can make sure that supplies are getting through.

If we are planning an education program (or an evaluation) for primary schools, we need to have a good understanding of the level of learning among primary-age children in the area. Who is falling behind, and who is not? What are the possible reasons that learning levels are low? What are the child absenteeism rates? What are the teacher absenteeism rates? (If children who attend regularly are learning well, child absenteeism could be the problem.) Or are children who attend regularly still falling behind? What do parents and children say about why they do not attend and why they find it hard to learn? What do teachers say about why learning levels are low? How are classes conducted? What material is covered? Is it appropriate to the level of learning of most children? Are children sick or hungry? Can they see and hear what is going on?

We also need to know if other providers are working in the area. What are they doing?

The answers to these questions can help us design a program to address the identified problems. If we are going to perform an impact evaluation, a needs assessment or descriptive survey will help us (jointly with the implementer) define a theory of change that will be used to design the evaluation (see Module 5.1). It will also help inform the design of our measurement tools (see Chapter 5) and provide input into our power calculations (see Chapter 6).

What methodologies are most useful for a descriptive or
needs assessment?

Needs assessments often include structured qualitative interviews with
individuals or focus groups. However, representative quantitative surveys are also extremely powerful tools for understanding a context,
informing the design of a program, and alerting us to problems in
existing programs. It is often possible to find relevant quantitative
data from other sources even if there is not sufficient funding to
undertake a new representative survey. In general, a combination of
both qualitative and quantitative techniques is useful in gaining a
good understanding of the context in which a program will be implemented or in which existing programs are being implemented.

The benefit of qualitative methodologies is that they allow for
open-ended questions. The free-ranging discussion that often results
makes it easier for new ideas and issues that the evaluator had not
previously thought of to more readily emerge. However, relying solely
on qualitative methods, even in a needs or descriptive assessment, can
be misleading, because people tend to give answers that they think we
want to hear. Beneficiaries may think it rude to point out the problems with existing services or programs. They may say they use a program or facility more than they actually do (just as people claim to
wash their hands more than they actually do).

Finally, people affected by a problem may not always understand
the problem they face. For example, parents in the Western Province
of Kenya did not realize that their children were infected with parasitic worms and that this was contributing to their skipping school.[1]
It is therefore helpful to go into a needs or descriptive assessment
with information about what other programs and research have found
elsewhere and to use this information to inform both qualitative and
quantitative methodologies. It is important to avoid preconceived
notions of local needs. But being well informed can help us ask questions more effectively. Chapter 5 discusses instruments for collecting
data on outcomes, but many of these approaches can also be used
during a needs assessment.

1. This study by Sarah Baird, Joan Hamory Hicks, Michael Kremer, and Edward
Miguel is summarized as Evaluation 1 in the appendix.

When is a descriptive needs assessment sufficient?

A needs assessment, or descriptive assessment, can sometimes be sufficient to raise serious issues and make us rethink our program before it is implemented. In other cases it can raise serious concerns about an existing program without the need for an impact evaluation. A descriptive assessment is sufficient in the following circumstances:

There is no real problem. For example, a program (or proposed program) may address a problem that exists elsewhere but does not exist locally or is less important locally than we thought. For example, we might assume that inadequate toilet facilities and sanitation products are leading girls to skip school, but a descriptive survey may reveal that girls are just as likely to attend school on days when they are menstruating as on days when they are not.[2]

The problem addressed is not a priority for the people or not as severe as we thought. We may plan to introduce new financial products but realize that existing informal networks of risk sharing and credit are already very sophisticated and decide that financial products are not the highest-priority intervention.

The cause of the problem is different from what we assumed. We may observe high rates of diarrhea in a population and assume that the drinking water source is contaminated. We design a program to prevent such contamination, building toilets and encouraging their use, but the rate of diarrhea remains high. We come to find out that if we had done a little more homework—checking levels of contamination at the water source, for example—we might have found that the drinking water when collected at the source has relatively low levels of contamination but becomes more contaminated while it is stored in households before being drunk. The more appropriate solution would have been point-of-use water treatment, such as the use of chlorine.

2. Emily Oster and Rebecca Thornton, "Menstruation, Sanitary Products, and School Attendance: Evidence from a Randomized Evaluation," *American Economic Journal: Applied Economics* 3 (2011): 91–100, and "Determinants of Technology Adoption: Private Value and Peer Effects in Menstrual Cup Take-Up," NBER Working Paper 148128, National Bureau of Educational Research, Cambridge, MA, 2009; J-PAL Policy Briefcase, "Menstruation as a Barrier to Education?" (Cambridge, MA: Abdul Latif Jameel Poverty Action Lab, 2011, http://www.povertyactionlab.org/publication/menstruation-barrier-education).

The basic conditions needed to make a program effective are not in place. Imagine that we are planning to provide incentives for expectant mothers to deliver in medical facilities. If a needs assessment finds a high rate of staff absenteeism at local facilities, we may want to rethink the program, because there is little point in encouraging mothers to show up if there is no one there to receive them.

The process evaluation

A process evaluation can tell us whether a program is being implemented as planned and how well it is functioning. It asks such questions as these:

- Are the program services being delivered (do the textbooks or building supplies reach the right people at the right time)?
- Are the outputs being delivered to the right people at the right time (was the bridge built, the training held, the vaccination given)?
- Are the program staff well informed and working hard?
- Is all the money accounted for?

When are process evaluations most useful?

Unlike impact evaluations, process evaluations need to be performed for every program. Most organizations will seek to answer these questions on an ongoing basis as part of their monitoring and evaluation systems. A key benefit of an ongoing process evaluation is that it can pick up implementation problems early so that these can be corrected. Another benefit is that the attendant monitoring can provide an incentive for better performance by program staff, boosting the quality of services. Process evaluations are also critical for good impact evaluations. If we find that a program has no impact, the implications of that finding are very different depending on whether the program was implemented well or not.

When is a process evaluation sufficient?

Process evaluations can tell us a lot about whether a program is failing and, if so, why. For example, if we find that textbooks are not being delivered to schools or new education software is not being used, there is no point in conducting an impact evaluation of these programs to learn whether the textbooks or new software have raised test scores.

What methodologies are used for a process evaluation?

We can use many different data collection instruments in a process evaluation. Chapter 5 discusses data collection issues in more detail. Below are the main approaches that are used.

Assessing operations on paper. For each step in the theory of change, an operations plan should articulate the tasks that must be performed to achieve it, by whom, and when. If there isn't one already, we must write one so that we will know how the program is supposed to be carried out. For example, imagine that we are conducting an antimalaria program that distributes mosquito nets at prenatal clinics.[3] We have to buy the nets, recruit the clinics into the program, deliver and store the nets, inform the target population, give the nets to the targeted people only, and so on. The operations plan outlines all the program tasks, and an analysis of this plan may reveal potential problems.

Following paper trails. We can then examine paper records to see if the operations plan has been followed. We would want to trace the flow of money, determine the delivery dates of inputs, ensure that time targets were met, and, where possible, assess the rates of use of the new facility or program.

Assessing operations in the field. A paper review should ideally be accompanied by some on-the-ground checking. The records may say that the attendance rate at a new school is high, but a good process evaluation will check the records against reality. A small number of random visits will quickly tell us whether the paper records are accurate and, if not, how great the gap is between the records and reality. We should also interview beneficiaries to hear their side of the story. Are they using the new school? How do they find it?

The literature review

A literature review is in a different category from the methodologies we have discussed so far. Instead of gathering new information about

---

3. This study by Jessica Cohen and Pascaline Dupas is summarized as Evaluation 6 in the appendix.

the context, process, or impact of a specific program, it seeks to summarize the information that existing studies have gathered on these issues. A literature review answers such questions as the following:

- What studies have already been done in this area?
- What is the quality of the evidence?
- Are there gaps in the evidence?
- How important are those gaps for making the decisions that need to be made?
- What are some of the general lessons that emerge from the many different studies?

When is a literature review most useful?

A systematic literature review can give us the state of knowledge of the subject we are studying, both empirical and theoretical. It tells us what solutions have been tried, what was effective and what was not, sometimes why the solutions were effective, and which of their components were important for their success or failure. It can also identify the underlying theories that help explain the problem we are trying to solve and why different approaches have proved to be effective or ineffective elsewhere.

Literature reviews are particularly useful when there is lots of good evidence to draw on. We can then use this evidence to improve a program's design and reprioritize our spending to focus on programs that have been found to be particularly effective. For evaluators, literature reviews can help identify the most important knowledge gaps and therefore where we want to perform our next evaluation. Where there is little rigorous evidence, a literature review can be completed quickly, draw attention to the lack of evidence, and stimulate more research. As discussed below, it is less useful to carefully document a large amount of poor-quality research.

When is a literature review sufficient?

After performing a literature review, we may decide that we have sufficient evidence to make a decision about how to move forward without an impact evaluation. For example, we may have been planning to offer a health program in schools in Rajasthan. We undertake a literature review of the evidence on different school health interventions and decide we want to help support the government in introducing mass school-based deworming in districts with a high intestinal worm load. We still need to perform a needs assessment to check which areas of the state have high worm loads, and we need to conduct a process evaluation to make sure that the pills actually get to the schools and are taken by children in the right quantity. An impact evaluation might be interesting, because no one has evaluated the impact of deworming in this environment. However, we may still decide that, given the pressures on resources and the existing evidence on the benefits of deworming, we do not need to perform an impact evaluation of our program.

What methodologies are used to conduct literature reviews?

When starting or commissioning a literature review we need to determine the scope of the review. Will it cover just impact evaluations, or would it be useful to include descriptive studies? Maybe the objective is to see what others have learned about improving processes, in which case it could focus on process evaluations. What should be its geographic and subject scope? Should it cover studies about primary school in the United Kingdom? Or do we want to include studies from other industrialized countries? Maybe we are particularly interested in low-income urban settings. As always, our study must be tailored to fit our objectives.

Once we have identified the scope of the review, we need to systematically identify studies that should be considered for inclusion in the review. This is likely to involve searching relevant journals and databases of studies (the Cochrane Collaboration provides guidance on how to perform systematic reviews).[4] A good place to start is with existing reviews. We can use these as a base and then update them with more recent studies or augment the scope of these reviews to meet our needs. Many development organizations commission and disseminate reviews of the evidence. For example, the World Bank publishes the World Development Report (WDR), which focuses each year on a particular issue or sector and often highlights important studies (with fuller literature reviews often published as background papers to the WDR). Research and evaluation units within multilateral organizations, such as the Development Impact Evaluation Initiative, also publish reviews. The International Initiative for

---

4. Julian Higgins and Sally Green, eds., *Cochrane Handbook for Systematic Reviews of Interventions: Cochrane Book Series* (West Sussex, UK: John Wiley and Sons, 2008).

Impact Evaluation (3ie) has commissioned a number of reviews of the results of impact evaluations in specific areas. Research centers dedicated to impact evaluation, such as J-PAL at MIT and Innovations for Poverty Action, often have reviews of the evidence in specific areas available on their websites.

Many scholarly journals routinely publish literature reviews. Often these reviews comment on the quality of particular studies, making it easier to weigh the conclusions. They also discuss the relations between studies and draw out more general lessons. In economics, for example, the *Handbook of Economics* series (which has volumes on agriculture, development, education, labor, and many other sectors), the *Annual Review of Economics,* and the *Journal of Economic Perspectives* are all good sources for reviews of recent literature.

The next step is to determine the quality threshold to apply when deciding whether to include a particular study in the review. A review that includes all studies related to a topic without any filter on quality can be unhelpful at best and potentially highly misleading. Take the example of an intervention (such as deworming) that generates positive externalities in that the benefits accrue not only to those who participate but also to their neighbors. Studies that do not take potential externalities into account will systematically underestimate the impact of the program (see Module 4.2). Imagine that there are 30 studies that evaluate this intervention: 24 of them fail to take the potential for externalities into account, while 5 do take them into account. If we average all the studies, regardless of quality, we may conclude that the intervention is not effective, whereas if we focus on the 5 more thorough studies we may find that the intervention is highly effective. Even if our literature review explains the difference in quality, it is not a good idea to spend a lot of time, if any, on poor-quality studies. Although we may want to briefly explain why certain studies are not of high quality, including too much information on bad studies detracts attention from the important information in the high-quality studies.

Exactly where the quality threshold should be drawn for any literature review depends in part on the depth of the evidence that is available. If there are no high-quality impact evaluations in the area, we will spend more time covering descriptive studies and some poorer-quality impact studies (while noting the caveats associated with the different studies). If there is a wealth of high-quality descriptive work and rigorous impact evaluations, we can be choosier about what we include. We will still want to include descriptive studies in order to be better informed about the problems and the context (Module 2.2 discusses the advantages and disadvantages of different nonrandomized impact evaluations, and Module 9.1 covers how to judge the quality of a randomized evaluation).

Another decision to make is how much interpretation to add to the study results. Some literature reviews present the results of different studies and do very little interpretation of how they fit together as a whole. Others try to put the results of many different studies into a combined theoretical framework. Done well, this latter approach can help us draw much broader lessons from existing studies, for example, by hypothesizing why we see the results we do and helping us extrapolate to other contexts. As we will discuss in more detail in Module 9.2, it is not possible to make good projections about whether and how results from one context will generalize to another without having some underlying theory, and the best literature reviews combine a review of the empirical evidence with theoretical underpinnings.

Cost-effectiveness projection or business case assessment

The final tool we mention here is a structured way to draw upon the evidence generated by others and use it to answer questions about a project without needing to undertake a full-blown impact evaluation. A cost-effectiveness projection, also called a business case assessment, asks hypothetical questions. If the proposed project had these costs and these impacts, would it be a cost-effective way of addressing the problem? If we wanted to transpose a project that was very cost-effective in one context to a different context, under what conditions would it still be cost-effective? Even in the best-case scenario for impact, could this project be cost-effective?

When is cost-effectiveness projection or business case assessment most useful?

This approach is most useful when we have cost-effectiveness analyses of similar projects or of projects seeking to address the same objective. A cost-effectiveness analysis of a similar project conducted in a slightly different context can allow us to think through, in a systematic way, how changes in cost in the new setting will impact cost-effectiveness. It also gives us the basis for performing a sensitivity analysis to see under what assumptions the project will be cost-effective in the new context. For example, would it still be cost-effective if the impact in the new context was 20 percent lower? Cost-effectiveness analyses from another project designed to achieve the same objective as ours can be useful in judging whether the new project will outperform the alternative approach.

In some situations, a business case assessment can still be useful even if we don't have many existing cost-effectiveness studies. This is particularly true in the case of very expensive programs: in these cases it is sometimes possible to calculate that the program would not be cost-effective in any plausible scenario.

Imagine that a proposed program is designed to boost farmers' income. The average farmer makes a profit of $400 a year. The program will provide inputs and training to 200 farmers at a cost of $1 million. In other words, it will cost $5,000 per farmer, meaning that it would have to increase farmers' income 12.5 times to break even. Even if there were spillovers—if, say, each farmer passed her knowledge on to 5 other farmers and they all doubled their incomes as a result—the program would still generate less than half the money for farmers that it cost to implement. A business case assessment would make this clear, allowing us to rethink the program, including whether it would be a judicious use of scarce resources.

What methodologies can be used?

A cost-effectiveness analysis tells us the cost of achieving a standardized unit of impact. For example, we can compare programs that use different approaches to reduce child diarrhea: improving water sources, providing chlorine, educating people about hand washing. To do that, we would calculate the cost of averting one case of child diarrhea for each program. This would allow us to compare the costs per unit of impact of different programs that have the same objective. (We discuss how to perform cost-effectiveness analyses in more detail in Module 9.3.)

In a cost-effectiveness projection we make assumptions about costs and impact to judge whether a proposed project or program would be effective under different assumptions. We can draw on cost and impact data from cost-effectiveness analyses conducted for other projects to inform our assumptions. We run our projections in multiple scenarios, including both best-case scenarios and realistic potential-impact scenarios. If these calculations show that our program would be less cost-effective than other alternatives, even if it achieved a best-case scenario and a huge impact, there is little point in implementing the program.

When is a cost-effectiveness projection sufficient?

A cost-effectiveness projection applied to a new context and a business case assessment of a new project are both projections and require assumptions. Nevertheless, the results may be sufficiently robust to different assumptions that we can make an investment decision without performing an impact evaluation. We may find that a project is unlikely to be cost-effective under most reasonable assumptions and conclude that we would prefer to invest our resources elsewhere. Alternatively, we may decide that the project will be highly cost-effective under a range of assumptions on cost and impact, so we should implement it. We will want to conduct a process evaluation to check whether our cost and take-up assumptions were correct, but we may decide to save our impact evaluation resources for a project with greater uncertainty about impact.

Example: Business case assessment of piped water in Zambia

Imagine that we specialize in funding water projects. We receive a proposal for piping clean water to houses in a poor area on the outskirts of Lusaka, where residents have no access to clean water. The objective of the program is to reduce the incidence of diarrhea. Is the program worth implementing and evaluating?

Fortunately, there have been a number of other impact evaluations of alternative approaches to reducing diarrhea. There was a randomized evaluation of a piped water program in an urban area of Morocco. This found no reductions in the incidence of diarrhea. But in Morocco people had already been using clean water from communal taps that drew water from the same grid as the water that was to be piped into their homes. The counterfactual was clean water from a communal tap. In Lusaka, the existing water used by the community is contaminated, so the example from Morocco is not relevant to this proposal.

Next we note that several randomized evaluations have shown positive health impacts from alternative approaches to addressing contaminated water sources, such as improving the water sources from which people collect their water or providing chlorine for people to add to the water they store in their homes. We use the results from these evaluations to estimate the cost-effectiveness of applying these approaches in our setting. Then we calculate the cost per head of the proposal in front of us. From this we can estimate how much diarrhea would need to be reduced to make piped water the most cost-effective way of reducing diarrhea in our context. We may find that building and maintaining the infrastructure to bring piped water to individual homes is so many orders of magnitude more expensive than the alternative approaches that no realistic reduction in diarrhea from introducing piped water will make it more cost-effective than the alternatives. Thus we may decide not to fund the proposal even without the results of a rigorous impact evaluation.

The results from this type of business case assessment need to be treated with caution. They are useful for putting a bound on the likely cost-effectiveness of a program and for ruling out some options as unlikely to be cost-effective even in the best-case scenario. Business case assessments are not, however, evidence of impact. A business case evaluation may suggest that even a modest impact would make a program cost-effective. This is useful to know, but without an impact evaluation we cannot know that even these modest impacts will be realized. However, if it is not possible to undertake an impact evaluation, a business case assessment may be an appropriate alternative. It can also help us decide if a project has the prospect of being cost-effective and thus is worth evaluating rigorously. Finally, a business case assessment or cost-effectiveness projection can, as we discuss in Module 6.4, provide useful input into our power calculations, which will help us determine how large a sample size we will need if we perform an impact evaluation.

Module 3.1 summary

- Descriptive surveys and needs assessments can help us design better programs by telling us what the problems on the ground are, what solutions already exist, and how well existing institutions and programs are functioning.

- Process evaluations tell us how well a program is being implemented. Sometimes this is all we need to know to evaluate a program.

- Reviews of the existing literature may answer many of our questions about how to design a good program and which programs to prioritize. Literature reviews can also highlight where additional impact evaluations would be most useful.

- Cost-effectiveness projections or business case assessments can tell us whether a proposed program would be cost-effective under a range of different assumptions. If we find that even in the best-case scenario the proposed program is unlikely to be cost-effective, we may decide not to proceed with the program even in the absence of an impact evaluation.

MODULE 3.2 Questions That Need an Impact Evaluation

An impact evaluation can answer the basic question of whether a program or policy works. But it can also answer a host of other questions. This module discusses the fact that some of these questions are particularly relevant to the organization running the program, but many are of much wider interest to the general antipoverty community.

What is the impact of the program?

We have a clearly defined program, and we want to know if the program as a whole works. This is the most basic question that an impact evaluation answers. The program may have one component or several. For example, it might provide free school uniforms to reduce the economic burden of staying in school. An impact evaluation of such a program can answer a very precise question, such as how much dropout rates fall when families no longer have to bear the burden of providing school uniforms. Alternatively, a program may provide a package of inputs to schools including textbooks, school uniforms, repairs to school buildings, and scholarships to help poor children attend school. In this latter case, the impact evaluation measures the impact of the package as a whole.

Which elements of the program matter the most?

We may also want to know which elements of a program matter the most for impact. For example, we know that *conditional cash transfer* (CCT) programs can be effective in improving health and education. But there are two elements to a CCT program: extra money and a conditionality (the requirement that families send their children to school and use healthcare services). Which element matters in terms of impact? If what is driving the results is the fact that a family has more money to invest in education and health, unconditional transfers may be better than conditional transfers. They do not exclude the poorest families, which are often the ones that fail to meet the conditionality, and they are also less expensive because we do not have to monitor compliance with the conditionality. But if the conditionality itself is what is driving the results, unconditional transfers may be less effective. Understanding which components of a program are most salient can help us design programs that are just as effective but less expensive, allowing us to reach more people with the same resources.

Which of two alternative strategies should we pursue?

We may want to test the relative effectiveness of alternative versions of a program so we can scale up the most effective version. Take the example of microfinance. A credit program can have group liability or individual liability. Which version increases loan repayments? In a typical microcredit program, borrowers have to start paying back the loan immediately, say, within a week of receiving the loan. How does varying the grace period change the type of project that the borrowers invest in? We may vary the length of the grace period or of the repayment schedule.

In an antimalaria program that provides vouchers for bed nets that can be redeemed at local pharmacies, we may vary the information we make salient in the marketing campaign (information about the negative health effects of malaria or about the positive savings from preventing malaria); we may also vary to whom we give the voucher (the male or female head of the household); and we may vary the size of the copayment, that is, the size of the subsidy we are providing (if the full price of a net is $6, we could provide vouchers worth $2, $4, or $6).[5]

Can we work on problems one at a time, or do we need to address all the related problems simultaneously?

Does a program have to address all aspects of a problem to be effective? Does an agriculture program, for example, have to include extension services to farmers as well as credit services, access to inputs and marketing, financial literacy training, and rural road improvements? A common assumption is that tackling any one of these barriers on its own will have no effect, and only a multipronged program will substantially change behavior and incomes. This hypothesis that there are strong complementarities between interventions is often voiced but rarely tested. Impact evaluations can be designed to test whether the impact of the joint program is greater than the

5. This study by Jessica Cohen and Pascaline Dupas is summarized as Evaluation 6 in the appendix.

impact of the sum of the individual components, which would provide evidence of complementarities.

Do results from one context translate into another?

An impact evaluation assesses the impact of a program or policy on a specific population at a given time. If we want to try the approach in a similar context, we may decide that we have enough evidence to move forward, but if we are working in a very different context, we may want to test whether the approach will also work there.

For example, CCTs have been replicated and evaluated in different countries of Latin America and the Caribbean. A country in that region, with comparable services, incomes, and so on, can be fairly confident that CCTs will have similar results there. A country in sub-Saharan Africa, however, may have a sufficiently different context that it is worth performing a new evaluation. The magnitude of cash transfers designed for Latin America may be beyond the budgets of most sub-Saharan African countries. Will the results hold if the transfers are much smaller in absolute terms? The health challenges may be very different in the new context; for example, HIV is a much larger problem in parts of sub-Saharan Africa than in much of Latin America. What impact will CCTs have on the health challenges in the new context? A series of impact evaluations have examined exactly this issue, adapting both the design of a CCT and the evaluation to the context in Malawi.[6]

In another example, researchers tested a program to give the ultrapoor productive assets (such as a buffalo) and mentoring to help them achieve financial sustainability in Bangladesh, Ethiopia, Ghana, Honduras, Peru, and Yemen.[7] The decision to test in several contexts came in part from a concern that the program's impact might be sensitive to context—for example, the assets provided to the ultrapoor would need to vary by context, and the market conditions in which the ultrapoor have to operate would also be different.

6. Hans-Peter Kohler and Pascaline Dupas, "Conditional Cash Transfers and HIV/AIDS Prevention: Unconditionally Promising?" *World Bank Economic Review* 26 (2012): 165–190.

7. This set of ongoing evaluations is discussed in Innovations for Poverty Action, "Ultra Poor Graduation Pilots," accessed January 2, 2012, http://www.poverty-action.org/ultrapoor/.

What fundamental processes underlie the observed behaviors and challenges?

The policy solutions and program designs that we introduce are based on our beliefs about the root causes of the problems. Impact evaluations can help us tease out what is driving the behavior we observe. For example, farmers in Africa are not adopting agricultural technologies that could improve their yield and ultimately their wellbeing. This could be for any number of reasons. The technology may be much less effective than we think. Farmers may not understand the technology well enough to use it effectively, in which case extension services may help. Farmers may not adopt the technology because they are risk averse; even though the technology has high returns, the returns are also more variable (riskier) than the returns from their current practices, in which case insurance or other risk-spreading mechanisms may help. Farmers may want to adopt the technology but find it hard to save the money they need to make the investment, in which case commitment savings may help.[8]

How can we find out which of these constraints underlie the low rate of technology take-up? We could ask farmers what they think and from their answers select likely hypotheses, but there are often motivators of behavior that people fail to articulate. Impact evaluations can test these alternative hypotheses and so identify the relevant process. By helping us understand the problems farmers face, they can also help us to generate new ideas on how to solve them.

MODULE 3.3 How to Prioritize among Impact Evaluation Questions

We can use the methods discussed in the first module to winnow the number of questions that need to be evaluated with an impact evaluation. However, we will still be left with a long list of questions that can be answered only with a new impact evaluation. This is particularly true if our impact questions go beyond "Does the program work?" to the many more complex questions that impact evaluations can answer (as we dis-

---

8. Kelsey B. Jack, "Market Inefficiencies and the Adoption of Agricultural Technologies in Developing Countries," Agricultural Technology Adoption Initiative, J-PAL (Abdul Latif Jameel Poverty Action Lab, MIT), and CEGA (Center for Effective Global Action, Berkeley), 2011, http://www.povertyactionlab.org/publication/market-inefficiences-and-adoption-agricultural-technologies-developing-countries.

cussed in the second module). That means we will have to prioritize. This module discusses how we choose which questions to answer with a randomized evaluation.

We should try to be strategic about investing in randomized evaluations and to have a plan for prioritizing different options. There are no simple rules for deciding between different impact evaluation questions, not least because of the need to balance so many criteria. Nevertheless, we discuss a number of factors to take into account when prioritizing questions that are candidates for impact evaluations.

What is the potential influence of the information yielded by the evaluation?

We evaluate in order to provide information that can help us and others in the international community to make decisions about which policies and programs to invest in and how to implement these programs. Our decision to invest in a randomized evaluation will depend on how influential the information generated by the results of the evaluation will be. To gauge the potential for influence, it is useful to ask the following questions.

Is the program or approach popular, or are significant resources invested in the approach?

When a program or approach is commonly used and substantial resources are invested in it, there is scope for the lessons from an impact evaluation to be influential and improve the effectiveness of how these resources are spent. All else equal, if a particular type of program represents a large portion of an organization's or a government's work, measuring the program's impact is a high priority. Similarly, if a type of program is commonly used across different countries and organizations, it is also a high priority for evaluation.

Is the program or approach likely to be expanded?

Some types of programs may not be large yet but may be scheduled for major expansion. This expansion represents a good opportunity to invest in understanding what works and how to structure programs that will be larger in the future. An added advantage is that there may be more flexibility to respond to the results of an evaluation before a program is expanded. Once a program is implemented at a massive scale, the stakes are higher and interests more vested. Then there can be considerable inertia with regard to making changes or cuts—even if the results of an impact evaluation show that there is little or no benefit from the program.

Is the approach inexpensive and easy to scale?

An approach may not be particularly common yet, but it may hold potential for being scaled up because it is relatively inexpensive and does not rely on scarce resources, such as highly motivated and skilled staff. An evaluation that finds that a low-cost, scalable approach is effective is likely to have much more impact on policy decisions than one that finds that an expensive and difficult-to-replicate program is effective.

What is the extent of existing evidence?

If many high-quality impact evaluations have already examined a particular evaluation question, that question should be a lower priority for additional evaluation. Although it is important to replicate evaluations to understand whether the results differ by context, we should be careful not to simply duplicate the efforts of others. All else equal, the amount to be learned from the fifth impact evaluation to examine a particular question is usually lower than the amount to be learned from the first impact evaluation on a question.

There are hundreds of randomized impact evaluations currently ongoing in different sectors across the globe. There are also thousands of different approaches to poverty reduction, which means that it is unlikely that we will find another evaluation of *exactly* the same program. Still, in prioritizing which evaluations to conduct, we should choose those that have the best potential to contribute new knowledge to the evidence base. So, if there are already many evaluations of similar programs, evaluating a class of programs that has not been studied as much may make a larger contribution.

Are the questions crosscutting or theory-driven?

Certain issues come up again and again in different programs and in different contexts. These make for very good evaluation questions. Thus we may decide to prioritize an impact evaluation that is able to address a fundamental issue, even if it would not be considered a high priority based on other criteria—for example, if it evaluates a small program that is unlikely to be scaled up. Examples of crosscutting questions include the following:

- What approaches help reduce public service absenteeism?
- What is the impact of price on health-seeking behavior?
- How important is class size to learning outcomes?
- What is the impact of greater community involvement in development projects?
- How much are people willing to pay for reduced air pollution?
- Does paying higher wages reduce corruption?

It may be that the answer to each of these questions is different in different contexts, but this in itself is an important issue to test empirically. As we gather more evidence on these important questions in different contexts, we will learn which results generalize and which do not.

When the question we want to answer is crosscutting, we must design our evaluation carefully so that we are isolating just the one factor we want to examine. For example, if we test a program that reduces class size but at the same time changes many other aspects of the classroom environment (the type of teacher, the level of inputs), we will not be able to isolate the impact of class size on its own without making additional assumptions. For this reason, evaluations that test crosscutting questions sometimes involve constructing somewhat artificial programs that would not necessarily be replicated without modification. The objective is to learn about a general issue that will feed into many different types of programs.

Example: An extra teacher program

Researchers set out to test three questions of fundamental importance to education in developing countries: how would test scores respond to lower class sizes, more accountable teachers, and tracking by initial learning level? They worked with a small NGO (ICS Africa) to establish a program that could answer each of these questions. Although the program used locally hired contract teachers, a strategy common throughout the developing world, the design of the program was very much driven by the evaluation design. For example, different types of teachers were assigned to classes randomly so that the impact of different types of teachers could be assessed. Thus half the time, higher-status teachers were assigned to lower-performing classes.[9] This is

9. This study by Esther Duflo, Pascaline Dupas, and Michael Kremer is summarized as Evaluation 3 in the appendix.

unlikely to be how the program would be implemented if it were rolled out on a large scale: higher-status teachers would likely demand to teach the better-performing children. But being less realistic in this case enabled researchers to disentangle the different channels through which the program achieved its impact, leading to greater general lessons for designing education programs. (The complex randomization design used in this case is discussed in more detail in Chapter 4.)

Can the question be answered well?

Some questions are very important but also very hard to answer with any precision through a randomized impact evaluation. In particular, some questions are about national-level policies and outcomes. Randomization at the national level would be required to answer them, but randomly assigning some countries to implement a policy is impossible. In other cases, the relevant outcome is very rare (which means that the sample size would need to be very large) or very difficult to measure. It may be that with a great deal of care and ingenuity or with large enough sample sizes it will be possible to perform a randomized evaluation. But undertaking an evaluation without the necessary sample size or with an inappropriate outcome measure would be a waste of time and money.

Example: The benefits and costs of using a fixed versus a floating exchange rate

It is impossible to evaluate fixed versus floating exchange rates using a randomized impact evaluation because we cannot randomize half the countries in the world to have a fixed exchange rate and the others to have a floating exchange rate. We might be able to use randomized evaluations to test some of the assumptions behind economic models that predict the impact of fixed or floating exchange rates (such as the extent to which prices and wages tend to stay the same even when there is good reason to change them—the "sticky wage" assumption). But we cannot use randomized evaluations to test the impact of the exchange rate system as a whole.

Example: Advocacy for inheritance rights for women

Another area in which it is hard to perform a randomized impact evaluation is lobbying efforts to achieve changes in laws. Again, the outcome measure is at the level of the country, making it hard to randomize. It may be possible to think of creative ways to test intermediate steps in the causal chain that can be randomized at a lower level. For example, we might encourage a random sample of lawmakers to attend an information session on legal rights for women and then see if their attitudes and knowledge are different from those of lawmakers not attending. Even here we would have to be careful, because those attending the session might pass information on to others not attending. If we think spillovers would be a major problem, we would need to see if it would be possible to account for that in the design of the evaluation. If we have no effective way of containing or measuring spillovers, it would be better not to perform an impact evaluation because we would risk producing misleading results.

Example: Programs to reduce gender-based violence

Gender-based violence is a major problem in many developing (and developed) countries, and which strategies are most effective in reducing it is a very important question. However, it is hard to perform a randomized evaluation of this question, not because the outcome is at a high level but because the outcome is hard to measure. There is a risk that a program designed to address gender-based violence will encourage more women to speak up about the violence they suffer. If this happens, there may well be more reported incidents in the treatment areas than in the comparison areas, making it look as though the program increased violence when in fact it reduced it. (We discuss measurement issues of this kind in Chapter 5.) The question of gender-based violence is too important to ignore, even if it is hard to measure, so we need to be creative in finding ways to measure accurately and objectively. On the other hand, it would be a waste of time and resources to launch an evaluation in this area without having solved the measurement issues. In other words, it is important to wait for the right opportunity to answer this question. Performing a bad impact evaluation with a poor outcome measure could be damaging by generating misleading information.

Can the question be answered with precision? Do we have a sufficient sample size?

It is wasteful and potentially counterproductive to undertake an impact evaluation that does not have sufficient statistical power to answer a question precisely. At the end of the evaluation, we will have an estimate of the impact of the program and a confidence interval around that estimate. If the confidence interval is large, we will not be able to say with confidence whether the program had a large or a small impact. We will have failed to generate much useful evidence despite all the resources that went into the evaluation.

There is also a risk that although the true effect of the program is large, we will fail to distinguish the effect from zero because of the wide confidence interval. This "failure to find an effect" may be interpreted as evidence that the program has no effect when in fact we can rule out neither a large effect nor a zero effect. This result, called an *imprecise zero*, is often the result of a poorly designed evaluation. A similar situation arises when an evaluation is designed to compare two alternative approaches but there is insufficient statistical power to distinguish with much precision between the impacts of the two alternatives.

Priority should therefore be given to questions that can be answered with precision, because we will learn much more from these evaluations. We discuss in considerable detail how to judge the likely precision with which an evaluation will answer different questions in Chapter 6.

Is the context, and the program, representative?

The objective of an impact evaluation is to generate as much general learning as possible. Choosing the right context for an evaluation can facilitate this. We usually want to avoid contexts that are special or unusual in some way. We may want to avoid an area that is high profile and may get special treatment or one that has particularly good communications or infrastructure. If we want to understand whether a program will work if it is scaled up much more widely, we will want to test it in an environment similar to where it will be scaled up.

Choosing a representative context is not just about the terrain of the area; it is also about finding a representative program and partner. For example, if we want to test the effectiveness of community-driven development, we may want to evaluate a program that is typical of other programs of this type—one that provides grants of sizes similar to those of other programs and is implemented neither more effectively nor more ineffectively than average. If we want to understand the impact of microcredit on people's lives, there are advantages in evaluating a program that is as representative as possible of the hundreds of different microcredit programs around that world. For example, most microcredit programs lend to groups of women and have some version of joint liability. They lend small amounts, at least initially, and require weekly repayment. The results of our evaluation are more likely to generalize to other programs if we evaluate a micro-credit program that shares these characteristics.

There are some situations, however, in which it is useful to evaluate a nonrepresentative program. For example, we may want to perform a *proof-of-concept evaluation*. In such an evaluation we ask the question "If this approach is implemented in the best possible way, what impact will it have?" Public health impact evaluations often test proofs of concept in this way. For example, an evaluation in Pakistan asked the question "If we get people in the slums of Karachi to wash their hands frequently with soap, how much will this reduce the incidence of diarrhea?" The program that was tested was too intensive to be scaled up in a cost-effective way, but it proved an important concept: that despite the many different possible pathways for fecal contamination to lead to diarrhea in these communities, hand washing on its own could have substantial impacts on the level of diarrhea, and thus it pointed the way toward possible solutions. A proof-of-concept evaluation can also be very helpful if it shows that even a gold-plated, best-case-scenario version of a program is not effective. One evaluation cannot, of course, tell us that all programs of a particular type are ineffective, but a proof-of-concept evaluation that finds no impact should raise serious questions about whether a particular approach is effective.

Another reason to evaluate a nonrepresentative program is that there is already good evidence on the typical program of a certain type and there is reason to think that an alternative version, which is not yet widely used, is either less expensive or more effective than the standard approach.

Is the program of the right maturity to evaluate?

There are disadvantages in evaluating a program that is very new. There are often implementation problems when a new program is launched that get sorted out after the first few months. It would be a waste of time and money to evaluate a program during a rocky start-up phase. We might find that the impact was very limited and then be left with the question of whether the impact would have been better if it had been evaluated later, once implementation issues had been sorted out. An additional concern is that programs are often adapted and changed in their early stages. It would be wasteful to evaluate version 1.0 only to have it replaced by version 2.0 very shortly after the evaluation was completed.

Yet there are also benefits to evaluating at an early stage. Precisely because new programs are in flux, implementers may be more ready to change the program in response to the findings of the evaluation. Also, if a program is not working, we don't want to wait until it is scaled up to millions of beneficiaries before finding that out.

Choosing the right time to evaluate a program is therefore a question of balance and one that depends on the precise objectives in a given case. If we are interested in testing the impact of a strategy that is used by many organizations and is already well rooted, we may want to choose a program that has a track record of smooth functioning rather than a start-up.

If we are working with an organization that is going into a new sector and wants to try out different approaches, we may decide to evaluate quite early, while policies are still in flux. However, even in the latter case it is advisable to at least run a small pilot of the program to make sure it functions and that the program design is tied down before the evaluation starts in order to avoid the risk of evaluating a moving target.

Do we have the right field partner?

To perform an effective randomized impact evaluation, it is important to have the full buy-in of those implementing the project being evaluated. This buy-in needs to be at several levels. The most senior levels of the organization need to be committed to finding out how effective their program is—and be willing to have the results published, whether they are good or bad. They need to be prepared to devote their time and/or the time of their staff to thinking through the details of how the evaluation will work, what objectives will be measured, and how, and to brainstorm solutions to the challenges that will inevitably arise. For example, implementation of the program may need to be delayed until the baseline survey has been completed. Transport costs for the program may have to be higher than usual because implementation is spread over a wider area to allow room for the comparison group. It is often useful to keep the design of the program relatively constant throughout the evaluation so that it is clear what exactly was evaluated, which may be at odds with some organizations' desire to constantly innovate during implementation. All of these are issues that can be overcome, but only with the goodwill and commitment of senior levels within the organization of the implementing partner.

The involvement and buy-in of midlevel and ground-level staff from the implementing organization are also critical for the design and implementation of a high-quality randomized evaluation. These staff will need to be closely involved in figuring out the logistics of providing the program to some people (the treatment group) but not to others (the comparison group). Their knowledge of the details of how the program works on the ground is critical in deciding how a multifaceted program can be divided into different components to be tested in different treatment arms or whether spillover effects are likely to be large and how they can be minimized. An implementation team that understands why randomization is important and how the evaluation is operating can spot threats to the integrity of the design, raise concerns in a timely manner, and thus prevent the threats from becoming serious. In contrast, ground-level staff who either do not understand or are not entirely committed to the evaluation can undermine experimental integrity in a multitude of ways. Examples include taking the initiative to reallocate resources, reaching out to comparison communities to offer them the program, or changing the design of the program.

If we are partnering with an implementing organization to evaluate a program that represents the majority of its portfolio, we need to realize that the stakes are high for the implementer, and this can raise some practical concerns. Some implementing organizations are keen to know the impact of their main program, whether the results are positive or negative. But this is not always the case. Other organizations may become defensive when they realize that an evaluation may find that their flagship program does not have an impact. This defensiveness can threaten their cooperation to implement the randomization according to the protocol. The organization may suddenly find many reasons that it is not possible, after all, to introduce an element of randomization into the program, even though initial discussions had suggested promising ways to introduce randomization. Or, even worse, an implementer that feels threatened by the possibility of negative results may sabotage the evaluation once it is underway.

Finding a partner that is really committed to evaluation and working with a local implementing team that buys in to the need for evaluation and understands the importance of randomization sometimes runs counter to the desire to evaluate a "typical" program with a "typical" implementation team.[10] This is, arguably, most true when randomized evaluation is new to a particular sector. The first partners to put themselves forward to be evaluated are usually somewhat special. As is so often the case, we have to trade off our different objectives in a particular context. But it is important to keep in mind that without partner buy-in there is no way to perform a good randomized impact evaluation.

How much would it cost to answer the question?

The cost of impact evaluations can vary enormously, from several thousand dollars to several million dollars. It is therefore relevant to think about the costs of answering different questions when deciding which questions to prioritize. For the same price, it may be possible to conduct several inexpensive evaluations of moderately important questions or one expensive evaluation of a very important question.

The key determinants of cost are the level of randomization (evaluations that are randomized at the individual level are less expensive; see Chapter 6 on power), the duration (evaluations of the long-term impact of a program are much more expensive), the outcome measure (some outcome measures, such as biomarkers, are expensive to collect, and others have a high level of variance, which means the sample size has to be larger), and location (for example, studies in urban India are much less costly than those in rural Africa because transport costs and the wages of high-skilled enumerators are lower).

However, if a question is important and if the information to be learned in an evaluation has the potential to significantly influence policies in many countries, even a very expensive evaluation can be worthwhile. (This is especially true when we compare the cost of the evaluation to the cost of misallocating funds to ineffective or potentially harmful programs.) In these cases, a good model is for foundations or aid agencies to pool resources to answer the key questions. This can take the form of creating funding pools that seek to answer a few key questions in a sector, then issuing a call for research proposals that can answer this question.[11] The agencies or foundations can then

10. An interesting discussion on this point appears in Hunt Allcott and Sendhil Mullainathan, "External Validity and Partner Selection Bias," NBER Working Paper 18373, National Bureau of Educational Research, Cambridge, MA, 2012.
11. For further information on J-PAL's research initiatives, see Abdul Latif Jameel Poverty Action Lab, "Policy Lessons," accessed January 2, 2012, http://www.povertyaction lab.org/policy-lessons. 3ie is another institution that pools resources. For more infor-

award the funds to the most promising proposals. This approach has the potential to generate much more useful learning than having every small organization hurry to conduct many small randomized evaluations just for the sake of randomized evaluations.

A case study from the field

In this module and the last we have stressed the importance of being strategic when prioritizing questions for impact evaluations and have discussed lots of possible criteria for making the selection. We can see an illustration of how these principles can be put into practice in the case of Seva Mandir, an Indian NGO that had worked for many years in the tribal communities of rural Udaipur District in Rajasthan and wanted to expand its work on health but wanted to find out how best they could do so with their relatively limited resources.

The first knowledge gap they identified was a descriptive one: what were the major health issues in the population? With the help of researchers, they undertook a detailed needs assessment (see Module 3.1). This took the form of a representative household survey that collected information on self-reported health as well as objective measures such as hemoglobin counts from blood samples. The survey also asked to whom household members went for treatment and what they paid. The public and private health providers mentioned by survey participants were also surveyed to understand what training and resources they had available.

The needs assessment highlighted four particularly common problems: (1) high anemia rates across age and gender, which had the potential to undermine productivity and health; (2) low immunization rates of children; (3) high rates of absenteeism of government health staff; and (4) high rates of diarrhea among children. All of these challenges were common in other contexts, and thus evidence of how to effectively address them would be relevant not only for Seva Mandir but also for other organizations in India and beyond.

The next step was to undertake a review of the approaches used by other organizations in trying to address these problems as well as the evidence of the effectiveness of these approaches. Some of the solutions being used elsewhere were inappropriate for the poor, rural, low-population density area in which Seva Mandir worked. For exam-

---

mation, go to 3ie, "Inform Policy," accessed January 2, 2012, http://www.3ieimpact.org/en/inform-policy/.

ple, centralized fortification of basic foodstuffs (like flour) is used in many contexts to address anemia but would not help in communities where people grow, process, and eat their own flour. Seva Mandir and the research team therefore looked to the literature on underlying behavior, particularly with respect to low investment in preventive health, to see if there were lessons there for designing new approaches to these fundamental problems.

Based on the needs assessment and literature review, discussions within the NGO and with other organizations, and evidence from previous evaluations in the education sector carried out earlier by Seva Mandir, different approaches were piloted. Some approaches were ruled out as impractical at the very early pilot stage. For example, one strategy that was piloted was to chlorinate local wells to reduce diarrhea rates. However, it was very hard to achieve the right level of chlorination without frequent monitoring, which was unlikely to be sustainable given the high levels of health worker absenteeism. Too-high levels of chlorine led the local population to complain about the taste, and too-low levels resulted in insufficient protection.

Three approaches were then designed to address the first three challenges (anemia, immunization, and absenteeism). All three were designed to be inexpensive and scalable, and all three were evaluated using randomized impact evaluations. In the end, one was highly successful: regular immunization camps with a small food incentive to encourage attendance at the camps increased full immunization rates from 6 percent to 39 percent. The other two approaches proved ineffective, although a lot of learning was generated about what does and does not work in addressing anemia and absenteeism.

For further reading

Banerjee, Abhijit, Angus Deaton, and Esther Duflo. 2004. "Wealth, Health, and Health Services in Rural Rajasthan." *American Economic Review* 94 (2): 326–330.

Banerjee, Abhijit V., Esther Duflo, and Rachel Glennerster. 2008. "Putting a Band-Aid on a Corpse: Incentives for Nurses in the Indian Public Health Care System." *Journal of the European Economic Association* 6 (2–3): 487–500.

Banerjee, Abhijit V., Esther Duflo, Rachel Glennerster, and Dhruva Kothari. 2010. "Improving Immunisation Coverage in Rural India: A Clustered Randomised Controlled Evaluation of Immunisation Campaigns with and without Incentives." *British Medical Journal* 340: c2220.

J-PAL Policy Briefcase. 2011. "Incentives for Immunization." Cambridge, MA: Abdul Latif Jameel Poverty Action Lab. http://www.povertyactionlab.org/publication/incentives-immunization.

Module 3.3 summary

- Approaches that are popular, have high levels of investment, or are about to be scaled up are high priorities for evaluation.

- Approaches that are cheap and easy to scale should also be given priority.

- Questions on which there is little evidence should have higher priority than those on which there is already quite a lot of existing evidence.

- Some evaluations are much less expensive than others. The cost should be compared to the usefulness of the evidence it will generate.

- We should carry out an evaluation only if we expect to be able to answer the question well—i.e., we have a sufficient sample size to answer the question with precision and we have reliable outcome indicators.

- Doing an evaluation too early risks testing an immature program, while doing it too late risks wasting resources on an ineffective program.

- We need to work in a representative context.

- Do we have a good implementing partner who is committed to understanding their impact?

4 Randomizing

There are many different ways to introduce randomization into a program. In this chapter we discuss how to decide which approach is best in a given context. We also cover the process and mechanics of randomization. This chapter has six modules:

MODULE 4.1: Opportunities to Randomize
MODULE 4.2: Choosing the Level of Randomization
MODULE 4.3: Deciding Which Aspects of the Program to Randomize
MODULE 4.4: The Mechanics of Simple Randomization
MODULE 4.5: Stratified and Pairwise Randomization
MODULE 4.6: A Catalog of Designs

MODULE 4.1 Opportunities to Randomize

In this module we explain the three aspects of programs (access, timing, and encouragement to take up the program) that can be randomly assigned to create treatment and comparison groups. We then outline nine common situations that lend themselves to randomized evaluation, illustrated with examples from recent evaluations.

What can be randomized?

In order to evaluate the impact of a program or policy, our randomly selected treatment group must have more exposure to the program than the comparison group. We can control three aspects of the program or policy to create this differential exposure:

1. Access: We can choose which people will be offered access to the program.
2. Timing of access: We can choose when to provide access to the program.
3. Encouragement: We can choose which people will be given encouragement to participate in the program.

Because we control these three aspects of the program, these are also the three aspects we can randomly allocate. Whether we vary access, timing of access, or encouragement to take part, we can vary each aspect by individual or by group. For example, we can randomize individuals within a community, offering access to some people but not to others, or we can randomize communities, offering access to all individuals in the chosen community.

Randomly assign the offer to access the treatment

Of the three possibilities discussed in this module, randomly assigning access to a program or policy is the most common. Imagine that we have enough resources to provide textbooks to only 100 schools. We would make a list of 200 eligible schools and then randomly select 100 to receive the textbooks during the evaluation period and then deliver the books to only these schools. The remaining 100 schools form the comparison group.

Randomly assign a time when people can access the treatment

We can randomly assign the time when people can access the program, designating who gets access first and who gets it later. Imagine a school-based deworming program in Kenya is planning to phase in their program to schools over three years. There are 75 eligible schools. We can randomly divide them into three groups of 25 each and randomly select which group starts the program in each of the three years (Figure 4.1). In the first year, Group A starts the program, and together Groups B and C form the comparison group. In year 2, Group B starts the program and, together with Group A, will make up the treatment group, while Group C is the comparison group. In year 3, Group C starts the program, and with all three groups now receiving treatment, there is no longer a comparison group. When we vary the timing of access, the difference in exposure to the program is created by delaying access for some people, as in this deworming exam-

Year	Group A		Group B	Group C	
Year 1	🧴	Treatment group	Comparison group	Comparison group	
Year 2	🧴	Treatment group	🧴 Treatment group	Comparison group	Evaluation ends
Year 3		🧴	🧴	🧴	No comparison group exists anymore

FIGURE 4.1 Random assignment of the timing of the treatment through phase-in design

Note: The pill bottles indicate which groups had received the treatment in each of the three years.

ple. It can also be created, as we will see in Module 4.5, by having people take turns in receiving access.

Randomly assign encouragement to take up the program

Sometimes we are unable to randomly assign access to a program itself, but we can randomly assign encouragement to take up the program. This approach is useful when we want to evaluate a program that is already open to all of the eligible recipients but only some are currently using it. The program continues to be open to all the eligible people, but only some of them (the treatment group) will receive extra encouragement to take up the program.

Imagine that we are evaluating a program that provides savings accounts for farmers growing cash crops. Any household that grows cash crops can sign up for an account, but only 50 of the 250 eligible households in the community have signed up for a savings account. It turns out that these 50 are much more likely to invest in inputs, and we want to know whether this is because the savings accounts help them save for their inputs. There are 200 eligible households remaining. We can split these into a treatment and a comparison group and give extra encouragement to open a savings account to the treatment group households. We send letters to these 100 randomly selected households telling them about the benefits of a savings account and offering to help them fill out the paperwork to open an account. For the other 100 households we do nothing. The hope is that a higher proportion of the encouraged households (the treatment group) will open an account. If, for example, 45 of the 100 households in the treatment group take up the program and 20 in the status quo comparison group take it up, the treatment group will have a higher proportion enrolled in the program—45 percent compared to 20 percent—and this gives us the difference in exposure to the program needed to measure program impact (Figure 4.2).

We can think of encouragement as making it easier for some people to take up a program. Because it is easier for them, they are more likely to take up the program, and we have the difference in exposure we need.

When is it possible to perform a randomized evaluation?

In general, opportunities to randomize arise when implementers want to design a new approach to addressing a problem, when a new program is being introduced, and when there are insufficient resources to provide a service to all those who could benefit. We cover 10 of the most common examples in Table 4.1. In most cases, conducting a randomized evaluation will not change the number of people who receive the program, and this is the case for all the opportunities listed here.

FIGURE 4.2 Encouragement as motivation for more people in the treatment group to take up the program

TABLE 4.1 Opportunities to randomize

Opportunity	Description
New program design	When a problem has been identified but there is no agreement about what solution to implement. The evaluators work with the implementers from the outset to design programs and then pilot-test them.
New programs	When a program is new and being pilot-tested.
New services	When an existing program offers a new service.
New people	When a program is being expanded to a new group of people.
New locations	When a program is being expanded to new areas.
Oversubscription	When there are more interested people than the program can serve.
Undersubscription	When not everyone who is eligible for the program takes it up.
Rotation	When the program's benefits or burdens are to be shared by rotation.
Admission cutoffs	When the program has a merit cutoff and those just below the cutoff can be randomly admitted.
Admission in phases	When logistical and resource constraints mean that not all the potential beneficiaries can be enrolled at one time and people can be randomly admitted in phases over time.

(See Module 2.4 for a discussion of ethics on this point.) There are cases on this list in which doing a randomized evaluation changes the approach to targeting under the program, and we discuss the ethical implications of this in Module 4.3.[1]

New program design

We may have identified a problem and concluded that it requires a new solution. In such cases, the evaluators can start working with the

1. For a more detailed discussion of ethics in randomized evaluations, see Glennerster and Powers in *The Oxford University Press Handbook on Professional Economic Ethics* (Oxford, UK: Oxford University Press, forthcoming), and William R. Shadish, Thomas D. Cook, and Donald T. Campbell, *Experimental and Quasi-experimental Designs for Generalized Causal Inference* (Boston: Houghton Mifflin, 2002).

implementing organization before there is a program or a set of alternatives to test and contribute to their design.

Example: A research partnership pilots a series of health programs.
The NGO Seva Mandir has been working for almost 60 years in the Udaipur District of Rajasthan, India. Its programs target education, the environment, microfinance, and health. In 2002 Seva Mandir partnered with researchers on a comprehensive survey to identify major health and healthcare needs. They jointly developed and pilot-tested three interventions in a series of randomized evaluations.[2]

New programs

When a program is new and its effects are unknown, a randomized evaluation often is the best way to estimate its impact. Randomly selecting the beneficiaries of a pilot program is also often perceived as the fairest way to allocate the program.

Example: The government pilots a new social welfare program in Mexico. The nationwide CCT program in Mexico was first introduced as a pilot program in rural areas of seven states under the name PROGRESA. Of the 506 communities that were sampled, 320 were randomly assigned to receive the pilot program. Those assigned to the comparison group received the program only after the evaluation, when the program had been found to be effective and was scaled up.[3]

New services

Programs evolve to meet new challenges. They can, for example, change the pricing or method of delivery, or they can add altogether new services. Much as in the case of the pilot test, the innovation can be randomly assigned to existing or new clients for evaluation.

Example: Microfinance institutions add new services. Besides credit for the poor, many microfinance institutions (MFIs) now offer additional services such as savings accounts, health insurance, and business training. For example, an MFI in India introduced health insurance; in the Philippines, an MFI introduced a loan product with individual liability in addition to its group liability product; and in India, an MFI introduced financial literacy training.[4] The rollout of

2. See Module 3.3 for further details.
3. This study by T. Paul Schultz is summarized as Evaluation 9 in the appendix.
4. Many of these studies are covered by Jonathan Bauchet, Cristobal Marshall, Laura Starita, Jeanette Thomas, and Anna Yalouris in "Latest Findings from Randomized Evaluations of Microfinance," in *Access to Finance Forum* (Washington, DC: Con-

these new services to existing customers was randomized, creating an opportunity for evaluation.

Example: An HIV education program in Kenya adds a risk information campaign. International Child Support (ICS, a Netherlands-based NGO) in Kenya piloted a program to improve the delivery of the national HIV education curriculum. The program had three existing components. Later an information campaign was added to address the danger of cross-generational sexual activity. This component was randomly assigned to 71 of the 328 participating schools.[5]

New people and locations

Programs expand by adding new people in their existing locations or moving to new locations. When there are not enough resources to cover all the new clients at once, randomizing may be the fairest way to decide who will be served first.

Example: A US state extends Medicaid to those just above the usual Medicaid cutoff. US state governments, with federal support, provide health insurance to millions of poor families. The state of Oregon had limited funding to extend the pool of people who were eligible for this program. They held a lottery among eligible low-income individuals to decide who would be offered services. Later researchers compared the outcomes of lottery winners and losers in terms of healthcare use, health status, and financial strain.[6]

Example: A remedial education program is expanded to a new city. In 2000 the Indian organization Pratham expanded their remedial education program to the city of Vadodara. There were 123 schools in the city, and each school received tutors, but the tutor was randomly assigned to either grade 3 or grade 4.[7]

---

sultative Group to Assist the Poor, 2011), http://www.cgap.org/gm/document-1.9.55766/FORUM2.pdf. For the smoking study in the Philippines, see Dean Karlan, Xavier Gine, and Jonathan Zinman, "Put Your Money Where Your Butt Is: A Commitment Savings Account for Smoking Cessation," *American Economic Journal: Applied Economics* 2 (2010): 213–235.

5. This study by Esther Duflo, Pascaline Dupas, and Michael Kremer is summarized as Evaluation 4 in the appendix.

6. Amy Finklestein, Sarah Taubman, Bill Wright, Mira Bernstein, Jonathan Gruber, Joseph P. Newhouse, Heidi Allen, Katherine Baicker, and Oregon Health Study Group. 2012. "The Oregon Health Insurance Experiment: Evidence from the First Year." *Quarterly Journal of Economics* 127 (3): 1057–1106.

7. This study by Abhijit Banerjee, Shawn Cole, Esther Duflo, and Leigh Linden is summarized as Evaluation 2 in the appendix.

Oversubscription

Often in developing countries, more people are interested in a program than the program has resources to serve. When demand outstrips supply, random assignment may be the fairest way to choose the participants.

Example: The government uses a lottery to decide who receives secondary school tuition vouchers in Colombia. A program in Colombia provided vouchers for private school to students from poor families. There were more qualified and interested students than vouchers. The municipalities assigned the vouchers by lottery to ensure fairness.[8]

Example: The US government uses a lottery to decide who receives vouchers for housing in more affluent neighborhoods. A pilot program in the United States provided vouchers for families to move from high-poverty housing projects to low-poverty neighborhoods. Demand for housing assistance in the United States often exceeds the supply of public housing available. The US Department of Housing and Urban Development randomly offered vouchers to families in order to rigorously evaluate the program and distribute the limited vouchers in a way that was fair.

Undersubscription

Sometimes program take-up is low and a program is serving fewer people than it could, even though there are enough resources to cover everyone and the program is open to everyone. One way to increase demand is to offer more encouragement to take up the program through either more information or more incentives. This additional encouragement can be randomized. Necessary but unpopular programs may also be undersubscribed (as in the case of the military draft for the Vietnam War or the quotas for women in politics in India). Lotteries are often seen as a fair way to distribute the burden of unpopular programs.

Example: A large American university encourages employees to sign up for retirement savings. Like many employers in the United States, a large American university has a retirement savings program. Every year the university organizes benefits fairs to provide information and enroll employees. One year the university offered a reward of

---

8. This study by Eric Bettinger, Michael Kremer, and Juan E. Saavedra is summarized as Evaluation 10 in the appendix.

$20 for attending the fair. This extra encouragement was randomly allocated.[9]

Example: A large South African lender encourages borrowers through direct mail. The lender provides loans to high-risk borrowers at a high interest rate. The firm used direct mailings to advertise its products and increase demand. The recipients and the content of the letters were randomized to measure the effects on demand.[10]

Example: The US government had too few volunteer soldiers during the Vietnam War. Young men who were eligible for the draft in the United States were entered into a lottery to determine whether they would have to serve in the armed services. Subsequently, academics used the lottery to determine the impact of serving in the armed services on future labor market outcomes.[11]

Rotation

Sometimes there are just enough resources to cover a portion of the people potentially eligible for a program, and the resources will remain fixed for a long time. Because everyone wants access to the program and they cannot all have it at once, one approach is to have people take turns. The order in which program resources or burdens rotate can be decided randomly, with the group in rotation serving as the treatment group. With this approach we have to worry about effects lingering after the program has rotated away to another group, improving or worsening outcomes in the next period.

Example: Some state governments in India randomly cycle political quotas among village councils. In India, a third of all rural village councils in each election cycle must elect a woman as president. To ensure that the reservations rotate fairly among the councils, some states determine the reservation schedule randomly.[12]

---

9. This study by Esther Duflo and Emmanuel Saez is summarized as Evaluation 11 in the appendix.

10. Dean Karlan and Jonathan Zinman, "Observing Unobservables: Identifying Information Asymmetries with a Consumer Credit Field Experiment," *Econometrica* 77 (2009): 1993–2008.

11. Joshua D. Angrist, "Lifetime Earnings and the Vietnam Era Draft Lottery: Evidence from Social Security Administrative Records," *American Economic Review* 80 (1990): 313–336.

12. This study by Lori Beaman, Raghabendra Chattopadhyay, Esther Duflo, Rohini Pande, and Petia Topalova is summarized as Evaluation 12 in the appendix.

Admission cutoffs

Some programs have admission cutoffs. These cutoffs may matter for program targeting, but the precise cutoff point is often somewhat arbitrary. For example, women with less than 1 acre of land may be eligible for special assistance. But how much less deserving of government support is a woman with 1.05 acres of land compared to one with 0.95 acre? Somewhat arbitrary cutoffs give us an opportunity to randomize.

Example: A rural bank in the Philippines uses credit scores. Eligibility for business loans at First Macro Bank in the Philippines depended on a credit score ranging from zero to 100. Those with scores of 30 and below were considered uncreditworthy and automatically rejected, and those with scores of 60 and above were considered very creditworthy and approved. A random sample of applications with scores between 31 and 59 (i.e., who were marginally creditworthy) were approved and formed the treatment group for the evaluation, while the rest of those in this range were rejected and formed the comparison group. The evaluation assessed the impact of giving credit to those who were marginally creditworthy.[13]

Admission in phases

Sometimes a program does not have the resources or logistical capacity to deliver the program to everyone at once. If resources are going to grow, then people may be admitted into the program as the resources become available. This presents an opportunity to randomize the order in which people are phased in.

Example: An NGO introduced deworming in phases. Because of logistical and financial constraints, ICS Africa could add only 25 schools a year to their deworming program in Kenya. The schools were randomly divided into three groups of 25, and one (randomly selected) group was phased in each year. At the end of three years, all the schools had been treated.[14]

---

13. This study by Dean Karlan and Jonathan Zinman is summarized as Evaluation 13 in the appendix.
14. This study by Sarah Baird, Joan Hamory Hicks, Michael Kremer, and Edward Miguel is summarized as Evaluation 1 in the appendix.

Module 4.1 summary

What aspects of a program can be randomized?

- Three aspects of a program can be randomized:
  1. Access to the program
  2. Timing of access to the program
  3. Encouragement to take up the program
- Randomizing access to the program is the most common of the three possibilities.
- We randomize the timing of access to a program when the program cannot reach all the people at the same time. The people are then admitted in phases. If the program effects are short-term and transient, the program can rotate access among the eligible.
- When we randomize encouragement to take up a program, we offer additional information or incentives to some of the people. We do this mostly when the program is open to all eligible people but is undersubscribed.

When do opportunities to randomize commonly arise?

- When the program is being pilot-tested
- When the program is adding new services
- When the program is adding new people
- When the program is adding new locations
- When the program is oversubscribed
- When the program is undersubscribed
- When the program has to be shared through rotation
- When the program has an admission cutoff
- When the program has to admit people in phases

MODULE 4.2 Choosing the Level of Randomization

This module describes how we decide whether to randomize individuals, households, communities, schools, clinics, or other units.

Most programs and policies seek to change the lives of individuals, but they often do so by working through groups such as schools, savings groups, households, or communities. When we design our randomized evaluation we have to decide whether to randomize individuals in or out of a program or to randomize whole groups in or out of the program.

Figure 4.3 describes the different steps involved in an individual-level and a group-level randomization. Panel A shows the steps involved in selecting a random sample of women farmers for involvement in an agricultural program in Sierra Leone. In partnership with those implementing the program we select from the three districts in Sierra Leone in which the program has the potential to operate three villages in which to run the program and the evaluation. Within these communities we determine who is eligible for the program (in this example, adult women). The women in these communities are then randomized into treatment and comparison groups. Those in the treatment group are offered access to the program, and those in the comparison group are not. Data are collected on all the women whether they are allocated to the treatment or the comparison group.

For a group-level randomization we again start by selecting a study site. As we discuss later in this chapter, we may want to choose our study sites randomly to ensure that the study is representative of a large geographic area. In this example we randomly pick three districts to be representative of the country as a whole. Again we use eligibility criteria to select participation in the program. We select medium-size villages (smaller villages will have few farmers who can benefit from our training, and large villages tend to have a higher ratio of nonfarmers). Among these communities we randomly select some to receive the training and others not to. In this case we do not need to survey everyone in the community; we survey only a random sample of eligible people within the community.

The most common levels at which to randomize are the individual and the community level, but we can also randomize by school, health clinic, agricultural cooperative, or grade.

Some programs operate at several levels. Many microcredit organizations make loans to individuals through lending groups that are part of centers. These centers are visited by credit officers who are responsible for several centers. For an evaluation we could randomize by individual, lending group, village, or credit officer. The higher the level

A Individual-level randomization

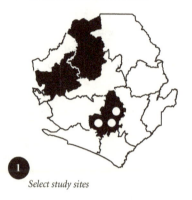

1 Select study sites

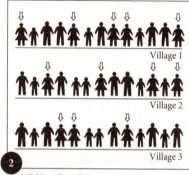

Village 1

Village 2

Village 3

2 Within selected sites,
apply eligibility criteria:

⟹ **Program available
to women only**

3 Randomize access to program
among eligible participants to
form the treatment group (T)

4 Survey people in both the treatment group (T)
(get program) and the comparison group (C)
(no program)

FIGURE 4.3 Randomization steps for individual- versus group-level
randomization

of randomization, the larger the number of people who are randomized together as a group.

Usually the unit of randomization is determined by the unit at
which the program is implemented. A program that works through
clinics will usually be randomized at the clinic level—with some clinics receiving additional support and others not. This is a matter of
practicality: it is usually infeasible to prevent some individuals from
having access to a program that is implemented at the community

B Group-level randomization

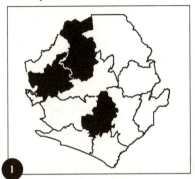

Optional: *Randomize selection* of districts

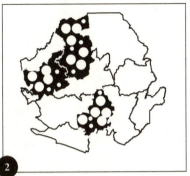

Within selected districts, *apply eligibility criteria:*

➡ ◯ **large villages only**

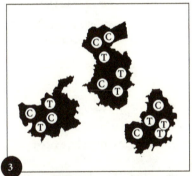

Among eligible villages, randomly assign some to treatment group (get program) *and the rest to comparison group* (no program)

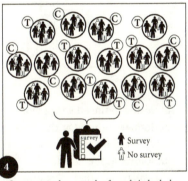

Survey a random sample of people in both the treatment group and the comparison group.

⬤ Survey
⬤ No survey

FIGURE 4.3 *(continued)*

level. But we do not always randomize at the level of implementation. As the microfinance example shows, a program may have many different levels at which it is implemented. But there are many other considerations. Six key considerations in determining the level of randomization are listed in Table 4.2.

Unit of measurement and unit of randomization

The level of randomization needs to be the same or higher than the level at which our outcome measure will be taken. Imagine that we are

TABLE 4.2 Technical and nontechnical considerations for choosing the level of randomization

Consideration	Question to be answered
Unit of measurement	What is the unit at which our outcome will be measured?
Spillovers	Are there spillovers? Do we want the impact estimate to capture them? Do we want to measure them?
Attrition	Which level is best to keep participants from dropping out of the sample?
Compliance	Which level is best to keep participants from dropping out of the sample?
Statistical power	Which level gives us the greatest probability of detecting a treatment? If we randomize at the group level, will we still have a large enough effective sample size?
Feasibility	Which level is feasible ethically, financially, politically and logistically? Which is easiest, and which is least costly?

interested in the effects of worker retraining on firm profits. We could randomize training at the worker level, but we can measure the outcome of interest (profits) only at the firm level. We therefore need to randomize at the firm level.

Similarly, a voter education campaign in India (implemented with the help of two local NGOs, the Sarathi Development Foundation and Satark Nagrik Sangathan) provided information on the quality of candidates. The evaluation authors were interested in the impact of this information on electoral outcomes. Voting in India is anonymous, so it is possible to collect only self-reported data on individual voting. The authors were concerned that self-reported voting data might be systematically different from actual voting—for example, that certain types of people might be unwilling to report how they voted. Actual voting reports are available only at the aggregate polling station level. So even though the treatment targeted individual households, the campaign was randomized at the polling station level.[15]

15. Abhijit Banerjee, Donald Green, Jennifer Green, and Rohini Pande, "Can Voters Be Primed to Choose Better Legislators? Experimental Evidence from Rural India," working paper, Massachusetts Institute of Technology, Cambridge, MA, 2009.

Spillovers and unit of randomization

Programs can have direct and indirect effects. The indirect effects are called *spillovers* or *externalities*. Spillovers can take many forms and can be positive or negative. They can occur through a number of channels:

- *Physical:* Children immunized by a program reduce disease transmission in their community. Farmers who learn pig husbandry from a program increase pollution.
- *Behavioral:* A farmer imitates the fertilizer application techniques her neighbor in a treatment group learned from a program.
- *Informational:* People learn about the effectiveness of insecticide-treated bed nets from others who received these nets through a program (also known as social learning).
- *Marketwide or general equilibrium:* Older workers lose their jobs because firms receive financial incentives from a program to hire young workers.

Why spillovers matter

The formal requirement for a randomized evaluation to be valid is that the outcome of one person does not depend on the group to which other people around that person are allocated. This assumption does not hold when we have spillovers. A farmer may be more likely to use fertilizer if his neighbor is allocated to the treatment group than to the comparison group because the farmer will observe his neighbor using fertilizer and copy her example.

The problem is that when an individual's actions depend on whether someone else was assigned to the treatment or the comparison group, the difference in outcomes between the treatment and the comparison group no longer represents the impact of the program. For example, if comparison group farmers learn about the benefits of fertilizer from their treatment group neighbors, these comparison group farmers no longer represent a good counterfactual: they no longer behave in a way that the treatment group farmers would have behaved if the program had not existed.

Choosing the level of randomization to limit spillovers to the comparison group

If the treatment and comparison groups do not interact, there will be no spillovers. For spillovers to occur, the different groups must have something in common, which can act as a transmission channel. All things equal, the greater the physical proximity and interaction between the treatment and comparison groups, the greater the spillovers. Choosing a unit of randomization so that most relevant interactions occur between people in the same group is the best way to limit spillovers to the comparison group.

Take the example of the relative risk HIV education program in Kenya. During a 40-minute class period, a program officer from ICS Africa shared and discussed information on the relative risk of HIV by age and gender. There was concern that children who attended the class would talk to their friends in other classes about what they had learned. To reduce the risk of spillovers, randomization took place at the level of the school.[16] The farther apart the schools were from each other, the more likely that the program effects would all be contained within the school where the program was offered.

Choosing the level at which to measure isolated spillover effects

If we want to measure spillover effects, we need within the comparison group a "spillover" group and a "no spillovers" group. In our analysis we compare outcomes for those in the treatment group with those in the no spillovers group to assess the impact of the program. By comparing outcomes from the spillover group and the no spillovers group we will assess the level of spillovers (Module 8.2). In choosing the level of randomization, we need to allow for this variation in exposure to spillovers. If we choose too high a level of randomization, there will be no contact between the treatment group and the comparison group. We will have eliminated the problem of spillovers but will not be able to measure them. If we choose too low a level of randomization, all of our comparison group will experience spillovers and we will not be able to evaluate the program because we will have no "pure" comparison.

We generate variation in exposure to spillovers by recognizing that the extent of spillovers will depend on the proportion of those around an individual who are treated. Consider physical spillovers. A cold is going around your office. The likelihood that you will catch that cold and be forced to take a sick day will depend on the number of coworkers with the cold. The same is true in the case of information

---

16. This study by Esther Duflo, Pascaline Dupas, and Michael Kremer is summarized as Evaluation 4 in the appendix.

spillovers: the higher the proportion of people in your circle who know a secret, the more likely you are to hear about it. This proportion of "treated" people is called the *treatment density*. We cover how to vary treatment densities in the last module of the chapter, but for now let's look only at what matters in choosing the level of randomization.

Untreated individuals in a treated group. In the HIV information campaign discussed above, only children in the final grade of primary school (grade 8) were treated, but it is possible that they shared what they learned with other adolescents in the grades below (grades 6 and 7). Comparing the outcomes of grades 6 and 7 girls in treatment schools with the outcomes of grades 6 and 7 girls in comparison schools enables us to measure the spillover effects: although both sets of girls were untreated, the first set was exposed to the program through spillovers.

Untreated units near treated units. In most cases, the nearer untreated units are to treated units, the more likely they are to be affected by spillovers. The evaluation of school-based deworming took this into account. Randomization was at the level of the school, but there was enough out-of-school mixing of children who went to different schools that a deworming program in one school had the potential to impact children in neighboring schools. The random variation generated by the phase-in design meant that some not-yet-treated schools were near treated schools, while others were not.

Using two levels of randomization to measure spillovers. If measuring spillovers is one of the main objectives of our evaluation, it may be useful to randomize at two different levels, usually the individual level and the group level. Take the HIV education example again. An alternative design would have been to randomly choose treatment schools where the HIV education would be given. Then one could have randomly picked some adolescents from these schools and called them to a meeting where the information on relative risk was given. The spillover group would then have been the adolescents in the school that did not attend the meeting, while the no spillovers group would have been adolescents at comparison schools who received no HIV education program.

Attrition and unit of randomization

Attrition is the term used when outcome data are missing from some of the people in the sample. This can happen because people drop out of the study, refuse to answer some questions, or cannot be found by enumerators during the endline survey. The level of randomization can play a role in reducing attrition.

Randomizing within a group can reduce cooperation when people are not assigned their preferred treatment. No matter how fair the randomization procedure itself may be, it is sometimes difficult to avoid the impression that the program is picking and choosing unfairly. This can lead to resentment. People in the comparison group, for example, might be less likely to cooperate with data collection when they see others receiving benefits from participating while they receive nothing. Randomizing at a higher level has the potential to reduce resentment because people living side by side are treated similarly, and it might therefore help reduce attrition. In practice, however, most attrition results from people's moving or finding the survey too long and onerous to complete.

Compliance and unit of randomization

We want as few departures as possible from the study plan or protocol. We want the program staff to execute the experiment as planned, and we want the participants to adhere as closely as possible to their assigned treatment. Choosing the right level of randomization can increase compliance by both the program staff and the participants.

Increasing the likelihood of compliance by program staff

An evaluation design that is seen as unfair by program staff or that makes the job of the program staff too complicated is likely to run into problems. If a staff member is faced with two equally needy children and is told to provide the program to only one of them, he may end up sharing the resources between the children, undermining the validity of the experiment. Or if a credit officer has to provide one type of loan to some clients and another type to other clients, she may become confused and give the wrong type of loan to some clients. The solution is to make sure that program staff are not faced with these difficult choices or confusing situations by adjusting the level of randomization. For example, we may want to randomize at the program staff level so that one credit officer delivers only one version of the program.

Increasing compliance by participants

Study participants themselves can sometimes "undo" the randomization. Good design can minimize this risk. For example, the Work and

Iron Status Evaluation studied the impact of iron supplementation.[17] To select the participants, all the screened subjects were placed in a pool, and a sample of individuals was drawn. Once an individual was chosen, his entire household was included in the study sample. The decision to assign treatment or comparison status at the household level was motivated by two concerns. First, household members might share iron pills with other members of the household. At a more pragmatic level, many of the older respondents in the study had limited literacy and there was concern that it would be difficult for respondents to keep track of which pills were to be taken by whom if not all household members were to be taking them.

In Module 7.1 we discuss other strategies to minimize noncompliance as well as the importance of measuring the level of noncompliance. In Module 8.2 we discuss analysis of results if there is noncompliance.

Statistical power and level of randomization

All things equal, the larger the number of units that are randomized, the higher the statistical power. When we choose to randomize groups such as schools or villages rather than individuals, we have fewer units to randomize. Even though the program may still serve the same number of individuals and we may collect the same amount of data as if the unit of randomization was the individual, the statistical power is likely to be dramatically reduced. This is because the outcomes of people in the same unit (the same village or same school) are not fully independent of each other. We will discuss this in much more detail in Chapter 6, but a rough rule of thumb is that for statistical power, the number of units randomized is more important than how many people are interviewed.

Feasibility and unit of randomization

We may have good technical reasons to randomize at one level over another, but in the end we have to ask if it is feasible. There are at least four factors to consider:

1. Ethics: Is the randomization ethical?

---

17. Duncan Thomas et al., "Causal Effect of Health on Labor Market Outcomes: Experimental Evidence," online working paper series, California Center for Population Research, University of California–Los Angeles, 2006, http://www.escholarship.org/uc/item/0g28k77w.

2. Politics: Is it permitted? Does the community consent? Is it perceived as fair?

3. Logistics: Can we carry out the tasks of delivering this program at this level?

4. Cost: Do we have the money? Is this the best use of the money?

Ethics and feasiblity

Module 2.4 sets out a commonly accepted framework for assessing the ethics of a given research design. We must respect the people involved in the trial and their wishes, balance any risks against likely benefits of doing the evaluation, and ensure that the benefits go at least in part to those who took part in the study. How do these principles impact our choice of the level of randomization?

We need to be careful to ensure that randomizing at an individual level does not create tensions that lead to harm if some in a community are seen as being unfairly chosen for benefits. If the process of randomization is not properly explained and accepted, having a few individuals in a community suddenly receiving large benefits compared to others might make them targets for criticism or worse.

Another key aspect of ethical behavior is ensuring that participants provide informed consent. (Module 2.4 has further details on different ways to seek informed consent that are appropriate to studies with varying levels of risk.) Randomizing at the group level raises difficult issues about seeking informed consent. Normally we explain the study and ask for consent when we interview an individual, but with group-level randomization we often do not interview all those who receive the program. Whether those who given the program but are not part of the data collection are part of the study and thus whether we need to ask their consent depends on the situation (definitions of study participants also vary by IRB). For example, it may depend on whether participation in the program is voluntary, how involved the evaluators are in the program design, and the level of risk. Usually evaluators seek to inform the community as a whole (through a community meeting) and get "community-level consent." We strongly advise discussing the appropriate approach with the relevant IRB regulator.

Politics and feasibility

Is the program allocation perceived as fair? Allocation is likely to seem arbitrary when people with equal needs who interact on a regular basis are assigned to different groups. To avoid the appearances of unfairness, it may be necessary to randomize at a higher level, such as the community. Randomizing at the community level helps partly because those in the treatment and comparison groups may not interact as regularly. In developing countries, at least, it is often considered normal for some communities to receive benefits (such as a well or a school from an NGO or a government agency) that others do not receive. This may be less true in developed countries where communities are used to national-level policies' dictating the allocation of programs.

Is it permitted? Sometimes the authorities may deny permission to randomize at the technically conducive level. For example, we may want to randomize across schools, but the authorities want every school to receive the program. This may require a design in which every school has one grade that benefits from the program but which grade benefits is randomized.

Logistics and feasibility

It is usually infeasible to randomize at a lower level than that at which the program is administered. If a program builds a new market center for a community, it is impractical to exclude some members of the community from purchasing produce there. Even when specific services are delivered to individuals, it is still sometimes easier to randomize across groupings of individuals (clusters) than across the individuals: delivering school meals to some children and not to others within a school would be logistically difficult because we would have to separately identify eligible children.

Cost and feasibility

If we randomize at the village level, we usually have to treat everyone in a village. Does the partner organization have the money to deliver the intervention at that level? Do we have the money to perform an evaluation at this level? Village-level randomizations tend to have much higher transport costs than those done at the individual level.

Reality check of units of randomization

Often the common units of randomization we mention above do not exist as neatly in real life as they do in textbooks. Official village boundary lines in government records may not correspond with the actual boundaries according to which people live and interact. Separate school classes may exist on paper, but in reality they may often be merged because of a lack of teachers or because teachers are chronically absent. For example, in Bangladesh the population density in rural areas is often so high that one "village" merges into the next, with no real distinction observable on the ground. In Kenya's Western Province, people live not in village clusters but on their farms, which are evenly spread out, making it difficult to randomize by "community." Administrative distinctions are not a good proxy for close social interaction in these cases, and we may have to come up with our own definition of the cluster (grouping of individual units) at which we want to randomize. We may want to use participatory methods to understand what local people consider their community. Alternatively, we can randomize using units not directly related to our program. For example, an agricultural program in the Western Province of Kenya used the primary school catchment area as its unit of randomization.

MODULE 4.3 Deciding Which Aspects of the Program to Randomize

We can randomize three aspects of the program: access to the program, the timing of access, and encouragement to access the program. In this module we discuss five research designs that we can use to create randomized variation in exposure to the program: the treatment lottery, the lottery around the cutoff, the phase-in design, the rotation design, and the encouragement design. This module reviews these four designs and a variation of the treatment lottery. The pros, cons, and ethical considerations of each are discussed.

The treatment lottery

Allocation. The units (individuals, households, schools, etc.) are randomly assigned to the treatment and comparison groups. The treatment group is offered access to the program; the comparison group is not. The two groups keep this status for the duration of the evaluation.

Difference in exposure to the program. This comes from offering access to the program to the treatment group but not to the comparison group.

When is the treatment lottery most workable?

When the program is limited in scale or being piloted. It is easier to justify a randomized evaluation when there are only enough resources to provide access to a small number of people or when the program is untested and the effects unclear.

When the program is oversubscribed. The lottery provides a conspicuously fair allocation mechanism.

When the evaluation will measure effects in the long run. The lottery allows us to measure the long-term effects of the program because there is always a comparison group that never receives the program.

What to consider when using the treatment lottery

Only in special circumstances can treatment lotteries be used to evaluate entitlement programs. Entitlements are programs that people receive as a legal right. Usually government regulations do not allow people to be randomized into and out of eligibility for entitlement programs. However, some countries have made exceptions to allow for the evaluation of their entitlement programs. In the United States, federal guidelines establish rules for federally supported entitlement programs (like Medicare). States are allowed to request waivers to deviate from these guidelines.[18] Waivers of welfare policy are conditioned on running a rigorous (usually randomized) evaluation of the revised program.[19] In these circumstances, individuals in a single state would experience different program benefits and conditions.

For example, in most US states, welfare benefits are based in part on family size. In the early 1990s, policymakers were concerned that giving more assistance to larger families encouraged women to have more children than they would have had otherwise. Several states applied for federal waivers to test new policies that would place a cap on the additional benefits families could receive if they had more children while on welfare. New Jersey was the first state to randomly assign a family cap to a subset of its welfare beneficiaries in order to evaluate its impact on childbearing beginning in 1992.[20]

18. Social Security Act. 42 USC 1315 §1115. http://www.ssa.gov/OP_Home/ssact/title11/1115.htm.

19. Prior to US welfare reform in 1996, waivers for states to redesign aspects of federal entitlement programs were conditioned on evaluating the new program. The Personal Responsibility and Work Opportunity Reconciliation Act of 1996 specified randomized evaluation as the preferred methodology. See the Office of Family Assistance 2012 information memorandum "Guidance Concerning Waiver and Expenditure Authority under Section 1115," TANF-ACF-IM-2012-03, http://www.acf.hhs.gov/programs/ofa/resource/policy/imofa/2012/im201203/im201203?page=all.

20. US General Accounting Office, "Welfare Reform: More Research Needed on TANF Family Caps and Other Policies for Reducing Out-of-Wedlock Births," GAO-01-924, 2001, http://www.gao.gov/new.items/d01924.pdf.

Attrition levels may be higher in lottery designs. Sometimes people drop out because they were not assigned their preferred treatment. In a treatment lottery, those in the comparison group will not receive the program in the future, and thus attrition may be more of a problem.

Ethical considerations in using the treatment lottery

Unlike in the case of some other methods of randomization, in a treatment lottery some participants in the study are never given access to a program. Is this ethical? The treatment lottery approach is often used when there are insufficient funds to provide the policy or program to all those who could benefit from it. For example, an NGO program may target scholarships to cover four years of secondary education but not have enough funds to cover all eligible children. We may use a lottery to decide who receives access to the program. Recalling the ethical principles described in Module 2.4, as researchers we must carefully weigh the benefits of the evaluation against the risk of harm and seek to minimize potential risks. Because the evaluation has not changed the number of beneficiaries of the program, we have not changed the risk–benefit profile. The only exception is if harm is caused by a participant seeing someone else's benefit while not benefiting herself. In this case we may need to think about randomizing at a higher level, as discussed above in the section on the unit of randomization.

But what if there is sufficient funding to cover all eligible participants? Is it ethical to use the treatment lottery in this case, when the lottery will reduce the total number of beneficiaries of the project, at least in the short run? Ethical guidelines suggest that we must trade off the potential harm of treating fewer beneficiaries as a result of doing an evaluation against the potential benefits of the evaluation. How can we do this? We need to take into account the level of uncertainty about the benefits of the program, how many people will have delayed access to the program because of the evaluation, and what the benefits would be of having more information about the impact of the program.

It can be ethical to proceed with an evaluation if any of the following conditions hold: if it is unclear whether the program will have positive effects, if there is some risk that the program will have negative effects, or if there are likely to be benefits to society in general and to one group (say, girls) in particular from learning the impact of the program. (Remember that the justice consideration means that benefits should accrue to the group in society that is undertaking the risks, and thus it is important that the benefits of doing the evaluation accrue to orphans in this example—not just to society in general.)

The benefits of undertaking the research may include being able to use the evidence of program effectiveness to raise more funding to expand the program so that it reaches more people in the long run, the gain from replacing the program with something more effective if we find its impact is disappointing, and the benefit of avoiding harm if we find that the program has unintended negative consequences and it is not scaled up as originally planned.

Lotteries and medical ethics. Medical trials have particular ethics rules that must be followed when using a lottery design. Under these rules, it is ethical to do an experiment to test two alternative treatments only if, at the start of the trial, we do not know whether the existing treatment or the new treatment is better. However, once it is clear that one approach is better than the other, there is an ethical obligation to end the trial early and scale up the effective treatment to all those in the evaluation.

In practice, this issue rarely arises in randomized evaluations of social programs. In medicine there is a presumption that everyone is receiving care and the question is which type of care is most effective. In most social programs, only some of those who could potentially benefit are receiving any program at all. Even if we know what is effective, there is often not sufficient funding to cover everyone. Additionally, we rarely have enough data to know for sure that a program is effective partway through the evaluation. In those cases in which we do have a lot of data in the middle of the program, we may not have the money to scale it up to everyone if we find midway that the program is succeeding, but we may want to consider stopping the program early if we find that it is having a negative effect.

The treatment lottery around a cutoff

Allocation. For programs that select participants based on qualifications (e.g., credit programs, secondary schools, need-based programs), a regular treatment lottery may not be feasible. Banks, for example, may not be willing to lend to any "random" applicant but may want to lend to all well-qualified applicants. Randomized evaluation, however, is still possible if we divide applicants into three groups: those who will be accepted into the program no matter what, those who will not be accepted into the program, and those who will have a random chance of being accepted into the program. Which group people fall into depends on how well qualified they are for the program.

Examples of groups that could be randomized around the cutoff include students seeking scholarships to go to university, applicants for loans, and families with assets slightly too great to qualify for an existing welfare program.

There are three slightly different versions of a lottery around the cutoff:

1. *A lottery among the marginally ineligible.* The program accepts all those it would have previously accepted, but now it is expanded to also include some who had previously just missed the cutoff. This tests the impact of expanding eligibility to the program—for example, expanding access to secondary education or expanding access to subsidized health insurance to those just above the poverty line. This design is possible only with additional program funding

2. *A lottery among the marginally eligible and marginally ineligible.* If there are no resources to fund additional participants, it is still possible to use the lottery around the cutoff design. Some of those who would previously have been eligible are put into the lottery along with some of those who would previously have fallen just below the cutoff. This design works best when new recruits are being accepted into the program. It is very hard to use a lottery to remove some existing participants from a program and at the same time accept others into the program. This design tests the impact of the program at the margin—both the impact of expanding and that of slightly contracting the program.

3. *A lottery among the qualified.* In this design there are only two groups, the eligible and the ineligible. The lottery takes place among all those who are eligible, but we still have a group that is entirely rejected. The only requirement is that we have more eligible people than we have places for. The advantage of this approach is that we are now testing the impact of the program on the average participant. This design is very close to the simple lottery described above.

Difference in exposure to the program. This comes from randomizing access to the program among a particular subset of those who apply.

What to consider when using the lottery around a cutoff

Does this design answer a relevant policy question? A lottery around the cutoff tests the effect of the program on a very specific population —those who are close to the cutoff. For example, the lottery among the ineligible tests only the impact of expanding the program to those not currently eligible. There is no comparison group of those currently eligible, because they all remain eligible. Sometimes whether there is a comparison group is exactly the question we want to answer because the policy question before us is whether to expand the program to those who are currently not eligible. For example, an evaluation in Oregon is examining the effect of making Medicaid available to those just above the current cutoff for Medicaid eligibility. Whether to expand health insurance to those who are poor but currently do not have access to medical insurance is a major policy question in the US currently. However, the evaluation will not be able to say what impact Medicaid will have because there is no comparison group among those currently eligible for Medicaid.

How large a range around the cutoff should we use? Imagine that we have 200 applicants for 100 places. We rank all the applicants from 1 to 200. Normally the program would accept the first 100 and reject the rest. For our evaluation, should we accept the first 50, reject the bottom 50, and randomize acceptance among the middle 100? Or should we accept the top 80, reject the bottom 40, and randomize among the remaining 80? The answer depends on program needs, perceived fairness, and statistical power. The program may have some basic requirements for its participants; those who do not fulfill these should be rejected.

We discuss ethical considerations and perceived fairness (political considerations) in more detail below. But it is worth noting that sometimes considerations around perceived fairness and statistical power may push us in different directions. In some situations it may be seen as unfair if some people are accepted into the program who score much lower on the qualification criteria than others who are rejected. For this reason, there may be pressure to keep the range of people from which we randomize quite narrow: for example, we could randomize among those who scored between 50 and 55 on the qualifying criteria. This difference is likely to appear small to most people, and it should be easy to convince the community that it is pretty arbitrary whether someone got a score of 50 versus 55, so randomizing participation is fair. But if we have a narrow range, this restricts the sample size we can use to estimate the impact of the program and thus the statistical power of measuring the impact. There is little point in performing the evaluation if our sample size is very small (see Chapter 6).

One way to try to balance these two competing pressures is to look for a point at which there are lots of people within a small range of scores and make that the randomization range. Then we can have a reasonable sample size and still randomize over a relatively small range of scores. As discussed above, our evaluation will test the impact of the program only on those whose scores fall within this range.

Ethical and political considerations

Usually when we introduce a lottery around the cutoff we do not change the number of beneficiaries, but we do change who receives access to the program. Is it ethical to deny access to those who are more qualified and give their places to people who are less qualified for the sake of the evaluation?

In assessing the trade-off between the costs and benefits of using a lottery around the cutoff, there are a number of issues to keep in mind. First, we are unlikely to know for sure that having access to the program is beneficial or we would not be doing the evaluation. As we discussed previously, there are degrees of uncertainty: the stronger the evidence that the program is beneficial, the more we have to be concerned about the harm of "denying" people access. In the case of a lottery around the cutoff, because we are changing the types of people who receive the program, a key question is whether we know that the benefits of the program are likely to be greater for those who are more qualified.

For example, imagine that we are evaluating the effect of giving access to consumer loans to people in South Africa.[21] The bank has a scoring system it uses to decide which applicants are creditworthy. The assumption is that those who score highly will be able to repay the loans, whereas those who score badly will not be able to repay, potentially getting themselves into a damaging debt trap. Both the bank and the participants are better off with scoring. But do we know that

---

21. This example is inspired by but is a simplified version of Dean Karlan and Jonathan Zinman, "Expanding Credit Access: Using Randomized Supply Decisions to Estimate the Impacts," *Review of Financial Studies* 23 (2010): 433–464.

the scoring system is good at determining who is a good risk and who is a bad risk? Maybe the system is good enough to detect the very good risks and the very bad risks, but does it do a good job of selecting people around the cutoff? The credit scoring system may be discriminating against people who are otherwise good risks but happen to receive a low score on some characteristic, such as living in a poorer neighborhood.

If there is uncertainty about the quality of the scoring system, a lottery around the cutoff can help us learn how good the system is and whether the cutoff has been placed at the right point. If we find that those just below the cutoff do just as well as those above it, then the bank will be encouraged to extend its loans to more people and those just below the cutoff will gain, as will the bank. There is a risk that the cutoff was at the right place initially and that those below the cutoff will get into debt as a result of being offered a loan they cannot repay. We have to take this risk into account when designing the study. We can ameliorate this risk by randomizing only above the cutoff (a lottery among the qualified), but this has other issues: we don't learn whether the cutoff was too high, and we reduce access among the qualified more than in other designs.

In general, the better the evidence we have that the cutoff is well measured and targets the program well, the more careful we need to be with a lottery around the cutoff. For example, researchers decided not to evaluate a feeding program for malnourished children because the criteria for selecting participants (height for weight and arm circumference) were relatively well designed. In contrast, credit score cutoffs used to gauge the creditworthiness of the poor clients served by MFIs do not have a lot of research behind them, and this level of uncertainty increases the benefits and reduces the probability of harm of changing the cutoffs.

One way to make a lottery around the cutoff more politically acceptable is to vary the probability that access to the program will depend on people's scores. For example, we could give those above the cutoff a higher (though still random) probability of being accepted into the program than we give to those below the cutoff. We call the probability of being assigned to treatment the *allocation fraction,* so in these examples we are varying the allocation fraction depending on the score. Figure 4.4 provides an illustration. In our example of randomizing access to credit around a credit score cutoff, we accept all those with a credit score above 60 and reject all those with a credit

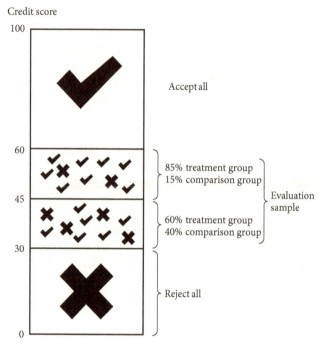

FIGURE 4.4 Lottery around the cutoff with varying allocation fractions

Note: Checkmarks indicate acceptance; x's indicate rejection.

score below 30. Those with a credit score between 45 and 69 have an 85 percent probability of being given credit, while those with a credit score between 30 and 45 have a 60 percent chance of receiving credit. In this design we have included an element of randomization, but each individual's probability of receiving credit is closely linked to her credit score.

The phase-in design

Allocation. When everyone must receive the program, we can randomly select who is phased in to the program first and who receives it later.

Difference in exposure to the program. The groups not yet phased in form the comparison group. They become the treatment group when they are phased in.

When is the phase-in most workable?

When everyone must be given access eventually. When everyone must receive program services during the evaluation period, the phase-in design allows us to still create a temporary comparison group.

When not everyone can be enrolled at once. When logistical or financial constraints mean that coverage must expand slowly, randomization may be the fairest way to choose who receives the program first. Programs with a heavy upfront training component will often fall into this category. If we are using a phase-in design because of financial constraints, we must be sure that we will have the funding and other resources to deliver the program later as we promise.

When anticipation of treatment is unlikely to change the behavior of the comparison group. People assigned to the later phases of a program could make choices based on expected treatment. Imagine a phase-in program providing capital grants of US$100. People know that next year they will receive a grant of US$100. They can borrow against that and have the capital this year, undermining our counterfactual. This is more likely to happen if the program is providing high-value transferable goods and services. If we are providing such untransferable goods as deworming pills to be swallowed on the spot, anticipation effects are unlikely.

When we are interested in the average program impact over different years. Often when we use a phase-in design we end up pooling the data across the several years of the experiment. However, with enough sample, we could look at each year separately and ask, "What was the impact of the program in year 1, when Group A was the treatment group and Groups B and C were the comparison group?" Then we ask, "What was the one-year impact of the program when Group B had had the program for one year and Group C was the comparison group?" Finally, we can ask, "What was the two-year impact of the program when Group A had had the program for two years versus Group C, which was the control?"

Usually we do not have enough statistical power to ask these three separate questions. Instead we perform one test that uses all our data. We implicitly assume that the effect on A in the first year of the evaluation is the same as the effect on B in its first year of the program but the second year of the evaluation. Alternatively, we may accept that the impact may vary in different calendar years but be satisfied with calculating the average effect of the program over the two calendar years. Note that in the phase-in setup we can account for changes in the general environment in different calendar years (for example, farmers do worse in the second year because of a drought) because we have our comparison group, Group C, which we use to factor out common-year effects. We can also pick up whether the program had more of an effect in its second year than in its first by comparing Group A in the second calendar year to Group B in the second calendar year (although we may not have much power to pick up small effects).

What to consider before using the phase-in design

Attrition may occur. Because it promises goods and services in the future, the phase-in design may increase the chance that the comparison group will continue to cooperate with the follow-up surveys and tests, which limits attrition.

Anticipation of treatment may induce behaviors that could mask the effects of treatment. As discussed above, anticipation of program goods and services can change the current behavior of those yet to be phased in, which can bias the impact estimates. Anticipatory effects can go in different directions: if the prospect of being given a free bed net makes people less likely to buy one now, the evaluation will overestimate the impact of the program. If anticipation of a grant tomorrow makes people more likely to invest today, the evaluation will underestimate the impact of the program. Anticipatory effects are one of the biggest drawbacks of the phase-in design. It means that this design is most workable when evaluating programs in which these effects are unlikely to exist. In some cases, program implementers do not tell individuals or communities that they will be phased into the program at a later stage because of concerns that the rollout may be prevented for some reason. This helps dampen possible anticipation effects, although it also reduces one advantage of phase-in programs, that communities will participate because they know they will receive the program later.

The time to effect (changes in outcomes) must be shorter than the time to the last phase-in. With each group phased in, the treatment group grows and the comparison group shrinks. If the phases are too short, there may not be enough time for the program to have a measurable effect. Imagine that we have three groups and are phasing in new participants every six months. All the groups will be phased in by the end of the first year. If the program takes two years to achieve its effect, the evaluation will find no impact. A well-articulated theory of change and logical framework, preliminary data collection, historical data, and existing literature can all help in guessing the time needed to achieve an impact.

Long-run effects cannot be measured unless the program targets a specific age or cohort, in which case some people will never receive the treatment. Once everyone is phased in, there no longer is a comparison group. The long-run effects cannot be estimated. One exception arises when people age out of the program before they are phased in. An example is education programs. If we are treating a given cohort, say children in the last year of school, every year the graduating cohort is aged out. If a school is randomly assigned to be phased in during the third year, two cohorts will age out before they receive the program. These children will never receive the program and can be used as a long-run comparison group.

Ethical considerations for phase-in designs. Because everyone is offered the program eventually, the ethical issues raised by the phase-in design center on the time to treatment. Even when they have enough funding, implementing organizations often face capacity constraints that force them to roll out programs slowly in the absence of an evaluation. For example, there may be enough funds to deworm all children in a district but not enough program staff to train all the teachers to provide the deworming medicine. In the absence of evaluation, the program will be rolled out based on the logistical preferences of the implementers: for example, those who live nearest the implementers' headquarters may receive the program first. What the phase-in design does is to formalize the rollout into rigid phases and randomize who is included in each phase. Implementers may face some costs associated with having the initial phases more geographically dispersed that would not have been incurred otherwise. These costs need to be weighed against the benefit associated with the evaluation.

A phase-in design can still be ethical even when there are sufficient financial and logistical resources to treat everyone immediately if the benefits of learning the impacts of the program are sufficiently high. In either case, the ethical principles described in Module 2.4 apply: we must carefully weigh the benefits of the evaluation against the risks of harm and seek to minimize potential risks.

The rotation design

Allocation. When everyone needs to receive a program but resources are too limited to provide access to everyone at once, we can rotate who receives the program. We can randomly divide those who are to receive the program into two groups, and the two groups can take turns receiving the program. The group that receives access to the program forms the treatment group for that period, and the other group forms the comparison group. Once it is the comparison group's turn to receive the program, it becomes the new treatment group, and the earlier treatment group switches to be the comparison group. We can randomly select the order in which the groups take turns.

Difference in exposure to the program. This comes from offering the program to one group and withholding it from the other at any given time.

When is rotation design most workable?

When resources are limited and are not expected to increase. When resources will remain limited for the duration of the evaluation and everyone has to be treated, the participants will have to take turns. The same applies when burdens have to be shared fairly.

When the primary concern is what happens to people during the time they have access to the program. For example, how do people behave when they are in office (and have official powers) or when they have access to insurance? In these cases, the potential effects of the program on behavior may go away once these individuals no longer have the program.

When the treatment effects do not remain after the treatment ends. Because the original treatment group switches and becomes the comparison group once they are out of it, we must be sure that the program has only short-term effects. If there are lingering effects, the original treatment group will not make a valid comparison group once their turn is over because their outcomes will reflect whatever program effects remain. These lingering effects will distort our impact estimate.

When we want to measure or document existing and induced "seasonal" influences. Rotation induces seasons: seasons when people have access to the program and seasons when they do not. But for some programs, there already are existing seasons. For example, schools can be in session or on vacation. Agricultural programs or antimalarial interventions are affected by the rainy seasons. How does this seasonality influence program outcomes? When and how is a seasonal program best delivered? How do the existing seasons and the "seasons" introduced by the rotating program interact? Because a rotation design introduces random variation as to when people are exposed to the program, it is possible to use it to measure the best time to run the program.

Imagine a tutoring program that is run both after school and during school vacations. Every three months children are rotated into and out of the program. Some children will experience the program as an afterschool program, and others will experience it during school vacation. At which time will they learn more—during the term, when the tutoring complements what they are doing in school, or during vacation, when their learning would perhaps decay rapidly given that they would not be doing any other schoolwork?

What to consider before using the rotation design

Rotation is common in everyday life and easy to understand. Here are some examples:

- *Vacation timeshares*   People take turns occupying a jointly owned vacation home.
- *Rolling blackouts or load shedding*   When electricity or water is being rationed in a city, the neighborhoods take turns having water and electricity at favorable times, such as rush hours.
- *Afternoon school and night school*   When there are more classes than classrooms, rotation is often used to share the classrooms.
- *Rotating savings and credit associations*   Members take turns using a collective savings pool.

Usually there is no pure comparison in the long run. Every group is treated at some point, so we cannot measure long-term impacts. The exception is if we rerandomize.

Rerandomizing can allow us to measure the effects of length of exposure to a program. The usual way to rotate the treatment is that groups take alternating turns repeatedly. For example, if we had two groups, A and B, the alternations would create one of the following treatment patterns: A, B, A, B or B, A, B, A. Instead we can rerandomize for each period. Imagine flipping a coin at the beginning of each time period to decide which group receives the treatment for that period. Sometimes the same group may receive the treatment again. For example, the repeated coin toss may create this pattern: A, B, B, A. If we compare the outcomes of Group B after two consecutive turns to those during the other periods, we may be able to disentangle the effects of length of exposure. For example, the political quotas for women in some states in India are rerandomized at each election, which creates variation in the length of time voters are exposed to women in political leadership.

Anticipation of having, or not having, treatment may change present behavior. As in the case of phase-in, the out-of-treatment group may behave differently in anticipation of receiving the treatment, and the in-treatment group may anticipate not having the treatment, which can undermine the validity of the comparison group.

The time needed to change outcomes may be shorter than the treatment period. The lag between the time of treatment and the time that the effect becomes detectable should be shorter than the treatment period. If the program rotates before then, impact estimates may be distorted.

The program must affect only those currently in treatment. Unless there are no lingering effects, we cannot have a "pure" comparison group. The exception is if we rerandomize after each cycle and by chance we have a group that is never treated. However, this would undermine one of the main rationales for using the rotation design: that everyone receives access to the program.

Ethical considerations. Ethical considerations for the rotation design are similar to those for the phase-in design. The difference is that in rotation people exit the program. It is therefore important to consider whether there are any risks associated with having a program withdrawn that are different from those of not having exposure to the program. For example, providing a short-term subsidy to address a long-term problem might be harmful. We would not want to provide antibiotics for only part of the time someone was sick. We might not want to provide a loan subsidy for only part of the time someone will have a loan because it might encourage people to take on unsustainable debt.

The encouragement design

Allocation. When a program is open to all, access cannot be directly randomized, but there is still an opportunity for evaluation if the program has low take-up. A treatment group is created by randomly assigning individuals or groups to receive encouragement to take up the program. The encouragement can be in the form of a postcard reminding people of the program, a phone call, a letter, or a reward.

The idea is to increase the probability of take-up by the encouraged. The comparison group still has access to the program but does not receive special encouragement to take it up.[22]

Difference in exposure to the program. Anyone who comes forward will receive treatment, regardless of whether they received the encouragement or not. Difference in exposure at the group level is created when a higher proportion of those in the treatment group take up the program than do those in the comparison group.

When is the encouragement design most workable?

When the program is open to all and is undersubscribed. The design works best when there are enough resources to treat everyone but take-up is low. This low take-up creates the opportunity to create higher take-up in the treatment group.

When the program is open to all but the application process takes time and effort. When the application process is burdensome, we can offer help with the application to some but not to others.

When we can find an encouragement that increases take-up but does not directly affect outcomes. The encouragement research strategy works only if the encouragement does not itself affect the behaviors and outcomes the evaluation is targeting and measuring. The challenge is to use a form of encouragement that creates a big difference in take-up rates between treatment and comparison groups without directly affecting outcomes. Here the encouragement is acting as an instrument in predicting take-up. In other words, this is a randomized form of the instrumental variables strategy we discuss in Module 2.2. The assumption that the encouragement affects outcomes only through its effect on take-up is exactly the same as the assumption for any instrumental variables strategy and is called the exclusion restriction. The benefit here is that we know the instrument itself is randomly allocated.[23]

Imagine that we are interested in the effect of a training program for pepper farmers that is taught in a local market town and is designed to

---

22. An early example of the encouragement design is Marvin Zelen's "A New Design for Randomized Clinical Trials," *New England Journal of Medicine* 300 (1979): 1242–1245.

23. For a more detailed description of the "exclusion restriction," see Joshua Angrist, Guido Imbens, and Donald B. Rubin, "Identification of Causal Effects Using Instrumental Variables (with Discussion)," *Journal of the American Statistical Association* 91 (1996): 444–472.

increase the quality of the peppers grown by farmers. We find that many local pepper farmers do not take up the training, and one of the reasons given is that they cannot afford the bus fare into the market town to attend the training. We therefore think about offering free bus passes to a random sample of pepper farmers as an encouragement to attend the class. We will measure the success of the program by examining the price at which the farmers sell their peppers (the theory is that the training helped increase the quality of their peppers and that higher-quality peppers receive higher prices). But our approach falls afoul of the exclusion restriction. The problem is that giving some farmers free unlimited transport to the local market town may affect the prices at which farmers sell their peppers even if they never attend the training or they learn nothing from it. Farmers without the transport subsidy may sell their peppers to middlemen who bear the transport costs of getting the peppers to market, while those with the free transport subsidy may sell their peppers in the local market town and receive higher prices because they cut out the middlemen. Our encouragement (the transport subsidy) may have increased take-up of the training, but it has also influenced our outcome measure (the sale prices of peppers) through a mechanism (place of sale) other than the effect of the program (increased training in improving pepper quality).

Often encouragement mechanisms involve some form of subsidy to take up the program, such as a small incentive tied to take-up. It is important that any subsidy be very small; otherwise the monetary benefit of the encouragement may have a direct effect on outcomes by making people richer. The most workable encouragement designs are specifically targeted to the take-up of the program.

It may seem hard to find an encouragement that is small enough not to have a direct effect on the outcome and yet have a large effect on take-up. But behavioral economics is increasingly finding that relatively small nudges can have surprisingly large effects on behavior. For example, helping people fill in the application form for a program may seem like a small incentive. If the service is valuable, surely people would fill out a form without help, we reason. But a number of studies have found that help with applications can have a large impact on program take-up.[24]

<hr />

24. See, for example, Céline Braconnier, Jean-Yves Dormagen, and Vincent Pons, "Willing to Vote, but Disenfranchised by a Costly Registration Process: Evidence from a Randomized Experiment in France," APSA 2012 Annual Meeting Paper, http://ssrn

What to consider before using the encouragement design

We have already set out a number of issues to consider when using the encouragement design while discussing the situations in which an encouragement design is most useful. Here we discuss two others.

Those who respond to the encouragement are a policy-relevant group. An encouragement design measures the impact of the program on those who respond to the encouragement. It does not tell us the impact of the program on those who had already taken up the program, nor does it tell us the impact on those who did not respond to the encouragement. Before we use an encouragement design, we should think carefully about the question we want to answer. Do we want to measure the impact of the program on the average person who takes it up, or do we want to measure the impact of the program on the marginal person who takes it up? If we want to measure the average impact across all those who take up the program, we want those who respond to the incentive to be comparable to those who have already taken up the program. But an encouragement design is particularly useful when we are especially interested in the impact on those who respond to the encouragement (were not taking up the program before). For example, if we want to know whether to invest in encouraging more people to take up the US food stamps program, we will want to know the impact of taking up food stamps on those who respond to an encouragement program.

The encouragement must not encourage some and discourage others. When we use an encouragement design, we must make what is called the *monotonicity assumption*. This means that everyone must be affected by the encouragement in the same direction. If we provide an incentive to take up a program, it must either increase the probability that someone will take up the program or not impact anyone at all. If the encouragement itself increases the take-up of some groups and reduces the take-up of others, we will likely get a biased estimate of the impact of the program. All too often, researchers play little attention to this assumption because it seems natural to assume that an incentive or an encouragement will have only a positive effect on take-

.com/abstract=2108999, and Florencia Devoto, Esther Duflo, Pascaline Dupas, William Pariente, and Vincent Pons, "Happiness on Tap: Piped Water Adoption in Urban Morocco," NBER Working Paper 16933, National Bureau of Economic Research, Cambridge, MA, 2011.

up. But there are some cases, like that of the provision of information, in which both positive and negative responses may be quite natural. For example, if we tell people the benefits of staying in school, in terms of increased earnings, this is likely to have different impacts on whether children stay in school depending on whether they had previously under- or overestimated the likely benefits of staying in school. The information may lead some to stay in school longer, while it may lead others to stay less long.

In Module 7.1 we explain why these "defiers" can undermine the validity of our experiment. For now, however, it is important to note that we need to carefully think through the channels through which an encouragement might work and make sure that it will not have perverse effects on (discourage) some people.

Ethical considerations

In some ways, encouragement designs ease some of the ethical and political concerns that may arise when randomized evaluations restrict access to certain programs. Everyone can have access to the program; we simply make it easier for some to have access than for others. But this difference is really a matter of degree. If we make it easier for some people to gain access to the program than for others we are still potentially (if the program works) giving a benefit to some over others, so we should consider whether the evaluation is changing those who access the program in a way that could be detrimental. In other words, we still need to go through the process of balancing the risks and benefits of the evaluation even in the case of an encouragement design.

Hybrid strategies in multistage experiments

Some research questions may require us to randomize more than once. We can use these multistage experiments to evaluate different components of an intervention or concepts underlying behavior. When we perform multistage randomization, we can use different randomization strategies at each stage to create hybrid strategies.

Hybrids when isolating spillover effects

As we discuss in Module 4.2, we may want to randomize in two stages to measure social interaction or spillover effects. For instance, researchers want to examine the social effects and information effects of participating in a retirement savings program offered by a large employer.

The employer offers information sessions about the program to employees. The organization is divided into many departments. We can use a combination of the treatment lottery and the encouragement design to generate variation in treatment density. We can randomize the proportion of employees in each department who will receive extra encouragement to sign up for the information session and then randomize which individuals in each department receive the encouragement.

Hybrids to isolate channels of underlying behavior

When there are multiple possible impact channels and we want to separately identify each, we may have to randomize more than once. An experiment in South Africa used a two-stage approach to isolate moral hazard and adverse selection, two concepts thought to explain why it is so hard to lend to the poor. In the first stage, clients of a South African lender received letters offering loans with randomly assigned high and low interest rates. This stage used the encouragement design. Those responding to low-rate offers were offered low-rate loans. (We call them the low-to-low group, because their repayment burden was low and remained low.) Those responding to high-rate offers were randomly split into two groups. This stage used the lottery. Half were randomly surprised with a lower-rate loan (the high-to-low group), and the other half were offered the original high rate (the high-to-high group).[25] The theory of moral hazard says that borrowers with little at stake face great temptation to default if the repayment burden becomes too large. If there is moral hazard, the clients who borrow at the higher rate are more likely to default because they have a large repayment burden. Decreasing the repayment burden for some reduces the chances that they will be subject to *moral hazard*. Comparing the high-to-high and the high-to-low groups identifies moral hazard. *Adverse selection* essentially says that, since the interest rate is supposed to reflect the risk, the less risky clients will refuse to borrow at high interest. If there is adverse selection, clients who agree to borrow at a higher rate are more likely to default. Comparing the high-to-low and the low-to-low groups identifies adverse selection.

25. Dean Karlan and Jonathan Zinman, "Observing Unobservables: Identifying Information Asymmetries with a Consumer Credit Field Experiment," *Econometrica* 77 (2009): 1993–2008.

Module 4.3 summary: Comparing the four basic strategies

Strategy	Randomization design	Most workable when	Advantages	Disadvantages
Basic lottery	• Randomizes access to program • Leaves treatment status unchanged throughout • Compares those with and without access to the program	• The program is oversubscribed • Resources are constant for the evaluation period • It is acceptable that some receive no program	• Familiar and well understood • Usually seen as fair • Easy to implement • Allows for estimation of long-term impacts	• Differential attrition—units in the comparison group may have little reason to cooperate with the survey
Lottery around the cutoff	• Randomizes access to the program among those close to an eligibility cutoff	• The program determines eligibility with a scoring system • There are large numbers of participants	• Program has considerable flexibility about who to enroll	• Measures the impact of the program only on those who are close to the eligibility cutoff
Phase-in	• Randomizes the timing of access • Switches units from comparison to treatment over time • Compares those with access to those who have not yet received access	• Everyone must eventually receive the program • Resources are growing over time • Treatment is being replicated	• Common • Easy to understand • The comparison group is more likely to cooperate in anticipation of future benefits	• The comparison group eventually goes away • Anticipation of treatment may affect the behavior of the control group • There is a limited time over which impact can be measured
Encouragement	• Randomizes encouragement to take up program • Treatment status constant throughout • Difference in exposure comes from higher take up among the encouraged	• Program is under-subscribed • When no eligible units can be excluded	• Allows evaluation of programs that cannot exclude anyone • Allows individual randomization despite group level implementation	• Measures impact only on those impacted by the encouragement • Encouragement cannot affect outcomes except through effect on take up

MODULE 4.4 The Mechanics of Simple Randomization

This module outlines the mechanics of random assignment. We discuss the ingredients we need, the steps involved, and the pros and cons of different devices we can use to perform the randomization.

The ingredients of random assignment

We need five ingredients to perform random assignment:

1. A list of eligible units (such as people, communities, schools)
2. The number of randomization cells
3. Allocation fractions
4. A randomization device
5. Initial data on the eligible units (for stratification or balance check)

The list of eligible units

The list of units eligible for our program can be individuals or groupings of individuals, such as households, villages, districts, schools, or firms. In the illustrations below, we consider the 26 letters of the alphabet as our list of eligible units (our *sampling frame*). In real life we have to create that list somehow. Here we provide some examples of commonly used methods for acquiring this list and sources of information that can be used.

Existing data from the government and other providers

Local governments. Local authorities typically have lists of all the schools or health centers in a given area. These lists can be useful when selecting a sample for a school-based or health-center-level program.

School registers. An experiment in Kenya on subsidies for long-lasting, insecticide-treated bed nets used school registers to create a list of households with children. This made sense for two reasons. First, primary schooling is free in Kenya, and nearly all the children are enrolled in school. Second, children are more vulnerable to malaria, so the subsidy program would target households with children, and a list constructed from the registers was as good as a census for identifying those households.[26] Had enrollment and attendance been low, the resulting list would have missed vulnerable households with out-of-school children.

---

26. This study by Jessica Cohen and Pascaline Dupas is summarized as Evaluation 6 in the appendix.

Resource appraisals Many programs target resources to those in need. Making the list of eligible people therefore requires us to assess who is "needy" according to the program definition. A number of ways have been developed to appraise the needy. These approaches may be used by program staff to create a list of people who are eligible for the program from which some will be randomized to receive it. They may also be used by evaluators to predict who is likely to receive the program in treatment and comparison communities. This latter approach is required if the program will assess need only in treatment communities but the evaluator needs to know who is potentially eligible in both treatment and comparison communities.

Census with basic needs assessment. If the program is going to target households lacking access to a given resource, such as households without a latrine at home or without a bank account, information about access to this specific resource can be measured through a census in which enumerators go from house to house and collect information on the assets of every household. A census is also useful if the program will define need based on an asset index (how many of a long list of assets a household has).

Community-driven participatory resource appraisals. Sometimes when eligibility is determined by outsiders based on a census as described above, the resulting list of eligible households may differ from the set of households the local community perceives to be most needy. Participatory methods capture the perceptions of the community about need. For example, a community may be asked to put forward the 10 poorest households, or the school committee or teachers may be asked to rank students by need.

Revealed need. The program inception can be delayed to reveal need. Imagine a program that targets scholarships to children who would not otherwise be able to attend secondary school. The school year starts in January. Instead of announcing the program and disbursing scholarships before the start of the school year, the program could be announced after the start of the school year, when all the children who would attend without help have already registered and are in school. The program can then target the qualified children who are still out of school for lack of fees.

Hybrids. Multiple approaches can be combined. For example, the results of the community participatory appraisal can be verified by a survey of assets, or the ranking by teachers can be checked against revealed need.

Random sampling to create a representative list of eligible units We may take a random sample of the population to create the pool from which we randomly allocate access to the program (the difference between random sampling and random allocation is discussed in Module 2.3). This makes sense for two reasons. First, there may be political constraints. We may have to achieve a balance of political groupings. If every political grouping (administrative district, ethnic grouping) must have a fair share, randomly sampling areas of the country to be part of the study can allow us to achieve this balance. Second, we may want to increase the external validity of the findings, so we would want the units in our evaluation to be as representative as possible of the population. (See Module 9.2.)

An education program in India did exactly this. An evaluation of a teacher performance pay program was conducted in Andhra Pradesh, which has three culturally distinct regions and 23 districts. Each district consists of five divisions, and each division has 10 to 15 subdivisions, each with about 25 villages and 40–60 government primary schools. The program was randomized at the school level. The pool of schools was created as follows: In each sociocultural region, five districts were sampled. In each district, a division was randomly selected, and in each division 10 subdivisions were randomly selected. In each of the 50 subdivisions, 10 primary schools were randomly selected using a probability proportional to school enrollment. That means that the 500 schools in the study were representative of the schooling conditions faced by a typical child in rural Andhra Pradesh.[27]

Number of randomization cells

In a simple evaluation that measures the impact of a program, we will randomize our list of eligible units into two *randomization cells:* treatment and comparison. In more complicated evaluations, we may have to divide our units into more than two cells. The number of cells will depend on the number of different treatments and the randomization strategy.

If we want to ask more complicated questions, such as which version of a program works better than another or how long the program

27. When we randomly select the sample for our study from a wider population, the whole of that wider population that is not treated is in effect part of the comparison group, even if we do not measure their outcomes. If we wanted to measure impacts more precisely later, we could go back and collect data or look at administrative outcomes from those areas that were (randomly) not picked for the study. This study by Karthik Muralidharan and Venkatesh Sundararaman is summarized as Evaluation 14 in the appendix.

has to persist before it has the effect we want to see, we have to have more than one treatment or treatment arm. We provide a number of examples of how multiple treatments can be used to answer complex questions in Module 4.6.

The research design can dictate the number of randomization cells. In the phase-in design, the number of time periods for the phase-in will determine the number of cells. For example, if the treatment is phased in over three periods, we will need three cells, one for each phase.

Allocation fractions

The *allocation fractions* are the proportions of the eligible units that we will assign to each group. The simplest allocation fraction is 50 percent, with 50 percent allocated to the treatment group and 50 percent to the comparison group. In most cases, dividing the sample equally between treatment and comparison maximizes statistical power. (See Module 6.4 for more details.)

Randomization device

We will need a randomization device. This can be mechanical (a coin, die, or ball machine), a random number table, or a computer program with a random number generator.

Mechanical devices We can use a mechanical device for *simple random assignment*. Examples include flipping coins, shuffling cards, rolling dice, using roulettes, picking the shortest straw, and picking names out of hats. Participants can be asked to pick a straw or to pick a ball from a transparent bowl. What should we consider before using mechanical devices? Four things: that they are ubiquitous and well accepted, they lend themselves to public randomization and transparency, they are limited to small sampling frames, and they can break down.

Ubiquitous and well accepted. A mechanical device has the advantage that it is perceived as fair, it can be used publicly, and it is universally familiar, used in raffles, lotteries, and other games of chance. For example, this type of device was used for the US 1969 military draft lottery for the Vietnam War.

Lend themselves to public randomization and transparency. Mechanical devices can facilitate public randomization and transparency. We can have the randomization in a public ceremony and can involve the participants and authorities in the randomization.

Limited to small sampling frames. For all their advantages, mechanical devices can be slow and tedious to use and are difficult to use with larger samples. Imagine picking names out of containers for 10,000 participants!

Subject to mechanical failures. Some mechanical devices will fail. For example, cards will stick together in a container, or people will grab two cards. The names put in first might never bubble to the top and never be drawn, resulting in non-equal probabilities of being drawn. These problems are real, and resolving them can undo the advantages of mechanical devices, especially the perception of fairness. For example, in the 1969 military draft lottery for the Vietnam War, the container was not well shaken, so the dates of birth put in last—those in October, November, and December—were drawn first.[28]

Avoid putting a large number of objects in one big sack because they may not shake and mix as well. Avoid cards that may stick together; use balls instead. Make sure that whatever you use is smooth and that someone putting a hand in the container cannot by touch know what number he is picking. Try to make the choice in a number of steps. For instance, instead of using 1,000 balls marked 000 to 999, use three containers with 10 balls apiece marked 0 to 9 and have someone choose the number by picking a ball from each urn. People may be less likely to feel cheated if the person making the selection has to draw more than once. Some mechanical devices may also be objectionable to some people because of their long association with gambling. Above all, though, keep it simple. A complicated and hard-to-understand public process will not help transparency.

Published random number tables A *random number table* is a list of unique numbers that are randomly ordered. Random number tables have been published from as early as 1927. For example, the RAND Corporation generated a large table by attaching a roulette wheel to a computer. The RAND table, published as the book "A Million Random Digits with 100,000 Normal Deviates," was used for experimental design. It is good practice when using random number tables not to start at the beginning of the book or table but to randomly pick where to start from. The use of random number tables has largely been supplanted by the use of random number generators on computers.

28. T. D. Cook and D. T. Campbell, *Quasi-Experimentation: Design and Analysis for Field Settings* (Chicago: Rand McNally, 1979).

Computerized random number generators Random number generators are available using web-based tools, spreadsheet software, or statistical packages. For example, both Microsoft Excel and the Google
Docs spreadsheet have a randomization function: `=rand()`.

Existing data on eligible units

We do not necessarily need to know anything about our units at the
time we randomize because randomization will yield balanced treatment and comparison groups if we have a very large sample. But with
smaller samples we may want to *stratify* or match units before randomizing to achieve balance on some key variables. This also helps us
achieve higher statistical power and precision. Data on some key characteristics of our eligible units will also help us check whether there is
indeed balance across our randomized study groups. This data may
come from administrative sources or from a baseline survey we have
conducted ourselves.

Steps in simple random assignment

The process of doing a simple random assignment is straightforward:
we take the list of eligible units as one big pool, and we randomly assign
them to different cells. If we are creating two cells (one treatment and
one comparison), this can be done by flipping a coin for each unit one
by one and assigning the unit to the treatment group if heads or to the
comparison group if tails (or vice versa). Obviously this procedure
can be quite time consuming if there are many units, and it is not possible to document that we undertook it fairly, so most evaluations use
computer-based randomization. Below we describe how to do this with
a spreadsheet in either Excel or Google Docs, but the procedural steps
are identical if done using a statistical package such as Stata. The most
commonly used process involves three simple steps:

1. Order the list of eligible units randomly.
2. Allocate units from the randomly ordered list into different
   groups, depending on the number of randomization cells.
3. Randomly choose which of the groups will receive treatment
   A, treatment B, and so on, and which will be the comparison
   group.[29]

---

29. It is increasingly common to avoid deciding which group is treatment versus
control until the very last step.

One advantage of this three-step process is that we do not know until the very end of the process which group is considered treatment and which comparison. However, this three-step process works only when all the treatment arms are of the same size. When the probability of ending up in different treatments is different (for example, 30 percent are allocated to treatment A, 30 percent to treatment B, and 40 percent to the comparison group), we usually have to accomplish our randomization slightly differently. Both of the following approaches are valid.

1. Decide the rule by which units will be allocated to different treatment arms and the comparison group (first 30 percent to treatment A, second 30 to treatment B, last 40 to the comparison group).

2. Order the list of eligible units randomly, and allocate units to the various arms following the prestated rule.

Whatever methodology is used, it is important to agree on it and document it beforehand.

Order the list randomly

To randomly order the list of eligible units, we assign a unique random number to each unit on the list and then sort the list in ascending or descending order. We illustrate this in Figure 4.5 by considering the 26 letters of the alphabet as our eligible units. We enter all of the units in the sample (A–Z) in column B of an Excel or Google Docs spreadsheet. Then, in column A (not shown in the table), we type =rand() for all 26 rows. Every letter now has its own random number next to it. We copy all of column A and "paste special-values only" in column C. We have to copy and paste values because both Excel and Google Docs assign a new random number whenever we do anything else on the worksheet. We then select columns B and C and sort them, ascending or descending, by column C. This gives us a randomly ordered list.

Allocate units to groups from the randomly ordered list

When the list has been randomly ordered, we can allocate units to the groups. Say we need two groups, a treatment and a comparison group, and our allocation fractions are 50-50. We can allocate in blocks, placing the top 13 entries into Group A and the bottom 13 into

B	C		B	C	
Random numbers assigned (column C) to each of the units in column B			Numbers sorted in ascending order (by column C) to get a randomly ordered list		
A	0.257540799		W	0.095374469	⎫
B	0.141977853		P	0.127155063	
C	0.377927502		B	0.141977853	
D	0.990857584		K	0.166217843	
E	0.948417439		O	0.221630819	
F	0.303441684		Q	0.257405314	
G	0.911827709		A	0.257540799	Group A
H	0.447802267		J	0.280958121	
I	0.287941699		I	0.287941699	
J	0.280958121		Y	0.299960876	
K	0.166217843		F	0.303441684	
L	0.871365641		C	0.377927502	
M	0.551764078		U	0.421965911	⎭
N	0.728706001		H	0.447802267	⎫
O	0.221630819		M	0.551764078	
P	0.127155063		R	0.564626023	
Q	0.257405314		N	0.728706001	
R	0.564626023		S	0.754678177	
S	0.754678177		V	0.87089069	
T	0.907811761		L	0.871365641	Group B
U	0.421965911		T	0.907811761	
V	0.87089069		G	0.911827709	
W	0.095374469		E	0.948417439	
X	0.987811391		Z	0.953142552	
Y	0.299960876		X	0.987811391	
Z	0.953142552		D	0.990857584	⎭

FIGURE 4.5 Randomizing on a spreadsheet

Group B. Or we can allocate at intervals, putting all the entries in even-numbered rows in A and all the entries in odd-numbered rows in B.

Randomly determine which group is treatment and which comparison

In the final stage we randomly decide whether A or B is the treatment group. This can be done by flipping a coin or using a random number generator. It is important to determine the exact procedure by which we plan to randomize before starting the process.

Using a statistical package

Most evaluators use a statistical package to do their randomization. The steps involved are identical to those described above. There are two key advantages in using a statistical package. First, when using complex stratification (we discuss what stratification is and why it is useful below), it is much easier to use a statistical package. More important, it is easier to record and replicate the randomization process. Statistical packages allow us to set a random seed. In other words, they pick a random number once and then remember this number. Once this is set, the program can be rerun and generate exactly the same random allocation. This allows an evaluator to prove that her allocation was random and exactly what stratification led to the random allocation that was derived. Examples of Stata code used to undertake randomization are available at the website accompanying this book (RunningRandomizedEvaluations.com).

Randomly order the list before selecting

Why do we need to order the list randomly? Can't we just order the list alphabetically or take the list as it was given to us and allocate every other entry to Group A and every entry between these entries to Group B? We randomly order the list because we cannot be entirely confident that any listing of the participants, no matter how haphazard, is not in fact ordered by some pattern.

For example, we may be tempted to assign people to the treatment or the comparison group based on whether their identification numbers (such as social security numbers) are odd or even. After all, it is random whether a given social security number is odd or even. However, we may worry that another program will also use odd- and even-numbered social security numbers for another evaluation. In this case, our program will not be the only systematic difference between those with odd and even ID numbers. It is unlikely, but why introduce the smallest risk into our experiment?

Use available data to check whether the groups we created are balanced

It has become standard practice to use baseline data (if we have it) or existing administrative data on some key observable characteristics of our eligible units to check whether, after the randomization, the groups are balanced along those characteristics. This check reports the mean of the treatment group and the mean of the comparison group for different variables and whether they are significantly different from each other (using a *t-test*).

Table 4.3 shows a balance check performed for the study Do Teenagers Respond to HIV Risk Information?, which was implemented in Kenya in 2004–05.[30]

Why are balance checks of this kind usually included in reports on randomized evaluations? After all, if we have randomized properly, the outcome of the process (balance or no balance) must be due to chance. That is, the allocation to the treatment or the comparison group was completely independent of the potential outcomes. So why report a check?

Some economists and statisticians argue that we should not do balance checks for precisely this reason, but for the most part evaluators do include them. The main reason is that balance checks can help make the case to a skeptical reader that the program was indeed randomized. Indeed, when a researcher does not have complete control over the randomization process, a balance check can alert us to problems. For example, if randomization is being done by pulling names out of a bowl and all the names being chosen start with W, X, Y, or Z, we may worry that the bowl was not shaken properly before the drawing took place. Or maybe agricultural extension workers are asked to set up a demonstration plot in a random field, and the randomization takes place on site. If we find that the treatment fields are much closer to the center of the village than the comparison fields, we may worry that the extension workers did not follow the randomization protocol correctly and chose the most convenient fields to study. We may have to start the project again. A better solution to this problem is to use a more foolproof randomization strategy in the first place, as we describe in the next module.

Lack of balance can occur by chance even when randomization was carried out correctly. Randomization creates balance only on average, with the chance of achieving balance in any specific case increasing as the sample size increases. Often, however, we have only modest

---

30. Pascaline Dupas, "Do Teenagers Respond to HIV Risk Information? Evidence from a Field Experiment in Kenya," *American Economic Journal: Applied Economics* 3 (2011): 1–34. This study is also summarized as Evaluation 4 in the appendix.

TABLE 4.3 The balance check from an experiment on the relative risk of HIV and a teacher training experiment

School characteristics at baseline	Relative risk information			Teacher training on HIV/AIDS curriculum		
	Comparison group (C) (1)	Treatment group (T) (2)	Difference (T – C) (3)	Comparison group (C) (4)	Treatment group (T) (5)	Difference (T – C) (6)
Class size	38.2 (15.9)	34.4 (17.4)	–3.8 (1.540)**	37.4 (16.9)	37.3 (15.7)	–0.06 (1.281)
Pupils' sex ratio (girls/boys)	1.07 (0.489)	1.12 (0.668)	0.049 (0.072)	1.06 (0.476)	1.10 (0.586)	0.040 (0.059)
Teacher/pupil ratio	0.026 (0.026)	0.026 (0.022)	0.000 (0.003)	0.025 (0.021)	0.027 (0.028)	0.003 (0.003)
Teachers' sex ratio (females/males)	1.033 (0.914)	0.921 (0.777)	–0.112 (0.119)	1.003 (0.92)	1.014 (0.852)	0.011 (0.099)
Exam results (2003)	251.0 (29.0)	249.4 (27.4)	–1.6 (3.9)	252.2 (28.6)	249.0 (28.5)	–3.2 (3.2)

Source: Pascaline Dupas, "Do Teenagers Respond to HIV Risk Information? Evidence from a Field Experiment in Kenya," American Economic Journal: Applied Economics 3 (2011): 1–34, table on 16. Reprinted by permission of the author and the American Economic Association.

Notes: The table shows the first five rows of Panel A of a multipanel table created for the above study. Standard errors are given in parentheses. ** indicates significant at the 5 percent level.

samples, particularly when we randomize at the group level (village, school, or district). There is a risk that the randomization can return unbalanced groups. Indeed, it is likely that if we look at a large number of different variables, we will find some significant differences in at least one variable. On average, one out of ten variables we compare across cells will be unbalanced at the 90 percent confidence level, and one out of twenty variables will be unbalanced at the 95 percent confidence level. We should not be concerned if we see this level of imbalance. In the example above, four different variables are compared between treatment and comparison groups for two different treatment groups. There is a significant difference for one variable in one of the comparisons. This is not a major problem, because it is close to what we would expect by chance and the variable, class size, is not a major factor in our theory of change.

Whether to avoid rerandomization if we do not achieve reasonable balance

What do we do if we find that, by chance, the treatment and comparison groups have very different characteristics? What if we are evaluating a business training program and our treatment group has much larger businesses than the comparison group at baseline? This may undermine our ability to draw clear conclusions from the results. If we find treatment group businesses grow faster than those in the comparison group, will we be certain that the difference is due to the program rather than to the tendency for better-capitalized larger businesses to grow faster than smaller ones? We will be able to check whether large businesses grow faster than small ones within the comparison group, or control for size of business in our analysis (see Module 8.2), but this difference at baseline is going to complicate the interpretation of our findings. The best approach is to avoid being in this situation by undertaking stratified random sampling as described in the next module.

If we do not stratify and randomization returns groups that are unbalanced along multiple dimensions of direct relevance, a common fix is to rerandomize, to try again. It used to be common practice to achieve balance by randomizing many times, selecting those random draws that achieved balance, and then randomly choosing one of these allocations for the experiment. But it is no longer considered good practice. The problem is that when we use this approach, not every combination of allocations is equally probable.

For example, if our sample happened to include one very rich person (a Bill Gates), any allocation that achieved balance would have to pair him with a large proportion of the poorest people in our sample. The other group would have to consist of the middle-income people in our sample. Whether Bill Gates and the very poor were assigned to treatment or comparison groups would be random, but certain people would always have to be in the same group to achieve balance.

The statistical rules we use to decide whether a result is significant assumes that every combination of people in the treatment and comparison groups is equally probable. But when we rerandomize, this assumption no longer holds because we reject certain combinations as unbalanced. If we deviate from this equally probable rule (as we do with stratification), we should usually account for it when we do our analysis. With stratification we know exactly what pairings we imposed:

they are the strata we constructed, and thus it is easy to control for these constraints in the analysis. With rerandomization, we can similarly control for the variables we used to balance check. However, we may not fully appreciate the precise restrictions we placed on pairings by requiring balance. In the above example, we may not realize that we forced Bill Gates and all the poorest people in the sample to be in one stratum, so we don't exactly replicate the constraints we placed on the data. It should be stressed that the practical implications of rerandomizing are unlikely to be great. However, our advice is to avoid using this technique, at least until there is more agreement in the literature about its pros and cons.

The final option is to abandon the evaluation. This is extremely costly because by the time we randomize we have usually developed a close partnership with the implementer, collected baseline data, and raised funding for the evaluation. However, it is also costly (in time and money) to continue an evaluation whose findings will be difficult to interpret.

The econometrics of stratification and rerandomization are complex, but our advice about what to do is simple. Stratified random sampling on a few key variables is usually a good idea so that we avoid the situation of having large differences between treatment and comparison groups on important variables and we can avoid rerandomization. If there are some differences between treatment and comparison groups on variables that are not the main outcomes variables of interest, it is normal and should not be considered a threat. There is no easy answer if you find large differences between the treatment and comparison groups on the baseline value of the main outcome variable, so avoid getting into that position by stratifying.

MODULE 4.5 Stratified and Pairwise Randomization

Stratified random assignment provides a way to ensure that our treatment and comparison groups are balanced on key variables. This module explains when stratified randomization is most useful and how to decide what variables to stratify on. It also covers pairwise randomization, which is a special form of stratified randomization.

Steps in stratified random assignment

In stratified random assignment, we first divide the pool of eligible units into strata and then within each stratum follow the procedure for simple random assignment. The steps to perform stratified random assignment are as follows:

1. Divide the pool of eligible units into sublists (strata) based on chosen characteristics.
2. Do simple random assignment for each sublist (stratum) by
   a. ordering the sublist randomly and
   b. allocating units to randomization cells from the randomly ordered sublist.
3. As a final step, randomly pick which cell is treatment and which is comparison.

Imagine that we have a pool of 200 farmers, 80 men and 120 women, with half from a high-rainfall region and half from a low-rainfall region. We can first divide them by region, then by gender, and end up with four categories (Figure 4.6). We then randomly assign half of the people from each group to cell A and half to cell B. Finally, we randomize whether either cell A or cell B is the treatment group.

Thus the treatment and comparison groups are balanced by rainfall and by gender, with each cell containing 20 percent high-rainfall men, 20 percent low-rainfall men, 30 percent high-rainfall women, and 30 percent low-rainfall women. We can think of this stratification as giving chance a helping hand, because it ensures that the treatment and comparison groups coming out of the randomization are fully comparable along the stratification variables.

When to stratify

We stratify to achieve balance, to increase statistical power, and to facilitate analysis by subgroups. A nontechnical reason for stratification is to comply with implementer or political constraints.

When we want to achieve balance. The smaller the sample size, the higher the chance that simple randomization may return unbalanced groups, so the greater the need for stratification.

When we want to increase statistical power. As we discuss in Module 6.4, stratifying on variables that are strong predictors of the outcome can increase our statistical power.

When we want to analyze the impact by subgroup. We should also stratify when we want to learn how the intervention affects subgroups, such as ethnic minorities or gender. Imagine that people in our target

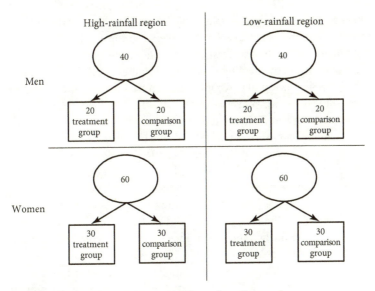

High-rainfall region | Low-rainfall region

Men

40

20 treatment group | 20 comparison group

Low-rainfall region

40

20 treatment group | 20 comparison group

Women

60

30 treatment group | 30 comparison group

60

30 treatment group | 30 comparison group

FIGURE 4.6 Stratified random assignment of 200 farmers

population belong to two ethnicities, K and R, with 80 percent of the people K. Outcomes have traditionally varied by ethnicity. With simple randomization we could, in the extreme, end up with no R people (or very few) in the treatment group. Stratifying by ethnicity would ensure that both ethnicities are well represented in both groups, which would facilitate analysis by subgroup.

When we need balance for political or logistical feasibility. Sometimes, for political or logistical reasons, the implementers want to achieve a particular distribution of treatment groups. For example, half the treatment groups need to be in the north of the country and half in the south, or there must be exactly equal numbers of men and women. Stratification (by region, gender, or ethnicity) is a way to ensure that these constraints are met.

Which stratification variables we should use

Variables that are discrete. Stratification involves placing units into different buckets and then randomizing within those buckets. It is therefore not possible to stratify on a continuous variable, like income or test scores, because there might be only one person in a bucket. For example, only one child might have a test score of 67, and perhaps no child has a test score of 68. We cannot then randomize within the bucket. Instead we put people in buckets if they have similar values for the continuous variable: for example, we group children into high-test-score or low-test-score strata. We can create even more precise test score strata by dividing children into more groups by test scores: for example, the top 10 percent of children by test score, the second 10 percent, and so on. When we say we stratify on test scores, we mean that we stratify on ranges of test scores.

Variables that are highly correlated with the outcomes of interest. We want balance because it simplifies the interpretation of our findings, increases their statistical power, and reduces the chance that differences in treatment and comparison groups could be driven by trends in confounding variables. Confounding variables are highly correlated with both the final outcome and participation. If available, the baseline value of the outcome of interest is a particularly important stratification variable. For example, if the outcome of interest is student test scores, a student's initial baseline score and her score at the end of the program will be correlated, so it is helpful to stratify by baseline test scores.

As we discuss below, there are usually practical constraints on the number of variables on which we can stratify. In choosing between them we should prioritize those that are most correlated with the outcomes of interest (including, potentially, the baseline value of the outcome of interest).

Variables on which we will do subgroup analysis. If, for example, we are going to be analyzing subgroups by gender, we will want balance on gender. We should stratify by gender to maximize power.

How many variables to stratify on

We want to stratify on variables that will explain a large share of the variation in the outcomes that interest us. But there may be many different variables that help explain the outcome. Suppose that we are measuring the impact of an education program on test scores. Age, mother's education, father's education, and baseline test score are all likely to be correlated with test scores. Do we stratify on all of them? Which do we choose? There are three considerations: stratum size, practicability, and loss of power.

Stratum size: Allotting as many units to each stratum as there are randomization cells. If we try to stratify on too many variables, we may find that we have strata with only one unit in them. We can't then split the people in that stratum randomly into both treatment and comparison.

Ideally, the number of units per stratum is a multiple of the number of randomization cells. For example, with two treatment cells and one comparison, it is easier to do stratified randomization if each stratum has 9 units than if each stratum has 10. Sometimes it is impossible to avoid having strata that are not multiples of the number of cells. The best approach in this case is to randomly allocate the "leftovers" to one of the treatment arms. Sometimes with this approach we will not get exactly the same number of units in each treatment arm, which will slightly reduce our power (see Chapter 6).[31]

Practicability: Trading off between balance on different variables. The greater the number of stratification variables, the harder it may be to achieve balance on all of them. Especially when we have continuous variables, we face a trade-off between achieving tight balance on one variable or achieving a less tight balance on many variables. This is particularly true with continuous variables like test scores. Imagine that we are testing a remedial education program and have the option of stratifying on baseline test scores and ethnicity. We have 200 students in our sample. If we stratify on only test scores we create 50 strata, each of which includes only four children, two of whom would be allocated to treatment and two to control and all of whom would have very similar test scores. If we also wanted to stratify on ethnicity and there were five different ethnicities, we could not do that with our existing test score strata because there would not be two children of each ethnicity in the top test score stratum. In order to stratify on other variables, we have to stratify less tightly on test scores. The easiest way to do this is to first stratify on ethnicity and then divide each ethnicity into those with high test scores and those with low test scores. We will achieve better balance on ethnicity but less balance on test scores. We have to decide which is more important to us. If past test scores are the best predictors of future test scores, we may decide to stratify only on test scores.

Statistical power: Trading off between low variance from more subgroups and loss of degrees of freedom from adding more restrictions. One

31. Another strategy is to put all the "leftover" units into a stratum of their own. This approach ensures an equal number of units in every research arm, but it is controversial among some evaluators.

problem with having many strata is a potential loss of degrees of freedom in the final analysis. There is some discussion in the literature about whether we have to include dummy variables in our analysis for all our different strata (see Module 8.2). The emerging consensus is that we may not have to, but usually it is helpful to do so. If we have lots of strata and decide to control for them, there is a theoretical risk that including all these dummies could reduce our power (for more detailed discussion on covariates and the precision of our estimate of impact, see Module 8.2). But usually this is not an issue because the need to ensure that we have at least as many units in our strata as we have randomization cells severely limits the number of variables we can stratify on.

The possibility of using stratified random assignment with a public lottery

If we are performing a public randomization, stratifying is still possible. For example, if we want the program allocation to be stratified by gender, we will want men and women to pick their randomized assignment from two separate containers, each containing half treatment and half comparison markers. If we want the program to be stratified by gender and poverty status, we will want four containers: one for poor women, one for nonpoor women, one for poor men, and one for nonpoor men.

Paired random assignment

In paired random assignment, two units are matched on a list of important characteristics, and then one of them is randomly assigned to treatment and the other to comparison. If there are three randomization cells (two treatments and one comparison), the units are placed into triplets, and within each triplet we randomly assign one unit to each of the three randomization cells. Paired random assignment is stratification with strata as small as possible. Pairing may take place on one continuous variable: in the education example above, we would create 100 strata with two children in each, starting with the two children with the highest test scores and working down. Alternatively, pairing can be done by creating strata using many different variables (gender, age, high test score or low test score, north or south) until there are only as many units in each stratum as there are randomization cells.

The reasons for pairing are the same as for stratification: to achieve balance and to increase statistical power. The impact on power is greatest when there is high variability in the outcome of interest and when we have small samples. For example, pairing would be important if we were randomizing across few clusters, such as only 10 districts.

Trade-offs on the number of variables to match

As in stratification, there are trade-offs to make on the number and types of variables to pair. Only here the trade-offs are even more pronounced. The loss of degree of freedom is even stronger because pairing is an extreme form of stratification.

Attrition

Like other strategies, attrition is a threat when pairing. In paired matching, for example, if we lose one of the units in the pair (say, because the participant moves out of the area) and we include a dummy for the stratum, essentially we have to drop the other unit in the pair from the analysis. That is because the remaining unit does not have a comparison. Some evaluators have mistakenly seen this as an advantage of pairing: they suggest that if one person drops out of the study, we can drop their pair and not worry about attrition. But in fact, if we drop the pair we have just introduced even more attrition bias. This is not a good approach (and can introduce bias) because we are dropping units in response to their actions and behaviors. As we will discuss in more detail in Module 8.2, we have to stick to our initial randomization; changing what we do based on any action after this point undoes our randomization.[32]

Our suggestion is that if there is a risk of attrition (for example, if the randomization and pairing are at the individual level), use strata that have at least four units rather than pairwise randomization (strata with two units). If we are randomizing at the group level and there is no risk of attrition at the group level, pairwise randomization is a reasonable strategy. For example, if we randomize at the village level and

32. If we do use pairwise randomization and have attrition, we could not include dummies for every stratum and thus not drop the pair of the unit that is lost to attrition. Not including dummies for strata can be controversial (although it probably should not be) and usually reduces our power. It would be possible to set out a complicated set of rules in advance about what dummies would be included if there was attrition. However, our advice is to keep the design simple and uncontroversial.

are confident that even if we can't find specific individuals in a village we will be able to find some people to interview in that village, we don't have attrition at the level of the randomization unit.

Some best practices in randomization

Bruhn and McKenzie conducted a review of how researchers are randomizing in practice and undertook some simulations comparing how different randomization strategies performed in virtual experiments.[33] From their analysis they came up with recommendations on randomization procedures, including the following:

1. *Improve reporting of the random assignment method used.* Evaluators should at least include the randomization method used; the variables used to achieve balance; how many strata were used, if any; and, if rerandomizing, what the balance criteria were.

2. *Improve reporting of the randomization procedures used in practice.* How was the randomization carried out in practice? Who did it? Using what device? Was it public or private? The CONSORT guidelines, available at http://www.consort-statement.org, provide a structured way to report how randomization was carried out.

3. *Avoid rerandomization as a way to achieve balance.* We discussed the issues associated with rerandomization earlier in this module.

4. *Stratify on baseline outcomes, geographic location, and variables for subgroup analysis.* The gains from stratification are greatest for variables that are strongly correlated with the outcome of interest. Often many of the variables on which we want to achieve balance are correlated with geographic indicators, such as the district, and with the baseline value of our main outcome variable. Stratifying on these usually means that we achieve reasonable balance on many other variables as well.

5. *Consider statistical power when stratifying.* The more strata we have, the lower the degrees of freedom we will have when esti-

---

33. Miriam Bruhn and David McKenzie, "In the Pursuit of Balance: Randomization in Practice in Development Field Experiments," *American Economic Journal: Applied Economics* 1 (2009): 200–232.

mating our outcomes. Stratifying on variables that are not highly correlated with the outcome can hurt power (see Module 6.2).

We would add two more:

6. *Where possible, ensure that the randomization procedure can be replicated.* To fully document our randomization, it is useful to do it on a computer using a randomly generated seed that can be saved so that it is possible to replicate exactly how the randomization proceeded and how it was carried out.

7. *Potential attrition when stratifying.* If there is a risk of attrition at the level at which we randomize, it is good practice to include at least twice the number of units in a stratum as there are cells over which we are randomizing. In other words, with two cells (treatment and comparison) we should make sure that all strata have at least four units in them.

MODULE 4.6 A Catalog of Designs

In this module we go over many examples of randomization in the field. These examples bring together the considerations from the four preceding modules. Each example gives the context of the study and the details of the randomization: how the opportunity to randomize came about, what was randomized and at what level, and what strategy (simple, stratified, or pairwise) was used to perform the randomized assignment.

Treatment lottery among the eligible: The Extra Teacher Program in Kenya

Context

In 2003 Kenya abolished primary school fees. Enrollment in primary schools rose 30 percent, from 5.9 million to 7.6 million, between 2002 and 2005. With this influx of children, class sizes in the first grade exploded. In Kenya's Western Province, for example, the average class size in first grade in 2005 was 83, and 28 percent of the classes had more than 100 pupils. The reform brought in many very poor children, and the result was not only larger classes but also classes with wide-ranging levels of preparedness.

Interventions

Reducing class size. To relieve overcrowding, ICS Africa implemented the Extra Teacher Program (ETP), which funded the hiring of extra teachers. The extra teachers were recent graduates of teachers' colleges. They were given one-year renewable contracts managed by the school committee, which had full control of the contracts, including hiring, remuneration, and termination.

Tracking students by prior achievement. To deal with the wide range of student preparedness, a tracking component was included. Students were assigned to one of two sections based on their scores on exams given at the beginning of the year. Students with below-average test scores were assigned to one section, and those with above-average test scores were assigned to another section. It was unclear whether tracking would help or harm students. If students learn from their peers, siphoning off the high-achieving peers into the upper section would hurt students in the lower section and benefit students in the upper section. But if reducing the range of preparedness in a class helps teachers tailor the instruction to the learning levels of the students, tracking would benefit all students.

Training school committees and formalizing their role. To prepare the school committee for its new role of managing the contract teachers, committee members were given short, focused training on monitoring teacher performance and attendance and on soliciting input from parents. Regular meetings between committee members and district education staff were also introduced. This component was called the School-Based Management Initiative (SBM).

Opportunity for randomized evaluation

The program was oversubscribed. ICS Africa had only enough funds to support the hiring of 120 teachers for two years. The study area included 210 rural primary schools from seven administrative districts in the Western Province.

Level of randomization

The program could not be randomized at the student level because the intervention introduced new teachers, affecting multiple students at once. It could not be randomized by grade because the overcrowding affected mainly the first grade, where ICS Africa wanted to focus its resources. The ETP funding was therefore randomized at the school level.

Questions and number of randomization cells

The effects of the ETP on learning could come from at least three channels: the reduced class size, the strong performance incentives faced by the contract teachers through the SBM, and the tracking. To disentangle the respective roles of these effects, each of the three components of the program (extra teachers, SBM, and tracking) was randomly assigned to one of three groups. The different randomization cells and the questions that could be answered by comparing different cells to each other are described in Figure 4.7.

Randomization

Stratification. Baseline data on enrollment, the pupil/teacher ratio, and the number of grade 1 sections were collected in 2004, prior to the start of the program. The schools were stratified by administrative district and by the number of grade 1 sections. There were a total of 14 strata.

Allocation. The schools were assigned to randomization cells in a multistage lottery using a computer.

Stage 1: Randomizing the ETP. There were 210 schools in 14 strata. The allocation fraction for the ETP program was two-thirds treatment (to receive funds for an extra teacher) and one-third comparison. In each stratum the schools were ordered randomly; the top two-thirds were assigned to receive funds, and the bottom third was assigned to the comparison group. In total, 140 schools received funds for an extra teacher. More schools were allocated to the treatment than to the comparison group because the treatment group was then going to be subdivided into several different randomization cells, and it was important to have sufficient samples in each to be able to compare different treatments to each other and to the comparison group.

Stage 2: Randomizing into tracking. Of those schools allocated to the ETP, half were allocated to the tracking treatment through the same stratified random ordering process described above.

Stage 3: Randomizing the SBM program. Two pools of schools were assigned to SBM or non-SBM: the 70 tracking schools and the 70 non-tracking schools. Half the schools in the tracking pool were randomly assigned to the SBM program. Similarly, half the schools in the non-tracking pool were randomly assigned to the SBM program. In other

Stage 1: Extra teacher — Treatment 1: Smaller class by adding contract teacher · Comparison to Treatment 1: Status quo

Stage 2: Tracking — Treatment 2: Tracking by initial test scores · Comparison to Treatment 2: No tracking

Stage 3: SBM — Treatment 3: School-based management training (SBM) · Comparison to Treatment 3: No SBM

Stage 4: Assign contract and government teachers — Contract teacher / Government teacher

	Treatment 2: Tracking by initial test scores				Comparison to Treatment 2: No tracking				Comparison to Treatment 1: Status quo
	Treatment 3: SBM		Comparison to Treatment 3: No SBM		Treatment 3: SBM		Comparison to Treatment 3: No SBM		
	Contract teacher	Government teacher	Contract teacher	Government teacher	Contract teacher	Government teacher	Contract teacher	Government teacher	
Randomization									
Contract	✓	✗	✓	✗	✓	✗	✓	✗	✗
Small Class	✓	✓	✓	✓	✓	✓	✓	✓	✗
Tracking	✓	✓	✓	✓	✗	✗	✗	✗	✗
SBM	✓	✓	✗	✗	✓	✓	✗	✗	✗
Research questions									
What is the effect of the class size reduction?	Treatment	Comparison	Treatment	Comparison	Treatment	Comparison	Treatment	Comparison	Comparison
How does a contract teacher compare to a civil servant teacher?	Treatment	Comparison	Treatment	Comparison	Treatment	Comparison	Treatment	Comparison	
What is the effect of tracking students by initial test scores?	Treatment	Treatment	Comparison	Comparison	Treatment	Treatment	Comparison	Comparison	
What is the benefit of SBM?	Treatment	Treatment	Comparison	Comparison	Treatment	Treatment	Comparison	Comparison	

FIGURE 4.7 Randomization cells and research questions for the Extra Teacher Program in Kenya

words, allocation to tracking was used as a variable for stratifying allocation to the SBM program.

Stage 4: Within-school randomization of teachers to sections. In addition, the teachers were randomly assigned to the different sections. Once an additional section had been created and the students had been assigned to sections, either with or without tracking, the contract teachers were randomly assigned to teach one section to make sure that the regular teacher did not always take the higher-level class when classes were tracked. The other sections were taught by the regular civil-service teacher.

For further reading

Duflo, Esther, Pascaline Dupas, and Michael Kremer. 2012. "School Governance, Teacher Incentives, and Pupil–Teacher Ratios: Experimental Evidence from Kenyan Primary Schools." NBER Working Paper 17939. National Bureau of Economic Research, Cambridge, MA.
This study is summarized as Evaluation 3 in the Appendix.

Treatment lottery among the marginally ineligible:
Credit in the Philippines

Context

First Macro Bank, a rural bank in the Philippines, provides business and consumer loans to poor clients. The bank uses a credit scoring algorithm based on the following characteristics: business acumen, personal financial resources, recourse to outside finances, personal and business stability, and demographic profile. Scores range from zero to 100. Applicants scoring below 31 are not considered creditworthy and are rejected automatically. The creditworthy applicants fall into two categories: the very creditworthy, those scoring above 59, who are automatically approved for a loan, and the marginally creditworthy, those scoring between 31 and 59.

Opportunity for randomized evaluation

The bank piloted a program to expand its services to a new client population: the marginally creditworthy. This program expanded credit to poor clients who might not otherwise receive credit. It also allowed the bank to gather data on these clients, which could be used to improve its credit-scoring model, risk management, and profitability.

Creating a sampling frame

Initial screening. Loan officers screened applicants for eligibility. To qualify, an applicant had to (1) be aged between 18 and 60 years, (2) have been in business for at least one year, (3) have been resident at his present address for at least a year if an owner and for at least three years if a renter, and (4) have a daily income of at least 750 pesos. Some 2,158 of the applicants passed the initial screening.

Credit scoring. Business and household information on these 2,158 applicants was entered into the credit-scoring software. Of these, 166 applicants scored between zero and 30 and were automatically rejected, 391 scored between 60 and 100 and were automatically accepted, and 1,601 scored between 31 and 59. These 1,601 were the sampling frame and were allocated randomly (see Figure 4.4).

Randomization

Stratifying by credit score and using different allocation fractions in the strata. The random assignment still took into account the credit scores. Among the 256 applicants with scores between 31 and 45, the probability of receiving a loan was 60 percent, but among the 1,345 applicants with scores between 46 and 59, the probability was 85 percent.

Allocation. Altogether, of the 1,601 applicants in this range, 1,272 were assigned a loan approval, and 329 were assigned a rejection. To reduce the chance that clients or loan officers would change the applications to improve the applicants' chances of getting a loan, neither group was informed of the algorithm or of its random component.

Verification of applicant information and final decision. The credit-score-based decisions were conditioned on verification of applicant information. Verification included a visit to each applicant's home and business, meeting neighborhood officials, and checking references.

For further reading

Karlan, Dean, and Jonathan Zinman. 2011. "Microcredit in Theory and Practice: Using Randomized Credit Scoring for Impact Evaluation," *Science* 332 (6035): 1278–1284.

This study is summarized as Evaluation 13 in the appendix.

Randomized phase-in: The Primary School Deworming Project in Kenya
Context

Worms affect more than 2 billion people in the world, causing, among other symptoms, listlessness, diarrhea, abdominal pain, and anemia.

Worldwide, 400 million school-aged children are at risk of worm infection. The World Health Organization (WHO) recommends pre-emptive school-based mass treatment in areas with high levels of worm prevalence. Treatment with deworming pills kills worms in the body. Although this reduces transmission, it does not prevent re-infection. Schools with a hookworm, whipworm, and roundworm prevalence of more than 50 percent should be mass treated every six months, and schools with a schistosomiasis prevalence of more than 30 percent should be mass treated once a year. ICS implemented a school-based mass deworming program that treated 30,000 pupils at 75 primary schools in Kenya's Western Province.

Opportunity for randomized evaluation

This was a pilot program; a key goal was to see whether, and how, deworming affected education. The program faced logistical and financial constraints.

The logistics were particularly complicated. The medication had to be acquired and parental informed consent to treat children obtained by having parents sign a ledger at the school. The prevalence of worms in the area had to be tested to see if a school qualified for mass treatment, and ICS public health officers and nurses seconded from the Ministry of Health had to be trained. Treatment dates had to be worked out with the schools, avoiding the two rainy seasons when the roads were hardly passable. In most cases children had to be treated twice a year because of the high infection rate in the area. Two categories of children who could not be treated had to be separated out: those whose parents had not given consent and all girls of reproductive age. (At the time it was thought that there was a risk of birth defects. It has now been found that there is no risk, and the recommendation is to treat all children.) Coverage could not be extended to all schools at once; for some of the schools, treatment had to be delayed. These logistical constraints made a phase-in design the most feasible.

Level of randomization

Most schools in the area met the WHO guidelines for mass treatment. The school was the natural unit of intervention for the school-based mass treatment program. Since worms are easily transmitted between children, spillovers were a major consideration. When there are no latrines, children relieve themselves in the bush around the school or around the home, creating the potential for spillovers around schools and homes. Randomizing at the school level would capture within-school spillovers in the impact estimate. The schools were far enough from each other that at least some schools would not be influenced by spillovers. The randomization was not heavily stratified to ensure that there was variation in treatment density in different geographic areas, allowing for measurement spillover effects (Module 8.2 discusses how the analysis measured spillovers in some detail).

Considerations for a phase-in design

Logistical constraints meant that ICS had to phase in the program, suggesting a randomized phase-in design. But it was unclear what the gap between different phases should be. There were two considerations: how fast could the program be phased in, and what was the likely timeline of impact?

Logistical constraints and resource availability. There would be enough financial resources for all schools by the beginning of the fourth year. Creating three phase-in groups with 25 schools each allowed ICS to benefit from economies of scale in training teachers for the program but did not overstretch their capacity.

Likely timeline of impact. Worms in the body would be killed immediately, but some of the benefits would become apparent only over time (for example, if children learned more or grew faster as a result of treatment). If the time between phases was very short, it might be difficult to pick up these benefits.

Randomization

Stratification. The schools were first stratified by administrative district and then by their involvement in other nongovernmental assistance programs.

Allocation. The schools were then listed alphabetically, and every third school was assigned to a group. This divided the 75 schools into three groups of 25. As discussed in Module 4.1, this strategy is less ideal than pure randomization, but in this case it arguably mimicked randomization.[34] Next the three groups of schools were phased into the program. In the first year, Group 1 schools were treated, while Groups 2 and 3 formed the comparison. In the second year, Group 2

---

34. The concern here would be if someone else used alphabetical order of schools to allocate their program. There is no reason to think that that occurred in this case.

was phased in. Now Groups 1 and 2 formed the treatment group, while Group 3 remained the comparison. In the fourth year, Group 3 was also treated, which ended the evaluation period because no comparison group remained.

For further reading

Baird, Sarah, Joan Hamory Hicks, Michael Kremer, and Edward Miguel. 2011. "Worms at Work: Long-run Impacts of Child Health Gains." Working paper, Harvard University, Cambridge, MA. http://elsa.berkeley.edu/~emiguel/pdfs/miguel_wormsatwork.pdf.
J-PAL Policy Bulletin. 2012. "Deworming: A Best Buy for Development." Abdul Latif Jameel Poverty Action Lab, Cambridge, MA. http://www.povertyactionlab.org/publication/deworming-best-buy-development. This study is summarized as Evaluation 1 in the appendix.

Rotation: Remedial education in India

Context

In 1994, Pratham, an Indian organization working in education, launched a remedial education program. Pratham hired and trained tutors and deployed them to schools. The tutors worked with children who had reached grades 3 and 4 without mastering the basic reading and math competencies taught in grades 1 and 2. The lagging children were identified by their teachers and were pulled out of their regular classes in groups of 20 and sent for remedial tutoring for half the school day.

Opportunity for randomized evaluation

In 2000 Pratham expanded their program to primary schools in the city of Vadodara in western India. The program was expanding to a new area and reaching a new population. There were not enough resources to cover all the schools at once, but the municipal authorities requested that all eligible schools receive program assistance.

Level of randomization

The municipal government and Pratham agreed that all the schools in the new area of expansion that needed tutors should receive them. This meant that the program could not be randomized at the school level. Nor could the program be randomized at the student level. Because this was a pullout program, randomizing at the student level would have meant that the teacher would identify the lagging students, and then half of those would be selected randomly. Both logistical considerations ruled this out. Instead, tutors were randomly assigned to a specific cohort, either grade 3 or grade 4. Every school still received a tutor but for only one of the two grades.

Randomization

Stratification. The schools were stratified by language of instruction, pretest scores, and gender.

Allocation. The schools were randomly assigned to two groups. In the first year, Group A would receive tutors in grade 3 and Group B would get them in grade 4 (Figure 4.8). In the second year, the groups would switch: Group A would receive tutors for grade 4 and Group B would get them for grade 3. After the first year of the program, the researchers could measure the impact of having a tutor for one year. Group A schools' grade 3 with a tutor were compared to Group B schools' grade 3. The reverse was true for grade 4.

After one year, the schools switched, with the tutors moving to grade 4 in Group A schools and the tutors in Group B moving to grade 3 (Figure 4.9). Because children progress from one grade to the next, this meant that children in Group A schools who moved from grade 3 to grade 4 had a tutor for two consecutive years, while their peers in Group B who moved to grade 4 did not have a tutor at all. This allowed the researchers to measure the impact of having a tutor for two years.

For further reading

Banerjee, Abhijit, Shawn Cole, Esther Duflo, and Leigh Linden. 2007. "Remedying Education: Evidence from Two Randomized Experiments in India," *Quarterly Journal of Economics* 122 (3): 1235–1264.

J-PAL Policy Briefcase. 2006. "Making Schools Work for Marginalized Children: Evidence from an Inexpensive and Effective Program in India." Abdul Latif Jameel Poverty Action Lab, Cambridge, MA. http://www.poverty actionlab.org/publication/making-schools-work-marginalized-children. This study is summarized as Evaluation 2 in the appendix.

Encouragement: Retirement savings at a large American university

Context

To increase savings for retirement, many employers in the United States offer to match employees' retirement contributions. Savings in these accounts also have lower tax rates than other savings accounts. But despite these incentives, many employees do not sign up for employer-matched retirement accounts. At a large American university, only 34 percent of eligible employees were enrolled. Because one

Schools in Group A

Year 1

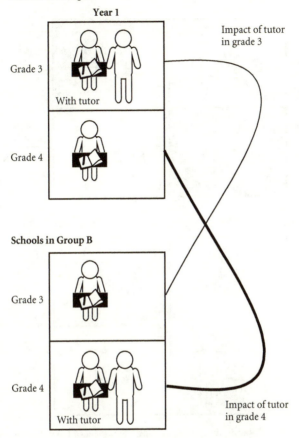

Grade 3

With tutor

Grade 4

Impact of tutor
in grade 3

Schools in Group B

Grade 3

Grade 4

With tutor

Impact of tutor
in grade 4

FIGURE 4.8 Rotation design: Measuring the impact of having a tutor for one year

reason employees did not sign up may be that they are unaware of the extent of the benefits, the university holds a fair yearly to educate employees about benefits.

Opportunity for randomized evaluation

The information fair was open to all university employees, but attendance was low. This meant there was room to increase take-up by offering employees a $20 reward for attending. This extra encouragement could be randomized.

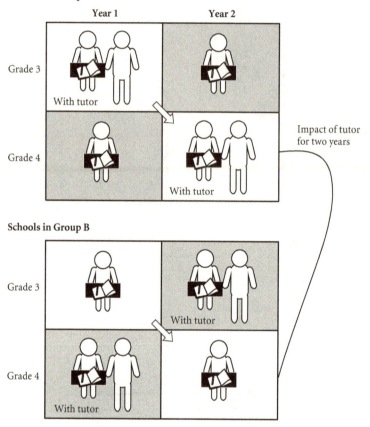

Schools in Group A

Year 1 · Year 2

Grade 3 · With tutor

Grade 4 · With tutor

Impact of tutor for two years

Schools in Group B

Grade 3 · With tutor

Grade 4 · With tutor

FIGURE 4.9 Rotation design: Measuring the impact of having a tutor for two years

Level of randomization

The fair targeted individual employees, who would decide whether to enroll for benefits and how much to contribute. But an employee's decision to attend the fair and to enroll in the account could depend on social interactions with colleagues. These spillovers could be both informational and behavioral. Employees could remind each other to attend the fair. The fair was held at two hotels some distance from the school, and people tended to go to the fair in groups by department. Someone was more likely to attend if there was a group from the department going. People who attended the fair could share information from the fair with people who did not attend. People could also mimic the investment decisions of their colleagues. The investment decisions themselves may have depended on social norms or beliefs about social norms. People may have wanted to conform to the savings norms they observed in their department.

Randomizing at the department level would capture the potential within-department spillovers, but savings could be measured at the individual level. Because the evaluators were interested in the social dynamics of saving, they randomized both at the department and the individual levels. There were 330 departments and 9,700 employees, of whom 6,200 were not enrolled in the retirement savings accounts. A week before the fair, a letter was sent to a randomly selected subset of employees to remind them about the fair and to inform them that they would receive a check for $20 if they attended.

Considerations for using the encouragement design

Why use money as an encouragement? Money is a good inducement because it is unrestricted and thus likely to draw the widest range of people in the population. By way of comparison, offering a free football or T-shirt would attract only certain types of people. The sum of $20 was likely chosen because it was too small to affect the level of savings on its own (the minimum annual contribution was $450) but large enough to encourage attendance at the fair. There might have been a concern that a $20 incentive would be more likely to attract those with lower salaries, but because these were the employees who were least likely to have employer-matched accounts, they were the main targets for the program.

Questions and number of groups

The objective was to isolate both the effects of peers on savings behavior and the effects of the fair on savings. This suggests randomization in at least two stages: one to create the experimental groups needed to isolate the social effects in the departments and the other to isolate the individual effects.

Randomization

Randomizing pairwise. The 330 departments were ranked by participation rates among staff and divided into 10 groups of 33. Within each group, the 33 departments were then ranked by size. Once ranked, the departments were divided into 11 groups of three, each containing three consecutive departments.

Randomizing the departments to estimate social effects. Within each triplet, two departments were randomly allocated to the treatment. In total, 220 departments were in the treatment group.

Randomizing individuals within departments to isolate individual effects. There were 6,200 employees who had not enrolled scattered in these departments. Of these, 4,168 were in departments assigned to treatment. Within each of the treatment departments, half of the employees were randomly assigned to receive the encouragement. This means that there were two treatments: a direct treatment (being encouraged to attend the fair) and an indirect treatment (being in the same department as someone encouraged to attend the fair). In the end, 2,039 employees received an encouragement letter one week before the fair, 2,039 employees had a colleague who had received encouragement, and 2,043 employees were in the 110 comparison group departments.

For further reading

Duflo, Esther, and Emmanuel Saez. 2003. "The Role of Information and Social Interactions in Retirement Plan Decisions: Evidence from a Randomized Experiment." *Quarterly Journal of Economics* 118 (3): 815–842.
This study is summarized as Evaluation 11 in the appendix.

Randomization as an instrumental variable: Delayed marriage incentive in Bangladesh

Context

Bangladesh has one of the highest rates of adolescent and child marriage in the world. Although the legal age of marriage for women is 18, it is estimated that nearly 50 percent of all girls and 75 percent of rural girls are married by age 15. Women who marry early have worse education, income, and maternal and child health outcomes. But does early marriage cause these negative outcomes, or is it a symptom of another underlying problem, such as poverty? To isolate the effect of early marriage we need to have random variation in age of marriage.

We cannot randomly assign the age of marriage, just as we cannot randomize many other variables of interest to policy. But we can randomize other variables that may influence the age of marriage as long as they do not themselves affect the outcome of interest. These variables are called instrumental variables, and they are very similar to the encouragement approach discussed above. Here the evaluators, working with Save the Children, mimicked delayed marriage by providing financial incentives to families of unmarried adolescent girls. If the incentives worked, randomized assignment of the incentives would generate the random variation in age of marriage needed to rigorously estimate the effects of early marriage.

Intervention

Research in Bangladesh has suggested that for each year a family delays the marriage of an adolescent girl, the dowry they have to pay increases by about US$15, creating a financial incentive for early marriage. In a random sample of villages in rural Bangladesh, Save the Children gave families with unmarried girls aged 15–17 a monthly transfer of cooking oil with a yearly value close to US$15. The incentive was given only to families of 15- to 17-year-olds because the funding for the incentive was severely limited and this was the age group with the highest marriage rate. A larger incentive might have had a greater impact on the age of marriage, which would have been useful in assessing the impacts of changing the age of marriage. But too large an incentive might have started to have direct impacts by changing the families' income in a significant way, which would have made it impossible to isolate the impact of change in the age of marriage from that of change in income. In addition, there were not sufficient funds to increase the incentive.

The delayed marriage incentive was part of a larger pilot empowerment program. That program had two versions. The basic package consisted of the establishment by the community of safe spaces where the girls could meet, such as the veranda of a home or a room in a school. In this safe space, girls received health education, homework support, and general empowerment training. A separate variant of the program added a financial readiness component to the training curriculum.

Opportunity for randomized evaluation

This pilot incentive program was designed to piggyback on an existing program working on the provision of food security and nutritional support to pregnant women and nursing mothers. But there were not sufficient resources to implement the adolescent girls' program everywhere the food security program operated, which created an opportunity for randomization.

Level of randomization

There were many considerations in choosing the level of randomization. For the delayed marriage incentive, individual randomization was ruled out because of the risk that this would create confusion and resentment. Individual randomization was also not possible for the safe spaces program because the community would decide the location of appropriate safe spaces. This meant that the program had to approach and sign up potential participants at the community level.

However, there was some flexibility about what a "community" was. We tend to think of a community as a simple and clearly defined geographical unit, but in practice there are often multiple ways for people to come together in a community. Deciding that the level of randomization is the community is just the first step. This is a particular concern in densely populated areas, such as rural Bangladesh or urban slums, where one community blends into the next. Adjacent neighbors may live in different administrative units, or the next farm in a village may be in another country.

One clearly identifiable unit was the cluster of houses around a common courtyard that make up a *bari*. Because there is substantial interaction within a *bari*, it could be considered a community. But a *bari* would not have enough adolescent girls for a viable safe space program.

Another option was to use the community units that were used by the food security and nutrition program to implement their intervention (i.e., to define which households should go to which food distribution center). However, if the nutrition program's concept of community were used, only a few communities could be covered because of resource constraints. There would not be enough different units for a good evaluation.

Another factor in the decision on randomization level was potential general equilibrium effects. If suddenly all the girls in an area married later, there could be an impact on the marriage market, particularly if men have a strong preference for marrying girls from the local area. There could be a short-run shortage of girls with a sudden shift in the age of marriage, which would even out if the delay in marriage persisted. It would be good to design the study to avoid picking this effect up, suggesting a unit of randomization that was smaller than the marriage market. There might be other general equilibrium concerns that would suggest a level of randomization at the marriage market level. For example, if girls were more educated when they married, this might mean that their families would seek more educated husbands. If the randomization level was smaller than the marriage market, treatment girls would marry more educated men in a way that would not be possible if the program were scaled up (it is unlikely that the program would lead to an increase in the number of educated men). However, it was decided that randomizing at the marriage market level would be too expensive. Instead, details on the characteristics of the husbands would be carefully documented to track whether the program led to changes in husband selection.

In the end, the evaluation identified "natural villages," geographic groupings that were small enough to allow a large sample size for evaluation but also represented groupings around which people on the ground would naturally organize themselves. Although most of these natural villages were not separate administrative units within the government system, they were recognized in addresses. The randomization was based on these natural villages. This approach, however, involved some risk that the lines between natural villages would not be clear enough in people's minds and that some girls from comparison villages would end up attending the safe space program, a risk that did in the end materialize.

Randomization

Altogether, communities were divided into six experimental groups of roughly 77 girls each; the first two were both comparison groups because of the importance the researchers gave to finding the precise impacts of the individual components of the program. So the groups were designated as follows: (1, 2) comparison; (3) safe spaces and education support; (4) safe spaces, education, and financial readiness; (5) safe spaces, education, financial readiness, and delayed marriage incentive; and (6) delayed marriage incentive. The randomization was performed using Stata and involved stratifying by union (a geographical cluster of roughly 10 villages). Within strata, villages were ordered by size. A random number between one and six was chosen: if the number six was chosen, the first community in the stratum was allocated to the delayed marriage incentive, the next two to comparison, the next to safe space with education, and so on.

For further reading

This study by Erica Field and Rachel Glennerster is summarized as Evaluation 7 in the appendix.

Creating variation to measure spillovers: Job counseling in France

To measure spillovers, we need variation in exposure to spillovers, which can be achieved by having variation in the treatment density. Treatment density is the proportion of units (individuals, schools, or communities) within a geographic area that receive the treatment. The higher the treatment density, the higher the chances of spillover effects on the average untreated person. We need to have some of our comparison group that we have good reason to believe do not experience spillovers; these will be the "pure comparison" group. In our earlier discussion of the deworming evaluation under randomized phase-in, we described how evaluators can use chance variation in treatment density to measure spillovers. Here we discuss an example in which evaluators have deliberately created (random) variation in treatment density. Another example is the study of savings in an American university discussed above, in which different departments were randomized to receive different intensities of encouragement.

Randomizing the treatment density

We can directly vary the treatment density. A study in France wanted to measure the negative spillover effects of job counseling. Here the fear is that providing counseling will help the counseled secure employment at the expense of those without counseling—that is, that there will be negative spillovers. Because the goal of the policy was to reduce unemployment, it was important to measure any negative spillovers.

The program was conducted through public employment agencies. There were 235 of these in 10 administrative regions. The randomization was at the employment agency level. Each agency was considered a small and autonomous labor market. The agencies were placed into groups of five based on size and population characteristics. There were 47 such groups. Within each group, the five agencies were randomized to one of the five treatment densities: zero percent, 25 percent, 50 percent, 75 percent, or 100 percent of the unemployed applicants were assigned to the treatment group. The unemployed were randomized as they applied. In agencies with zero percent, none were treated; in those with 25 percent, a quarter were treated, and so on. The study examined whether an untreated (not counseled) unemployed person in an agency where 75 percent of the unemployed were treated (counseled) has a *lower* chance of obtaining employment than an untreated unemployed person in an agency where only 25 percent of the unemployed were treated. In other words, were the untreated people in areas where they had to compete with a higher proportion of counseled people worse off? If yes, there were negative spillover effects.

For further reading

Crépon, Bruno, Esther Duflo, Marc Gurgand, Roland Rathelot, and Philippe Zamora. 2012. "Do Labor Market Policies Have Displacement Effects? Evidence from a Clustered Randomized Experiment." NBER Working Paper 18597. National Bureau of Economic Research, Cambridge, MA.

———. 2011. "L'Accompagnement des Jeunes Diplômés Demandeurs d'Emploi par des Opérateurs Privés de Placement." *Dares Analyses* 94: 1–14.

This study is summarized as Evaluation 8 in the appendix.

5 Outcomes and Instruments

This chapter covers planning for data collection. It gives practical advice for choosing what data to collect, selecting good indicators and instruments, and choosing the time, place, and frequency of data collection. The chapter has the following modules:

MODULE 5.1: Specifying Outcomes and Indicators
MODULE 5.2: Specifying Data Sources
MODULE 5.3: Assessing and Field Testing Outcome Measures
MODULE 5.4: A Catalog of Nonsurvey Instruments

MODULE 5.1 Specifying Outcomes and Indicators

The programs we evaluate aim to improve the outcomes of participants, but to get the most out of an evaluation, it is useful to track outputs and intermediate outcomes as well as final outcomes. This module describes how developing a theory of change helps us map potential pathways of impact and ensure that we have indicators for each step of the process that are relevant to our particular context. It also shows that it is useful to include standard indicators that allow us to compare our findings to those of other studies in the literature.

We can use a theory of change to specify outcomes and indicators

Specifying good outcomes and the indicators we will use to measure them requires a deep understanding of the program being developed, the objectives of those implementing the program, and potential pathways through which the program or policy can impact lives, both positively and negatively. Some of the terms we use are defined with examples in Table 5.1. A theory-of-change framework is a useful tool to use in systematically thinking through potential pathways to an impact and is best developed in close cooperation between those implementing and those evaluating a program. This theory of change is likely to lead us to develop indicators that are very specific to the context.

A *theory of change* is a structured approach used in the design and evaluation of social programs. It maps the logical chain of how program inputs achieve changes in outcomes through activities and outputs. We can go further and explicitly set down the assumptions that are needed to get from one step to another and the possible risks. For each step in the theory of change, we specify outcomes and indicators we will measure to help us understand whether the program has worked and also how it has worked. If the program is not successful, having indicators for these intermediate steps helps us understand at which step in the chain the program failed.

Indicators are observable signals of change

Outcomes are changes our program aims to achieve. Often these changes are conceptual, such as "economic empowerment of women"

TABLE 5.1 Data collection jargon

Term	Definition	Examples
Outcome	A change or impact caused by the program we are evaluating	Increase or decrease in women's empowerment, child health, corruption
Indicator	An observable signal used to measure outcomes	The number of women who spoke at a meeting, child arm circumference
Instrument	The tool we use to measure indicators	A survey question, achievement test, direct observation record
Variable	The numeric values of indicators	Self-evident
Respondent	The person or group of people we interview, test, or observe to measure the indicators	Individuals; their teachers, colleagues, or family

or "improved learning." *Indicators* are observable signals of these changes, such as "monthly income of women in a village" or "ability to read a simple paragraph." Indicators measure whether the changes the program is designed to bring about are in fact happening. Test scores, for example, can be an indicator of the more abstract concept of learning. For an indicator to be any good, there needs to be a strong logical link connecting it to the relevant outcome we are ultimately trying to measure.

The logical validity of the indicator depends on the context

Not only must the indicator logically follow from the outcome concept, but this logic also has to be valid for the context.

Say our outcome of interest is teacher effort. We need to choose indicators that measure how our program is affecting the efforts of teachers. In rural areas with remote schools, teachers face high travel costs. In a context of high levels of teacher absenteeism, whether teachers show up at school could be a good indicator of teacher effort. However, teacher attendance as an indicator of effort would not work as well in urban areas where teachers face very low travel costs and shirking may instead take the form of socializing with colleagues in the staff room rather than teaching. In this context, better indicators of effort might be "time spent with students after school," "time spent teaching instead of socializing in the staff room," or "frequency of assigning homework."

Module 5.3 discusses in more detail how to assess the validity of indicators in a given context.

Specifying outcomes from the literature

If an evaluation is to be influential in broader policy debates, it is useful if its results can be compared with those of other leading studies in the field. To facilitate comparison, it is helpful to include outcome measures and indicators that are commonly used in the literature for assessing programs with similar objectives.

Take for example the goal of increasing the quantity of education. Some studies only look at enrollment rates of students, but an increasing number of studies also examine attendance rates by counting how many children are at school during unannounced visits. Collecting attendance data allows an evaluator to calculate the total increase in schooling generated by a program (measured in weeks or years of additional schooling). For a policymaker choosing between alternative approaches to increasing schooling quantity, it is useful to be able to see which of many approaches is the most cost-effective, but this is possible only if outcomes are defined in the same way across projects. (Module 9.3 discusses ways to calculate and use comparative cost-effectiveness analyses.)

Consensus on the best outcome measures and indicators is always evolving. Examining the recent literature for the most current measurement standards allows us to benefit from what others have learned about assessing outcomes reliably and accurately. This is particularly important in social and economic evaluations whose content overlaps with that of other disciplines. For example, a microfinance program aiming to empower women will incorporate frameworks from the economics, sociology, and psychology literatures; a health program will be influenced by the medical and public health literatures and an education program by the education and cognitive science literatures; and a political empowerment project can incorporate aspects of the political science and psychology literatures. These literatures are a deep source of useful outcomes and indicators, and many have their own conventional outcome measures. For example, in cognitive development there is a battery of standardized tests; for learning there are internationally standardized achievement tests; and for nutrition there are measures of arm circumference, weight for age, and weight for height.

Case studies on specifying outcomes and indicators

The following case studies illustrate a two-step process for selecting outcomes and indicators during program evaluation: (1) mapping the theory of change and (2) determining indicators that are the logical consequences of each step in the theory of change, when possible drawing on the existing literature. We also give examples of specifying assumptions needed to move through the theory of change.

Example: An HIV education program in Kenya

A program in Kenya provided in-service training for teachers to improve their delivery of HIV prevention education in primary schools. The training focused on how to teach HIV/AIDS prevention best practices while teaching other subjects and how to start and run after-school student health clubs devoted to HIV/AIDS education.[1]

---

1. This study by Esther Duflo, Pascaline Dupas, and Michael Kremer is summarized as Evaluation 4 in the appendix.

A simple theory of change for the program says that (1) teacher training (2) increased HIV education, which (3) increased knowledge of prevention best practices, which (4) reduced unsafe sexual behavior, which (4) led to reduced HIV infection rates. The theory of change links five steps: teacher training, HIV education, knowledge of best practices, sexual behavior, and incidence of HIV infection. Although the policy variable of interest is HIV status, the program directly targets only the intermediate outcome of unprotected sexual behavior and knowledge.

For each of the concepts in the causal chain, we need to find a concrete indicator in the real world that we can observe and measure (Table 5.2).

HIV status is the ultimate outcome of interest. If we can measure HIV status in both our treatment and our comparison groups, we can know whether our program changed HIV infection rates. Although testing HIV status is common in the literature, it may be too expensive as well as ethically, politically, or logistically infeasible in our context. If this is the case, we can use other indicators as proxies for HIV rates. In the literature it is common to use a broader range of sexually transmitted infections (STIs) as a signal of unprotected sex. In this case, our observable indicators would include biomarkers for a range of STIs common in this context, such as herpes, syphilis, gonorrhea, chlamydia, hepatitis, and human papillomavirus. The results of tests for these STIs are commonly used in the literature as indicators of risky sexual behavior. Childbearing would also be a good proxy for STIs and HIV infection, because the same unsafe sexual behavior that leads to childbearing can also lead to STIs and to HIV infection.

We may also be interested in more proximate outcomes, such as changes in knowledge, that are not captured by HIV status. Indeed, HIV status is not a valid measure of *knowledge* of best practices, because someone may know the best prevention methods but choose to not practice them. Measuring these intermediate outputs and outcomes would allow us to learn about the underlying mechanisms that can translate program inputs into impacts. For example, if the program failed to achieve the desired impact, did it fail because it did not change knowledge or because changing knowledge did not change behavior?

Example: Achieving political reservations for women in local politics
India amended its federal constitution in 1992, devolving the power to plan and implement development programs from the states to rural

TABLE 5.2 Logical framework for HIV education program

Inputs, outputs/outcomes	Objectives hierarchy	Indicators	Assumptions or threats
Inputs (activities)	Teachers are trained to provide HIV education.	Hours of training implemented	Teachers engage with the training and learn new concepts.
Outputs	Teachers increase and improve HIV education.	Hours of HIV education given; application of the program's teaching methods	Teachers are receptive to changing their HIV education approach, and outside pressures do not prevent them from implementing a new curriculum.
Outcome (project objective)	Students learn prevention best practices.	Test scores on HIV education exam	Students engage with the new curriculum and understand and retain the new concepts.
Impact (goal, overall objective)	Students reduce their un-protected sexual behavior; incidence of HIV infection decreases.	Self-reported sexual behavior; number of girls who have started childbearing; HIV status	The information students learn changes their beliefs and their behavior. Students can make decisions and act on their preferences for engaging in sexual behavior.

village councils. Councils now choose what development programs to undertake and how much of the village budgets to invest in them. The states are also required to reserve one-third of council seats and council chairperson (*pradhan*) positions for women. Most states developed lotteries so they could use random assignment to create a schedule as to which third of the villages are required to reserve the council chair position for a women in a given election cycle.[2] The lotteries created an opportunity to assess the impact of reservations on politics and government by answering the following questions: Do policies differ when there are more women in government? Do the policies chosen by women in power reflect the policy priorities of women?

A basic theory of change for the evaluation was (1) legislation mandating quotas for women leaders is passed, (2) more women are made chairs of their village council, (3) investment decisions better reflect the preferences of women, and (4) the quality of public goods preferred by women increases. In this case there were relatively few standard indicators in the literature for the researchers to rely on, and most of the indicators were specific to the evaluation context.

Legislation mandating quotas for women leaders is passed Even after quotas for women was mandated by the Supreme Court, the necessary legislation had to be passed in each state. This input could be confirmed through legislative records.

More women are made chairs of their village councils Once the legislation was passed, it still had to be implemented at the village level. Implementation could be checked by determining the gender of council chairs in office from official records.

Women's participation in village councils increases To ensure that the council investments reflect the community's priorities, the amendment included two requirements that allow members of the community to articulate their priorities. First, the councils must hold a general assembly every six months or every year to report on activities in the preceding period and must submit the proposed budget to the community for ratification. Second, the council chairs must set up regular office hours to allow people to submit requests and complaints.

2. Two studies on this policy, one by Raghabendra Chattopadhyay and Esther Duflo and the other by Lori Beaman, Raghabendra Chattopadhyay, Esther Duflo, Rohini Pande, and Petia Topalova, are summarized as Evaluation 12 in the appendix.

Having female council leaders may embolden women to voice their policy preferences at general assemblies, and being able to direct their queries to other women could further encourage these women to express their views. If women become empowered, they will take advantage of available political channels. Our observable indicators of this behavior are women's attending and speaking at general assembly meetings and their submitting requests and complaints.

Investment in public goods better reflects the preferences of women The councils decide which development programs to implement and how much to invest in them. They have to choose the programs from a list of development areas, including welfare services (services for widows, care for the elderly, maternity care, antenatal care, child healthcare) and public works (providing drinking water, roads, housing, community buildings, electricity, irrigation, and education).

We can rely on public records for estimates of or expenditures on public goods and services. But we also want to verify that the officially recorded public goods and services were actually delivered on the ground. We can do this by taking an inventory of public goods of different types in the community and asking when they were built and when they were last repaired.

We also need to determine which public goods are preferred by women. It takes time and potentially courage to speak up during a general assembly meeting or to submit a service request or complaint. Speaking up about one's priorities can also have real consequences, such as affecting the sectors or projects in which public money is invested. This means that people are unlikely to speak unless they have a compelling interest in the issue at stake. Thus an observable indicator of people's true preferences is the public goods they address in their requests, complaints, and speeches to the general assembly. Sorting the issues raised by gender should help us determine the policy preferences of men and women. It is worth noting that we would not expect to see a change in investment in a good that was highly valued by women but also highly valued by men. In this case there would be investment in both quota villages and non-quota villages, so the introduction of quotas would not change the pattern of investment.

The quality of public goods preferred by women increases Quotas for women would not benefit women if they led only to increases in investment in goods preferred by women but not to improvements in the quality or quantity of these goods. We can measure the quality of goods. In the case of water quality, for example, we can test for the presence of microbes in the water.

Assumptions, conditions, and threats

Our theory of change rests on a number of assumptions and conditions that must be met for the chain of events in the theory of change to hold. In the logical framework for our evaluation of the program to increase women's participation in village councils (Table 5.3), we map these assumptions:

- *Reservations for women were implemented properly.* The amendment directed the states to (1) establish the rural councils, (2) devolve all powers to plan and implement rural development programs to the councils, (3) ensure that council elections are held every five years, and (4) ensure that one-third of all council seats and council chair positions are reserved for women.

- *Seeing women leaders encourages other women to participate more fully.* When quota legislation was passed there was concern that women leaders would have power in name only. In this scenario there would be little reason for other women to become more active participants in village councils, to speak up, or to voice complaints.

- *Women have different preferences from those of men.* This implies that if we sort preferences by gender, we will see a difference. For this we need to catalog the content of queries made by type (water, roads, agriculture, etc.) and check whether men and women have different preferences and in which areas.

- *Some democracy exists.* There should be elections every five years, with councilors popularly elected to represent each ward. The councilors should elect from among themselves a council chairperson. Decisions should be made by a majority vote, and the chairperson should have no veto power. That there is democracy implies that investments would reflect the preferences of the constituents.

- *The democracy is imperfect.* If there were perfect democracy, elected officials would perfectly channel the wishes of all their constituents, and the leader's gender and preferences would not

TABLE 5.3 Potential indicators of the outcomes of a policy to increase women's participation in village councils

Inputs, outputs/outcomes	Indicator	Assumptions and threats
Inputs Quotas for women are passed.	Passage of legislation in state legislatures	Supreme court mandate is translated into effective legislation at state level.
Outputs There are more women leaders.	Number of women leaders in council chair positions	Quota legislation is implemented as designed in villages.
Political participation increases.	Number of complaints brought by women	Seeing women leaders encourages women to voice complaints.
	Number of women speaking at general meetings	Seeing women leaders emboldens women to speak up at meetings.
Impact Public goods investments more closely match women's priorities.	Types of public goods mentioned in women's queries versus men's queries	Women's preferences for public goods differ from men's.
	Number of public goods of different types	The system is democratic enough to respond to an increase in women's queries and public statements but not democratic enough to have taken their views into account prior to having women leaders.
	Repairs to public goods of different types	Responses to political pressure from women will impact repairs as well as new investments.
	Recently built public goods by type	New investments will be more in line with women's needs than were older investments.
The quality of public goods that are priorities for women improves.	Reduced presence of microbes in drinking water	Greater investment in areas of priority to women will translate into better-quality services.

matter. But the chairperson is the only councilor with a full-time appointment and so wields effective power. That the democracy is imperfect implies that investments would reflect the preferences of the leader.

- *Increases in investment translate into more public goods of better quality.* Political pressure from women could lead to more investment in the goods that they prefer, but that does not necessarily translate into more or better-quality goods if the money is spent poorly. Some commentators were concerned that because women leaders were inexperienced the investments would not translate into real gains. If indicators such as repairs of goods preferred by women were to be good measures, the investments would have to take the form of repairs as well as new building.

MODULE 5.2 Specifying Data Sources

Once we have specified our outcomes of interest and selected the indicators we plan to use to measure those outcomes, we need to specify how that data will be collected. This module discusses how we go about choosing how we will collect the data (whether to use existing data or collect our own through survey or nonsurvey instruments), when we will collect the data, who will perform the data collection and from whom they will collect it, and where they will collect it.

Finding existing data sources or collecting new data

We must decide between using existing administrative data sources and collecting our own data through surveys or nonsurvey instruments.

Using administrative data

How will we acquire data on our outcomes of interest? In some cases, existing administrative data can be a good source. Administrative data are records collected by governments or civil society organizations, usually in the context of program administration.

First, we must evaluate whether the administrative data will be suitable for answering our research questions. The following issues should be considered:

- Do the data actually exist?
- Have the data been consistently collected?

- Does the data set cover our population of interest?
- Do the data cover the outcomes that interest us?
- Are the data reliable and unlikely to have been manipulated?

Limitations Administrative data tend to come in two kinds: basic data that are collected on everyone (for example, results on school completion exams) and more detailed data that are collected on a random sample of individuals (most government statistics come from representative surveys). Typically, administrative data that are collected on all individuals are not very detailed and may not be sufficient to answer all the questions we have. There are exceptions: for example, medical records contain detailed information about the treatment and outcomes of all patients, and prison records can contain quite a lot of information on prisoners.

Large-scale national surveys tend to collect very detailed data but only for a subset of the population. For example, the Demographic and Health Surveys collect rich data from individuals sampled to be nationally representative. In most cases, however, not enough people from our treatment and comparison groups will have been sampled for the survey to give us sufficient sample size for the analysis.

Example: Electoral outcomes of politicians In Brazil a policy randomly assigned the timing of corruption audits of municipalities. Researchers were then able to use existing administrative data on electoral outcomes to evaluate the impact on the electoral outcomes of incumbent mayors of making information on corruption available.

For further reading
Ferraz, Claudio, and Frederico Finan. 2008. "Exposing Corrupt Politicians: The Effects of Brazil's Publicly Released Audits on Electoral Outcomes." *Quarterly Journal of Economics* 123 (2): 703–745.
J-PAL Policy Briefcase. 2011. "Exposing Corrupt Politicians." Abdul Latif Jameel Poverty Action Lab, Cambridge, MA. http://www.povertyactionlab .org/publication/exposing-corrupt-politicians.

Example: Collecting overdue taxes in the United Kingdom The Behavioral Insights Team in the Cabinet Office of the United Kingdom tested different ways to encourage taxpayers to pay off their debts to the government. Roughly 70 percent of those in arrears paid up after receiving a letter from the authorities, but the government wanted to see if they could increase this rate, because taking further steps toward litigation is expensive. They developed alternative ways to draft the letter requesting payment, drawing on lessons from behavioral research. They then randomized which debtor was sent which letter. Outcomes were measured using tax administration records.

For further reading
Cabinet Office Behavioral Insight Team. 2012. "Applying Behavioral Insights to Reduce Fraud, Error, and Debt." Accessed May 28, 2013. https://update .cabinetoffice.gov.uk/sites/default/files/resources/BIT_FraudErrorDebt_ accessible.pdf.

Example: Test scores of high school graduates Researchers evaluated the impact of a policy that randomly selected families to receive vouchers for private schooling. Later the researchers examined administrative records on registration and test scores from a government college entrance examination. The test scores also gave the researchers a good proxy for high school graduation, since 90 percent of all graduating high school seniors take the exam.

For further reading
Angrist, Joshua, Eric Bettinger, and Michael Kremer. 2006. "Long-Term Educational Consequences of Secondary School Vouchers: Evidence from Administrative Records in Colombia." *American Economic Review* 96 (3): 847–862.
This study is summarized as Evaluation 10 in the appendix.

Collecting our own data

In many cases we cannot rely only on data collected by others to measure our outcomes because the data do not exist, they are unreliable, or the sample size is insufficient. Collecting our own data allows us to create a custom data set on exactly those outcomes that are most relevant to our research questions. However, collecting data is expensive, and we will face many trade-offs in deciding exactly what data to collect and when.

Surveys The most common method of collecting data for impact evaluation is to administer surveys. Surveys are good for collecting data on lots of different questions from the individuals in our study. They are relatively quick, and (compared to some nonsurvey instruments) relatively inexpensive. However, for some outcomes we may worry that the information people report in surveys is unreliable because they may have forgotten what happened in the past or they may misreport potentially sensitive information.

Nonsurvey instruments Although using surveys is the most common way to collect data, there are also a host of nonsurvey instruments that can help us quantify difficult-to-measure outcomes. These range from simple vignettes an enumerator presents to respondents, often as part of a survey (discussed in greater detail later in this chapter), to the collection of complex biomarker data. These instruments enable us to rigorously quantify activities or outcomes that participants would not report in a survey (such as corruption or discrimination), that they may not know (such as whether they have an HIV infection or subconscious racial or gender bias), or that need more nuanced measurement (for instance, small changes in health outcomes such as levels of anemia).

Nonsurvey instruments also have important limitations, which vary by instrument. In Module 5.4 we discuss a number of nonsurvey instruments in detail, noting the advantages and limitations of each. Many nonsurvey instruments, however, are quite expensive for the number of outcomes they measure compared to a survey that can cover many outcomes in one survey.

Specifying the subjects and respondents

Who will be our subjects and respondents? This question encompasses many others: Who is a representative unit of observation? Who is the respondent that knows the information we need about the unit of observation? Who is the respondent that will give the most reliable information? Who is the efficient respondent that will allow us to gather the most information at one time?

Who will be our subjects and respondents?

Who is subject to the treatment? The person whose outcomes we will measure depends on the question we are trying to answer. For example, if we want to know whether a business training program increased knowledge of business practices, we will test the participants. But the choice is not always so straightforward.

If we provide a clean water program and want to study its health effects, we can look at the health of everyone in a family because they are all likely to suffer from diarrhea if they drink unclean water. However, it probably makes sense to focus only on diarrhea among children under age 5 for two reasons: (1) children under that age are much more likely to die of waterborne diseases, and thus we care more about diarrhea in this age group, and (2) the incidence of waterborne diseases is higher in this age group, so it will be easier to pick up an effect in this age group.

In contrast, for microfinance programs we may want to look not only at the person who got a loan (if the MFI lends to women only, the female head of the household) but also at her spouse. Maybe we would see no effect if we looked only at spending on the female head but would see a change in total household consumption or in the size of a business owned by the male head.

The question of whom to use as respondents in collecting data is less obvious when we are dealing with aggregates such as households. Whom do we include in the aggregate? How, for example, do we define a household when dealing with nonnuclear families or polygamous families?

Who is representative? In many cases we do not measure every person in the treatment and comparison group, and in these cases we need to choose whom to sample. For example, imagine that we are doing a communitywide iron supplementation program. We decide that it would cost too much to take blood samples from everyone in both the treatment and the comparison communities. A key consideration then becomes from whom we will take blood so that our subsample is representative.

One common sampling methodology is to go to the center of the community and interview someone in every second (or third) house to which the interviewer goes. Another is to go to the center of a community and start talking to passersby. But the people we meet in the middle of the day in the middle of a community are not random. In many countries richer people tend to live near the center of a community and many people will be out working in the middle of the day, so it is a very special group of people we meet in the middle of the day. The only way to be sure that we get a truly representative group of people for our data collection is to get a listing of everyone who lives in an area and then randomly select people or households to be measured.

Who knows the information we need? We want to interview respondents who have the information that we are looking for. If, for example, we are collecting information on child health—say, the number of cases of diarrhea in the past week—we want to go to the primary caregiver. And we want to make sure that we obtain comparable responses; in other words, if we decide to interview the mother because she is the primary caregiver, we should make sure to systematically interview mothers and not substitute aunts or sisters for convenience. Allowing no substitutions can be costly. If enumerators arrive in a household and the mother is absent, they might have to come back another day to interview her.

In contrast, if we want information on the number of public works projects in a village over the past year, we can do a participatory appraisal in which we simultaneously interview a group of, say, 20 villagers to get an aggregate picture of these projects. This will give us information that is more accurate than that we would get from interviewing one person, no matter how well chosen.

Who is unlikely to manipulate the information? Which respondent has the least incentive to manipulate the information? Some questions are sensitive, and respondents may have an incentive not to be straightforward in their answers, in which case we need to think carefully about the incentives of different potential respondents.

Consider teacher attendance. Both students and teachers can supply this information. But the teacher has a stronger incentive to misreport her attendance because she may fear sanctions from supervisors, or she may misreport simply because she does not like to think of herself as shirking. If we cannot directly observe attendance and have to rely on reported information, the attendance reported by the students may be closer to the truth than that reported by the teacher.

Who will be most efficient in reporting data? Efficiency has to do with the amount of information we can get from one person in one sitting. If, for example, we want information on child health and education and our indicator for the former is test scores on report cards, the parents may be a more efficient source than the teachers. From the teachers we will get only test scores, but from the parents we can get both the test scores and the health information.

Who will do the measuring?

It is important to think carefully about whom we will choose to be the enumerators who collect the data.

The same people must interview both the treatment and the comparison groups. It can seem expedient to have program staff who are already working with the treatment group interview them and hire others to interview the comparison group. However, it is critical that the same approach be used and the same team interview both the treatment and the comparison group. Otherwise it is possible that differences in the data will be due to differences in interviewing style, procedure, or social interaction—not the program.

Enumerators should not be program staff or anyone the participants know from the program It can be tempting to try to save on costs and human resources by using program staff to conduct the survey with both treatment and comparison groups. However, the treatment group may feel less free to answer questions honestly if the enumerator is someone they recognize from a program that provided services. Also, it is important to have well-trained enumerators who are skilled in administering surveys and know how to avoid asking leading questions. We cannot simply hand a survey (even a well-designed one) to general staff and hope they can administer it well.

The characteristics of the enumerator can matter We need to think carefully about the social interaction between the enumerator and the respondent. In some cases, for example, it is best if the enumerator is the same gender as the respondent. Minimizing language barriers is also very important: ideally, enumerators will be fluent in all the local languages spoken in the area in which they conduct surveys. When enumerators work in small teams, at least one enumerator should be fluent in each relevant language.

We should have a plan to check for cheating and announce it in advance We need to have a carefully made plan in place to check for cheating or carelessness by enumerators. Enumerator shirking could take a number of forms. Enumerators may save time by filling in surveys without ever interviewing the respondents. But an enumerator can also cheat by not being careful to track the correct respondent and simply substituting another person who happens to be present for the person in our sample. Or she may save time by taking advantage of skip patterns in the survey. For example, often there are certain questions in a survey on which a "yes" answer will lead to many more questions than a "no." If the enumerator writes down a lower number of household members in response to an early question, she will have fewer people about whom to ask questions. Similar problems could arise in response to questions about the number of crops grown, whether a person has ever taken a loan, or whether the household has experienced episodes of illness. Cheating and carelessness of this kind can invalidate the entire evaluation.

Different researchers have different approaches to checking for cheating, but the most common forms are performing random back-checks and looking for patterns in the data. In random back-checks, a separate team of enumerators randomly selects people in the sample, whom they then visit and administer a short survey. The survey asks whether someone recently visited them to ask some questions and repeats a few objective questions from the survey to which the answers are unlikely to change over time. Back-checking is most effective when enumerators are warned in advance that their work will be checked in this way and when every enumeration team is back-checked in the first few days of data collection so the threat is credible.

One rule of thumb is to administer back-check questionnaires to approximately 10 percent of the people surveyed. For larger surveys, slightly fewer than 10 percent may suffice, but for small surveys about 15 percent may be needed. The important guiding principle when deciding how many back-checks to do is to make sure that every team and every surveyor is back-checked as soon as possible. One option to consider is to have a more aggressive back-check process in the first few weeks of the survey and then reduce it to 10 percent of surveys through the rest of the surveying phase.

We also need to check for patterns in the data that suggest cheating. For example, the management team for the data collection process can check in real time for a high number of "no" answers to questions that let enumerators skip forward in the survey. Providing enumerators with clear definitions can also be helpful. For example, because there is an incentive to shrink household size so that the enumerator has fewer people about whom to ask questions, we must clearly define what we mean by a household. This will be culturally dependent, but a common definition is people who eat together.

Finally, computer-assisted interviewing using such things as GPS-enabled devices can make it easier to monitor for some kinds of cheating. Requiring enumerators to fill in the GPS locations of different households or interview sites makes it possible to check whether the enumerators did in fact visit those locations rather than filling in all the surveys at one location. If data are collected electronically and quickly downloaded onto a main server, it also becomes much easier to spot suspicious patterns in the data early in the data collection process.

Specifying the time and frequency

We need to decide when and how often to collect data. Should we conduct a baseline survey before the program is rolled out? Should we collect data throughout program implementation? How long do we wait before doing an endline survey? How often should we visit, and how long should these visits be?

Should we conduct a baseline survey?

A *baseline* survey could be worthwhile when (1) the sample size is limited, (2) the outcomes are specific to individuals, (3) we want to show that our treatment and comparison groups were balanced at the start of the evaluation or (preferably) ensure they are balanced by doing a stratified randomization, (4) we want to analyze the data by subgroup or include control variables in the final analysis.

Limited sample size Collecting baseline data can help us increase our statistical power, which is particularly important when our sample size is small. In other words, for a given sample size we will be able to detect smaller program effects with baseline data than otherwise. In our analysis we can use baseline data to reduce unexplained variation in the outcomes of interest. For example, children vary widely in their test scores. If we have a test score for one child both before the program starts and after it ends, our statistical analysis can use those baseline data to make our estimate of the impact much more precise. However, a baseline can be expensive, so we will want to trade off the cost of doing a baseline with the cost of increasing our sample size. (For details, see Chapter 6 on statistical power.)

Individual-specific outcomes A baseline is particularly useful when the outcomes are person specific. For example, cognitive abilities, test scores, and beliefs tend to be highly correlated over time for a given individual. If we collect baseline and endline data on the same individuals for these variables, we will be able to explain a lot of the variance between individuals. For other variables, such as agricultural yields, there is much lower correlation over time for the same person.

In such a case, having a baseline will provide less additional statistical power.

Balance Sometimes the luck of the draw means that our randomized assignment results in unbalanced treatment and comparison groups; for example, the treatment schools may have a disproportionate number of the more educated teachers. Thus, if we find that children in treatment schools have higher test scores than those in the comparison schools, it may be due to the program or it may simply be due to the imbalance of educated teachers. Imbalance is more likely when the sample is small, and it makes interpreting the results more difficult.

Having baseline data can be reassuring if it confirms that our randomization led to good balance between treatment and comparison groups. This balance can also help confirm that randomization was in fact carried out (for example, if we are relying on a randomization done by others). However, a baseline can also reveal that our groups are not balanced, and there is little we can do if this is the case. A better strategy (as discussed in Chapter 4) is to do a stratified randomization. Baselines are useful for generating the data on which to stratify the randomization. This approach does require that the baseline data be collected, entered, and cleaned before randomization takes place and before the program is rolled out. If we are taking this approach, it is important to explain to those implementing the program that there will need to be a delay between the baseline and the rollout of the program.

Subgroup analysis and baseline controls Baseline data allow us to define subgroups for analysis. For example, if we have income data, we can categorize people by income brackets and then check how the effects of the program vary by income. Or if we have pretest scores, we can check whether the program benefited all students or just those who, based on pretest scores, were already doing well. It is not possible to do this if we have data on outcomes only after the program was implemented because we don't know who was poor or doing badly before the program began. Analyzing effects by subgroup often helps us answer important policy questions.

Similarly, baseline data allow us to include baseline characteristics such as income as control variables in our final analysis, which can help increase our statistical power (see Modules 6.4 and 8.2).

When should we start data collection after the program rollout?

How long after the program rollout should the follow-up data collection begin? That depends on whether there are novelty effects and on the lag between the program's inception and its impact.

Novelty effects arise when some aspect of a new program excites the participants and artificially raises outcomes in the short term. For example, if we monitor teacher attendance with cameras, the cameras themselves may cause excitement and temporarily increase the attendance of both students and teachers. It may be better to measure impact when this novelty has worn off in order to get a better estimate of the medium-term impact of monitoring.

Program impacts are rarely instantaneous. Impact should be measured after the program has had time to achieve its effects. For example, even if a program reduces teacher absenteeism instantaneously, the effect of more regular teaching may take time to show up in learning and test scores.

How frequently should we collect data?

The more frequent our data collection, the more likely we are to capture intermediate outcomes and patterns in the outcomes.

A benefit of frequent collection is that it can enrich the explanation of program impacts. A study in Kenya evaluated a program in which teachers were paid based on attendance, with school principals responsible for recording absences and awarding regular attendance bonuses.[3] The researchers did random spot checks three times a month to measure attendance independently. The resulting data allowed them to cross-check the attendance data they received from the principals and also to see the pattern of attendance over the course of the program. They found that the attendance level was high at the beginning, but after six months it deteriorated to its normal level again, and that change coincided with an increase in the number of absences marked as presences. This analysis was possible only because the researchers collected intermediate outcomes frequently. If they had measured attendance only at the end of the evaluation period, that would have sufficed to estimate the program's impact, but they would

---

3. Michael Kremer and Daniel Chen, "An Interim Report on a Teacher Attendance Incentive Program in Kenya," Harvard University, Cambridge, MA, 2001, mimeo.

not have seen the full story of the initial attendance gains that were later undermined by principal discretion.

A downside of frequent data collection is the cost, not just to the evaluation but also to our respondents, who have to admit enumerators to their homes or classrooms and fill out the surveys. In deciding on frequency, we face a trade-off between detail and cost.

Sometimes too-frequent surveying can itself become an intervention and change outcomes. Another evaluation in Kenya estimated the effect on child health and diarrhea of distributing chlorine for household water purification. In the treatment and comparison groups, the researchers varied how frequently they visited families to ask them about their use of chlorine in their drinking water. They found that visiting the families frequently caused them to increase their use of chlorine. In a sense, the data collection acted as a reminder to chlorinate the water. The comparison group with frequent data collection no longer provided a representation of chlorine use in the absence of the program.[4]

When should we end the data collection?

When should we do the endline survey? When the program ends? After the program ends? And if we want to know the long-term effects, how long after the program ends should we wait? The decision is usually a trade-off between waiting to get longer-term results and getting a result in time for the findings to inform decisionmaking. Attrition is also an important factor for long-term follow up. The longer we wait to do the endline survey, the higher the attrition rate is likely to be, because people will move and even die over time.

How does the randomization design influence the timing of data collection? The timing of data collection may vary with the randomization design, particularly for the comparison group.

In an *encouragement design* it may take a while for those who are encouraged to take up the program. If we wait too long to collect data, however, even those who have not been encouraged may take up the program. We need to do the endline survey at a point when take-up is high in the encouraged group but not yet high in the group not encouraged.

4. Alix Peterson Zwane et al., "Being Surveyed Can Change Later Behavior and Related Parameter Estimates," *Proceedings of the National Academy of Sciences USA* 108 (2011): 1821–1826.

In a *phase-in design* we need to conduct the endline survey before the last group receives the program. However, in some versions of a phase-in design it is still possible to measure long-term results. The comparison for the long-term effects is between those who had the program for a longer period and those who had it for a shorter period of time. For example, see the evaluations of the school-based deworming program in Kenya.[5]

In a *rotation design* we must collect data each time the treatment rotates between the two groups.

Specifying locations: What locations make for efficiency?

Imagine that we are running an after-school book club to see whether it helps increase reading comprehension. We randomize some schools to receive the club. We could test children on reading comprehension at school or at home. It will be much more efficient to test them at school because most of them will be gathered in one place at one time. The schools (even the comparison schools) may be happy to cooperate because they will receive feedback on their students. We may still have to do some tests at home to follow up on students who have dropped out of school or are absent when we do the test, but this will still be less expensive than doing all the tests at school.

MODULE 5.3 Assessing and Field Testing Outcome Measures

Now that we have a list of indicators, how do we decide which are best for our evaluation? This module discusses the need to look for four qualities in an indicator: it must be logically valid, measurable (observable, feasible, and detectable), precise (exhaustive and exclusive), and reliable.

Criteria for a desktop assessment of potential indicators

We will have a long list of potential indicators after we review the literature and map outcomes and indicators to the program's theory of change. This list may be too long. It would be too costly, not to mention confusing, to measure every possible variable that could be

5. Sarah Baird, Joan Hamory Hicks, Michael Kremer, and Edward Miguel, "Worms at Work: Long-Run Impacts of Child Health Gains," working paper, Harvard University, Cambridge, MA, October 2011. http://www.economics.harvard.edu/faculty/kremer/files/KLPS-Labor_2012-03-23_clean.pdf. See also Evaluation 1 in the Appendix, which summarizes this study.

changed by the program. Ultimately, we need to test our indicators by piloting them in the field. Before doing that we can conduct a "desktop assessment" of our potential indicators. We can compare them according to four qualities of a good indicator to winnow our list of potential indicators to the most promising ones.

Logically valid

In the specific context of the program we evaluate, there must be a logical link connecting our outcome of interest at the conceptual level and the indicator we observe and measure.

Example 1: HIV status is a logical indicator of unsafe sexual behavior HIV status is a valid indicator of unsafe sexual behavior. The logical link is as follows: unsafe behavior can lead to infection with HIV, infection causes the body to produce HIV antibodies after a certain period, and an HIV test determines whether these antibodies are present in the blood.

Example 2: HIV status is not a logical indicator of knowledge of safe sexual practices HIV status is not a valid indicator of knowledge of safe sexual practices; someone may know the best prevention methods but not practice them.

Example 3: Childbearing is a logical indicator of unsafe sexual behavior Unprotected sex can lead to pregnancy, which can lead to the birth of a child. Thus childbearing is a valid measure of unsafe behavior.

We must also consider whether there is any potential for the program to change the logical relationship between an indicator and the outcome we are trying to measure. An indicator could be correlated with our outcome of interest, but if the intervention changes that correlation, it is no longer a good indicator. For example, having a sheet metal roof is a good proxy for wealth in many communities in developing countries, so we often ask about the roofing material of a house to understand wealth levels. But if our intervention involves supporting house renovation and we see more corrugated iron roofs in our treatment group than in our comparison group, we cannot necessarily assume that general wealth has increased as a result of the program.

Measurable

A measurable indicator is observable, feasible, and detectable.

Observable An indicator must be a behavior or state that can be observed in the real world. Thus happiness is not an indicator, but laughter or self-reported happiness could be. Learning is not an indicator, but being able to read and do arithmetic are. This is an important distinction to maintain. We are not done defining our outcomes until we have identified some indicators that are observable.

Feasible Indicators must be feasible to measure—politically, ethically, and financially. Being feasible is context specific. Thus HIV status is observable in theory, but it may not be a good indicator for a school-based HIV education program if it is infeasible to test children for HIV. If certain questions are too sensitive to ask, indicators derived from those questions are not feasible.

Detectable Indicators must be detectable with the instruments and statistical power of our specific experiment. Thus infant mortality (number of deaths of children aged 12 months or younger per 1,000 live births) might not be a good indicator for a maternal and child health program. If infant mortality occurs relatively infrequently, even if the program has an effect there may not be enough of a change in the numbers of deaths to detect the effect. If we are testing a program to improve water quality, we might want to measure the number and severity of diarrheal episodes as a more detectable alternative.

In our HIV education example we are targeting children in the last grade of primary school, age 15 years on average. The government does not authorize testing of primary school children for HIV, nor do we have the infrastructure to test for HIV, meaning that measuring HIV status is not feasible. This also means that we do not know the starting incidence of HIV and cannot gauge whether a change in HIV infection rates would be detectable. Of course we could make guesses to do a power analysis, but given the cost of the infrastructure we would need for an HIV biomarker study, we want to know the real incidence in our sample before choosing that indicator. We can postpone using HIV status as an indicator until the next round of the evaluation. If the program proves to be effective based on the indicators we do have, it might be worthwhile to do a biomarker follow-up study to determine the program's effects on HIV rates, which is an important consideration for replication and scale-up. Table 5.4 shows a range of possible indicators for this study assessed as to whether they are observable, feasible, and detectable.

TABLE 5.4 Potential indicators and their measurability

Outcome	Indicators	Measurable		
		Observable	Feasible	Detectable
Amount of HIV education	Number of hours teachers spent on HIV curriculum	Yes	Yes	Yes
Modes of HIV education	Use of lecture time to teach about HIV	Yes	Yes	Yes
	Use of playtime to teach about HIV	Yes	Yes	Yes
Knowledge of safe practices	Number of correct answers on test	Yes	Yes	Yes
Unsafe sexual behavior	Number of unprotected sexual encounters	No	No	No
	Incidence of childbearing	Yes	Yes	Yes
Protected sex	Condom use	No	No	No
	Self-reported condom use	Yes	Yes	Yes
HIV infection	HIV status	Yes	No	Unknown

Precision

The more exhaustive and exclusive the indicator, the more precise it is.

Exhaustive indicators An outcome can be measured by more than one indicator, all of them logical ramifications of the outcome. More exhaustive indicators capture more instances of the outcome we need to measure. They improve how accurately we can measure impact. Imagine that a microfinance program increases savings and that it leads to 100 instances of saving. The more comprehensive our indicators, the more of these instances they would capture. We need to think through all the possible manifestations of the concept "savings" in the program's context. People may prefer saving by investing in durable assets rather than by saving money in a bank account. They may buy a goat, buy jewelry, bury money in a jar, or deposit money in a bank. If we measured only money deposits in a bank, we would miss all the other instances of saving. The indicator "money deposited at the bank" would not be an exhaustive indicator of our "savings" outcome.

Is our childbearing indicator an exhaustive indicator of unsafe sexual behavior in our HIV education example? As Figure 5.1 shows, the concept "unsafe sex" has many other effects in the real world besides childbearing. In using childbearing as an indicator of unsafe sex, we are following only the path, marked in boldface, from unsafe sex to vaginal sex to pregnancy to childbirth. Only unprotected vaginal sex leads to pregnancy, and it does so only some of the time. Exhaustiveness concerns how much childbearing captures the incidences of unsafe sex. The question to ask is "If there are 100 instances of unsafe sex in the population, how many result in childbirth?"

In contrast to our childbearing indicator, HIV status is an exhaustive measure of HIV infection. If there were 100 instances of HIV infection and we tested all 100 people at the right time, we would probably have close to 100 HIV-positive tests. HIV status captures all the instances of HIV infection.

Exclusive indicators An exclusive indicator is an indicator that is affected by the outcome of interest and by nothing else. Tears are an example of a nonexclusive indicator. Tears come when people are happy, when they are sad, when they are in pain, and when they cut onions and their eyes become irritated, and some people (actors and politicians) can cry on cue. On their own, tears are an ambiguous sign

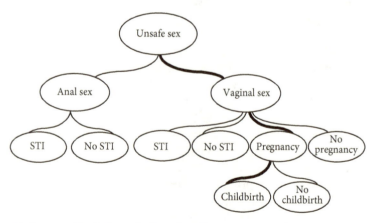

FIGURE 5.1 A logical tree for "unsafe sex"

Note: STI = sexually transmitted infection.

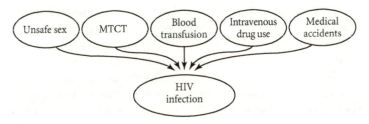

FIGURE 5.2 Possible sources of HIV infection

Note: MTCT = mother-to-child transfer.

of the state of an individual's feelings. If our outcome of interest was sadness, tears would not be a precise indicator.

Although childbearing is not an exhaustive indicator of unsafe sex, it is (in the Kenyan context) exclusive. If we see childbearing, we know for sure that there was an instance of unprotected sexual behavior. Is HIV status an exclusive indicator of unsafe sex? This depends on the context (Figure 5.2). It is possible to become HIV positive without having had unsafe sex. HIV infections can also result from mother-to-child transfers or contact with contaminated blood (through transfusions, intravenous drug use, and medical accidents), although it is rare for 15-year-olds in the Kenyan context to be HIV positive as a result of these alternative transmission routes.[6]

Reliability and social desirability bias

An indicator is reliable when it is hard to forget, counterfeit, or misreport. Say, for example, that we are interested in the incidence of STIs. We could ask people if they have an STI, or we could test them for STIs. People may not tell the truth about their STI status, perhaps because they claim to be abstinent. Test results, on the other hand, are hard to counterfeit. When possible, it is better to choose an indicator that is harder to counterfeit.

Maybe we want to evaluate an HIV prevention program that promotes abstinence and condom use. Neither of these can be directly observed, which leaves us relying on reports from respondents. There are two possible threats: forgetting and deliberate misreporting.

6. This study by Esther Duflo, Pascaline Dupas, and Michael Kremer is summarized as Evaluation 4 in the appendix.

People could simply forget whether they used a condom. To improve the reliability of the variable, we can narrow the question and make it more specific. We could ask, "In how many of your last 10 sexual encounters did you use a condom?" A more reliable question would be, "Think of the last time you had sex. Did you use a condom?"

People could also deliberately misreport. Respondents may lie because they suspect what the "right" answer should be. For example, in contexts in which social stigma is attached to unmarried individuals' being sexually active, some respondents may deliberately lie about being virgins. For example, a study in Kenya found that 12 percent of women who reported being virgins were HIV positive and most had other sexually transmitted infections, making it unlikely that they acquired HIV nonsexually.[7] It may also be the case that people suppress memories that embarrass them or make them unhappy; in other words, they may not even know they are misreporting. When programs encourage certain practices, participants may have a particularly strong desire to report that they are doing these "right" things, so they will report that they are abstaining and using condoms, saving, and not discriminating against their daughters, among other encouraged and socially desirable behaviors. When people misreport because they want to show that their behavior is aligned with what they perceive as socially desirable, the resulting distortion is called *social desirability bias.*

A desire to say what is socially desirable can lead to overreporting as well as underreporting. For example, if microfinance clients are told to invest what they borrowed in a business, clients may state that this is how they used their loans, even if many used them to pay off other loans instead.

Proxy indicators A good way to get around self-reporting bias is to use a proxy indicator that can be measured directly. If the outcome changes, we can predict that the proxy and the unobservable indicator will both change.

For example, the childbearing indicator of unprotected sex used in the HIV education study discussed above is a proxy that helps us avoid social desirability bias. This is particularly important given that

---

7. J. R. Glynn, M. Caraël, B. Auvert, M. Kahindo, J. Chege, R. Musonda, F. Kaona, and A. Buvé, "Why Do Young Women Have a Much Higher Prevalence of HIV than Young Men? A Study in Kisumu, Kenya and Ndola, Zambia," *AIDS* 15 (2001): S51–60.

the HIV education program being tested promoted abstinence before marriage and fidelity in marriage, so there is a risk that teenagers in the treatment group will be even more likely to misreport unprotected sex than those in the comparison group. Childbearing is a good proxy because it is difficult to counterfeit.

Ensuring that incentives are properly aligned for good reporting We must be careful that we do not use as an outcome something that is incentivized for the treatment group (but not for the comparison group) or for which one group faces a higher incentive than the other. For example, imagine that we are evaluating a program that uses school attendance records to incentivize teachers. Bonuses are given to teachers whose classes have the highest attendance rates as recorded in class registries. Class registries are not a reliable data source in this context. The same problem holds if the incentive is present in both groups but one group faces a higher incentive than the other (for example, if teachers in the treatment group receive 100 rupees for each day they are recorded as present, while comparison group teachers receive 20 rupees for each recorded presence).

As soon as a system is used as the basis of an incentive, we have to worry that there will be manipulation of the data. The problem is even worse if the manipulation is likely to be correlated with our treatment groups. In this case, those who have the incentive (or have a higher incentive) are more likely to manipulate the data. Instead we need to use as our indicator an independent source of information on attendance (such as spot checks). If the independent source shows that the data on which the incentive is based have not been manipulated, we can potentially use them as a supplement to our independent data but we will always need some independent data in these cases.

Ensuring that data are being collected in an identical manner in the treatment and comparison groups All the characteristics of what makes a good measure that we have discussed are important regardless of which type of study we are doing. However, for randomized evaluations there is an additional consideration. Everything about the data collection (who does it, how it is done, how frequently, and with what tools) must be identical between the treatment and comparison groups. Often we may have data for the treatment group (from running the actual program) that we do not have for the comparison group. For example, a program in India incentivized teacher attendance at schools with cameras that produced date- and time-stamped images. The researchers thus had very detailed attendance information for the treatment group. They could not use this same method of cameras to collect attendance data in the comparison group because that mechanism was part of the treatment. Instead the researchers conducted random spot checks to measure teacher attendance. These spot checks were conducted in an identical manner in both treatment and comparison schools.[8]

Field testing

There is only so much progress that can be made toward developing a good data collection plan in the office. Any plan, however well thought out, needs to be tested in the field. It is not enough to do a desktop assessment, because even indicators that make sense and have been used with success elsewhere may still fail in this evaluation, in this context, with this population. This module discusses some considerations for conducting a field test and checking whether our assumptions about our indicators were right.

Have we chosen the right respondents?

Field testing may reveal that the respondents we have chosen do not know the information we are asking about. For example, in an agriculture program it may be reasonable to assume that the head of the household would know about planting decisions. But if in our context men and women are responsible for different crops, the male head of the household will know only about men's crops.

Alternatively, we may find that there are key respondents who know the outcomes of many individuals or of the community as a whole, so we don't have to ask every individual all of the questions but can get the information from a centralized source. The distance to the nearest clinic is a good example of such an indicator.

Do our instruments pick up variation?

The data collection instrument must be sensitive to the variation found in the population where the evaluation is done. If measuring test scores, the test should not be so easy that most participants score 100 percent or so hard that most score 0 percent. Field testing the instrument will help make sure that this is the case.

---

8. Esther Duflo, Rema Hanna, and Stephen Ryan, "Incentives Work: Getting Teachers to Come to School," *American Economic Review* 102 (2012): 1241–1278.

Is the plan appropriate given the culture and the politics of this context?

If, for example, our program is designed to promote collective action, we will want to ask questions about specific types of collective action that make sense in the specific cultural context. What are the types of activities that cohesive communities in this part of the world engage in collectively? Do they improve local schools? Collectively tend community farm plots? Plan community celebrations? Some of these insights can be gained from talking to experts and reading the literature, but there is no substitute for spending time in the communities, doing qualitative work, and then developing and testing good instruments.[9]

Are the questions phrased in a way that people understand? A question may make sense to us but not to a participant. A common measure of social capital is the number of groups a person belongs to. Early in the field testing of an evaluation in Sierra Leone, we included a question about how many social groups respondents belonged to, but we quickly realized that the question was not well understood. One man claimed to belong to no social groups. After some general discussion it emerged that he was an active member of the local mosque. In addition to attending a prayer group there, he and some of the other elderly members of the mosque had joined together to buy seeds to work some communal land. It became evident that we needed to ask specifically about membership in common groups if we wanted a complete answer to our question about the number of groups someone belonged to.

Are administrative data collected? Do they seem reliable? We may wish to rely on administrative data, such as child enrollment data held by schools or police records. Often it is required by law that these types of records be collected, but that is no guarantee that they exist, and it is certainly no guarantee that they are accurate. Field visits will give us an indication of how well these records are kept.

9. For an example of detailed questions on collective action specific to the local context, see the study by Katherine Casey, Rachel Glennerster, and Edward Miguel, summarized as Evaluation 15 in the appendix. All the survey instruments for this evaluation are available through the J-PAL website at http://www.povertyactionlab.org/evaluation/community-driven-development-sierra-leone.

Is the recall period appropriate? The field test can also help us figure out the right recall period. Is it better to ask about outcomes over the last week or over the last year?

Are the surveys too long? A field test will help us determine how long it takes the average respondent to go through our questions. Fatigue can decrease the quality of the data. But remember that with training and time, our enumerators will get better at administering the questionnaire and the completion time per respondent will fall.

What is the best time and place to find the respondents? The respondents may be less available at some times than at others to answer questions. Field testing will help us plan our survey timetable by answering these questions: How many people will we be able to reach before they go to work? How many can we survey during the middle of the day? Are there days of the week when people are more likely to be found at home? How many times will we have to go back to find the people we missed?

MODULE 5.4 A Catalog of Nonsurvey Instruments

This module gives examples of nonsurvey instruments we can use to quantify difficult-to-measure outcomes such as corruption, empowerment, and discrimination. For each instrument, there are trade-offs to be made between richness of data, cost, and avoidance of reporting bias.

Direct observation

In many cases we can choose to directly observe the behavior of interest in real time, when it happens. We can use random spot checks, mystery clients, or incognito enumerators or can observe group behavior.

All the direct observation instruments discussed here share the advantage of reducing misreporting due to poor memory and deliberate misrepresentation. They can also provide rich, detailed data. However, all direct observation instruments suffer from the drawback of capturing one very specific point in time.

Random spot checks

In a random spot check, an enumerator directly observes and records the indicator of interest at the study site. The timing of the visit is selected randomly. The idea is to capture the normal state of things. Although any single visit may pick up the unusual behavior of any individual being observed, with a sufficient number of spot checks the average values observed should be a good reflection of reality. For example, a single random spot check is not a good way to assess whether an individual teacher attends regularly. For this we would want to visit at different times on different days. However, if we visit all the teachers in our sample once, visit different teachers at different times on different days of the week, and have a large enough sample of teachers, overall we will get an accurate reflection of absenteeism in our sample. The more frequent the visits, the more expected the visits become and the more polished and less normal the behavior being observed.

When are they useful? Random spot checks are useful when we are measuring outcomes subject to corruption or when participants have incentives to hide their failures or absence. One spot check can also yield rich data on a number of outcomes in one short visit, because we can also observe what an individual is doing, not just whether he is there.

Limitations To ensure that our spot checks give us an accurate picture of reality, we have to conduct a large number of them. These are expensive and require highly trained and well-monitored enumerators. The spot checks also have to measure something that can be quickly observed before people can change their behavior in response to seeing the enumerator.

Example: Spot check of teacher attendance and effort Spot checks have been used to check on the attendance and participation of both providers and beneficiaries. For example, an education project in Indian schools used spot checks to measure teacher and student attendance and teacher effort.[10] Given that the evaluation was sending an enumerator to a school to check whether the teacher was present, she could also quickly record three indicators of teacher effort during an unannounced visit: Were the children in the classroom? Was there anything written on the board? Was the teacher teaching? As for the

10. This study by Abhijit Banerjee, Shawn Cole, Esther Duflo, and Leigh Linden is summarized as Evaluation 2 in the appendix.

students, a roll call was taken on each visit to see who was present. The data from these spot checks are likely to be more reliable than the attendance data recorded in the teacher's register because the teacher may face an incentive to misreport student attendance.

The spot check worked well to check teacher attendance and teaching behavior because these were one-room schools with one teacher. The enumerator can arrive and immediately see what the teacher is doing. In a larger school, a spot check may be able to measure whether teachers are present, but word may spread as the enumerator goes from classroom to classroom, and teachers may quickly start teaching, even if they were talking to colleagues in the staff room when the enumerator arrived.

For further reading
Duflo, Esther, Rema Hanna, and Stephen P. Ryan. "Incentives Work: Getting Teachers to Come to School." *American Economic Review* 102 (4): 1241–1278.

Example: Spot check of environmental audits of industrial pollution An evaluation in Gujarat, India, tested whether changing the incentives of third-party environmental auditors would make them report more accurately. These auditors visit industrial plants three times a year to measure pollution, which they report to the environmental regulator. The evaluation randomly selected some audit visits and had independent agencies spot check them by taking the same pollution readings at the same plant that had just been audited. The person doing the back-check would enter the plant and immediately go to the pollution source (e.g., a boiler stack or chimney) to take a reading before the firm could shut down machinery or take other actions to lessen the pollution it was emitting. These back-checks enabled the researchers to see whether the auditors were telling the truth in their audit reports and formed a valid indicator of misreporting by third-party auditors.

For further reading
Duflo, Esther, Michael Greenstone, Rohini Pande, and Nicholas Ryan. 2012. "Truth-Telling by Third-Party Auditors: Evidence from a Randomized Field Experiment in India." Working paper, Massachusetts Institute of Technology, Cambridge, MA.

Mystery clients

The data collection process itself can be made incognito with mystery clients. An enumerator visits the location of interest and pretends to be a typical client or citizen. The enumerator can then observe and record the quality of the service he receives and any other indicators of interest. In some cases, the "mystery client" can take the form of a paper application sent to an organization instead of a visit by a live person.

If the people the enumerator is visiting and observing do not know that they are part of a research study, the researcher usually has to request a waiver from his or her institution's IRB. A waiver is usually required for not acquiring informed consent before collecting data on someone and for engaging in deception—that is, claiming to need a service when in fact the objective is to collect data. Having the mystery client disclose her purpose after the interaction is complete and not collecting identifying information (i.e., names, locations, or job titles) can help ensure that using mystery clients is compatible with IRB rules. More discussion of IRB rules and judgments as to when research is ethical can be found in Modules 2.4 and 4.2.

When are they useful? Mystery clients are particularly useful for measuring antisocial or illegal activities, such as discrimination or corruption, to which individuals or institutions will not otherwise admit. The use of mystery clients enables us to carefully control an interaction. For example, we can send in mystery clients of different races or genders or have them wear different clothes to gauge how these characteristics affect the interaction.

Limitations If mystery client enumerators must disclose their purpose at the end of the visit, people may change their future behavior in response to knowing that they have been observed and may tell other participants in the study that there are mystery clients in the area.

Example: Using mystery clients to measure the quality of police responsiveness in India An evaluation in Rajasthan, India, tested the effectiveness of different policing reforms on the responsiveness and service of the police. To measure whether police responsiveness to citizens' reports of crime had improved, the researchers sent enumerators on unannounced visits to police stations, where they attempted to register cases posing as victims of various types of crimes. The enumerator did not disclose his identity except when it appeared that the police would actually register the case (to avoid registering a false case, which is illegal) or when circumstances required that the enumerator disclose his identity—for instance, if the police threatened to prosecute him for filing a false case. The enumerator then recorded his success or failure in registering the crime, the attitudes and actions of the police, and other details, such as the total time taken and the names of the officers with whom he interacted.

This use of mystery clients provided rich indicators of police responsiveness. However, when the police at a station knew that they had been observed in this way, they changed their behavior. In fact, the decoy visits, which had been intended only as a means of collecting outcome data, ended up having a greater effect on the likelihood that a future crime would be registered than did the actual interventions the evaluation tested.

For further reading
Banerjee, Abhijit, Raghabendra Chattopadhyay, Esther Duflo, Daniel Keniston, and Nina Singh. 2012. "Can Institutions Be Reformed from Within? Evidence from a Randomized Experiment with the Rajasthan Police." NBER Working Paper 17912. National Bureau of Economic Research, Cambridge, MA.

Example: Measuring race discrimination in hiring processes in the United States Racial, gender, and ethnic discrimination are difficult to measure in the United States because they are illegal. A randomized evaluation sent decoy resumes to firms to see whether employers discriminate based on race in inviting candidates to interview for open positions. The researchers mailed identical resumes to different employers, but some were randomly selected to have a stereotypically white name at the top (e.g., Emily or Greg), while others were randomly selected to receive a resume with a stereotypically African-American name (e.g., Lakisha or Jamal). They then counted the number of callbacks to numbers given for the white-sounding names and the African-American-sounding names. Although discrimination is not directly measurable, these callbacks were, and they formed a good proxy indicator of discrimination.

For further reading
Bertrand, Marianne, and Sendhil Mullainathan. 2004. "Are Emily and Greg More Employable than Lakisha and Jamal? A Field Experiment on Labor Market Discrimination." *American Economic Review* 94 (4): 991–1013.

Incognito enumerators (ride-alongs)

An incognito enumerator experiences the process we wish to measure and records indicators of the outcomes of interest during the process. The enumerator observes the process firsthand and simply counts the number of incidences in a process. Unlike a mystery client, the ride-along does not pose as a client, ask questions, or actively engage in the process she is observing.

When are they useful? These are useful when we need to see a whole process and a single "snapshot" is not enough. Ride-alongs can help us measure the quality of service the participants experience, such as how long it takes to be served or how many steps there are in the process. They are also often used to get an accurate estimate of corruption.

Limitations Ride-alongs can be used only when having a person observing won't change the process. They are expensive because they require extensive training and monitoring, and the process of observation takes a considerable amount of time. We must also come up with an objective way to compare observations across instances and across different enumerators. For example, we can randomly assign enumerators to locations so that differences in how enumerators interpret a script or record events do not bias our data.

Example: Riding along with truckers to record bribes paid at road blocks A study of the corruption of traffic police in Indonesia used this method. The enumerators, traveling incognito, simply rode along with the truckers and counted the number of solicitations for bribes and the number and amount of bribes paid at each roadblock.

For further reading
Olken, Benjamin, and Patrick Barron. 2009. "The Simple Economics of Extortion: Evidence from Trucking in Aceh." *Journal of Political Economy* 117 (3): 417–452.

Observing group interaction and structured community activities

An enumerator can visit a scheduled event that lets him or her observe group interactions. In most cases, however, there will not be a pre-scheduled event that occurs in both treatment and comparison communities that we can plan to attend. In this case we need to prompt the interaction we wish to observe. This approach is known as structured community activities (SCAs).

When is this useful? Sometimes the outcomes that interest us can best be observed when a group of people are interacting. For example, if we are interested in power dynamics or empowerment, observing how people speak or relate to each other can give us information we could not glean from self-reported information in a survey or even from observing individuals.

Limitations This approach works only when the presence of an enumerator is unlikely to change the outcomes we are measuring. Additionally, the type of interactions we want to observe may occur only rarely, so if we simply turn up and wait, we may have to wait a long time before seeing the interaction we want to observe. Unless an interaction, such as a meeting, follows a set schedule, we may have to prompt the interaction that we want to observe.

Example: Prompting a community meeting so we can observe and measure empowerment In cases in which there are no previously planned events to observe, the researchers can prompt an event to occur and use that occasion to observe group interaction. For example, researchers in Sierra Leone conducted SCAs to measure the extent to which a community-driven development program was successful in increasing the participation of women and youth in community decision-making. There were no formally scheduled meetings. Instead a village chief called a meeting whenever a decision had to be made on issues such as how to repair a bridge or how much to contribute to local public works projects.

The researchers therefore created a situation in which the community would have to make a decision. The night before the survey started, the enumerators announced that they would like to address the community as a whole and asked the chief to gather community members the next morning. At that meeting the enumerators said that to thank the community for taking part in the household survey they would like to give the community a gift of either batteries or small packages of iodized salt. They then stood back and let the community decide which gift they preferred. Unobtrusively they observed how many women and youth attended and how many spoke at the meeting. They also noted whether a small group of elders at any point broke away from the main meeting to "hang heads," that is, deliberate privately about which gift they wanted the community to choose.

For further reading
This study is summarized as Evaluation 15 in the appendix.

Other nonsurvey instruments

When we cannot directly observe the behavior we want to measure, we can use one of many other nonsurvey instruments to record the outcome of interest.

Physical tests

When are these useful? Physical tests are not subject to deliberate misreporting or psychological bias in reporting. A wide variety of physical tests can be used to measure a range of different behaviors and outcomes.

Limitations Physical tests measure one specific outcome. Some tests have high error rates and can produce a noisy (although unbiased) measure. Some physical tests can be difficult to perform in the field and may require specialized technical knowledge. They can also be expensive.

Example: Audit of materials used in public infrastructure projects A program in Indonesia measured corruption on road construction projects. Corruption on construction projects can take the form of diverting funds or using inferior or fewer materials that cost less than the amount allocated and siphoning off the rest of the funds for private use. It can also take the form of diverting the materials themselves, using fewer materials and siphoning the rest for sale or for private use. Here the audit took the form of digging up randomly selected spots on the road and measuring the amount of material used. These data were then used to estimate the total quantity of material used and compare it to official records of expenditures on materials and labor. The gap between the two formed a quantitative indicator of corruption.

For further reading
J-PAL Policy Briefcase. 2012. "Routes to Reduced Corruption." Abdul Latif Jameel Poverty Action Lab, Cambridge MA.
Olken, Benjamin A. 2007. "Monitoring Corruption: Evidence from a Field Experiment in Indonesia." *Journal of Political Economy* 115 (2): 200–249.

Example: Spot check to test whether chlorine is being used in home drinking water An evaluation in Kenya tested the impact of giving households small bottles of chlorine with which to purify their water. To see whether households were using the chlorine, enumerators tested the drinking water in the family's home to see if residual chlorine was present.

For further reading

Kremer, Michael, Edward Miguel, Sendhil Mullainathan, Clair Null, and Alix Peterson Zwane. 2011. "Social Engineering: Evidence from a Suite of Take-up Experiments in Kenya." Working paper, Harvard University, Cambridge, MA. <http://elsa.berkeley.edu/~emiguel/pdfs/miguel_chlorine dispensers.pdf>.

Biomarkers

Using biomarkers is a highly objective way to test the effects of a program, because biomarkers cannot be manipulated by the subject or respondent. The biomarker used may be directly related to the program (a deworming program checks for worm load) or may be an outcome of a social program that did not directly target health (an education program tests for changes in child health). Some tests of biomarkers include the following:

- STI and HIV tests
- Diagnostic tests for illnesses such as malaria or tuberculosis
- Measures of weight, height, body mass index (BMI), arm circumference
- Tests of toenail clippings for substances such as arsenic
- Pregnancy tests
- Urine tests
- Saliva swabs for cortisol (a stress hormone)

When are these useful? Biomarkers can be much less biased than self-reported information.

Limitations Collecting biomarker data can be very expensive and logistically complicated. There is a risk of high refusal rates if collecting the biomarker is intrusive or painful. We may also be under an ethical obligation to treat those we find have serious medical conditions through biomarker testing. Especially given the expense, it is important to assess in advance whether there will be sufficient variation in the biomarker we choose for us to detect differences between treatment and comparison groups. (See Chapter 6 on statistical power.)

Example: Anemia and a decentralized iron fortification program An evaluation in India tested the impact of a program that sought to address anemia by giving a fortified premix to local millers to add to flour when they ground it for local farmers. Blood samples were taken from respondents to test for anemia. However, many respondents refused to have blood samples collected, and there were higher rates of refusal in comparison communities than in treatment communities (where community members felt thankful for the program and were more willing to cooperate with the enumerators). This high and differential rate of attrition made it hard to interpret the results.

For further reading
Banerjee, Abhijit, Esther Duflo, and Rachel Glennerster. 2011. "Is Decentralized Iron Fortification a Feasible Option to Fight Anemia among the Poorest?" In *Explorations in the Economics of Aging*, ed. David A. Wise, 317–344. Chicago: University of Chicago Press.

Example: BMI as a measure of how families invest in girls Researchers tested the impact of sending job recruiters to villages near Delhi to advertise positions in the business outsourcing industry. When families learned about these well-paying jobs for educated young women, they changed how they invested in their daughters. In addition to educational attainment, girls' BMI increased, which was a good indicator that families invested more in the nutrition and/or health of girls.

For further reading
Jensen, Robert. 2012. "Do Labor Market Opportunities Affect Young Women's Work and Family Decisions? Experimental Evidence from India." *Quarterly Journal of Economics* 127 (2): 753–792.

Mechanical tracking devices

Mechanical tracking devices such as cameras or fingerprinting devices can be used to track the attendance of teachers, students, doctors, nurses, or other service providers or to record events or activities. As they have become cheaper and cheaper, mechanical devices have found a lot of use in data collection.

When are these useful? Mechanical devices can overcome problems of distance and timing: a GPS unit can track where someone is on a continual basis without the need for constant observation. For example, a teacher and a principal could easily collude in submitting inaccurate timecards, but an automatic system that relies on a fingerprint to clock the teacher in and out of work prevents corruption.

Limitations Putting a tracking device on someone can alter his behavior, so we need to use tracking devices similarly in the treatment and comparison groups. Moreover, we must understand that the members of our comparison group are not the same as the rest of the population because they know that they are being tracked. Tracking devices can break. If they are intentionally destroyed, breakages may vary by treatment and comparison group.

Example: Measuring road quality with video cameras on cars in Sierra Leone In Sierra Leone researchers studied the impact of a road-building project. To get an objective indicator of road quality and to measure road usage, they mounted video cameras with GPS units on cars. They used the cameras to measure the speed of the car, the width of the road, and how much traffic was on the road.[11]

Spatial demography

GPS readings, satellite images, and other artifacts from spatial geography can be useful in data collection. For example, GPS devices can be used to accurately measure the distance between places (e.g., between a house and its nearest school) or to measure the size of a farm.

When is this useful? Spatial data allow us to make more use of distance in our analysis. For example, we can use distance to predict take-up rates. We can also use spatial data to measure spillovers. For example, we can define villages within a fixed radius of a treatment village as spillover villages and those farther from the treatment villages as pure control villages. Satellite imagery allows us to collect data over much larger areas than would be feasible using survey data.

11. Lorenzo Casaburi, Rachel Glennerster, and Tavneet Suri, "Rural Roads and Intermediated Trade: Regression Discontinuity Evidence from Sierra Leone," 2012, http://ssrn.com/abstract=2161643 or http://dx.doi.org/10.2139/ssrn.2161643.

Limitations When we use distance in our analysis, we are often interested in the travel time between two points. Distance as measured by GPS does not always match travel time—for example, if roads, rivers, or difficult topography connect or separate two locations. GPS information is not always 100 percent accurate because of bad weather during data collection, poor reading of the GPS output by enumerators, or poor-quality machines. Using a GPS device that digitally records the reading (rather than having enumerators write it down) is recommended, but if this is not feasible, enumerators must be thoroughly trained to use the GPS devices appropriately. Satellite imagery is of very mixed quality in different parts of the world, detailed in some (mainly rich countries) and limited in many poor countries. The availability and quality of satellite imagery are improving over time.

Example: Satellite imagery to measure deforestation Research in Indonesia used data from satellite imagery to track changes in deforestation. Researchers constructed a data set that combined satellite imagery with GIS data on district boundaries and land-use classifications. This enabled them to construct a data set that captures deforestation across localities.

For further reading
Burgess, Robin, Matthew Hansen, Benjamin Olken, Peter Potapov, and Stefanie Sieber. 2011. "The Political Economy of Deforestation in the Tropics." NBER Working Paper 17417. National Bureau of Economic Research, Cambridge, MA.

Example: Using GPS to estimate the effect of distance on program take-up An evaluation in Malawi tested how people respond to incentives to learn their HIV status and the impact of distance on take-up of learning one's HIV status. The researcher used GPS data on the location of the study participants in order to group households into zones. Then the location of the temporary HIV test results center was chosen randomly within each zone. This allowed the researcher to see how distance to the center might reduce the probability that people would collect their test results.

For further reading
J-PAL Policy Briefcase. 2011. "Know Your Status?" Abdul Latif Jameel Poverty Action Lab, Cambridge, MA.

Thornton, Rebecca L. 2008. "The Demand for, and Impact of, Learning HIV Status." *American Economic Review* 98 (5): 1829–1863.

Participatory resource appraisals

These appraisals use a number of dynamic approaches to incorporate local knowledge and opinions in the data collection process. They are used, for example, to find out the amount of resources that are available in a village, or to estimate the wealth of a given family, or to decide who is eligible to be a program beneficiary.

When are these useful? A participatory approach is useful when interaction between people can give us more information than asking people questions individually. Each individual person may only know part of the picture, but as they talk they prompt each other, and something one person says reminds another person of more details. This can be useful when we want information from a long time period (e.g., the village's investments in public goods over the past five years), and asking one person at a time may produce less accurate data than asking a group at once.

Limitations One concern with participatory appraisals is that people may not be willing to make certain comments in front of others. In particular, if it is likely that members of the community elite will be present in the group, it may be difficult for nonelite members to criticize them openly. Participants may not be willing to contradict a neighbor or admit that they don't know the answer to a question. Choosing the right group of knowledgeable participants and asking the right questions is important for participatory appraisals to work well.

Example: Recording when and where wells were built and how they were maintained Researchers wanted to test whether quotas for women in local politics affected how public goods were supplied. They wanted to see whether there were more wells or whether existing wells were better or worse maintained in villages where the chief village councilor position had been reserved for a woman. In each village, no single person would know the history of all the wells in the area. However, enumerators could gather a group of informed people from the village and engage them in a conversation about the wells. They drew up maps of the village, and as people shared information on where and when wells were built and when they were repaired, they added that information to the maps. One person might say that the well near the school was dug five years ago, which prompted another to mention that it was actually six years ago, because it was dug before her child left school. This reminds a third person to mention that the well was repaired the previous spring. At the end of the conversation, the enumerators could select some of the villagers for a walkabout to check the accuracy of the recollections of the resources on the map and note the condition of the wells. The key is that interaction between the local people as they prompted and corrected each other helped a much more accurate and comprehensive picture to emerge.

For further reading
Chattopadhyay, Raghabendra, and Esther Duflo. 2004. "Women as Policy Makers: Evidence from a Randomized Policy Experiment in India." *Econometrica* 72 (5): 1409–1443.
J-PAL Policy Briefcase. 2006. "Women as Policymakers." Abdul Latif Jameel Poverty Action Lab, Cambridge, MA. http://www.povertyactionlab.org/ publication/women-policy-makers.
This study is also summarized as Evaluation 12 in the appendix.

Example: Gathering tracking information on program participants An HIV education program in Kenya targeted adolescents in the final years of primary school. The main outcome was a biological proxy for unsafe sexual behavior: the incidence of pregnancy and childbearing among girls. The data were collected during six visits to the schools in the three years following the intervention.

To limit attrition in this extended follow-up, the researchers collected tracking information on program participants by conducting participatory group surveys of students enrolled at each participant's former school. At each visit the list of all participants in the original baseline sample was read aloud to students enrolled in the upper grades. For each participant, a series of questions was asked to prompt conversation about the student: Is she still going to school? If yes, to which [secondary] school, in what grade? Does she still live in the area? Is she married? Is she pregnant? Does she have any children? If yes, how many children does she have? One person might remember that the girl moved to a different area. This reminded another person that when he last saw her, she was pregnant and no longer attending school.

The participatory process connects bits of information that "live" with different people. In this case, the participatory group survey generated very accurate data. In a subsample of 282 teenage girls who were tracked at their homes and interviewed, 88 percent of those who had been reported to have started childbearing had indeed started, and 92 percent of those who had been reported as not having started had not started. The accuracy rates were similar across treatment groups.

For further reading

Duflo, Esther, Pascaline Dupas, and Michael Kremer. 2012. "Education, HIV and Early Fertility: Experimental Evidence from Kenya." Working paper, Massachusetts Institute of Technology, Cambridge, MA.

Dupas, Pascaline. 2011. "Do Teenagers Respond to HIV Risk Information? Evidence from a Field Experiment in Kenya." *American Economic Journal: Applied Economics* 3: 1–34.

J-PAL Policy Briefcase. 2007. "Cheap and Effective Ways to Change Adolescents' Sexual Behavior." Abdul Latif Jameel Poverty Action Lab, Cambridge, MA.

This study is also summarized as Evaluation 4 in the appendix.

Using purchase decisions to reveal preferences

Sometimes difficult-to-observe behavior or preferences can be inferred from how individuals choose to spend money. Although someone may give an inaccurate answer on a survey to please the enumerator, it is likely that when people's own resources are on the line their purchasing decisions will better reflect their true preferences. People may still buy a token amount to please the enumerator, but overall it is likely that when people spend their own money, their purchases reflect their true preferences more closely than does self-reported information in a survey.

When is this useful? Using purchase decisions is useful when we think that there is a strong social desirability bias in people's answers to survey questions about how much they value a good or how often they would buy it. For example, if we ask in a survey how often children in a household get sick from unclean water and then ask people how much they value clean water, they are very likely to overestimate the true value they place on it. Similarly, people may be unwilling to admit that they don't use condoms. Observing purchasing decisions allows us to test for demand at prices that may not exist in the market. If we ask about existing purchases, we find out only about demand and the current price. However, we can manipulate the price to see what people would buy at different prices.

Limitations Although spending real money reduces the risk of social desirability bias, it does not eliminate it. People may well buy a token amount to please the enumerator. It is useful, when possible, to offer larger amounts to distinguish between token purchases and substantial purchase.

Example: Inferring sexual behavior from condom-purchasing behavior A program in Malawi provided free HIV tests in a door-to-door campaign and offered small cash incentives to people to collect their results at temporary mobile voluntary care and testing centers in their community. Later interviewers visited the homes of participants and offered them the chance to buy subsidized condoms. Whether people chose to buy the subsidized condoms revealed the impact that learning their HIV status could have on this proxy for sexual behavior.

For further reading
J-PAL Policy Briefcase. 2011. "Know Your Status?" Abdul Latif Jameel Poverty Action Lab, Cambridge, MA. http://www.povertyactionlab.org/publication/know-your-status.
Thornton, Rebecca L. 2008. "The Demand for, and Impact of, Learning HIV Status." *American Economic Review* 98 (5): 1829–1863.

Example: Learning whether free distribution reduces future purchases of bed nets An evaluation in Kenya tested whether people who had received free bed nets in the past would feel "entitled" to free bed nets indefinitely and thus were less likely to purchase bed nets in the future. In a survey the enumerators could have asked people whether they would purchase a bed net in the future, but the researchers obtained far more reliable data by offering bed nets for sale both to people who had been randomly selected to receive free bed nets in the past and to those who had had to pay for bed nets in the past.

For further reading
Cohen, Jessica, and Pascaline Dupas. 2010. "Free Distribution or Cost-Sharing? Evidence from a Randomized Evaluation Experiment." *Quarterly Journal of Economics* 125 (1): 1–45.
Dupas, Pascaline. 2009. "What Matters (and What Does Not) in Households' Decision to Invest in Malaria Prevention?" *American Economic Review* 99 (2): 224–230.
———. 2012. "Short-Run Subsidies and Long-Run Adoption of New Health Products: Evidence from a Field Experiment." NBER Working Paper 16298. National Bureau of Economic Research, Cambridge, MA.

J-PAL Policy Bulletin. 2011. "The Price Is Wrong." Abdul Latif Jameel Poverty Action Lab, Cambridge, MA. http://www.povertyactionlab.org/publication/the-price-is-wrong
This study is also summarized as Evaluation 6 in the appendix.

Example: Learning about collective action by offering matching funds for community fundraising In an evaluation in Sierra Leone, communities were given vouchers that could be redeemed at a local building supply store if the community also raised its own funding. For approximately every US$2 raised by the community, the voucher would allow the community to receive an additional US$1. Because it was always worthwhile for the community to redeem the vouchers, the number of vouchers redeemed at the store by each community was used as a measure of how well the community was able to coordinate to raise funding for local projects.

For further reading
This study is summarized as Evaluation 15 in the appendix.

Games

Sometimes having the subject play a "game" can measure social qualities such as altruism, trust, and fairness. Normally this is done in a controlled laboratory experiment, with participants' behavior in the game as the outcome of interest. Examples of standard games include the dictator game, which measures altruism, the trust game, and the ultimatum game, which measures fairness or reciprocation.[12]

When are these useful? Games can be useful when we want to test theories of how people will respond to different incentives and scenarios. We can run lots of different scenarios in one day with games. If we tried to run the same range of scenarios in real life, it would take us many years and hundreds of thousands of dollars to run. Games can help us differentiate between different types of people. For example, games can identify people who are risk averse and those who are risk loving.

12. A description of a trust game and an example of how it can be used in a randomized evaluation can be found in Dean Karlan's "Using Experimental Economics to Measure Social Capital and Predict Financial Decisions," *American Economic Review* 95 (December 2005): 1688–1699. A description of the ultimatum and dictator games can be found in Robert Forsythe, Joel Horowitz, N. E. Savin, and Martin Sefton's "Fairness in Simple Bargaining Experiments," *Games and Economic Behavior* 6 (1994): 347–369.

Limitations Unlike most aspects of randomized evaluations, games are not played in the "real world," and thus the findings from them may not be easily generalized to other settings. Participants in games sometimes think they are being judged and play a certain way; for example, they may demonstrate substantial altruism in the hope that this will make them eligible to receive rewards or participate in projects.

Example: Using games to identify attitudes toward risk and impulsiveness An ongoing evaluation in Uganda is measuring the impact of a small grants program on the livelihoods and empowerment of at-risk women. The evaluation will use games to identify specific attitudes and traits in participants to see if the program has a differential impact on people based on these traits. The researchers are trying to assess the role that attitudes toward risk, impulsiveness, altruism, trust, and public mindedness can play in group and poverty dynamics. They are using behavioral games to measure attitudes toward risk, time preferences, in-group trust, honesty, in-group altruism, group coordination, and in-group public goods contributions both before the intervention begins and at the conclusion of the program. The games have three goals: (1) to associate game behavior with individual characteristics (e.g., are wealthier individuals more risk averse?), (2) to correlate game behavior with long-term outcomes (e.g., do more patient individuals benefit the most from business skills?), and (3) to serve as outcome measures themselves (e.g., does group formation increase the level of trust and cooperation?).

For further reading
Annan, Jeannie, Chris Blattman, Eric Green, and Julian Jamison. "Uganda: Enterprises for ultra-poor women after war." Accessed January 2, 2012. http://chrisblattman.com/projects/wings/.

Example: Public goods games to test collective action Researchers conducted a randomized evaluation to test the impact of introducing local democratic governance institutions in northern Liberia. The intervention sought to strengthen the ability of communities to solve collective action problems. Five months after the intervention was completed, the researchers used a communitywide public goods game as a behavioral measure of collective action capacity. They found that treated communities contributed significantly more in the public goods game than did comparison communities. The researchers then used surveys of the game players to try to understand the mechanisms by which the program had affected contributions.

For further reading
Fearon, James, Macartan Humphreys, and Jeremy M. Weinstein. 2009. "Development Assistance, Institution Building, and Social Cohesion after Civil War: Evidence from a Field Experiment in Liberia." CGD Working Paper 194. Center for Global Development, Washington, DC.
————. 2011. "Democratic Institutions and Collective Action Capacity: Results from a Field Experiment in Post-Conflict Liberia." Working paper, Stanford University, Stanford, CA.

Standardized tests

Giving participants a standardized test is a simple way to measure what the participants learned as a result of the program. The most common example is subject tests given to schoolchildren. Tests do not need to be a pen-and-paper test. Sometimes a paper test will measure skills other than the ones that interest us. (For example, we may be interested in measuring problem solving but end up simply measuring literacy.) Visuals, manipulable puzzles, and other devices can enable testing in which language and literacy do not get in the way of our measurement.

When are these useful? These tests are useful when we want to test a large number of people quickly and we are interested in their knowledge of a specific set of topics.

Limitations Test scores are only an intermediate outcome. What we really want to know is whether a program has led to learning that will improve the lives of children later in life. A particular concern is whether the program makes the relationship between test scores and later life outcomes less reliable. For example, if we think that the program makes it more likely that teachers will teach to the test, test scores become a less reliable outcome measure because there is a systematic difference in how well test scores measure learning between the treatment and comparison groups. We may need to see if results persist or administer other tests that are not incentivized to try to measure reliable outcomes in this instance.

Example: Testing basic math and reading skills in India In India, the NGO Pratham administers standardized tests to assess very basic literacy and numeracy skills in children. An evaluation of Pratham's remedial education program used simple tests that were targeted to the actual learning levels of the children to measure whether the program improved learning. The set of tests were designed to pick up different levels of very basic skills, ranging from deciphering letters to reading words to reading a sentence. Had the evaluation used tests designed to measure whether children were meeting grade-level standards (i.e., a third-grade test used for a third-grade child), most of the children would have failed the test. From the standpoint of the evaluation, this would not have been useful for detecting changes in learning levels because the tests used should not be so difficult (or so easy) that most children have similar scores (either acing or failing the tests).

For further reading
Banerjee, Abhijit V., Shawn Cole, Esther Duflo, and Leigh Linden. 2007. "Remedying Education: Evidence from Two Randomized Experiments in India." *Quarterly Journal of Economics* 122 (3): 1235–1264.

J-PAL Policy Briefcase. 2006. "Making Schools Work for Marginalized Children: Evidence from an Inexpensive and Effective Program in India." Abdul Latif Jameel Poverty Action Lab, Cambridge, MA. http://www.poverty actionlab.org/publication/making-schools-work-marginalized-children. This study is also summarized as Evaluation 2 in the appendix.

Using vignettes to assess knowledge

Vignettes are hypothetical scenarios presented to respondents to measure their skills.

When is this useful? Vignettes can give more information than a standardized test by seeing how a respondent analyzes a "real-life" scenario.

Limitations Vignettes do not always tell us what people will do when faced with the same situation in real life; when we use a vignette, they know they are being tested.

Example: Assessing doctors' ability to diagnose common illnesses Clinical vignettes were used to measure the knowledge and competence of doctors in India. Doctors were presented with patients' symptoms and given the opportunity to ask questions about their case histories. The cases included examples such as those of an infant with diarrhea, a pregnant woman with preeclampsia, a man with tuberculosis, and a girl with depression. The doctors were then asked which tests they would prescribe and which treatments they would give. A competence index was constructed based on the questions asked by the doctors and their treatment decisions. Although the test measured how much doctors knew, the authors found that many doctors did better in vignettes than when they faced real patients. The vignettes were useful in pointing out this difference between knowledge and action.

For further reading
Das, Jishnu, and Jeffrey Hammer. 2007. "Location, Location, Location: Residence, Wealth, and the Quality of Medical Care in Delhi, India." *Health Affairs* 26 (3): w338–351.

———. 2007. "Money for Nothing: The Dire Straits of Medical Practice in India." *Journal of Development Economics* 83 (1): 1–36.

Using vignettes and hypothetical scenarios to assess unstated biases

We can create multiple identical vignettes that differ only by the sex or race of the person in the hypothetical scenarios. We can then randomly select which respondents hear which version. If the respondents, on average, rate the vignettes differently based on the race or sex of the person in the scenarios, this is a measure of bias.

When is this useful? Vignettes are useful for measuring unstated or socially undesirable biases and discrimination. They allow the researcher to control exactly what the respondents hear—enabling them to isolate the one difference they want to study.

Limitations This type of vignette is designed to measure the differential response to one very specific attribute, such as gender. This can be an expensive way of measuring one outcome. It is thus most useful when the one outcome is the main focus of the study and when a survey response is likely to be unreliable.

Example: Recorded speeches by male and female leaders in India An evaluation in India measured the effect of quotas for women in local politics. The researchers wanted to measure whether villagers would rate a speech given by a woman lower than an identical speech given by a man. Each respondent heard a short tape-recorded speech in which a leader responded to a villager complaint by requesting that villagers contribute money and effort. Some respondents were randomly selected to hear the speech read by a male voice and others to hear it with a female voice. They were then asked to evaluate the leader's performance and effectiveness.

For further reading
Beaman, Lori, Raghabendra Chattopadhyay, Esther Duflo, Rohini Pande, and Petia Topalova. 2009. "Powerful Women: Does Exposure Reduce Bias?" *Quarterly Journal of Economics* 124 (4): 1497–1539.
Chattopadhyay, Raghabendra, and Esther Duflo. 2004. "Women as Policy Makers: Evidence from a Randomized Policy Experiment in India." *Econometrica* 72 (5): 1409–1443.
J-PAL Policy Briefcase. 2006. "Women as Policymakers." Abdul Latif Jameel Poverty Action Lab, Cambridge, MA. http://www.povertyactionlab.org/publication/women-policy-makers.
———. 2012. "Raising Female Leaders." Abdul Latif Jameel Poverty Action Lab, Cambridge, MA. http://www.povertyactionlab.org/publication/raising-female-leaders.
This study is also summarized as Evaluation 12 in the appendix.

Example: Grading bias by caste in India An evaluation in India tested whether teachers discriminate based on sex or caste when grading exams. The researchers ran an exam competition through which children competed for a large financial prize and recruited teachers to grade the exams. The researchers then randomly assigned child "characteristics" (age, gender, and caste) to the cover sheets of the exams to ensure that there was no systematic relationship between the characteristics observed by the teachers and the quality of the exams. They found that teachers gave exams that were identified as being submitted by lower-caste students scores that were about 0.03–0.09 standard deviations lower than they gave exams that were identified as being submitted by high-caste students.

For further reading
Hanna, Rema, and Leigh Linden. 2009. "Measuring Discrimination in Education." NBER Working Paper 15057. National Bureau of Economic Research, Cambridge, MA.

Implicit association tests (IATs)

An IAT is an experimental method that relies on the idea that respondents who more quickly pair two concepts in a rapid categorization task associate those concepts more strongly.

When are these useful? IATs can measure biases that participants may not want to explicitly state or biases that participants do not even know they hold.

Limitations Although IATs allow researchers to quantify biases, they still provide only approximations. They rely on the assumption that immediate categorization results from a strong association between two concepts and that the strong association results from biases or stereotypes. For example, people may be aware that society reinforces stereotypes and may deliberately try to counter their own stereotypes when they face situations in real life.

Example: IATs to measure biases about female leaders in India An evaluation in India measured whether villagers who had been exposed to female leaders through a quota system had increased or decreased their bias against female leaders. During the IAT, respondents were shown sets of two pictures on the left-hand side of a computer screen and two pictures on the right-hand side. They were shown one of two picture configurations. The "stereotypical" configuration showed a picture of a man next to a picture of a leadership setting (such as a parliament building) on one side and a picture of a woman next to a picture of a domestic setting on the other. In the "nonstereotypical" configuration, the picture of the woman was placed next to the leadership setting and the picture of the man next to the domestic setting. Respondents were then played recordings or shown pictures in the middle of the screen that represented different concepts or activities. These could include things like cooking, washing, mechanics, politics, children, and money. Each respondent would then press a button to indicate whether the concept or activity belonged to the right- or left-hand side of the screen. If a participant more strongly associated leadership with men and domestic skills with women, she would more quickly sort leadership activities to the correct side if that side also had a picture of a man and domestic activities to the correct side if that side also had the picture of the woman. The researchers then calculated the difference in average response times between the stereotypical and nonstereotypical picture configurations as the quantitative measure of bias: the larger the difference in sorting time, the stronger the implicit stereotype.

For further reading
Beaman, Lori, Raghabendra Chattopadhyay, Esther Duflo, Rohini Pande, and Petia Topalova. 2009. "Powerful Women: Does Exposure Reduce Bias?" *Quarterly Journal of Economics* 124 (4): 1497–1539.
Chattopadhyay, Raghabendra, and Esther Duflo. 2004. "Women as Policy Makers: Evidence from a Randomized Policy Experiment in India." *Econometrica* 72 (5): 1409–1443.
J-PAL Policy Briefcase. 2006. "Women as Policymakers." Abdul Latif Jameel Poverty Action Lab, Cambridge, MA. http://www.povertyactionlab.org/publication/women-policy-makers.
———. 2012. "Raising Female Leaders." Abdul Latif Jameel Poverty Action Lab, Cambridge, MA. http://www.povertyactionlab.org/publication/raising-female-leaders.
This study is also summarized as Evaluation 12 in the appendix.

Using list randomization to quantify hidden undesirable behavior

List randomization enables respondents to report on sensitive behavior without allowing the researcher to identify individual responses. Half of the survey respondents are randomly selected to receive a short list of activities; they are asked *how many* of the activities on the list they have engaged in, but they are not asked to report which specific activities. The other half of the survey respondents sees the same list of activities but the key sensitive activity (the one of interest to the researchers) is added. Again, respondents report the number of activities on the list that they have engaged in before. The researchers can then average the number of activities respondents in the two groups have previously engaged in. The difference in the average number of activities of the two groups lets the researchers estimate the proportion of respondents who engage in the sensitive behavior.

When is this useful? List randomization can allow us to estimate how common a sensitive, forbidden, or socially unacceptable activity is. This is especially useful when program beneficiaries may fear that telling the truth may disqualify them from receiving program benefits in the future.

Limitations This technique can supply only aggregate estimates of how common an activity is, not individual-level information.

Example: Estimating how many microfinance clients use business loans for personal consumption Researchers conducting evaluations in the

Philippines and Peru used list randomization to estimate how many microfinance clients used loans that were intended for business investment to pay off other loans or to purchase personal household items. For example, one group was presented with a list of different uses for a loan (such as purchasing merchandise or equipment for a business), and the second group received the same list, plus one more statement such as "I used at least a quarter of my loan on *household items,* such as food, a TV, a radio, et cetera." The difference in the average number of activities people reported engaging in between the two groups let researchers estimate the percentage of people who spent their loans on household items, which was much higher than the percentage of people who self-reported that behavior in surveys.

For further reading
Karlan, Dean, and Jonathan Zinman. 2010. "Expanding Microenterprise Credit Access: Using Randomized Supply Decisions to Estimate the Impacts in Manila." CGD working paper, Center for Global Development, Washington, DC.
———. 2011. "List Randomization for Sensitive Behavior: An Application for Measuring Use of Loan Proceeds." Working paper, Yale University, New Haven, CT.
This study is also summarized as Evaluation 13 in the appendix.

Using data patterns to check for cheating
When people face an incentive or penalty based on data they submit, they may be likely to cheat and falsify the data. Researchers can conduct checks on the data sets to look for certain patterns that indicate cheating. For example, a teacher seeking to boost the test scores of her students may fill in the correct answers to any questions the students left blank when they ran out of time at the end of a section. In the data we would then see a pattern of all correct answers at the ends of test sections.

When is this useful? It is useful to check for cheating by program participants or by the evaluation's enumerators.

Limitations Sometimes patterns may look like cheating and not be. For example, if a class is doing badly on a test and then everyone gets one question at the end right, it may be because of cheating or because the class was taught about that subject very recently and they all remember it. Usually there is no reason to think that these coincidences will be more common in treatment than control groups (or vice versa), but we need to watch out for these possibilities.

Example: Corruption in smog tests in Mexico A study in Mexico tested for corruption in emission checks of cars by running a statistical test for specific patterns in the data of readings from emission checks. In this context, cheating can occur when a customer bribes an emission testing technician to use a clean testing car that has passed the emission test, commonly called a "donor car," to provide the emission readings for the bribing costumer's dirty car. A donor car is needed because emissions cannot be entered manually into the center's computer. The car's information, on the other hand, has to be entered manually into the computer, which allows the technicians to enter the information from a dirty car and match that with emissions from a clean car. When technicians run an emission test multiple times in a row on the same clean car but falsely label those readings as being from dirty cars, the data will reveal a pattern. Consecutive emission readings look similar, despite being labeled as belonging to cars of different years, makes, and models. This can be detected with statistical tests for serial correlation.

For further reading
Oliva, Paulina. 2012. "Environmental Regulations and Corruption: Automobile Emissions in Mexico City." Working paper, University of California, Santa Barbara.

Measuring social interaction and network effects

Collecting rich data on social networks opens a whole set of possibilities for data analysis and research on issues such as peer effects, spillovers, and social diffusion of knowledge. This type of data is typically collected with surveys or participatory appraisals, and it is very important to acquire comprehensive data.

When is this useful? Randomized evaluations are increasingly looking at the question of how technology and information spread within and between communities. Is it possible to train a few people in a community on a new technology or on improved health prevention approaches and have them spread the word to others? How do we identify the relevant people in a community to train or pass information to? In order to answer these questions, we need to collect information on social connections and use this to draw a map of the social networks in the community. From the basic information on whom different individuals know and talk to—about, say, agriculture—we can describe the social network in a given community. Is a community best described as composed of different groups who share information within their respective group but don't share across groups very much? Or are social links much more fluid, with many connections across subgroups? If there are distinct subgroups, who are the connectors: the people who can pass information from one subgroup to another in a community? If we see that a technology initially introduced to one farmer has spread to another farmer, how close was the new adopter to the original adopter? Within the first two years of the introduction of a new technology, did it spread mainly to farmers who were one or two social links away from the original adopter?

Limitations Although it is relatively straightforward to collect basic information about whether someone has lots of friends, it is hard to perform a full-scale social network analysis. If we want to be able to ask how many social links a technology passed through in a given amount of time, we have to have a complete mapping of every social link in the entire community. In other words, we have to ask every single person in the community whom they know and talk to, and we also have to be able to match the information given by one person about her social contacts with the information given by those social contacts. This matching can be difficult and imprecise when a single person may have different names (for example, a formal name and a nickname), when names are misspelled by enumerators, and when many people in the same village have the same name (as is common in many countries).

A further limitation is that even small errors in data collection can sharply undermine the quality of the network description. Usually when we collect data, small errors creep in: people cannot remember exactly how long ago they were sick or how much rice they planted. Errors also arise when data are entered. But these errors usually even out because some people overestimate and some underestimate, with the result that the errors don't affect averages very much. But because everything is connected to everything else in a network, a small data error (such as confusing Mohammed Kanu with Mommed Kanu) can radically change the connection map.

Imagine a village that is socially very divided—by religion, caste, income, or simply by geography. The true social network is described below (Figure 5.3A), with each farmer represented by a dot and a lowercase letter and the lines representing people they talk to about agriculture. For information to pass from a to c it has to go through two connections, from a to b and then from b to c. Now imagine that in collecting our data we made one mistake. Farmer a told us that she talks to b, e, and f about agriculture, but we ended up recording that she talks to b, e, and g about agriculture. Our mistaken view of the network is that described in Figure 5.3B. Although in reality information has to pass through a few central figures, our view of the network dramatically shortens the information links between the two groups. And suddenly farmer b has become an important nodal figure through whom information has to pass, when in fact he does not play this role.

Example: Social networks in Karnataka, India Researchers collected data on social networks in 75 villages of Karnataka, India. A census of households was conducted, and a subset of individuals was asked detailed questions about the relationships they had with others in the village. This information was used to create network graphs for each

A True social network

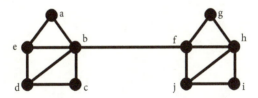

B Recorded social network

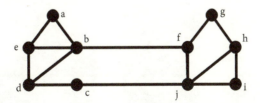

FIGURE 5.3 Social networks

Note: Each dot with a lowercase letter represents a farmer. The lines represent their interactions.

village that could be used to study the diffusion of microfinance throughout the villages.[13] More information about this process, including the original data and a set of research papers that have made us aware of the social networks data, can be found at the MIT Department of Economics website: http://economics.mit.edu/faculty/eduflo/social.

13. Abhijit Banerjee, Arun G. Chandrasekhar, Esther Duflo, and Matthew O. Jackson, "The Diffusion of Microfinance." NBER Research Paper w17743, National Bureau of Economic Research, Cambridge, MA, 2012.

6 Statistical Power

In this chapter we explain what power is, how it is determined, and how we can use power analysis to determine what sample size we need, the level at which to randomize, how many different treatment groups we can test, and many other design issues. It contains the following modules:

MODULE 6.1 The Statistical Background to Power

This module covers the basic statistical concepts we will use in our discussion of power, including sample variation, standard errors, confidence intervals, and hypothesis testing.

We have completed our evaluation of a program designed to improve test scores in a poor community in India. We find that the average score on the test we administer is 44 percent in the treatment group and 38 percent in the comparison group. Can we be reasonably confident that this difference of 6 percentage points is due to the program, or could it be due to chance? We perform a statistical test designed to check whether the difference we observe could be due to chance. We find that the difference between the treatment and comparison groups is not statistically significant, that is, there is a reasonable likelihood that the difference is due to chance. The program was inexpensive, so an improvement of 6 percentage points in test scores would be considered a great success and possibly a target for scale-up and replication, if we could be reasonably confident the difference was due to the program. But we cannot rule out that the difference is due to chance because our evaluation produced a result that was not very precise. A wide range of program impacts are plausible from our results: we can be confident only that the impact of the program was somewhere between –2 and +14 percentage points on the test we administered. Our evaluation was not designed well enough to avoid such a wide range of plausible values. It did not have enough statistical power.

Statistical power can be thought of as a measure of the sensitivity of an experiment (we provide a formal definition at the end of this module). Understanding power and doing power analysis is useful because it helps us decide whether to randomize at the individual or the group level, how many units (schools, communities, or clinics) to randomize, how many individuals to survey, how many times to survey each individual over the course of the evaluation, how many different program alternatives to test, and what indicators to use to measure our outcomes. It helps us design more sensitive evaluations.

Before we formally define power and discuss what determines it, we need to go over some of the basic statistical concepts that we will need to determine the power of an evaluation, in particular sampling variation, standard errors, critical values, and hypothesis testing.[1]

Sampling variation

When we want to measure characteristics of a population, we usually do not collect data on everyone in the population. We can get a pretty accurate picture of what the population looks like by taking a random sample and collecting data on that sample. For example, if we want to know the average test score of a third grader in Mumbai, we do not have to test every child in the city. We can take a random sample of children and assume that they will be representative of the total population of third graders in Mumbai.

---

1. A more thorough but still accessible introduction to the statistical concepts discussed here is given by William Greene in *Econometric Analysis* (New Jersey: Prentice-Hall, 2011).

But how many children should we test? And how accurate will our estimate of learning be? Imagine we choose a random sample of 200 children from across Mumbai to test. There is some chance that we will include some very high-scoring children and very few low-scoring children. We will then overestimate the true level of learning. There is also a chance that we will pick particularly poorly performing children and underestimate the true level of learning. Because we are selecting our sample at random, the chance of underestimating should be the same as the chance of overestimating the true level of learning, but that does not mean that we are guaranteed to get exactly the true learning level if we take a sample of 200 children. We will get an *estimate* of the true mean level of learning in Mumbai (the population mean) by taking the mean of learning in our sample (the sample mean). If we take a sample multiple times, we will get a slightly different estimate each time. If we do this and plot the frequency of the number of times we get different estimates, we will end up with something like Figure 6.1.

The sampling variation is the variation between these different estimates that we get because we are testing only a small proportion of the total population. There are other possible sources of variation between our estimate of the mean and the true mean in the population. For example, our test might not be administered correctly and give us a bad measure of learning. But in this chapter and when we perform power analysis, we are concerned only about sampling variation.

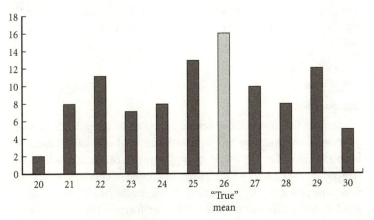

FIGURE 6.1 Frequency of 100 estimates of average learning levels in Mumbai

The extent to which our estimates will vary depending on whom we draw in a particular sample, and thus how confident we can be that our estimated mean is close to the true mean, depends on the variation in test scores in the population as a whole and on how many people we sample. The more people we sample, the more likely that our estimated (sample) average will be close to the true (population) average. In the extreme, if we sample everyone in the population, the sample mean and the population mean will be identical and there will be no sampling variation. In the example below we assume that the sample is small relative to the full population.

The more dispersed the scores are in the population, the more likely that we will include in our sample a child who is far from the mean. Therefore, the less dispersed the sample, the fewer people we have to sample to be confident our estimate is close to the true mean. In the extreme, if everyone in the sample were identical (there was zero variance in the population), we would have to sample only one person to know the true mean.

Standard deviation

A useful measure of the extent of dispersion in the underlying population is the *standard deviation, sd.* To calculate a standard deviation of test scores, we take every third grader in Mumbai, calculate the mean test score for the whole sample, and then for each child calculate the difference between that child's test score and the sample mean and square this difference. Then we add up all the squared differences and divide by the number of children in Mumbai. Finally we take the square root. The algebraic formula for a standard deviation is given as

$$sd = \sqrt{\frac{\sum_{i=1}^{n}(x_i - \bar{x})^2}{n}}.$$

Standard error

Remember that if we take a sample of 200 children and calculate our estimate many times we will get a distribution of estimated means. We have said that the dispersion of our estimate of the true mean will depend on two things—the size of the sample of children we test and their dispersion in the test scores of the underlying population. We need to make this relationship a bit more formal. The *standard error* (*se*) measures the standard deviation of our estimate. But we don't usually take many estimates and so can't calculate the standard deviation of the estimates as we did when we calculated the standard deviation of the test scores of children. But if we know the dispersion of the test scores of children themselves, we can use this to calculate the likely dispersion of the estimates. Specifically, the standard error of the estimate is equal to the standard deviation of the population divided by the square root of the sample size:[2-4]

$$se = sd/\sqrt{n}.$$

Central limit theorem

Under certain assumptions (which hold in most of the situations we deal with in this book), the central limit theorem applies.[5] This theorem states that the distribution of the estimated means is close to normal as long as our estimate is based on a large enough sample. A normal distribution is a bell-shaped curve with a particular shape in which approximately 68 percent of all estimates will be within 1 SD of the mean. This is true even if the underlying distribution is not normal. This is important because many of the variables we will use will not be normally distributed. For example, because test scores usually cannot go below zero, we may have a cluster of scores and zero, and the distribution of scores may not be symmetrical around the mean. That our estimate is normally distributed is very useful because if we know the standard deviation of a normal distribution, we know the percentage of times an estimate will fall any distance away from the mean. For example, in a normal distribution we know that approximately 68 percent of all the estimates will be within one standard deviation of the true value and that approximately 95 percent of all estimates will be within two standard deviations of the true value. The standard deviation of the distribution of estimates of the mean is the

2. Technically this holds true when we are sampling a small proportion of the population. Remember that if we sample the whole population we don't have any sampling error and the standard error is zero.

3. For a detailed algebraic derivation of the standard error of an estimate, see John A. Rice, *Mathematical Statistics and Data Analysis* (Belmont, CA: Wadsworth and Brooks, 1988), 182–184.

4. We don't actually observe the standard deviation of the population, so we usually estimate this using the standard deviation of the sample.

5. A key assumption for the central limit theorem to hold is that the population has a mean and a variance, which is true if the population is finite. A formal exposition of the central limit theorem and a discussion of its practical applications can be found in Rice, *Mathematical Statistics and Data Analysis*, 161–163.

standard error; this means that there is a 95 percent chance that our estimate of the population mean will be within two standard deviations of the true mean.[6]

Confidence interval

When we calculate an estimated mean we get a single number, sometimes called a single point estimate. But we know that there is some uncertainty around this estimate. A *confidence interval* is a range of estimates around a single point estimate. When poll results are reported in the run-up to an election, they are reported with a margin of error, reflecting this uncertainty. For example, we might hear that support for a given candidate is 45 percent ± 3 percent. In other words, the confidence interval is between 42 and 48 percent.

Confidence level

A confidence level will often be reported alongside the confidence interval and the point estimate. A 95 percent confidence level means that if we constructed 100 confidence intervals we would expect 95 of them to contain our parameter.

Hypothesis testing

Measuring differences in averages

Until now we have been drawing just one sample from a population and asking whether our estimate (the average of that sample) is close to the true average of the population. But when we perform a randomized evaluation we are drawing two samples and comparing them to each other. Instead of being interested in estimating the mean of one population, we are interested in estimating the difference between a large hypothetical population that is treated and a population that is untreated.[7] We can estimate this by comparing a randomly chosen sample that is treated and a randomly chosen sample that is not.

6. Unfortunately we never observe the true SD (unless we measure the entire population). We therefore use the SD in our sample as an estimate of the SD in our population. However, this adds another layer of uncertainty to our estimate that we need to account for. Using the t-distribution allows us to account for this additional uncertainty. The t-distribution is similar to the normal distribution except that it has fatter tails (in other words, it has a larger number of more extreme values) than the normal distribution and it follows a different distribution depending on the size of the sample. With large sample sizes the t-distribution approximates the normal distribution.

7. We say hypothetical here because our statistical tests assume that we are testing two small random samples from two large populations, one that received the program

To tell whether the program affects test scores, we want to see whether the mean of the treatment sample is different from the mean of the comparison sample; in other words, our estimate of interest is now the difference between the two samples. Fortunately, just as the average of a random variable has a distribution that approaches normal, so does the difference between two averages. In other words the distribution of our estimate will asymptotically approach a normal distribution—that is, it will approach a normal distribution as we run our experiment thousands of times. We can still calculate the standard error of the estimate in the same way and our standard error can give us a confidence interval around our estimate.

The null hypothesis and the research hypothesis

When we estimate the impact of our education program in Mumbai we start with a hypothesis. Our hypothesis is that the program increases test scores and therefore that the average test score of the group exposed to the program is higher than that of the group not exposed to the program:

Hypothesis: Remedial education led to higher test scores.

By convention, every study proposes two hypotheses, the null hypothesis and the research (or alternative) hypothesis. The *null hypothesis* states that the treatment effect is zero, in other words, that the test scores of those exposed and not exposed to the program are the same. The null hypothesis is conventionally denoted H_0:

H_0: Treatment effect = 0.

We sample a subset of the population and expose it to the program while not exposing another subsample. Given that these samples are chosen at random from the same population, without the program these two groups would, on average, have the same test scores. The null hypothesis states that we do not expect any difference between the treatment and comparison groups. Of course, even if the null

---

and one that didn't. Sometime this is the case. For example, when we randomize at the group level we often test only a small proportion of those who receive the program. In individual-level randomization, however, we often test everyone who received the program. In this case we think of our treatment group as a sample of what we would have seen if we had treated a much larger group of individuals.

hypothesis is true, we can find that in a particular sample the mean test score is 44 percent and in another sample it is 38 percent. The null hypothesis is not inconsistent with an observed difference of (say) 6 percentage points between the two samples; it says that this difference is due to chance (as a result of sampling variability) and that if the program were scaled up it would not affect the average test scores of the population of Mumbai students.

The *research hypothesis* says that the treatment effect is not zero. It is also called the alternative hypothesis and is designated H_1:

H_1: Treatment effect $\neq$ 0.

This states that the means of the underlying populations from which the two samples were drawn are not the same. This is the most common form, but the research hypothesis can be more elaborate and say something about the direction of the underlying difference—that one mean is smaller or larger than the other:

H_1: Treatment effect > 0, or else H_1: Treatment effect < 0.

Irrespective of the form it takes, the research hypothesis is the logical opposite of the null hypothesis. (Note that if our research hypothesis is that the program has a positive effect, the null hypothesis is the logical opposite, that is, that the difference is zero or less than zero. Traditionally, we stick to a null hypothesis of zero effect and a research hypothesis of an effect that could be positive or negative, because we want to be able to test whether the program does harm.)

The practice in hypothesis testing is not to test our main hypothesis directly but instead to test its logical opposite. Because the two hypotheses are logical opposites, they cover all the possible inferences that we can reach in a statistical test. So we *test the null hypothesis*. A key notion related to this type of test is that of the "p-value," which is the probability of obtaining outcomes such as those produced by the experiment had the null hypothesis been true. A p-value of below 0.05 implies that there is only a 5 percent chance or less that an outcome was generated under the null hypothesis. This suggests that we should reject the null hypothesis. If we "reject" the null hypothesis of zero effect, we conclude that the program had an effect. We say that the result is "significantly different from zero." If we "fail to reject" the null hypothesis, we need to ask ourselves. "Is it really true that there is zero effect, or is it simply that our experiment does not have enough statistical power to detect the true effect?"

Statistical inference and statistical power

The program is hypothesized to change the outcome variable (test scores). There is an underlying truth, that the program either would or would not change test scores in the population of students in Mumbai. But we never observe the underlying truth; we observe only the data from our samples. We test whether the means of treatment and comparison samples are statistically different from each other. (In Chapter 8 we go over in detail how we test whether the treatment and comparison samples are different from each other.) But we must remember that statistical tests are not infallible. They only ever give us probabilities because of sampling variation.

The four possible cases

Both the statistical test and the underlying reality have an either/or quality. For the statistical test, either the difference is significant (we reject the null hypothesis) or the difference is not significant (we fail to reject the null hypothesis). For the underlying reality, either there is a treatment effect or there is no treatment effect. This makes four cases possible (Figure 6.2).

1. *False positive* We have a *false positive* when we find a statistically significant effect even though the program did not actually have a treatment effect. We wrongly infer that the program had an effect. (We reject the null hypothesis when in fact the null hypothesis is true.)

If the program has no effect, the probability of making a false positive error—also called a Type I or alpha error—is called the significance level and denoted α. The convention is that it should be no larger than 5 percent. This says that if the treatment effect is zero—if the null hypothesis is true—the probability that the observed difference is due to chance alone is 5 percent or less. In other words, we have a 5 percent rate of false positives.

2. *True zero* We have a *true zero* when we find no statistically significant effect and there truly is no treatment effect. We correctly fail to reject the null hypothesis and infer that the program does not work.

The probability that we do not find a statistically significant effect if the treatment effect is zero is called the confidence level. It is the com-

The underlying truth:
Is there a treatment effect?

Statistical test: Is the observed difference statistically significant?	Treatment effect (H_0 false)	No treatment effect (H_0 true)
Significant (Reject H_0)	True positive Probability = $1 - \kappa$	False positive Probability = α Type 1 error
Not significant (Fail to reject H_0)	False zero Probability = κ Type II error	True zero Probability = $(1 - \alpha)$

In reality, one thing is true. Either there was a treatment effect or there was no treatment effect. But when we combine the possibility of two underlying realities with two possible outcomes from our statistical tests, there are four possible cases we could face with given probabilities: (1) false positive with probability α; (2) true zero with probability $(1 - \alpha)$; (3) false zero with probability κ; and (4) true positive with probability $(1 - \kappa)$. Power is the probability of attaining a true positive. It is the probability that we will detect a treatment effect when there is one.

FIGURE 6.2 Four possible cases, only one of which is true

plement of the significance level. In other words, it is equal to $(1 - \alpha)$. Testing at the 5 percent level, then, gives a confidence level of 95 percent, which says that if the true effect is zero there is a 95 percent probability that we will fail to reject the null hypothesis.

3. *False zero* We have a *false zero* when we do not find a significant treatment effect (fail to reject the null hypothesis) even though there truly is a treatment effect. We wrongly infer that the program does not affect test scores.

The probability of making a false zero error—also called a Type II error—is denoted here as κ. Some people use a rule of thumb that studies should be designed to have a κ of 20 percent or less. κ can be defined only in relation to a given treatment effect. In other words, a κ of 20 percent means that if the true treatment effect is of a given level, there is a 20 percent chance of failing to find a significant effect. The level of the treatment effect that we want to design our study to be able to distinguish from zero is a whole separate topic that we cover in great detail in the next module.

Power is the probability that we will not make a Type II error. In other words, it is the probability that (if the true effect is of a given size) we will find an effect that is statistically different from zero. Power is therefore shown as $(1 - \kappa)$. If we aim for a κ of 20 percent, we are aiming for 80 percent power.

4. *True positive* We have a *true positive* when we find a statistically significant effect (reject the null hypothesis) and there truly is a treatment effect. We correctly infer that the program works.

The probability of finding a true positive when there really is an effect of a given size is $(1 - \kappa)$. This probability is our statistical power. If the probability of detecting a significant effect (when there is one) is 80 percent, we say that we have 80 percent power.

What level of certainty do we need?

By convention, the significance level—the chance of finding a false positive—is set at just 5 percent.[8] At this low probability, if there is no treatment effect, we are highly unlikely to conclude that there is one.

8. See, for example, Howard S. Bloom, *Learning More from Social Experiments* (New York: Russell Sage Foundation, 2005), 129, as well as the discussion in Alan Agresti and Barbara Finlay, *Statistical Methods for the Social Sciences* (New York: Prentice-Hall, 1997), 173–180.

Usually the chance of a false negative (failing to reject the null hypothesis when the truth is that the program had an effect of a given size) is set at 20 percent (or sometimes 10 percent). Typically we worry more about false positives than about false negatives. If we set the chance of a false negative (for a given effect size) at 20 percent, we are saying that we want 80 percent power, that is, we want an 80 percent chance that (for a given effect size) we will find a statistically significant effect.

Module 6.1 summary

Statistical background to power

- Sampling variation is the variation in our estimate due to the fact that we do not sample everyone in the population: sampling variation is the reason we do power calculations.

- Standard deviation is a measure of the dispersion of the underlying population.

- Standard error is the standard deviation of our estimate and is related to the size of our sample and the standard deviation of the underlying population.

- A confidence interval gives a range of values around a given estimate.

- Statistical significance uses standard errors to say whether we can be confident that the true estimate is different from a given value: for example, whether we can be confident that the estimate is not zero.

Hypothesis testing

- The null hypothesis is the opposite of our research hypothesis: if our research hypothesis is that we expect the treatment group to have different outcomes from the comparison group, the null hypothesis says that there is no difference between the two groups.

- Traditionally we test the null hypothesis, not the research hypothesis.

- Type I error is rejection of the null hypothesis when in fact it is true (false positive).

- The significance level (traditionally 5 percent) is the chance we are willing to take that Type I errors will occur.

- Type II error is failure to reject the null hypothesis when in fact there is a difference between the treatment and comparison groups (false negative).

- Power measures the probability that we will avoid Type II errors, and we conventionally design experiments with 80 percent or 90 percent power.

MODULE 6.2 The Determinants of Power Explained Graphically

This module explains which factors determine the power of an experiment and how different features of the evaluation design and analysis can affect power. In this module we show graphically and intuitively how power is related to its key components. In the next module we provide a more formal, algebraic explanation of power determinants.

At the end of the previous module we defined power as the probability that (if the true effect of a program is of a given size) we will find a statistically significant effect. To understand the determinants of power we need to return to the issue of sampling variation (discussed in the previous module), in particular the question of how we can tell whether a difference between our treatment and comparison groups is due to chance. In other words, could the difference we see between treatment and comparison groups be due to the fact that we happened to sample individuals with slightly different characteristics in our treatment and comparison groups?

Figure 6.3 is a frequency chart with the results from one randomized evaluation of an education program in India. It shows the number of children who achieved different test scores in both the treatment and the comparison groups on the same chart. It also shows the estimated means for the treatment and comparison groups.

We can see that the mean of the treatment group is slightly higher than the mean of the control group. But is the difference statistically significant? To find this out we must examine how accurate our estimate of the difference is. Accuracy in this case means how likely our estimate is to be close to the true difference.

If we run a perfectly designed and executed experiment an infinite number of times, we will find the *true difference*. Each time we run the experiment, we will get a slightly different estimate of the difference

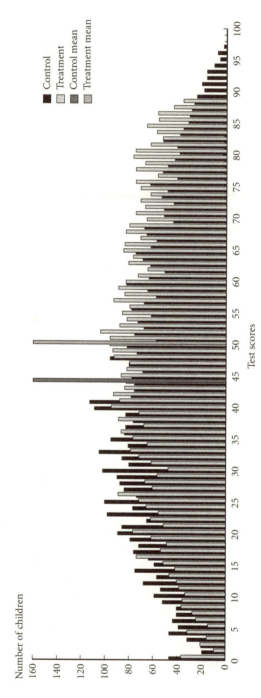

FIGURE 6.3 Test scores of treatment and comparison groups in an educational program

between the treatment and comparison groups and thus of the impact of the program. One time we run the evaluation we might by chance get most of the really motivated children in the treatment group and thus overestimate the impact of the program because these children would have improved their test scores a lot even without the program. Another time we run it, the motivated children might be mostly in the comparison group and we will underestimate the true impact of the program. Because we are running a randomized evaluation and therefore have no selection bias, the average of all our estimated program impacts, if we run the evaluation many times, will be the same as the true impact. But we cannot guarantee that every individual evaluation will give us exactly the same impact as the true impact. Sometimes, by chance, we will get an estimated difference that is much higher or lower than the true difference.

If the true difference (the true effect size) is zero, a very large number of experiments will generate a bell-shaped curve of estimated effect sizes centered on zero (H_0). In other words, the most common result of the many experiments we run will be a difference near zero. But the tails of the bell curve show the number of times we will get an estimated effect that is far from zero.

It is useful to introduce a little bit of notation here. Let us use β to represent the true effect size. If we hypothesize that the true effect is zero, we say that we assume that $\beta = 0$. What if the true effect size is β^*, that is, what if $\beta = \beta^*$? Then running a very large number of experiments will result in a bell-shaped curve of estimated effect sizes centered on β^* (Figure 6.4).

In this example there is considerable overlap between the curves for $\beta = 0$ and $\beta = \beta^*$. This means that it is going to be hard to distinguish between these two hypotheses. Imagine that we run an evaluation and get an estimated effect size of $\hat{\beta}$. This effect size is consistent both with the true effect size's being β^* and with the true effect size's being zero. The heights of points A and A′ show the frequency with which we would get an estimated effect size of $\hat{\beta}$ if the true effect size was β^* or zero, respectively. A is higher than A′, so it is more likely that β^* is greater than zero, but there is still a reasonable probability that the true effect size is zero. The more the curves overlap, the more likely we are to get a result that could come from either hypothesis and thus the less likely we are to be able to tell whether there was an effect. If there are lots of estimated effects that have a reasonable prob-

Frequency of estimate

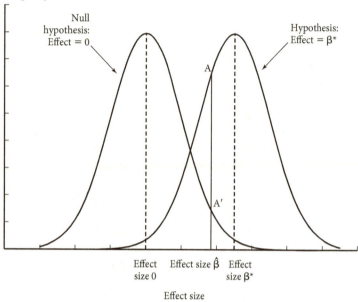

FIGURE 6.4 Frequency of estimated effect sizes from running multiple experiments under both the hypothesis $\beta = 0$ and the hypothesis $\beta = \beta^*$

ability of being generated by the null hypothesis or by the $\beta = \beta^*$ hypothesis, we have low power.

We will always have to live with some overlap between our two bell curves because there is always a small chance of an estimated difference that is far from the true difference. How much overlap are we willing to live with? As discussed in Module 6.1, traditionally we are willing to reject the null hypothesis if there is only a 5 percent chance that it is true. This occurs if the estimated treatment effect falls in the thin tails of the distribution of likely effect sizes under the null hypothesis, above (or below) the 95 percent significance level. The value of the estimated treatment effect that exactly corresponds to the 95 percent significance level is called the *critical value*—anything above this is statistically significantly different from zero, while anything below it is not. This 95 percent critical value is shown in Figure 6.5. We can see that, in the example drawn here, the bulk of the mass of the research hypothesis curve (on the right) is above the critical value of 95 percent for the null hypothesis curve. This means that we are likely

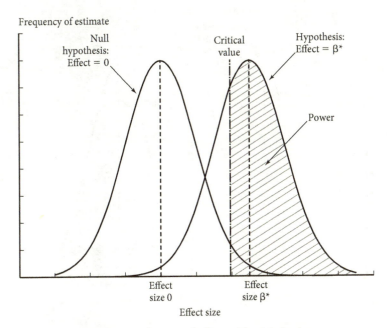

Frequency of estimate

Null hypothesis: Effect = 0

Critical value

Hypothesis: Effect = β*

Power

Effect size 0

Effect size β*

Effect size

FIGURE 6.5 Distribution of estimated effects with critical value

to find a significant effect if there truly is one of the anticipated size. What is the precise chance that we will be able to reject the null hypothesis if the true effect is β*? This is given by the percentage of the research hypothesis curve that is above the critical value for the null hypothesis. In Figure 6.5, this is the percentage of the total area under the research hypothesis curve that is shaded. This percentage is the definition of the power of the experiment. In Figure 6.5, 70.5 percent of the area under the curve is shaded, meaning that there is 70.5 percent power.

Figure 6.5 shows a *one-sided test*; in other words, it tests whether the program has a positive effect. This test is based on our assuming that a negative effect is not possible. Normally we do not want to impose this assumption, so we test the null hypothesis of no effect against the research hypothesis of either a positive or a negative effect. Although there is usually no strong reason that the positive minimum detectable effect (MDE) size should be the same as the negative MDE, we test symmetrically. In other words, the symmetry of the normal distribution implies that if we want to be able to pick up a positive

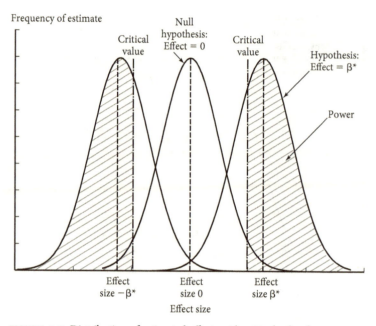

Frequency of estimate

Critical value

Null hypothesis: Effect = 0

Critical value

Hypothesis: Effect = β*

Power

Effect size −β*

Effect size 0

Effect size β*

Effect size

FIGURE 6.6 Distribution of estimated effects with critical value for a two-sided test

effect of magnitude β (with 80 percent power) we should use a two-sided test, which also has 80 percent power to pick up an effect size of −β with 80 percent power. Note, however, that the MDE is always just a point on a continuum; in other words, if we do this we will have some power to pick up a less negative effect than −β. We will have more than 80 percent power to pick up an effect that is more negative than −β. This is shown in Figure 6.6. For the rest of this section, however, we show only a positive research hypothesis in our graphs because it makes the figures easier to follow.

Minimum detectable effect size and power

In Figure 6.7 we can see that power is greater and the overlap between the curves is smaller the farther the two curves are away from each other (i.e., the greater the true effect size). In the case shown here, the true effect size is twice what it is in Figure 6.4 and power is 99.9 percent.

So power is related to the true effect size, but we never know what the true effect size is. We are running the experiment to estimate it. So

Frequency of estimate

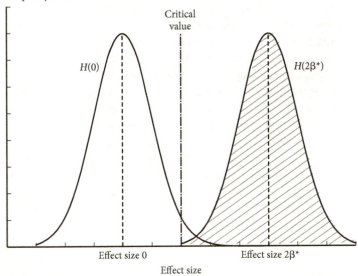

FIGURE 6.7 Distribution of estimated effects with a doubled effect size

how do we calculate power? The answer is that we draw up hypotheses. We say, "What would be the power if the true effect was β^* or $2\beta^*$?" What a power calculation can answer is "What chance do we have of finding a statistically significant effect if the true effect size is β^*?" Or "Given this sample size, what is the minimum level of true effect at which we would have enough power to reject the null hypothesis using a 95 percent significance cutoff?" This hypothesized β is our MDE (see Module 6.1). Choosing the right MDE is a critical part of power analysis, and in the next module we discuss how to choose one in more detail.

Residual variance and power

The hypothesized effect size determines how far apart the two bell curves are. But what influences the shapes of our bell curves of estimated effect size? The width of the bell curves reflects the variance in our estimate of the difference. As we discussed in Module 6.1, variance in our estimate comes from sampling variance; in other words, it comes from the fact that we are testing only a sample of the population, and we may by chance choose people with different outcomes for our treatment group and our comparison group. The greater the variance in the underlying population, the greater our sampling variance will be (for a given sample size). In the extreme case, if all the children in the population had identical test scores, every time we drew a sample of them we would get the true value of test scores in our population, and we would know that any difference we saw between the treatment and comparison groups was due to the program and not to sampling variation. The larger the sample size, the lower the variance in our estimate (i.e., the narrower our bell curves).

Some of the differences in test scores between children will be correlated with observable factors such as age or parental education. If we include age and parental education as "control variables" in our final analysis, we sharply reduce the likelihood that we will misestimate the true effect if, by chance, we have more children with highly educated parents in our comparison group than in our treatment group. The most important control variable to include is usually the baseline level of our final outcome variable. Our estimate of the effect size is more precise, our bell curve is narrower, and our power is higher. Thus our power depends on the residual variance after we have controlled for other available variables. Residual variance depends on the underlying variance of the population and the extent to which this variance can be explained by observable factors for which we have data that we intend to use as controls in the final analysis. In the equations that follow (Module 6.3) we denote residual variance as σ^2.

In the case study at the end of this chapter we show just how important control variables can be for power. For example, including baseline test scores in an education program designed to improve test scores can reduce residual variance by up to 50 percent, allowing for a sharp reduction in sample size for a given power.

When we are performing a group-level randomization, the variance of our estimate of the effect will depend on a few other factors. We discuss these when we discuss power for group-level randomization below.

Sample size and power

The sample size of the experiment will also affect the width of the bell curves. The larger the sample, the more accurate the estimated difference will be and thus the narrower the bell curves. Figure 6.8 shows how in the remedial education example above, the shape of the bell curve of estimated effect size changes as the sample size increases. The

A

Frequency of estimate

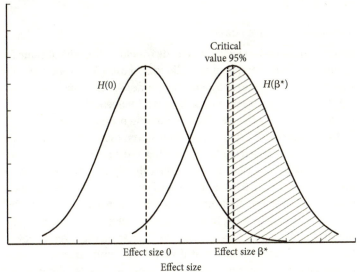

Critical
value 95%

$H(0)$

$H(\beta^*)$

Effect size 0

Effect size β^*

Effect size

B

Frequency of estimate

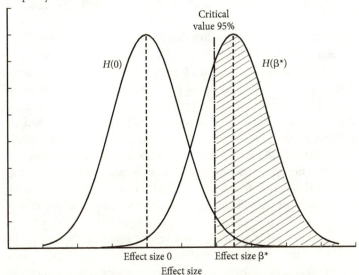

Critical
value 95%

$H(0)$

$H(\beta^*)$

Effect size 0

Effect size β^*

Effect size

FIGURE 6.8 Distribution of estimated effects with a small sample size (A) and with a large sample size (B)

larger the sample, the more accurate our estimate, which we can see in the narrower bell curve and higher power. We denote sample size as N.

Significance level and power

Power also depends on what we decide should be the critical value for significance. For example, it is traditional to use a 5 percent cutoff for statistical significance. A 5 percent significance level means that we reject the null hypothesis only if there is a 5 percent chance or less that the result is due to chance. There is nothing magical about 5 percent, and some academic papers show results even though they are significant at only the 10 percent level (showing a 10 percent probability that the result is due to chance). Loosening the significance level moves the threshold to the left (as shown in Figure 6.9). This increases the shaded area to the right of the critical value, increases the chance that we will reject the null hypothesis (i.e., we will find a statistically significant difference if there is one), and increases the level of power. However, we should realize that if we loosen significance to increase power (and therefore reduce the likelihood of Type II false zeros) it comes at the cost of increasing the chance of false positives. In the power equation, the critical value is denoted as α and the proportion of the curve to the left of the critical value is given by t_α. We show how the critical value changes with α in Figure 6.9.

It may seem counterintuitive that moving from a 5 percent to a 10 percent cutoff level for significance increases power, so let us use an analogy. Imagine that we are the jury in a murder trial and we have to decide whether Xi is guilty or not guilty of poisoning Yi based on evidence presented in court. The prosecution submits 20 pieces of evidence. Because not one of us on the jury was present when the poisoning took place, there is always a chance that we could reach the wrong verdict, either saying that Xi is not guilty when he really did poison Yi or saying that he is guilty when he really is innocent. Recognizing this, we decide to set a standard for how stringent we should be. We say that we will convict Xi only when the probability that we could be wrong is 5 percent or less; if it's any higher we will say that he is not guilty. That is, each of us will vote to convict only if we find at least 19 of the 20 pieces of evidence put forward convincing and at most 1 of them unconvincing. If 2 are unconvincing, we vote not guilty. At the 10 percent level, we will need at least 18 convincing pieces of

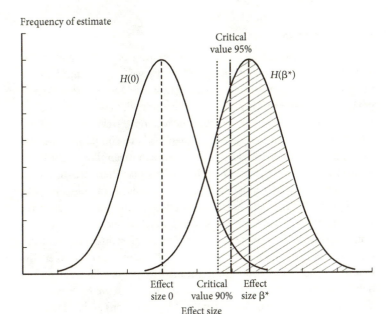

Frequency of estimate

Critical
value 95%

$H(0)$

$H(\beta^*)$

Effect
size 0

Critical
value 90%

Effect
size β^*

Effect size

FIGURE 6.9 Distribution of estimated effects with two thresholds for the critical value

evidence and allow for two unconvincing pieces. We will vote not guilty if 3 are unconvincing. Power is the probability that we will find Xi guilty when he really did commit the murder. We are more likely to find him guilty the more pieces of unconvincing evidence we choose to ignore. At the 5 percent level, we will find him guilty even if one piece of evidence is unconvincing, but at the 10 percent level we will do so if 2 pieces are, at the 30 percent level if 6 pieces are, and so on. The less stringent we are, the more likely we are to convict Xi when he is guilty but also when he is not guilty.

The point to realize is that significance is not so much about the underlying truth, which we cannot know, as about how high we set the standard for conviction. If the standard is low, we are more likely to convict when the defendant is truly guilty (we find an effect when there truly is one); we have more power. But we are also more likely to convict when he is not guilty (we find an effect when there is not truly an effect). This means there is a trade-off, and increasing the significance threshold to increase power is not a panacea.

Allocation ratio and power

Another determinant of power is the fraction of the sample that is allocated to the treatment group. Normally we assume that half the sample will be allocated to the treatment group and half to the comparison group, but this is not necessarily optimal, as we discuss below.

Why does the allocation fraction impact our level of power? If we allocate more of the sample to treatment than to comparison we will have a more accurate measure of the treatment mean than of the comparison mean. Usually this is inefficient, because there are diminishing returns to adding more sample size: increasing sample size from 10 people to 20 improves our accuracy a lot, but increasing our sample size from 1,010 to 1,020 does not make much difference. Each additional person we add makes a smaller and smaller difference in accuracy. So, all else equal, our estimate of the difference between the treatment and comparison group means is maximized if we allocated half the sample to treatment and half to control. If we have two randomization cells (one treatment and one comparison) and P is the proportion of the sample allocated to treatment, we achieve the highest power when $P = 0.5$. There are exceptions in which it is useful to create unequally sized groups; we discuss these later in this chapter.

Power with clustering

Until now we have assumed that we randomly assign individuals to either a treatment or a comparison group. But sometimes we randomize at the level of the school, clinic, or community rather than at the level of the individual. In our remedial education example, rather than randomly picking children to be part of the program, we may choose 50 schools to be part of the program and then randomly select 20 children per school to interview. What does this do to our power calculations? Randomizing at the group level reduces power for a given sample size because outcomes tend to be correlated within a group. The more correlated people are within a group, the more that randomizing at the group level reduces our power.

For example, in Sierra Leone the Agricultural Household Tracking Survey (AHTS) was designed to estimate, among other things, how much rice the average farmer grew in the past year.[9] If we had ran-

9. Results from the Government of Sierra Leone's Agriculture Household Tracking Survey can be found at Harvard's dataverse website: http://dvn.iq.harvard.edu/dvn/.

domly picked 9,000 farmers from across the country, we would have gotten a pretty accurate estimate of rice production by smallholder farmers in Sierra Leone. We might have been tempted, for logistical reasons, to randomly pick three districts and survey 3,000 farmers from each of these three districts. But this would have given us a much less accurate picture of rice production for two reasons. Some districts (such as Koinadugu) tend to grow less rice than the other parts of the country because the land and climate there are suitable for livestock. In the year in which the AHTS was conducted, the district of Bonthe in the south was hit by a damaging flood, which suppressed the rice harvest. In other words, both long-run conditions and short-run shocks meant that rice production levels were correlated within the district. This within-district correlation made an estimate of the average harvest that was based on collecting data from a few districts much less precise for a given sample size.

The same problem occurs when we are trying to estimate the impact of a program, in this case a program to promote increased rice production. In the extreme, if we randomize one village to receive the program and one to be the comparison group, we will never be able to distinguish whether any difference we find is due to village-level factors including weather shocks or to the program. Even if we survey 100 farmers in each village, we cannot isolate the village-level shocks from the program effect. It is almost as if we had a sample of 2, not 200.

So we have to randomize over many villages, some treatment and some comparison. But how many villages do we need, and how does that number change with the number of farmers per village whom we survey? Let us think back to our power-calculation bell curves, which represent the probability of finding different effect sizes if we run the same experiment multiple times. If we randomize 600 individual farmers into treatment and comparison groups, we will get pretty similar results from our experiment each time we run it because farmers will be drawn from all over the country each time. If we randomize 15 villages into a treatment group and 15 villages into a comparison group and survey 40 farmers per village, we are likely to get different estimates of the effect size each time we run the experiment. Sometimes we will pick more villages in heavy rice-growing areas for the comparison group, sometimes the other way around. Sometimes bad weather will decrease output more in treatment villages than in comparison villages, sometimes the other way around. For a given sample size, the variance of the estimator will be larger when we randomize by village than when we randomize by individual because our sample is less diversified. Our bell curves are wider, and thus our power is lower.

How much lower is our power? That depends on how many clusters (villages) we group our sample into. The more clusters, the better. It also depends on how similar people in our clusters are to each other compared to how similar they are to the population in general. If the people in our clusters are very similar to each other (i.e., the within-cluster variance is very low), our power is much lower when we move to a group-level randomization. If the people in our clusters are just as varied as the population as a whole, moving from individual-level randomization to group-level randomization does not much change our power.

A specific example brings all these factors together. An evaluation was seeking to estimate the impact on yields of the introduction of a new high-yielding rice variety in Sierra Leone called New Rice for Africa (NERICA).[10] Seed rice for the new variety was roughly twice as expensive as traditional rice seed, so the project concluded that it would be successful only if NERICA yields were at least 20 percent higher than those of traditional varieties. The average rice yield in the area of study was 484 kilograms per hectare, so a 20 percent increase would be an increase of 97 kilograms per hectare. The standard deviation of rice yields is 295, so the standardized MDE is 97/295, which is 0.33 standard deviations. The intracluster correlation in rice yields was 0.19. If the project were to be randomized at the individual level, the sample size needed to detect a MDE of 20 percent would be 146 individuals per treatment cell and 292 in total (assuming 80 percent power, 5 percent alpha, and the same number of individuals in both groups). However, given the likelihood of spillovers within villages (if farmers were to pass the new seed on to their neighbors), it was decided that the randomization would need to be at the village level. Because roughly 25 percent of any survey costs in rural Sierra Leone are accounted for by the transport costs of reaching remote communities, it made sense to interview more than one farmer once a survey team had reached a village. With 5 enumerators on each team, it was estimated that it would be possible to survey 10 farmers per day. Thus a one-day visit to a village would produce 10 surveys. So, assum-

10. This example is inspired by an ongoing study by Rachel Glennerster and Tavneet Suri.

ing 10 farmers interviewed per village, two treatment cells (one treatment and one comparison), an equal allocation fraction, reaching an MDE of 20 percent would require surveying 80 villages (40 treatment and 40 comparison) and 800 farmers in total.

The algebraic formula for power, as well as an algebraic explanation of the formula, is given in the next module.

MODULE 6.3 An Algebraic Exposition of the Determinants of Power

Power analysis uses power functions to calculate the sample size necessary to identify a given effect size. In the previous module we explained the intuition behind why the different ingredients of the power equation affect power. In this module we explain the relationship algebraically for both individual and group-level randomization. This module is designed for those with greater familiarity with statistics. Those with less familiarity with statistics should feel free to move directly to the next module.

Individual-level randomization

As we discuss in Module 8.2, we usually analyze the results of a randomized evaluation by running a regression of our outcome variable against a dummy variable that takes the value one for those in the treatment group and zero for those in the comparison group. The coefficient of this dummy variable gives us the difference in the means of the outcome variables for the treatment group and the comparison group. We can also include control variables in the regression, which can help us explain the outcome variable. More formally,

$$Y_i = c + \beta T + X_i \gamma + \varepsilon_i,$$

where Y_i is the outcome variable for individual i, β is the coefficient of the treatment dummy T, X_i is a set of control variables for individual i, and ε_i is the error term. In this framework the constant c is the mean of the comparison group.

In this framework, the variance ($\hat{\beta}$) of our estimate of β is given by

$$Variance\ (\hat{\beta}) = \frac{1}{P(1-P)} \frac{\sigma^2}{N},$$

where N is the number of observations in the experiment; σ^2 is the variance of the error term, which is assumed to be independent and identically distributed (IID); and P is the proportion of the sample that is in the treatment group. Note that we have included control variables in our equation, and thus σ^2 is the residual variance. As discussed above, including controls in this way reduces residual variance and increases power. If α is our significance level (traditionally taken as 5 percent), the critical value $t_{\alpha/2}$ is defined as

$$\Phi(t_{\alpha/2}) = 1 - \alpha/2$$

for a two-sided test, where $\Phi(z)$ is the standard normal cumulative distribution function (CDF), which tells us the proportion of the mass under the curve to the left of a particular value (in this case $t_{\alpha/2}$). Then, as illustrated in the graphical representation in Module 6.2, we can reject the null hypothesis H_0 if $\hat{\beta}$ (the estimated effect size) falls above or below the critical value—that is, if

$$\frac{|\hat{\beta}|}{SE(\hat{\beta})} > t_{\alpha/2}.$$

Note that here we are assuming a two-sided test—that is, that we are testing whether β is either larger or smaller than H_0—so we have two hypothesis curves to which to compare the null hypothesis (Figure 6.10). Usually we have a strong reason to pick the MDE that we do on the positive effect size; in contrast, we usually don't have a particular hypothesized negative effect size that we want to be able to test for. But traditionally we test symmetrically—in other words, it is as though we were testing two hypotheses, one assuming an impact of β^* and one assuming an impact of $-\beta^*$. If we are interested in testing only whether the program has a positive effect, we can perform a one-sided test, which has more power, and we replace $t_{\alpha/2}$ with t_{α}.

The curve to the right in Figure 6.10 shows the distribution of effect sizes if the true effect is β^*, that is, the distribution of $\hat{\beta}$ if the true impact is β^*. The one to the left shows the distribution of estimated effect sizes if the true effect size is $-\beta^*$. (For simplicity here and in the earlier graphical representation, we provide the intuition by focusing on the positive curve. But the algebra is all for a two-sided test.) The power of the test is the percentage of the area of the $\beta = \beta^*$ curve that falls to the right of the critical value. For a given κ, this proportion can be found from the value

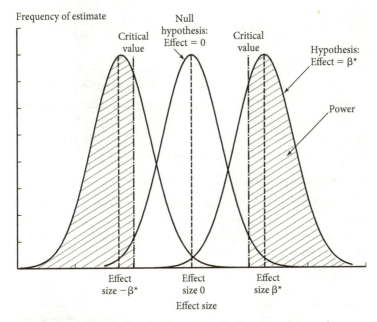

Frequency of estimate

Critical value

Null hypothesis: Effect = 0

Critical value

Hypothesis: Effect = β*

Power

Effect size −β*

Effect size 0

Effect size β*

Effect size

FIGURE 6.10 Distribution of effect sizes under the null and research hypotheses

$$1 - \Phi(t_\kappa) \equiv \Phi(t_{1-\kappa}).$$

The MDE is the minimum level of β that we can pick up with a given power. In other words, assuming that we want a power of 80 percent, the MDE is the minimum distance between the β = β* and null hypotheses for which 80 percent of the $H(\beta*)$ hypothesis curve falls to the right of the critical value $t_{\alpha/2}$. This is given by

$$MDE = (t_{(1-\kappa)} + t_{\alpha/2}) \times \sqrt{\frac{1}{P(1-P)}} \sqrt{\frac{\sigma^2}{N}}.$$

We can rearrange the equation to get

$$t_{(1-\kappa)} = \left[MDE \times \sqrt{P(1-P)} \times \sqrt{\frac{N}{\sigma^2}} \right] - t_{\alpha/2}.$$

Hence the power is given by

$$1 - \kappa = \Phi(t_{(1-\kappa)}) = \Phi\left(\left[MDE \times \sqrt{P\,(1-P)} \times \sqrt{\frac{N}{\sigma^2}}\right] - t_{\alpha/2}\right).$$

From this we can confirm the intuition represented graphically earlier in this module. A larger MDE size gives higher critical value and thus higher power (because the CDF is monotonic increasing); a larger sample size and/or smaller variance gives higher power, as does a smaller critical value. And we can see that for a given sample size, MDE, and critical level, power is maximized if $P = 0.5$.

Group-level randomization

When we randomize at the group rather than the individual level, we have to worry about two types of variation: those at the individual level and those at the group level. Our analysis equation is now

$$Y_{ij} = c + \beta T + X_i \gamma + v_j + \omega_{ij},$$

where Y_{ij} is the outcome of individual i in group j. We assume that there are J clusters of identical size n.[11] We have two error terms: one that captures shocks at the cluster level v_j, which is assumed to be IID with variance τ^2, and one that captures shocks at the individual level within a cluster, ω_{ij}, which we assume is IID with variance σ^2. The ordinary least squares estimator of β is still unbiased, and its standard error is

$$\sqrt{\frac{1}{P(1-P)}} \sqrt{\frac{n\tau^2 + \sigma^2}{nJ}}.$$

As in the case of the individual-level randomization, P is the proportion of the sample that is in the treatment group.

Comparing the standard error for the estimate of β with group-level randomization and individual-level randomization, we can see that the precision of the estimate now depends on both the within-cluster variance (τ^2) and the between-cluster variance (σ^2). The share of the total variation that is explained by cluster-level variance is given by *intracluster correlation*, ρ:

11. If clusters are of similar but not exactly equal size, we will slightly underestimate our power if we assume that they are the same. However, given the many assumptions going into power equations, it is rarely worth it to adjust the power equation for unequal clusters. The issue of unequal-sized clusters also arises during analysis (Module 8.2).

$$\rho = \frac{\tau^2}{\tau^2 + \sigma^2}.$$

Intracluster correlation is a key component of the design effect (D), which is a measure of how much less precise our estimate is, for a given sample size, when we move from an individual-level random-ization to a group- or cluster-level randomization:

$$D = \sqrt{1 + (n-1)\rho}.$$

The design effect says that for a given sample size, the more people we survey per group, the fewer groups we have, so the less power we have. This trade-off (more people per group but fewer groups) diminishes our power most when ρ is high because the more people within groups look like each other, the less we learn from interviewing more people in the same group.

The reduction in precision of our estimated effect that comes with a move to group-level randomization has implications for sample size calculations. Specifically, Bloom shows that the MDE with J groups of size n each is given by

$$MDE = \frac{M_{J-2}}{\sqrt{P(1-P)\,J}} \sqrt{\rho + \frac{1-\rho}{n}\sigma^2},$$

where $M_{J-2} = t_{\alpha/2} + t_{1-\kappa}$ for a two-sided test.[12]

This formula summarizes the relationships between power, MDE, variance, and sample size—the intuition of which we discuss in de-tail in the previous module. For the most part, evaluators use sta-tistical packages to perform the calculations, but it is important to understand the intuition of how the elements relate because this allows us to design more powerful experiments, as we discuss in the next module.

Module 6.3 summary

How power relates to each of the following:

- *Significance level:* The lower the level of significance we require, the more likely we are to reject the null hypothesis and find a

12. Howard S. Bloom, "Randomizing Groups to Evaluate Place-Based Programs," in *Learning More from Social Experiments* (New York: Russell Sage Foundation, 2005), 115–172.

statistically significant effect (i.e., the higher the power). However, we are also more likely to make false positive (Type I) errors.

- *MDE:* The larger the minimum detectable effect size, the higher the power.

- *Variance:* The lower the variance of the outcome of interest in the population, the lower the variance of the estimated effect size and the higher the power.

- *Sample size:* The larger the sample size, the lower the variance of our estimated effect (the closer it is to the true effect) and the higher the power.

- *Allocation fractions:* The more evenly the sample is distributed between treatment and comparison groups, the higher the power.

- *Level of aggregation in the unit randomized:* Individual randomization is more powerful than group-level randomization with the same sample size.

- *Intracluster correlation:* The more correlated outcomes are within groups in a group-level randomization, the less power.

MODULE 6.4 Performing Power Analysis

A power function *relates power to its determinants: (1) the level of significance, (2) the MDE size, (3) the unexplained variance of the outcome of interest, (4) the allocation fractions, (5) and the sample size. But where do we find these ingredients? In this module we first discuss how to find and calculate the ingredients necessary to calculate power. We then provide examples of statistical packages that can be used to perform power analysis.*

Ingredients for a power calculation
Desired power

Common levels of power that are used are 80 percent and 90 percent. If our power is 80 percent, in 80 percent of the experiments of this sample size conducted in this population, if there truly is an effect, we will be able to measure a statistically significant effect (i.e., we will be able to reject the null hypothesis).

MDE size

Choosing the most appropriate MDE size is probably the hardest and most important part of performing a power calculation. There is no right size; it is a matter of judgment. The true effect size of a program is a simple concept: it is the difference in the mean outcomes of the treatment and the comparison groups.

When we present the results of our experiment, we present the mean outcomes of the treatment and comparison groups and the difference between them in whatever units are most intuitive to understand. But for a power calculation we need to measure the effect size in a standard way; specifically, we measure it in standard deviations. We calculate the standardized effect size by dividing the effect size by the standard deviation of the outcome of interest:

Standardized effect size = (mean of treatment group − mean of comparison group) / standard deviation of outcome.

We can perform this calculation only when we know the actual effect size (i.e., after we have done the experiment). What we need for a power calculation is the smallest effect size that we want to be able to pick up in the experiment. Any effect below this threshold may well be indistinguishable from zero and may well be interpreted as a program failure. Some people think of the MDE size as a prediction of the effect of the program or as a goal as to how well the program might perform. This is not a good way to think about MDE sizes. To understand why, let's return to the example of remedial education.

The first in a series of studies of Pratham's remedial education program was carried out in urban India. It found an effect size of 0.27 standard deviation (SD).[13] Subsequent evaluations looked at alternative versions of the same program—for example, testing the impact in rural locations. So in this case the researchers had a pretty good idea of what the effect size might be. Should subsequent evaluations use the effect size from the first evaluation as a guide to the MDE for power calculations?

---

13. This study by Abhijit Banerjee, Shawn Cole, Esther Duflo, and Leigh Linden is summarized as Evaluation 2 in the appendix.

This strategy is risky. The effect size found in the first evaluation (0.27 SD) was large considering how cheap the program was to run. Even if the program had an impact of 0.2 SD, it would still be cost-effective. Imagine that a subsequent evaluation had chosen an MDE of 0.27 SD and the true effect size was 0.2 SD. There would have been a high probability that the subsequent evaluation would not have been able to distinguish the program effect from zero, raising concerns about whether the program was effective. Thus choosing too large an MDE might have made the evaluation too likely to fail to find an impact, even though the program in fact had an impact large enough to make it a cost-effective policy choice.

To discover the right way to think about MDE size, answer this question: "What size of effect would be so small that, for all practical purposes, it would be equivalent to zero?" There are three ways (not equally valid) to think about the right MDE size:

1. Using "standard" effect sizes

2. Comparing various MDE sizes to those of interventions with similar objectives

3. Assessing what effect size would make the program cost-effective

Let's look at each of these in detail. Usually it is worth thinking about our MDE in all three ways.

Using "standard" effect sizes There are rules of thumb about what constitutes a large effect size that are used by some researchers and appear in the literature. Based on the results of a large number of experiments on education, a view has emerged that an effect size on test scores of 0.2 SD is small but respectable, whereas an effect size of 0.4 SD is large.

Should we conclude that we can translate these rules of thumb to other sectors or even to other questions in the education sector? Maybe it is much easier to change outcomes such as school attendance than test scores and it is harder to change, for example, the height and weight of newborns than test scores. Maybe a reduction of 0.2 SD in the number of children suffering from anemia would be considered large. Even in the test score example, an effect size of 0.2 SD due to an inexpensive program in a district where few programs have been found to be effective might be hailed as a great success.

So although rules of thumb about what constitutes a large effect size are attractive because they can be taken off the shelf and used in any context, this independence of context is also its main weakness. The results of the evaluation will enter into the policymaking process as a basis for decisionmaking. As such, it seems that the optimal way of determining what is a small, medium, or large effect should come from the policy context. It is only in the policy context that even the idea of a minimally important effect size makes sense. Knowing the rules of thumb in a given sector can be a useful starting point for thinking about MDE sizes—but it should be only a starting point.

Comparing various MDE sizes to those of interventions with similar objectives Because a given program is usually one of several alternative policy options, one place to get a MDE size is from published evaluations of similar programs. By *similar programs* we mean programs that had similar goals. For example, programs that aimed to increase the number of years of schooling and have been rigorously evaluated include school input programs, scholarship programs, information programs, cash transfer programs, and health programs. Although they had very different designs and were evaluated in different countries, they had the same goals, and they all have reported effect sizes and costs. At the very least, we want our effect size to be comparable to those of other programs of similar cost. Ideally we would like to figure out what MDE size would make our program cost-effective compared to the alternatives.

For example, a school meals program intended to increase attendance can be compared to other programs that reduce the cost of education, such as programs offering school uniforms, conditional cash transfers, or deworming. What matters is that the comparable programs' costs are of the same magnitude and their stated goals are the same as those of our program.

However, if the alternatives have a very different cost per person reached than our program, then simply looking at the effect sizes of other programs is not sufficient. We need to be thinking about what MDE size would make our program cost-effective.

Assessing what effect size would make the program cost-effective Rational policymakers who want to achieve a certain goal—for example, increasing the number of children attending primary school—and have a fixed budget constraint would first invest in a program that increased school attendance by the most days for a given budget. If that program was very inexpensive and was able to be implemented throughout the country, state, or district, they might then invest in the second most cost-effective approach—and so on until their budget ran out.

If as evaluators we want to affect policy, we need to be able to distinguish whether our approach is in the range of cost-effective interventions. Given our estimate of the cost of the program, we can calculate what the effect size would need to be for the program to be cost-effective. This implies that MDE sizes will be smaller for less expensive programs because such programs are cost-effective even if they have small impacts. In other words, ironically, inexpensive programs are the most costly to evaluate because they require a large sample size for the evaluation to detect those small effects.

For cost-effectiveness comparisons, and indeed any comparisons of alternative policy options, we care not only about distinguishing our effect size from zero; we also care about having a precise estimate. Imagine that we determine that a remedial education program would be cost-effective if it achieved a test score improvement of at least 0.15 SD. If we pick 0.15 as the MDE size and 80 percent power, that means that there is an 80 percent chance that (if the effect really is 0.15) we will be able to distinguish the effect size from zero (in other words, that the confidence interval around our estimated effect size will not include zero). But we may well have a large confidence interval around our estimated effect. It may range from 0.28 to 0.02. If we are trying to compare this program with alternatives, such a wide confidence band may make it hard to make clear-cut comparisons. If we want to be able to measure the effect size precisely, we have to take this into account when setting the MDE. For example, if an effect size of 0.15 SD would make the program cost-effective, an effect size of 0.05 would mean that the program was not cost-effective, and we wanted to be able to distinguish between the two, we would need to have a MDE of 0.1.

Policymakers are influenced by many factors other than cost-effectiveness comparisons. They may, in particular, be influenced by absolute changes. If a program is inexpensive but creates only small absolute improvements, it may not receive as much support as one that is less cost-effective but produces improvements that are more visible. It may be worth asking the hypothetical questions "What size of change would be so small that it would not be considered worth it?" and "How much change would we need to see to act on the information?"

Choosing the number of clusters

As we discussed when we derived the power formula, for a given sample size we achieve the highest power by having the largest number of groups and one person per group. But sample size is typically constrained by our budget, and it is usually less expensive to interview one more person in the same group than one more person in a new group. For example, there are usually transport costs involved in traveling to a school or village. These fixed costs have to be paid regardless of the number of people we interview in the village.

Imagine that it costs $100 ($90 fixed cost + $10 per person) to interview the first person in a village and $10 per person after that. If our budget is $1,000 we can interview 1 person in each of 10 villages (with a total sample size of 10) or 11 people in each of 5 villages (for a total sample size of 55). Unless we have a very high degree of intra-cluster correlation, we will probably get more power from interviewing 55 people from 5 villages than 10 people from 10 villages.

There may be other practical considerations that make it more efficient to interview several people in one cluster. For example, the survey may be set up with one supervisor for a team of five enumerators. But a supervisor cannot effectively supervise if his five team members are each in a different village. Interviewing one person per village would mean that there would need to be one supervisor for every enumerator (which would be very expensive) or that enumerators would have to go to villages without a supervisor (which can lead to low-quality data).

So the marginal power from each additional person interviewed per cluster declines, but so does the marginal cost of each additional person interviewed per cluster. To maximize our power within a budget constraint, we have to trade off these two factors. In practice, costs tend to be lumpy. For example, if every enumerator can interview an average of 2 households in one day, it will not be very practical to interview 15 households per village with teams of five enumerators and one supervisor. It would be better to interview either 10 households (with each team spending one day in a village) or 20 (with each team spending two days in a village). With transport time and costs, if we try to interview 15 households, the teams will probably end up spending two days per village anyway.

Allocation fractions

Earlier we noted that in general, power is maximized when the sample size is allocated equally among all groups. More precisely, for a given sample size when there is one treatment and one comparison group, power is maximized when the allocation fraction is 0.5. However, we also noted that there are situations in which it makes sense not to distribute the sample equally between groups. In this section we examine each of these exceptions in turn.

When one budget pays for both program and evaluation

If there is one pot of funding to both run and evaluate a program and the only limits to our sample size are financial, maximizing power will involve having a larger comparison group than treatment group. This is because one additional treatment community or individual is more expensive than each additional comparison community or individual.

Imagine that we have $240,000 to both run a training program and evaluate it. It costs $1,000 per person to run the program and $100 per person to perform the evaluation. The randomization is at the individual level. Each additional person we add to the treatment group costs $1,100, while each additional comparison person costs $100. With an allocation fraction of 0.5, we could afford to have 200 people in treatment and 200 in the comparison group. When the allocation fraction is 0.5, we get the same increase in power by adding 1 treatment person as we do adding 1 comparison person. If we reduce the number of people in treatment by 1 and increase the number in the comparison group by 1, we reduce our power, but only very slightly, because we are still very close to balance between the groups. However, in this example we can reduce our treatment group by 1 and increase our comparison group by 11 within the same budget envelope. This will increase our power.

As we shift more of the sample from treatment to comparison, the power benefits diminish. At some point, reducing the treatment group by 1 and increasing the comparison group by 11 will actually reduce our power, even though it increases our sample size. This is clear if we think about the extreme case. When there is no treatment group left and only a comparison group, we have no power.

So how do we calculate the allocation fraction at which we maximize power? We can use the following formula, which says that with a set budget that must pay for both the program and evaluation, the optimal allocation fraction is equal to the square root of the ratio of the cost per person in the comparison group (c_c) to the cost per person in the treatment group (c_t):

$$(P_T/P_C) = \sqrt{(c_c/c_t)}.$$

In the example above, we maximize power with an allocation fraction of 22 percent.

If this approach sounds too complex, an alternative is to calculate different combinations of sample size and allocation fractions that we can afford with our budget and plug them into a program that calculates power (for example, in the Stata or Optimal Design software discussed below) and see which one gives the greatest power or the lowest MDE size.

When the MDE size varies by treatment group

If we have more than one treatment group, we may want to have different MDE sizes for the different treatment groups. In particular, if treatment 1 is much less expensive than treatment 2, treatment 1 would be cost-effective with a MDE size smaller than that for treatment 2. We will want to have a MDE that is at least as small as the cost-effectiveness cutoff, which suggests that we might choose a smaller MDE size for treatment 1 than for treatment 2. If we are interested only in comparing each treatment group to the comparison group, we will put more of the sample into treatment 1 than into treatment 2.

However, our decision is more complex if we are also interested in directly comparing treatment 1 with treatment 2. The appropriate MDE for a comparison between the two treatments may be even smaller than that between treatment 1 and the comparison. This is particularly true if the two treatments are variants of the same program with relatively similar costs. Even quite small differences in effect might be enough for us to conclude that one is better than the other. If we really want to be able to pick up these subtle differences between the two treatments, we will have to have large sample sizes in both treatment groups. We will discuss this conundrum more below. But the general point remains: with more than one treatment we may have more than one MDE and thus may want uneven allocation fractions.

When the comparison group plays a particularly important role

When there is more than one treatment, there is more than one pairwise comparison that can be analyzed. We can compare treatment 1 with treatment 2, treatment 1 with the comparison, and treatment 2 with the comparison. We sometimes want to compare all the treatments combined against the comparison (if, for example, the two treatments are two variants of the same program that are not very different from each other). As we mentioned above, it can be hard to distinguish one treatment from the other. If costs are similar, if one treatment is even slightly more effective than the other, it would be of policy interest. One approach is to have a large enough sample to pick up even small differences between treatments, but most experiments cannot afford the very large samples this requires. The alternative is to recognize that we are unlikely to be able to distinguish between the two effect sizes and that the core of the experiment will be comparing the different treatment groups to the comparison group. If this is the case, the comparison group will play a particularly large role.

Consider an evaluation in which the main questions of interest will involve comparing

> Treatment 1 versus the comparison
> Treatment 2 versus the comparison
> Pooled data from treatments 1 and 2 versus the comparison

In this case, data from the comparison group are used in all three pairwise comparisons, while data from treatment group 1 are used in only two of the three. In one of the pairwise comparisons, treatment 1 data are pooled with treatment 2 data and there will be more data points in the combined treatment group than in the comparison group. Thus if we add one person to the comparison group we help improve the power of three of the pairwise comparisons; if we add one person to treatment 1 we improve the power of only two comparisons, and for one of these comparisons we already have more power than for the other cases.

For these reasons, researchers often allocate more of the sample to the comparison group than to individual treatment groups. They are particularly likely to do this if they think they are unlikely to have enough power to directly compare the different treatment groups with each other even if they have an equal allocation fraction.

There is no formula for deciding how much extra sample to put into the comparison group when it does more work, mainly because it is a matter of judgment which pairwise comparisons we care most about. A procedure that is helpful, however, is to write out all the pairwise comparisons in which we are interested. Calculate the MDE size that could be detected for the different comparisons assuming equal allocation fractions. Then rearrange the sample in a number of different ways, including placing more samples in the comparison group. Recalculate the MDE for the different comparisons with these different allocation fractions. This can help us understand where our priorities are and the trade-offs we are making in the precision with which we will answer different questions under different scenarios.

When there is greater variance in one group than another

Some treatments may have a direct effect on the variance of the outcome of interest, either increasing it or decreasing it. We might think, for example, that a program that encouraged retirees to invest their retirement savings in an annuity would reduce the variance in the income of retirees. We might therefore want to sample a larger number of people in the comparison group in order to accurately measure their highly variable income and a smaller number of people in the treatment group, whom we expect to have less variable income.

Researchers, however, very rarely use uneven allocation fractions for this reason. They may feel that they don't have enough information to judge whether variance will rise or fall because of the program, or they may decide that although they have good reason to think the program will decrease variance in one indicator it will not decrease that in other indicators of interest. Take the example of an evaluation of weather insurance. Weather insurance, if it is effective, should reduce the variance of farmers' incomes. However, researchers may be interested to see if the reduced risk from the weather changes the crops farmers plant: weather insurance may actually increase the variance of crops planted. In other words, insurance may reduce variance in one indicator while increasing it in another.

Calculating residual variance

Residual variance is the variance in the outcome variables between people (or units) that cannot be explained by the program or any control variable (e.g., gender or age) we may use in our analysis. But we perform our power calculation before our analysis. So we need to use substitutes to estimate what the residual variance will be. Specifically, we can use (1) historical data from the same or a similar population or (2) data from our own pilot survey or experiment. We usually assume that the program will not increase variance, in which case residual variance can be calculated from data collected before the program is implemented. For example, we can run a regression with our outcome variable against all the variables we plan to use as controls. Most statistical packages will then show the residual variance from the regression. This can be used for power calculations.

Historical data include data collected by the investigator in past experiments or data collected by others, including national Demographic and Household Surveys. The World Bank is a good source of survey data from which variances for particular populations can be estimated. J-PAL also posts data from previous experiments at its website (www.povertyactionlab.org). Research papers often show the variances of their samples in descriptive statistics tables. However, these will give the total variance, not the residual variance after controlling for those variables that will be used for stratification or as controls in the final analysis. A power calculation done using total variance will underestimate power or overestimate the sample size we need.

The number of repeat samples

We need to decide if we are going to conduct a baseline as well as an endline survey and whether we want to collect data between these two points as well (i.e., a *midline*). The more times we collect data on the same people, the more we will reduce the residual variance and the more power we will have. However, there are diminishing returns, and for a given budget we may find that we get more power from increasing our sample size than from adding more intermediate surveys. The increase in power from collecting more than one data point on one person depends on how correlated outcomes are for individuals over time. A person's height tends to be highly correlated over time, so conducting a baseline and an endline will allow us to reduce unexplained variance a lot. In contrast, agricultural variables such as yield tend to be less correlated over time because they are highly dependent on weather shocks, which are not constant over years. The documentation for the Optimal Design software has a useful tool for estimating the effect of multiple rounds of surveys on power.[14] It is worth noting that if we interview 100 people five times each, our sample size is 100, not 500.

We discuss other factors that affect the decision of whether to conduct a baseline survey in Chapter 5, on data collection.

Temporal correlation (for power calculations with repeat samples)

If we plan to collect data on the same person more than once—for example, with a baseline and an endline survey—and we want to undertake a power calculation that reflects this, we need to include an estimate of the *intertemporal correlation* (i.e., how correlated outcomes for individuals are over time). It can be hard to find a good estimate of temporal correlation. Even if we conduct a pilot survey, we may have only one data point for each person. Only if we run a full pilot evaluation with a baseline and an endline will we have more than one estimate, which we can then use to calculate the correlation between two data points on the same individual. The alternative is to find panel data from a similar population that has been made publicly available. Panel data (which include data on the same person over time) are much less common than other types of data (Demographic and Household Surveys are usually not panel surveys, whereas data from previous randomized evaluations often are). Because it is hard to get good estimates of temporal correlation in a relevant population and researchers are nervous about overestimating temporal correlation and thus having an underpowered experiment, many researchers simply ignore the fact that they will have both baseline and endline data when they perform their power calculations. They think of this as a power buffer. In other words, they know that their power is greater than they calculated, but they do not know by how much.

Intracluster correlation (for group-level randomization)

Remember that the intracluster correlation is the percentage of the total variance in the sample that is explained by the within-cluster

---

14. Jessaca Spybrook, Howard Bloom, Richard Congdon, Carolyn Hill, Andres Martinez, and Stephen Raudenbush, "6.0: Repeated Measures Trials," *Optimal Design Plus Empirical Evidence: Documentation for the "Optimal Design" Software Version 3.0*, accessed January 3, 2013, http://hlmsoft.net/od/od-manual-20111016-v300.pdf.

variance. We can estimate the intracluster correlation by using data from other surveys of similar populations or from pilot data. Most statistical packages will be able to calculate rho from a data set that includes the outcome variable and a cluster variable (for example, village ID). Our power calculations will be sensitive to this factor, so it is worth trying to track down as good an estimate as possible.

Some tools for power calculations

Once we have the ingredients for a power calculation, how do we actually conduct it? Most statistical packages, such as Stata, have sample size functions. Free tools are also available, such as Optimal Design. Although these tools will undertake the mechanics of power for us, it is important to have a solid understanding of the principles behind them.

Stata

Stata has a command, `sampsi`, which allows users to plug in all the ingredients (including the desired level of power) to calculate the sample size needed to achieve the desired power. If the sample size is entered, `sampsi` will give the level of power. The default in Stata is that power is 90 percent, the significance level is 5 percent, the number of randomization cells is two, the allocation fraction is 0.5, the variance is the same for treatment and comparison groups, and a two-sided test is being performed.

Rather than a MDE size, Stata asks for the mean of the treatment group and the mean of the comparison group (recall that the MDE is the difference between the two). Imagine that we are performing an individual randomization of a program designed to increase test scores. We use existing data on test scores to determine that the average test score prior to the intervention is 43 percent with an SD of 5 percentage points. We decide that we want to be able to detect a 2 percent change in test scores with 80 percent power, so we enter

```
sampsi 0.43 0.45, power(0.8) sd(0.05).
```

Stata will return a sample size of 99 for the treatment group and 99 for the comparison group, assuming a 95 percent critical value (reported as an alpha of 5 percent).

If we decide we want to do the same evaluation but randomize at the class level and there are 60 children per class, we can use `sampclus`

—which is currently an add-on to Stata, so has to be downloaded the first time it is used. We first do `sampsi` and then adjust the sample size for the clustering by indicating either how many observations there will be per cluster or how many clusters we intend to use. We will also need to input the intracluster correlation, rho (calculated, for example, using existing data and the `loneway` command in Stata). In this example we would input

```
sampsi 0.43 0.45, power(0.8) sd(0.05)
```

and

```
sampclus, obsclus(60) rho(0.2).
```

The result of moving to a class-level randomization in this case is that the sample size needed to detect a change in test scores of 2 percentage points increases to 1,268 students for the treatment group and 1,268 for the comparison group, or 43 classes in total.

There are a number of options for performing more complex sample size calculations in Stata, for example, if we are collecting data more than once on the same individual or unit (in which case the extent to which outcomes are correlated over time for a given unit must be specified).

Optimal Design

An alternative software package is Optimal Design, which is specifically designed to calculate power. One advantage of Optimal Design is that it shows graphically how power increases with sample size at different levels of MDE size or intracluster correlation. This can be helpful for seeing the magnitude of some of the trade-offs we have discussed in this chapter. It is possible to see, for example, just how quickly the returns to adding more individuals per cluster diminish with different levels of intracluster correlations. Another advantage of Optimal Design is its detailed manuals, which take the user through the different types of evaluation design and which options to use. Optimal Design also allows for three levels of data collection; for example, if we are evaluating a program designed to inform voters about the records of their parliamentarians, we might collect data on individuals who are clustered into polling stations that are themselves parts of constituencies.

It is important to note that when Optimal Design reports the necessary sample size for a given MDE, the software is assuming that we have two treatment cells (i.e., one treatment and one comparison cell). If we have two treatment groups and one comparison group we need to take the reported sample size and divide by two (to get the sample size per cell) and then multiply by three (the number of randomization cells in our experiment).

Optimal Design may be downloaded free from the University of Michigan at http://sitemaker.umich.edu/group-based/optimal_design_software.

The best package for you: What you are used to

Tools will differ in their execution of power calculations. For example, one difference between Optimal Design and Stata is their treatment of binary variables in clustered designs. While Stata will prompt for rho (the level of intracluster correlation), Optimal Design avoids using rho in this context (because of concerns that rho is not accurate at the tails of the binary distribution). Our understanding is that a new version of Optimal Design is under development that will provide more accurate estimates of power for binary outcomes when the mean of the outcome variable is close to one or zero.

Finally, a warning: in practice, power calculations involve some guesswork. One way to reduce the amount of guesswork is to run a pilot on our population. This will help us get a better estimate of the mean and the variance in our population and may also help us estimate what compliance rates will be. Having better parameters will improve our calculations. But even rough estimates tell us something. So even when we don't have all the parameters we need for a full power calculation, it is still worth doing some calculations based on our best estimates of parameters.

To launch into a study without having undertaken power calculations risks wasting a massive amount of time and money. Power calculations can tell us (1) how many treatments we can have, (2) how to trade off between clusters and observations within clusters, and (3) whether the research design, at least in this dimension, is feasible or not.

Case study of calculating power

In this section we work through an example of calculating sample size for a group-level randomized evaluation of a remedial education program in Mumbai. A number of other examples and exercises on power are given at www.runningrandomizedevaluations.org.

We want to test the effectiveness of a remedial education program for third-grade students in Mumbai. We are at the early stage and want to know how many schools we will need to include in the study and on how many children in each school we will need to collect data.

We need many pieces of information for our power calculation, including the mean and variance of test scores in Mumbai. We also want to have a chance to test our data collection instrument (an academic test we have designed specifically for this evaluation). We therefore perform a pilot data collection exercise in six schools, testing all the third-grade children in these schools. On average there are 100 third-grade children in each school (no school has fewer than 80 third-grade children).

With these pilot data we calculate some basic descriptive statistics:

- The mean test score is 26 percent.
- The SD is 20.
- We also calculate the intracluster correlation as 0.17.

Note that the only use of the SD is to calculate the standardized MDE because we are doing a group-level randomization.

After looking at the impacts and costs of other education programs, we decide that we want the program to have at least a 10 percent impact on test scores—in other words, a change in the mean of test scores of 2.6 percentage points (a 10 percent change from a starting point of 26 percent). Anything less will be considered a failure. This will be our MDE size, but we have to translate it into a standardized MDE size. To do this we divide by the SD. In other words, our standardized MDE is 2.6/20 = 0.13 SD.

We are now ready to start looking at some examples of sample sizes. We set alpha to 0.05 (this gives us a significance level of 95 percent, which is standard). We start by assuming that we will test 40 children in each school. We use Optimal Design to learn that we will need 356 schools in our sample (Figure 6.11, panel A)—in other words, 178 for the treatment group and 178 for the comparison group. We decide that it will be hard for the program to work with 356 separate schools. Because this is a school setting and therefore it is relatively easy to increase the number of individuals in a group that we test, we decide to test the maximum number of children per school, which

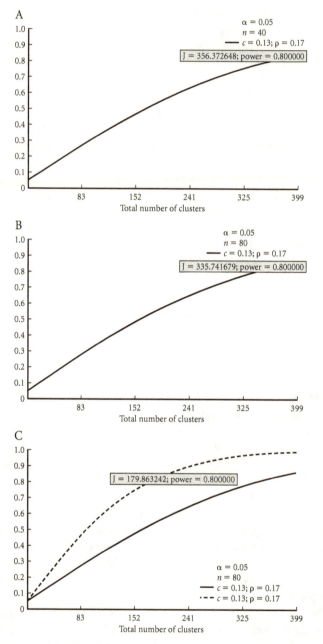

FIGURE 6.11 Number of clusters and power under different assumptions

Source: Optimal Design.

Notes: The assumptions are as follows: panel A, 40 children per school; panel B, 80 children per school; panel 3, with and without adjusting for baseline scores.

is 80. We rework the power analysis and find that for 80 percent power we will need 336 schools (Figure 6.11, panel B). In other words, doubling the number of children we test per school reduces the number of schools we will work in by only 20 out of 356, or 6 percent. Then we realize that we will make two observations on each child: before the program and after the program. Previous studies in similar populations have found that 50 percent or more of the variation in test scores in the endline survey can be explained by baseline test scores. Putting this into Optimal Design gives us a revised number of schools: 180 (Figure 6.11, panel C).

Originally we had wanted to test two different versions of the program against each other. But looking at the power analysis, we realize that we cannot afford to do this. Specifically, we had been interested in the benefit of increasing the length of the remedial sessions with children by half an hour per day. We would have considered the new version a success if it had led to a 15 percent increase in test scores compared to a 10 percent increase in test scores for the basic program. But in order to test between the two versions of the program we would have needed to be able to pick up a difference between an average test score of 28.6 (for treatment 1) and 29.9 (for treatment 2). In other words, our standardized MDE would be 0.065. The number of schools needed for this MDE (assuming that 80 children were tested per school and including baseline controls) if we were just comparing treatment and comparison groups would be 712 (356 for treatment and 356 for comparison). But we now have two treatments and a comparison group, so in fact our sample size would be $356 \times 3 = 1,068$ schools. This is well beyond our budget.

We therefore decide to evaluate just one treatment with 180 schools and 80 children per school for a total sample size of 14,400.

Module 6.4 summary

Where do we find the ingredients of a power calculation?

The following table summarizes the parameters we need for power calculations and where we can find them.

What we need	Where we can find it
Significance level	Conventionally set at 5 percent.
Mean of outcome in comparison group	Previous surveys conducted in the same or a similar population

What we need	Where we can find it
Residual variance in outcome of comparison group	Previous surveys conducted in the same or a similar population (the larger the variability is, the larger the sample size for a given power)
MDE size	Smallest possible effect size that would be considered important. For example, the smallest effect size that would make the program cost-effective. Drawn from discussions with policymakers and cost-effectiveness calculations.
Allocation fractions	We decide on this based on our budget constraints and prioritization of different questions. When there is only one treatment group, the allocation fraction is usually 0.5.
Intracluster correlations (when randomizing at the group level)	Previous surveys in the same or similar populations
Level of power	Traditionally, 80 percent power is used.
Number of repeat observations and intertemporal correlation	Number of times we plan to interview the same person (for example, baseline and endline). Other evaluations may have data on how correlated over time outcomes are for an individual.

MODULE 6.5 How to Design a High-Powered Study

We have to plan for power, weighing the impact of our design choices and constraints. The determinants of power suggest ways we can ensure high power at each stage of the evaluation, from design through analysis. Features of the evaluation design affect power. The most important of these are the number of treatments, the outcome measures, the randomization design, control variables, stratification, and compliance with the research design. In this module we discuss how to design and implement high-powered experiments.

When designing the evaluation

The number of questions we attempt to answer determines the number of treatment groups that we will need to have. When we calculate power, we do so for one particular pairwise comparison, say, treatment 1 versus comparison or treatment 1 versus treatment 2. Our sample size is the sample involved in that pairwise comparison. Thus if we have 180 people in the total sample and four treatments groups of equal size (45 people), our total sample size for comparing one treatment with another is 90. All things equal, the fewer the groups, the higher the power we can achieve for a given total sample.

Choose a decent sample size

A sufficiently large sample is crucial. It increases the accuracy with which we estimate impact and thus increases power. It can be a fairly expensive way of increasing power, because adding subjects increases the size of the study and, if not the number of people to be treated, at least the amount of data to be collected.

Use fewer treatment groups

Reducing the number of treatment groups increases power, but fewer groups come at a cost of fewer questions answered. As is so often the case in economics (and life), we have to make a trade-off: should we try to answer a few questions with greater precision and be reasonably confident that we will be able to detect a statistically significant effect, even if the treatment effect is quite small, or should we try to answer more questions and risk finding imprecisely estimated coefficients?

In general, it is good to have at least one question in an experiment that we can answer with a reasonably high degree of precision. For example, we may be interested in testing two different versions of a program against each other. We may not have much power to distinguish between the different versions, but we probably want to design our experiment so that it can show us whether the program as a whole has any impact with a good degree of certainty. To do this, we can combine both versions of the program into one large treatment group and compare it to the comparison group. This will give us much more power to answer this question, because the number of observations in the combined treatment group will be quite large in this case.

Randomize at the lowest level possible

The randomization level is one of the most important determinants of power. As discussed above, when randomization is done at the group level rather than person by person, the impact estimates are usually much less precise. This is because a single shock can hit an entire community, changing the outcomes of many people in that community in a correlated way. Power is much more sensitive to the number of units over which we randomize than to the number of people we survey. Often we get the same order of magnitude of power when we randomize 100 people as when we randomize 100 villages, even if the sample size in the latter case is 10 times larger (e.g., if we survey 10 people per village).

Use a design that increases compliance

Partial compliance dilutes the effect size because there is less contrast in exposure to the treatment between treatment and comparison groups. Thus the power is lower. Imagine that the true effect of a remedial education program on children who participate is 0.3 SD. But some of the children who are randomized into the treatment group fail to show up at school, and the remedial teacher in another school resigns and is not replaced. In the end, only half of the children randomized to receive the program actually complete it. The average test score difference between treatment and comparison groups is now only 0.15 SD because of lack of compliance. Because of the way sample size and effect size are related in the power equation, we need four times the sample size to pick up an effect size that is half as large.

Partial compliance can also result when some of the comparison group receives the program. In our remedial education example, imagine that there is a mix-up in the school, and some children who were randomized into the control group end up attending remedial education classes. This diminishes our measured effect size even further because it reduces the distinction between treatment and comparison groups. As above, assume that the true effect size of the program is 0.3 SD and only 50 percent of the treatment group receives the program. Now assume that 25 percent of the control group ends up receiving the program. The difference in take-up between the treatment and control groups is now only 25 percentage points; that is, the treatment group is only 25 percentage points more likely to receive the program than the comparison group. The overall effect size is only $0.3 \times .025$ or 0.075 SD. This is a very small effect size and will be difficult to pick up. In this case, our MDE is a quarter as large as it would have been with full compliance. This means that our sample size must now be 16 times larger.

More formally, the MDE size with noncompliance is related to the MDE size with full compliance in the following way:

$$MDE_{\text{partial compliance}} = MDE_{\text{full compliance}}/(p_t - p_c),$$

where p_t is the proportion of the treatment group that is treated and p_c is the proportion of the control group that is treated.

We can also express this in terms of sample size, namely

$$N_{\text{partial compliance}} = N_{\text{full compliance}}/(p_t - p_c)^2.$$

This suggests that a high level of compliance is vital. But sometimes take-up of a program is a critical question we want to find out about, so we don't want to be too active in encouraging participation beyond what a normal program would encourage. However, when testing the impact of a program on those who take it up, it is of critical importance to ensure that the participation rate is higher in the treatment group. As we discuss in detail in Module 8.2, it is also important to design the study to minimize the existence of defiers (individuals who take up the treatment only when they are placed in the comparison group), although in this case the problem is not so much their impact on power as the fact that they bias our estimated effect.

Encouragement designs by their nature tend to have less than full compliance because the treatment involves telling people about a program or giving them a modest incentive to participate. Encouragement designs therefore need large sample sizes. One benefit of encouragement designs, however, is that they normally involve randomization at the individual level, which does help with power.

Use a design that limits attrition

When people drop out and cannot be measured, our sample size effectively goes down, and that reduces our power. Attrition can introduce all sorts of other problems, as discussed in Module 7.2. For these reasons, and for the sake of power, choose a design that limits attrition. Ways to limit attrition are also discussed in Chapter 7.

Use stratification

As discussed in Module 4.4, when we stratify we first divide the sample into smaller groups composed of people with similar observable outcomes (such as gender or district) and then randomize from these groups into the treatment groups. This ensures that the groups are similar on the stratification variables. Stratification ensures that even in small samples, the treatment and comparison groups are balanced and have exactly equal numbers of people with different characteristics.

Stratification makes our estimate more precise for a given sample size, increasing power. By ensuring that the treatment and comparison groups are balanced on key characteristics, stratification reduces the chance that, for example, all the children with high test scores will happen to be in our treatment group and we will overestimate the treatment impact as a result. We can be sure that our estimated effect will be closer to the true effect. In terms of our power equation, balance means that there is less residual variance, which means that for a given sample size, the power is higher. In general, the more outcomes we stratify on, the better. However, it is theoretically possible to overstratify if we stratify on variables that don't have any impact on the outcome variable. We discuss the variables on which we should stratify and how to calculate residual variance with stratification in Chapter 4, on design.

Stratification is most important for small sample sizes because the law of large numbers ensures that randomization will lead to balance only in very large sample sizes.

Choose an allocation fraction

For a given sample size, power is maximized if we allocate equal shares to the treatment and comparison groups. As discussed in detail in Module 6.4, sample size may not be fixed, and there may be cases in which equal allocation fractions are not optimal.

When planning the data collection

Choose proximate outcome measures

As discussed in Chapter 5, the proximity of an outcome measure is defined by how far down the logical chain it is. In our immunization example, reducing child mortality is the ultimate objective, but it is not proximate.[15] The logical chain involves several steps: (1) camps are established and transfers provided to improve access, reliability, and incentives; (2) mothers take children to be immunized; (3) children are immunized; (4) child immunity improves; (5) children do not become sick when exposed to disease; and (6) children do not die from exposure. At each step, factors other than the program are at play:

---

15. Abhijit Banerjee, Esther Duflo, Rachel Glennerster, and Dhruva Kothari, "Improving Immunisation Coverage in Rural India: Clustered Randomised Controlled Evaluation of Immunisation Campaigns with and without Incentives," *British Medical Journal* 340 (2010).

mothers attend camps for reasons other than the program, and children die for reasons other than exposure to the diseases against which the immunization protects. All these other factors become part of the variance in outcomes that cannot be explained by the program. Unexplained variance makes our estimate less precise and reduces our power. In our immunization example, we may want to use immunization rate rather than child mortality as our outcome of interest.

Some outcome measures can be too proximate to be of interest, even though they have high power. If our outcome measure is whether the camps operated, we will have power but will not have learned much about the impact of the program on people's lives. As is so often the case, a balance needs to be struck between two objectives: our desire for power and our desire to follow the logical chain as far as we can toward the ultimate impact.

Collect data on control variables

Including control variables that are strong explanitors of the outcome variable can limit the amount of unexplained variance. By reducing the amount of unexplained variance, we reduce the sample size needed to detect an effect of a given size. In other words, by reducing variance we decrease the MDE for our sample size. We discuss why this is important and how to calculate power when control variables are used below.

Collect multiple observations on one person

Individuals have idiosyncrasies that cannot be fully explained by their observable characteristics, such as their age or income. Some people are harder workers than others of a similar age and education, for example. These characteristics often persist over time: once a hard worker, always a hard worker. If we have multiple observations on the same person, such as a baseline and an endline, we can calculate a fixed effect for each person. These individual idiosyncrasies become part of the explained variance rather than the unexplained variance, which increases our power. Having a baseline also helps with stratification, because it provides variables on which we can stratify. However, it is costly to conduct additional rounds of surveys. Whether collecting more rounds of data on a small sample or expanding the sample will give us more power depends on how correlated outcomes are over time. If they are weakly correlated, a larger sample may give us higher power than a smaller sample with two survey rounds.

Plan data collection to limit attrition

Data collection strategies include collecting cell phone numbers, having a tracking module in the baseline that collects contact information on people who will know where the subject is even if he or she moves, and providing subjects with cell phones and free credit if they check in at regular intervals throughout the study.

Limit procedural variation

The fewer fluctuations there are in how a program is implemented and how the data are collected, the less variability there is in the outcome data. Some forms of measurement variation can be limited by simplifying the data collection procedures and training staff thoroughly. Limiting variability reduces the variance of our impact estimates, increasing power.

When implementing the evaluation—managing threats

Increase compliance

Strategies for increasing compliance during implementation include using a higher level of randomization between treatment groups, providing incentives to participate to all subjects, and treating only those in the cluster at the time of randomization. (For example, if we are providing school uniforms, we can give uniforms to the children already in the treatment schools at the time the program is announced. Otherwise, comparison group children may transfer to the treatment schools to obtain the uniforms.) Of course, these have to be balanced with other considerations. For example, we said above that we can increase power by using a lower level of randomization, and now we are saying that we can increase power by using a higher level of randomization. Which is it? The fact is that different effects go in different directions. When faced with this type of trade-off, it can be helpful to make some assumptions about what the crossover would be at different levels of randomization and undertake a power analysis for the different designs to see how the two factors balance out in a particular context.

Limit attrition

As discussed above, limiting attrition helps improve power. Preventing attrition needs to be a focus at all times in an evaluation, including during implementation. If the budget allows, it is useful to check in with participants (in the treatment and comparison groups) as the program is rolled out to become aware of whether participants are moving.

When undertaking the impact analysis

Use control variables

Controlling for covariates reduces unexplained variance, which increases power. Any variable we want to add as a covariate should not be influenced by the treatment, which usually means that we must use variables that were collected before the intervention started. If we collect data on covariates and use it in the analysis, this will increase the power of our tests. In our remedial education example, final test scores are correlated with lots of factors other than the program, including participants' ages, genders, and, most important, baseline test scores. If we conduct our analysis in a regression framework and put in age, gender, and baseline test scores as control variables, the unexplained variation decreases. Even if we end up having more children who are older in our treatment group than in our control group, if we use control variables we will not attribute the higher test scores associated with age to the treatment. Our estimated effect size will, on average, be closer to the true estimate (it will be more precise), and we will have more power. Control variables reduce the "background noise." This makes it easier to detect the true impact, and thus increases the power, of the experiment.

Choose a significance level

The conventional significance level is 5 percent, and it makes sense to use this when performing power analysis. Using a larger significance level may formally give us more power, but only because we have changed the rules of the game. When we write up our results, we may want to point out where there are effects, even if they are significant only at the 10 percent level, but these results will always be looked at with some hesitation. We should not plan from the outset to be able to pick up only effects with 10 percent significance.

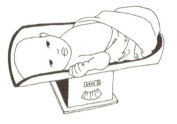

7 Threats

Our randomization design and data collection plan describe how the study is meant to proceed. But rarely does everything go according to plan. This chapter covers common threats to the integrity of the experiment. Each module covers one threat and explains ways to design an evaluation to limit these threats. The modules in this chapter are as follows:

MODULE 7.1 Partial Compliance

Some of the participants may not receive the treatment that was assigned to them in the protocol. When some of the people are noncompliant, we say that there is partial compliance. This module discusses why partial compliance is a threat and how we can limit it.

What is partial compliance?
When people in the treatment group are not treated

Some of the people in the treatment group may never be treated. For example, some students assigned to a training program may never attend the training. Some parents whose children are assigned to receive deworming drugs may not give their consent. Or impassable roads in the rainy season may keep a program from delivering fertilizer to some farmers in time for planting. We can measure the extent of this partial compliance from process data collected throughout the implementation as we check records of how many people attend the training program or how many parents do not give permission for deworming drugs.

When people in the treatment group do not complete the treatment course

People sometimes stop participating in a program before it is over. For example, some students in a training program may drop out after a few sessions. Some farmers in a fertilizer program may save fertilizer for the next planting season instead of using it for the current season as intended. Instead of using their fertilizer, some farmers may sell it. In the latter case, we may not know the extent of noncompliance until we complete a final survey and ask farmers how much fertilizer they used in the previous season.

When people in the comparison group receive the treatment

People in the comparison group may be exposed to the program. This may happen through a number of channels. First, some members of the comparison group may have been receiving the program already. For example, if we introduce a deworming program, some parents whose children are in the comparison group may already be investing in deworming medicine and treating their children at home. Second, members of the comparison group may move to a treatment group location. For example, if we are running a deworming program through schools, parents may transfer their children from comparison schools to treatment schools. Third, outside actors may deliver the treatment to the comparison group. For example, if we are providing insecticide-treated mosquito nets to pregnant women through prenatal clinics assigned to the treatment group, another NGO might come in and decide to distribute similar nets to pregnant women through clinics that do not yet have a net distribution program (i.e., our comparison clinics).

When implementation staff depart from the allocation or treatment procedures

Implementation staff can depart from the protocol. For example, program managers could deviate from the randomized allocation and extend services based on their own judgment of need or on personal relationships. In other words, they might choose to provide the program to some of the people allocated to the comparison group and fail to provide the program to some people allocated to the treatment group. They could also change the actual treatment.

Imagine a training program for female entrepreneurs. The staff we hire to deliver the training might decide to add an "empowerment" module to the regular business training modules we have designed. The staff may have a good rationale for adding the empowerment module, but then the intervention we are evaluating is not just a business training program; it's a business training and empowerment program.

Finally, program staff could decide to compensate people in the comparison group by providing them with something—some gift or cash to make them feel that they are not left out. Sometimes minimal compensation is part of the study protocol and is given to those surveyed in both treatment and comparison groups to encourage them to stay in the study. But program staff's decision to compensate without discussion of the implications for the evaluation is a threat to the integrity of the study.

When people (defiers) exhibit the opposite of compliance

In some unusual cases, providing access to a program or encouraging take-up of the program may have a perverse effect and reduce take-up. Similarly, excluding people from a program may make them think they are missing out on something great and end up generating greater take-up. People who behave in this counterintuitive way are called *defiers*. Not only are these people noncompliers; they are in a sense negative compliers in that they are reacting in exactly the opposite way to what we predicted in our protocol. Although this situation is rare, it is a major threat to our experiment. (We discuss defiers in more detail in Module 8.2.)

How is noncompliance a threat?

Noncompliance can reduce the difference between the treatment and comparison groups in exposure to the program

For us to be able to detect the impact of a program, our treatment group must be significantly more likely to receive the program than are those in the comparison group. Partial compliance narrows the gap in actual treatment rates between the groups. In the extreme, if the treatment rate is comparable in the two groups, our ability to estimate the impact breaks down. For example, in our bed net program, if all the health clinics in the comparison group receive bed nets from another NGO, the rate of exposure to bed nets does not differ between our treatment and comparison groups. Because there is no contrast in treatment rates between the two groups, we cannot measure the impact of the program.

Noncompliance can reduce comparability between the treatment and comparison groups

In a randomized evaluation, the program we want to evaluate should be the only systematic difference between the treatment and comparison groups. Partial compliance by implementation staff can reduce comparability between the two groups. Say that we want to test the effect of distributing bed nets at prenatal clinics. Our program manager may be concerned about the health of the women at the comparison clinics and decide to implement a health education program teaching women how to prevent malaria in the comparison clinics. But now the program we want to evaluate (distributing bed nets) is no longer the only systematic difference between the treatment and comparison groups. Because the malaria education program introduces another difference, we can no longer be sure that differences in outcomes between the two groups are caused by the bed net distribution program.

Defiers can make it impossible to estimate the true impact of a program

The problem of defiers is most likely to arise when we use an encouragement design and the encouragement in some cases encourages and in other cases discourages people from taking up the program. As we discuss in Module 4.3, a kind of encouragement that may create defiers arises when we give information about the benefits of an action in the hope that it will spur more people to take the action. However, if some people have previously overestimated the benefits, when they receive information about the true benefits, these people may decide not to take the action as a result of the information. Here we explain why defiers make it impossible to identify the true impact of a program.

Imagine that we wanted to evaluate the impact of staying in secondary school on the rate of teenage pregnancy. Previous studies have suggested that providing information to children and their parents about the returns to staying in school reduces dropout rates. We therefore randomize some girls to receive information about the returns to staying in school. On average, those who receive the information do stay longer. We measure pregnancy rates and find that those who received the information also have lower teenage pregnancy rates.

The problem with this design is that although most girls may previously have underestimated the benefits of staying in school, some girls may have overestimated the benefits. The information may cause this latter group to leave school earlier than they would have otherwise. These girls who are discouraged by our encouragement are defiers; they respond in a way that is opposite to what we would expect and to the way others respond.

If the effect of staying in school on pregnancy rates were the same for all girls, the monotonicity assumption would still hold. But we know that these girls are different from the norm because they react differently to the information we give: isn't it possible that schooling has a different effect on their pregnancy rates, too? A numerical example may help explain the problem. The numerical example may be hard to follow for those who are not familiar with how we analyze encouragement designs. We go through this in Module 8.2.

Suppose that 80 percent of girls are pessimists, have seen very few girls complete secondary school and get good jobs, and underestimate the benefits of staying in school. Learning the real returns to schooling leads this group to stay in school one more year. The remaining 20 percent of girls are optimists (maybe they have seen older siblings get well-paying jobs) and overestimate the benefits of staying in school. Learning the real returns to school makes these girls drop out two years earlier than they would have.

The effects of staying in school on the pregnancy rates of the two groups of girls are also different. For the pessimists, an additional year of school reduces teenage pregnancy by 10 percentage points. For the optimists, who have low rates of teenage pregnancy, schooling is less of a factor, reducing teenage pregnancy by only 1 percent.

The experiment is designed to test the effect of schooling on pregnancy for the population. To calculate the true effect, we have to calculate the effect of the program separately for the pessimists and the optimists. For the pessimists, who are 80 percent of the population, one more year of schooling reduces teenage pregnancy by 10 percentage points. For the pessimists, who are 20 percent of the population, one more year of schooling reduces teenage pregnancy by 1 percentage point. A weighted average of the two effects is 8.2 percent.

But if we assume that there are no defiers and look at the average effect of the encouragement on the whole population, we will get a different result. The encouragement increases schooling, on average, by 0.4 year (the average of a one-year increase for the pessimists and a two-year decrease for the optimists). We see that the average pregnancy rate falls by 7.6 percent (the weighted average of an 8 percent drop in pregnancy among the pessimists and a 0.4 percent increase in pregnancy among the optimists). If we get a 7.6 percent reduction in pregnancy from an increase in schooling of 0.4 year, we assume that we would get a 19 percent reduction in pregnancy from a full year of additional schooling (0.076/0.4). In other words, our estimated effect of schooling on pregnancy is almost double the true effect.

How can we limit partial compliance?

We can start limiting partial compliance at the design stage.

Make take-up of the program easy

Complicated application procedures can sharply reduce take-up, as can inconvenient locations. If we make take-up easy and convenient we are likely to have a much higher rate of take-up. A study in Sierra Leone was examining the impact on voter knowledge and voting behavior of screening debates between rival candidates for parliament.[1] Randomization was at the level of the polling station. To ensure high levels of exposure to the debate, it was decided that the debate should be screened not only at the main community center but also in outlying hamlets. If the program was being implemented without an evaluation, these extra screenings might not have been offered, because there were far fewer viewers at these satellite screenings. However, for the evaluation it was important to ensure high rates of exposure.

Incentivize take-up of the program

We may want to encourage take-up by providing a small incentive. We do not want the incentive to be so large that it will change outcomes, but it is surprising how effective very small incentives can be in promoting take-up. In case of the Sierra Leone parliamentary debate discussed above, those individuals who were part of the study were given a very small incentive for attending the debate (the incen-

---

1. This study by Kelly Bidwell, Katherine Casey, and Rachel Glennerster is ongoing.

tive was a set of ten "Maggi cubes"—local flavorings to be added to dishes while cooking, rather like stock cubes and costing only a few cents each). In this example it is unlikely that receiving a Maggi cube would have changed how someone voted in the election (especially because there was no clear "right way to vote"; that is, there was not a particular way to vote that would have pleased the enumerators).

Compartmentalize and routinize field tasks

We can limit partial compliance by reducing the chances that staff will have to make on-the-spot decisions in the field. We can do this by assigning and training staff to offer specific treatments. For example, an empowerment program for adolescent girls in Bangladesh had two modules. Each village was offered either a basic module or an expanded package with both modules. To avoid confusion, a given staff member was trained in either the basic or the expanded program and only ever had to deliver that one version of the program.[2] This compartmentalization may have increased compliance by staff with the randomization. When they were in a village, they did not have to trouble themselves about what service they were supposed to be delivering and to whom. (We may worry, especially in small programs, that the staff allocated to deliver one package may be better than those allocated to the other package, in which case the difference between the two program results may reflect both the difference in the program and the difference in staff quality. In some cases evaluators randomize the staff to the different packages to avoid this. In other cases this may not be appropriate because the different packages require different technical skills, in which case staff effects are an integral part of the program.)

Randomize at a higher level

To minimize the comparison group's exposure to the treatment, we can randomize at a different level. For example, we can randomize at the village level rather than at the individual level. The risk of having the comparison group exposed to the treatment is more likely when people assigned to different treatments interact. This may be because of spillover effects (discussed below) or because treatment individuals share with their neighbors or family. One solution is to randomize at

2. This study by Erica Field and Rachel Glennerster is summarized as Evaluation 7 in the appendix.

a higher level. We discuss pros and cons of randomizing at different levels in Module 4.2.

Include a basic program that everyone receives, including the comparison group

Sometimes it may be difficult to implement an evaluation that involves having a comparison group that receives no service. For example, program staff may be reluctant to implement a randomized evaluation unless they feel that everyone in the study receives at least something. Having a basic program that everyone receives and a more advanced program that is restricted to the treatment group can be a way to estimate the effect of the more advanced program. This strategy has important drawbacks. In particular, we won't be able to know if the basic program has any impact. (Because all units will receive it, there will be no comparison group for it.) And we won't be able to know how the advanced program compares to no program at all because there will be no pure comparison group. But we will be able to say how the advanced program compares to the basic program.

How can we document compliance and identify defiers?

To account for partial compliance in the analysis, we have to document compliance in the treatment and comparison groups in the same way. This usually means adding questions on take-up of the program to the endline survey. But it is also useful to document the level of compliance during implementation so that we can take action to limit it while the implementation is ongoing.

Document who receives what treatment

To know the level of compliance, we must document who receives what treatment and when. Some of this information can be collected as part of routine monitoring. For example, we can use monitoring data to see how many people are taking part in the program and compare this to how many eligible people there are in the community in general. We can also monitor where those attending the program come from (whether any people are attending from comparison communities). But monitoring data are not comprehensive because people may gain access in other ways. For example, children not attending schools with a mass deworming program may be given deworming drugs through a clinic. We therefore need to ask about participation in our endline survey so that we have a comprehensive measure of compliance that is consistently collected for treatment and comparison individuals.

In determining the timing and frequency of compliance monitoring, we have to worry about generating demand effects. Asking people about the treatments they are or are not receiving encourages them to seek treatment. We discuss the risk of changing behavior by asking about it in Module 7.4 when dealing with evaluation effects.

Usually we cannot use monitoring data to document compliance during the analysis phase because monitoring data are not usually collected in the comparison group. If our randomization is between two versions of a program with no participants who do not receive the program, we may be able to use monitoring data to adjust for compliance levels in the analysis.

Identify defiers

If there is a risk that there will be defiers (people who take up the program less because they are encouraged to take it up), it is important to identify these people. As long as we can identify defiers, we can estimate the impact of the program on them separately and then find the true impact of the program. When we develop our theory of change (discussed in Module 5.1) we need to think through why some people might react perversely to being offered or encouraged to take up a program. This should help us come up with indicators of these people. In our example of providing information on the benefits of education we said that defiers are likely to be those who had previously overestimated the benefits of education. If we include a question in our baseline survey about how wages rise with education, we will be able to identify who previously overestimated the benefits of education and thus might be a defier.

MODULE 7.2 Attrition

Attrition occurs when outcomes cannot be measured for some study participants. This creates a problem of missing data. This module discusses how attrition is a threat and what we can do to limit attrition.

What is attrition?

Attrition is the absence of data because the researchers are unable to collect some or all of the outcome measures from some people in the sample. This can occur when participants drop out and cannot be measured; when they are still participating but are not measured, for example, because they refuse to be interviewed; or when they refuse to answer some of the questions. Attrition creates a problem of missing data.

When people drop out of the study and can no longer be measured

The starkest example occurs when people die. But people can also move out of the area or withdraw their cooperation. In any of these cases, we cannot measure the outcomes of all the people we planned to study.

When people are still participating but cannot be measured

Sometimes people who are still in a program cannot be found. They are not at home when the enumerators visit or are not at school on the day the test is administered. They may participate in the program but refuse to cooperate with the evaluation. They may not have time to sit down to answer survey questions.

When people refuse to answer some questions

Sometimes people refuse to provide answers to some of the questions asked. For example, they may refuse to answer questions about their sexual or illegal behavior. They may refuse to answer questions about how they earn their money or how much money they earn. A survey may simply be too long, and people may tire of answering questions.

How is attrition a threat?

Attrition can reduce the comparability of treatment and comparison groups

When we lose people's data through attrition, the comparability of the treatment and comparison groups may be undermined if the rates of attrition or the types of attrition differ between treatment and comparison groups. In a (successful) remedial education program, for example, the low-achieving children assigned to the treatment group are more likely to start doing well and not drop out, but the low-achieving children assigned to the comparison group may drop out of school altogether. When looking at test scores later on, if we observe only the test scores of those still in school, we will be comparing a bag of apples and oranges to a bag of apples only. In the treatment group we have both low- and high-achieving children in our sample, but in the comparison group we only have high-achieving children because all the low-achieving children have dropped out. We will wrongly conclude that the remedial program reduces test scores when in fact it helps low-achieving children stay in school.

Imagine that a program increased the test scores of low-achieving students from an average score of 10 to an average score of 15 (Figure 7.1). Overall, the average score for the class increased from 15 to 17.5. And because the low-achieving students in the treatment group were given support, they did not drop out of school, as many of their peers in the comparison group did. However, if we had measured the test scores only of those children who stayed in school, we would have concluded that the program worsened test scores, from 18.3 in the comparison group to 17.5 in the treatment group.

Even if the attrition rates are the same, if different types of people drop out of the two groups, we may still get a biased measure of im-

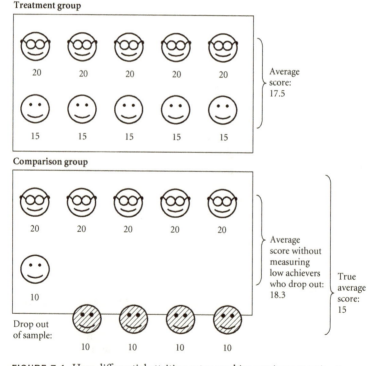

FIGURE 7.1 How differential attrition rates can bias our impact estimate

Note: The faces with eyeglasses represent high-achieving students; those without eyeglasses represent low-achieving students.

pact. Imagine the same remedial program. Parents of high-scoring children in the school with the remedial program are unhappy that the class size is larger than in other schools and there are so many children getting remedial help. They move their children to private school. If we test children at school, we find that four children have left the treatment school, so we have no scores for them, and 4 children have left the comparison school, and we similarly have no scores for them (Figure 7.2). Although the attrition rate (the amount of missing data) is the same in the treatment and comparison groups, we are missing data for different types of children in the treatment and comparison groups, so our estimated impact is biased. In this example, the

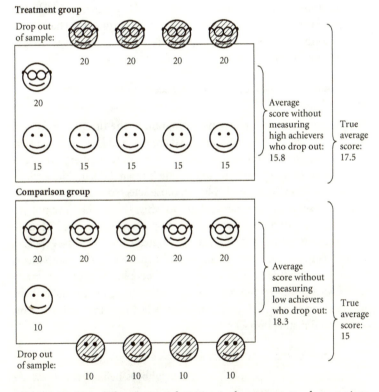

FIGURE 7.2 How different types of attrition in the treatment and comparison groups can bias our impact estimate

Note: The faces with eyeglasses represent high-achieving students; those without eyeglasses represent low-achieving students.

average score of the treatment group is now 15.8 and that for the comparison group is 18.3. If we don't take attrition into account, we might think that the program reduced scores when in fact it increased them.

Attrition lowers statistical power

As discussed in Chapter 6, statistical power depends on sample size. Attrition reduces the sample size, reducing power. The experiment loses sensitivity; now the impact of the program must be larger in order for the evaluation to detect it. If we do not find a statistically significant impact, we cannot tell whether there truly is no impact or whether the attrition diminished our statistical power to detect the impact.

How can we limit attrition?

We can limit attrition in three ways: we can (1) use a research design that promises access to the program to all over time, (2) change the level of randomization, and (3) improve data collection (survey design, administration, and tracking).

Use a research design that promises access to the program to all over time

People who anticipate receiving a program in the future may be less likely to refuse to participate in the study. We could use a design that creates this expectation. Instead of using a treatment lottery, we could use a phase-in design in which everyone is treated during the evaluation period. During the early phases, those selected to receive the program first serve as the treatment group while those who have not yet received the program serve as the comparison group (see Module 4.3). There are some drawbacks to this strategy, however. The expectation of benefits can lead to changes in behavior in the comparison group (see Module 7.4). For example, if people are promised assistance with fertilizer purchases in the future, that might make them less likely to invest their own resources in fertilizer in the short term. This would distort impact estimates.

Change the level of randomization

It is possible that if people see their neighbors being treated but are not treated themselves, this can lead to resentment, and resentment can lead to attrition. One work-around is to randomize at a higher level to ensure that people in close interaction receive the same treatment. However, we are unaware of cases in which too low a level of randomization has led to attrition.

Improve data collection (survey design, administration, and tracking)
There are a number of ways to improve data collection.

Pilot the data collection instruments and procedures Poorly designed data collection instruments and procedures can lead to missing data. Surveys that are too long and complicated are more likely to have missing data, and people may refuse to participate in follow-up surveys. Confusing skip patterns (for example, if the recipient answers, then skips the next three and a half pages of questions) can lead to missing data. Poor administration, such as having men ask women sensitive questions about reproductive health, can make people reluctant to answer surveys (and may even get a survey team thrown out of a community). These types of attrition can be avoided or reduced by better survey design. Piloting our measurement instruments and protocol helps to identify these issues in advance (see Module 5.3).

Follow up on everyone originally randomized We can reduce attrition by following all participants, no matter where they go. In a remedial education program in India, for example, attrition was minimized by returning to the schools many times to administer the test to children who had been absent on the day of the first test. In the end, the enumerators tracked missing children at home and gave them the test there.[3] This ensured that test scores were available from everyone, regardless of whether the children had dropped out of school.

Don't wait too long to follow up The longer the gap between surveys, the higher the attrition rate is likely to be. The longer the wait, the more likely that households will have moved, children will have left home, or individuals will have died. In addition, the longer the wait, the more likely it is that neighbors will have lost track of where people have moved to. In long-term studies we face a trade-off between examining longer-term impacts and keeping attrition low.

3. This study by Abhijit Banerjee, Shawn Cole, Esther Duflo, and Leigh Linden is summarized as Evaluation 2 in the appendix.

Improve follow-up by collecting tracking data routinely Baseline surveys should include tracking modules that include questions on such things as the likelihood of migration, likely migration destinations, cell phone numbers, and contact information of relatives and friends who would not migrate with the families in the study but would know their new contact information in case of migration.

When tracking information collected in the original survey is out of date, peers can be a good source of information. It often works better to use participatory methods to source contact information rather than asking only one person. For example, an HIV prevention program in Kenya targeted adolescents in the final years of primary school. The main outcome was childbearing among school-age girls. The data were collected during six visits to the schools in the three years following the intervention. To limit attrition in this extended follow-up, the researchers used tracking information collected in participatory group surveys of students enrolled at the participants' former school. At each visit, the list of all participants in the original baseline sample was read aloud to students enrolled in the upper grades. For each participant, a series of questions was asked: "Is 'Mary' still going to school? If yes, in which school, in what grade? Does she still live in the area? Is she married? What's her husband's name?" This type of information made it much easier to find Mary and survey her.[4]

Reduce attrition through survey timing The appropriate timing of surveys (both through the day and through the year) can contribute to reducing attrition. When people work far from their homes it is important to survey them at the beginning or the end of the day. There may also be times of the year when people traditionally travel to see relatives. This can be either a help or a hindrance depending on whom we are trying to track. For example, if we are surveying professionals in Paris, we will want to avoid conducting our survey in August, when many Parisians take their annual vacation. Similarly, if we are studying factory workers in China, we may want to avoid the Chinese New Year, because many workers will travel back to their families in rural China. On the other hand, a study of adolescent girls in rural Bangladesh was attempting to track girls who had gone through the pro-

4. This study by Esther Duflo, Pascaline Dupas, and Michael Kremer is summarized as Evaluation 4 in the appendix.

gram, many of whom had moved to Dhaka to work in textile factories. For those girls who could be found neither during the initial survey round nor during the tracking round in Dhaka, a special survey round was carried out during the Eid holiday, when many girls return to their home village from the factories. This "Eid tracking" substantially reduced attrition.[5]

Reduce attrition for a subsample Sometimes it is too expensive to intensively follow up all those in the original sample who have moved. As we will discuss in more detail in the chapter on analysis (Module 8.2), it is important to show how sensitive our results are to attrition, which in turn depends on how different the people who dropped out are from those who didn't. But we can't tell this unless we know a lot about the people who dropped out. One approach, therefore, is to take a random sample of those who have dropped out, follow up with them very carefully, and assume that the dropouts we follow up with will have the same characteristics as those dropouts we did not follow up with. If we undertake this strategy, it is critical that we find virtually all the subset of dropouts that we attempt to follow up with.

Provide incentives Again, we can use the fact that small incentives can have large impacts on behavior—this time to reduce attrition. Studies that involve long surveys may provide limited compensation to encourage participants to complete the survey. The incentive can be provided to all participants or to particular subgroups that are particularly hard to reach. For example, in the survey of adolescent girls described above, married girls were given a small incentive (a melamine plate) to compensate them and their families for their time. Girls who were working in Dhaka were given 100 *taka* in cash ($1.25) because these girls worked very long hours in factories and it was hard to persuade them to give up their very limited free time to respond to a survey. Finally, incentives can be a particularly useful complement to the approach of following up on a small subsample of attriters when it is particularly important to have very low attrition and thus where large incentives can be very worthwhile, as discussed above.

5. This study by Erica Field and Rachel Glennerster is summarized as Evaluation 7 in the appendix.

Spillover effects are the indirect effects of a program on those who have not been treated. This module discusses how spillovers are a threat, what we can do to prevent them, and how we can measure these indirect effects.

What are spillovers?

Programs can have spillover effects, or externalities (as discussed in Chapter 4). Spillovers can take many forms and can be positive or negative. They can occur through a number of channels:

- *Physical:* Children immunized by the program reduce disease transmission in their community. Farmers who learned pig husbandry from the program increase pollution.

- *Behavioral:* A farmer imitates the fertilizer application techniques her treated neighbor learned from the program.

- *Informational:* People learn about the effectiveness of insecticide-treated bed nets from others who received this knowledge through the program (known as social learning).

- *Marketwide (or general equilibrium) effects:* Older workers lose their jobs because firms receive financial incentives from the program to hire young workers.

Spillovers are common and natural. People learn from their peers, they imitate others, they transmit disease. Where spillovers are positive, programs should actively try to harness them to ensure that a program has maximum impact. For example, if people learn about the effectiveness of preventive health products from each other, encouraging a few people to invest in those products might be all it takes to trigger mass adoption. If people are more likely to save for retirement if they are surrounded by savers, we would want to increase the number of savers and the resulting spillovers. When spillovers are negative, programs should attempt to minimize them.

Overall, the presence of potential spillovers has two main implications for our evaluation design. First, we want to anticipate spillovers, so we can choose the appropriate level of randomization. Second, we may want to measure the spillovers to identify the optimum number of people to treat (the density of treatment) to achieve optimal impact.

In Chapter 4 we discussed these implications in terms of the level of randomization. This section focuses on identifying potential spillovers and understanding why they can undermine the evaluation design.

How are spillovers a threat?

Spillovers reduce the quality of the counterfactual

People outside the treatment group can experience indirect effects of the program. When, as often happens, these people make up our comparison group, the outcomes of the comparison group will reflect the indirect program effects. This means that the comparison group is no longer as good a counterfactual because their outcomes reflect indirect program effects, not the outcomes in the absence of the program.

Spillovers become a threat to the evaluation if we do not take them into account in the design and/or analysis phase

If the evaluation does not capture or account for *positive* spillovers from treatment to comparison, the impact of the program will be *underestimated*. If it does not capture or account for *negative* spillovers, the impact will be *overestimated*.

Imagine a deworming program randomized at the individual level within a school. Treated children have lower worm loads, which reduces worm transmission in the population. Reduced disease transmission benefits untreated children in the comparison group because they will have lower worm loads, despite not having been treated for worms. Comparing treated children to untreated children within a school will lead us to underestimate the impact of the program.

How can we manage spillovers?

Identify potential spillovers

The first step in managing spillovers is to anticipate them. That means asking the following questions: What, who, how? What is spilling over? From whom do the spillovers come, and to whom do they accrue? How do the spillovers work, by what pathways, and to what effect (i.e., are they positive or negative)?

We can use common sense, previous studies, existing theories, and logical frameworks to anticipate potential spillovers. Critically, we need to think both of potential *positive* and *negative* spillovers. It may be a lot more alluring to think through potential positive spillovers, but anticipating potential negative spillovers is very important, too.

Reduce spillovers to the comparison group

As discussed in Chapter 4, the presence of spillovers has implications for our choice of the level of randomization. Take an evaluation of an HIV information program on girls' behavior. We could randomize the program classroom by classroom, but adolescents would probably share information with their friends in other classes. Instead we can randomize at the school level. If a financial literacy program is implemented at the business level but we anticipate spillovers in the marketplace (because businesses compete for a fixed pool of clients), we should randomize at the marketplace level.

Estimate the spillover effects by measuring outcomes of the untreated in or near the treated units

Many programs have a clear target population. For instance, microfinance organizations often target women exclusively. Bed net distribution programs target pregnant women and mothers of young children.[6] HIV information programs typically target schoolchildren and often miss out-of-school youths. How do these programs affect untreated people nearby? Do they have positive or negative spillovers on these other populations? Knowing the answers to these questions can have important implications for program design.

To make sure the evaluation can answer this question, we need to systematically collect data on outcomes for those not directly treated but whom we expect to be affected indirectly. If we anticipate that neighbors of pregnant women may learn about the effectiveness of bed nets by observing the pregnant women's health, we should monitor the adoption of bed nets among the neighbors of both our treatment and our comparison groups. If we anticipate that husbands of women targeted by microfinance might be able to borrow from their wives, we should measure the business outcomes of the spouses of women selected for microloans and the spouses of the women in the comparison group.

---

6. This study by Jessica Cohen and Pascaline Dupas is summarized as Evaluation 6 in the appendix.

MODULE 7.4 Evaluation-Driven Effects

The fact of being part of an evaluation can change the way people behave, independent of any impacts of the program. This module discusses why this poses a threat and how we can limit the threat.

What are evaluation-driven effects?

Being part of an evaluation can change behavior independent of the treatment. This evaluation-driven behavior can take at least six main forms:[7]

1. *Hawthorne effects:* The treatment group works harder than normal.

2. *John Henry effects:* The comparison group starts competing with the treatment group.

3. *Resentment and demoralization effects:* The comparison group resents missing out on the treatment.

4. *Demand effects:* The participants change their behavior in response to their perception of the evaluators' objective.

5. *Anticipation effects:* The comparison group changes their behavior because they expect to receive the treatment later on.

6. *Survey effects:* Being surveyed (frequently) changes the subsequent behavior of the treatment or the comparison group.

Hawthorne effects: When the treatment group works harder

People in the treatment group may exert a greater effort than they would if everyone got the program because they have been "chosen." One reason could be that they feel lucky and do not want to waste the "rare" opportunity. For example, a student who wins a scholarship through a lottery among many eligible students may work especially hard because she feels she has been given an unexpected opportunity. But this extra effort from being "chosen" would not have been there if the scholarships had been given to all the eligible students.

---

7. William R. Shadish, Thomas D. Cook, and Donald T. Campbell provide a good discussion of evaluation effects in *Experimental and Quasi-experimental Designs for Generalized Causal Inference* (Boston: Houghton Mifflin, 2002).

Gratitude may also lead a community to exert greater effort. The treatment group may work especially hard because they are thankful and do not want to fail the program. This gratitude and the work it generates is a natural part of the program and not an evaluation effect unless it is generated by seeing that the program is being evaluated and there is a strong desire to see positive results from an evaluation so that the program can be scaled up to others.

Evaluation-driven behavioral changes in the treatment group are sometimes called Hawthorne effects. In a series of studies carried out at the Hawthorne site of Western Electric Company outside Chicago in the 1920s and 1930s, it was thought that workers responded to being under observation by increasing their productivity.[8] Later studies showed that this was not the case, but the name caught on and survives.

John Henry effects: When the comparison group competes with the treatment group

People assigned to the comparison group may start to compete with the treatment group. For example, regular teachers may compete with the contract teachers introduced during an evaluation. In a program evaluating the impact of contract teachers, the regular teachers may work especially hard over the course of the experiment, harder than they normally would, to influence any policy decision about how many contract teachers to hire. Once the experiment is over, the policy decision has been made, and they are no longer under observation, they might revert to their normal work habits. Competition, including between regular teachers in comparison schools and contract teachers in program schools, makes outcomes in the comparison group higher than they normally would have been if there had been no evaluations.

Evaluation-driven behavioral changes in the comparison group are sometimes called John Henry effects, after a legendary American steel driver of the late nineteenth century. According to a US folk song, John Henry worked laying railway track using long-handled hammers. When steam drills were introduced, threatening steel drivers with redundancy, John Henry is said to have challenged a steam engine to a drilling competition, telling his captain, "A man ain't noth-

8. Elton Mayo, "Hawthorne Effect," in *The Oxford Companion to the Mind* (Oxford, UK: 1929), 303.

ing but a man. Before I am bitten by that steam drill, I'm gonna die with this hammer in my hand." He won the competition but died from overexertion, with the hammer still in his hand. A comparison of the productivity of the steam driver versus John Henry on that day would not have been a good way to evaluate the impact of steam drivers.

Resentment and demoralization effects: When the comparison group resents not being given the treatment

People assigned to the comparison group may become demoralized or resentful. This could lead them to behave in ways that worsen their outcomes, which means that the comparison group would no longer be a good counterfactual for what would have happened in the absence of the program.

Demand effects: When the participants change their behavior in response to their perception of what the evaluator is trying to test

Demand effects are a particular problem for lab experiments in which participants are asked to take part in many different games with somewhat different parameters. The participants may start to ask themselves, "Why am I being presented with these different scenarios? What is the researcher trying to test?" The participant may consciously or unconsciously try to confirm or undermine the hypothesis they think the evaluator is trying to test.

During an evaluation of a program, participants may well attempt to change their behavior to meet the expectations of those running the program, but this is an integral part of the program. It is a program effect rather than an evaluation effect and is a problem only if that behavior is stronger in small pilots than in large programs.

Anticipation effects: When the comparison group changes their behavior because they think they will receive the program in the future

The phase-in design and the rotation design rely on delayed treatment to create the comparison groups (see Module 4.3). This can generate evaluation-driven behavior changes if people anticipate the rollout. For example, if we are using a phase-in design to roll out a microfinance program, the comparison group could change their behavior in anticipation of the loan. They might take out other loans, expecting to repay them with the anticipated microloan. Even if there is no phase-in design, people in the comparison group might still think that they will possibly receive the program in the future and change their behavior in response.

Survey effects: When being surveyed can change future behavior

To measure the impact of a program, we conduct surveys, but frequent surveying can itself change how the participants behave. In an education program, frequent testing can mean that the children get very good at test taking. In a water treatment program in Kenya, one of the outcomes was the incidence of diarrhea. To test for survey effects, a random sample of participants were interviewed every week about the occurrence of illness incidence and about their use of water purification products. The survey itself provided a reminder to invest in water purification products and changed behavior.[9]

How are evaluation-driven effects a threat?

Evaluation effects can undermine power and generalizability

Evaluation-driven behavior can lead to outcome changes that would not occur in the absence of the evaluation. If those changes are common to both the treatment and the comparison groups (such as survey effects), they do not affect the comparability of the two groups, and therefore they do not introduce bias into the estimate of the program's impact. But survey effects, even if they are equal between treatment and comparison groups, may well reduce the power of the evaluation to detect the treatment effect and reduce the generalizability of the results.

Take the example of the antidiarrhea program above. Imagine that 40 percent of the people in an area already add chlorine to their water, another 40 percent sometimes do and are relatively open to efforts to persuade them to chlorinate their water, and a final 20 percent are very unlikely to chlorinate their water under any circumstances. A highly effective program might increase water chlorination from 40 to 70 percent. But frequent surveys produce an increase in water chlorination to 60 percent in the comparison group. The program is now effectively operating in an environment with higher-than-average water treatment. It becomes harder for the program to have as great

9. Alix Peterson Zwane, Jonathan Zinman, Eric Van Dusen, William Pariente, Clair Null, Edward Miguel, Michael Kremer, et al., "Being Surveyed Can Change Later Behavior and Related Parameter Estimates," *Proceedings of the National Academy of Sciences USA* 108 (2011): 1821–1826.

an impact in these conditions because many of the easily convinced people have already changed behavior due to the frequent surveying. It thus becomes harder to judge if the program is effective. On the other hand, the surveying and the program may act as complements to each other, with the constant reminders from the frequent surveys making people more responsive to the program. We are still getting an unbiased impact of the program in a particular context (one in which surveys are frequent), but the results may not generalize to other situations in which the level of chlorination is lower and people are not being frequently reminded of the reasons to take part in the program.

Evaluation-driven effects can undermine comparability

Even worse, if the evaluation-driven behavior is group specific (affecting only the treatment or only the comparison group), it undermines the comparability of the two groups. This threatens the integrity of the evaluation strategy. Imagine a secondary school scholarship program that targets poor children. Scholarships are awarded by lottery. Those who win the lottery are able to attend secondary school, but those who lose the lottery have to discontinue their education. Those who have to discontinue, though equally qualified, could become demoralized and put less effort into their work or informal studies. The comparison group now has worse outcomes than they would have had if the evaluation had never been conducted at all. This exaggerates the difference in outcomes between the treatment and comparison groups.

Evaluation-driven effects can bias impact estimates

Hawthorne effects and social desirability effects can inflate the estimated impact of a program compared to its true impact by artificially boosting outcomes among the treatment group. John Henry effects deflate the estimated impact of the program by artificially boosting outcomes in the comparison group. Demoralization effects inflate the estimated impact of the program by artificially depressing outcomes in the comparison group. Anticipation effects might either inflate or deflate estimated effects, depending on the situation.

How can we limit evaluation-driven effects?

Identify potential sources of evaluation-driven behavior change

One place to start this process is to identify the interactions between the evaluation team and the treatment and comparison groups that would exist only in the evaluation context and would not exist if the program were not being evaluated.

Use a different level of randomization

One way to limit evaluation-driven behavior among the comparison group is to limit the treatment-comparison interactions that generate demoralization, anticipation, and competition. This can be done by changing the level of randomization (see Module 4.2).

Do not announce the phase-in

When planning to do a phase-in or rotation design, we may choose not to announce it, to avoid anticipation effects. Not announcing the phase-in means that we cannot rely on anticipation of treatment to reduce attrition. As in many other instances in designing the evaluation, we would have to make trade-offs, deciding what works best for our evaluation and in our particular instance.[10]

Make sure the staff is impartial

To reduce Hawthorne effects, it is important to ensure implementation staff do not feel their job is threatened if the evaluation does not show a positive effect. In general, implementing organizations feel less threatened by an evaluation that includes different alternatives than by a simple "program versus nothing" evaluation.

Make sure the treatment and comparison groups get equivalent interaction with evaluation staff

To make sure survey effects do not affect comparability, the treatment and the comparison groups must get the same interaction with evaluation staff—both in terms of quantity and quality. If we spend more time and interact differently with the treatment group, we are likely to generate differential evaluation-driven behavior change across groups. So whatever we do to the treatment group, we do to the comparison group, except, of course, giving them access to the program. We use the same surveys for both groups, use the same procedures, and use the same enumerators.

---

10. Researchers should check with their IRB whether it is ethical not to announce that all communities in the study will receive the program eventually. However, program implementers will often not want to announce future plans because of concerns that funding may change and they will not be able to fulfill their promises.

Measure the evaluation-driven effects on a subset of the evaluation sample

We could measure the evaluation-driven effects if we expect them to be important. We would have to create random variation in evaluation procedures to measure the effects. This is what was done in the Kenya water program discussed above. The randomized study of chlorination included a sample of 1,500 households. Of these, 330 were randomly selected as the sample to measure survey effects. One hundred and seventy of the households were randomly assigned to be surveyed every two weeks, as is common in epidemiological studies, for over 18 months. The other 160 were randomly assigned to be surveyed only three times, or once every six months (an approach more commonly used by economists). That study, and others like it, found that frequent surveying changes behavior and therefore program impacts. This implies that we should carefully consider whether, how, and how much to survey the participants.[11]

11. Zwane et al., "Being Surveyed Can Change Later Behavior and Related Parameter Estimates."

8 Analysis

This chapter covers how to analyze the data from a randomized evaluation and make inferences about the impact of a program. The analysis of the simplest of randomized evaluations can be relatively straightforward. However, more sophisticated analysis can help us understand who and what are driving the results. In addition, we need to make corrections if we use stratified or group-level randomization, if we face threats such as spillovers, or if we have multiple outcomes.

MODULE 8.1: Basic Intention-to-Treat Analysis
MODULE 8.2: Catalog of Corrections
MODULE 8.3: Pre-analysis Plans

MODULE 8.1 Basic Intention-to-Treat Analysis

This module introduces intention-to-treat (ITT) analysis, which should be the first step in the analysis of any randomized evaluation. We discuss how to add control variables, estimate multiple treatments, and go beyond average treatment effects.

Prior to analysis

Before we start any analysis, we need to prepare (or "clean") our data and make sure we have a good understanding of their properties. This usually involves taking the following steps:[1]

---

1. A good discussion of some of the challenges of collecting and preparing data can be found in Robert M. Townsend, Sombat Sakunthasathien, and Rob Jordan, *Chronicles from the Field: The Townsend Thai Project* (Cambridge, MA: MIT Press, 2013).

- Correcting obvious errors in the data
- Checking for outliers
- Calculating attrition rates
- Calculating compliance rates
- Plotting and describing the data

Correcting obvious errors in the data

It is good practice to look at our data and make sure that we have corrected obvious errors in the data (sometimes called "cleaning the data"). Errors can occur when a respondent misunderstands the question, when an enumerator fills in the questionnaire incorrectly, or when data are entered incorrectly. In Chapter 5 we discussed a number of processes to limit errors in the data, including supervisors' checking completed surveys at the end of each day of data collection to look for inconsistent answers. Errors that are caught early in the field can be corrected by going back to respondents to ask clarifying questions. If data are collected electronically, software can be programmed so that answers that are outside the feasible range will not be accepted by the data collection device. Similarly, if two answers within a survey are inconsistent with each other, a data collection program can prompt the enumerator to ask a clarifying question. In Chapter 5 we discussed back-checking (or redoing) a subsample of surveys to spot enumerators and questions that are not reliable. We also discussed entering the data that have been collected on paper twice to reduce errors at the data entry stage. Part of the "cleaning" process involves comparing the outcomes from the two data entry efforts. When the results differ, the paper record is checked to see which is correct.

The next step is to check for responses that are outside the feasible range. It is not possible that a child is 2 centimeters tall or that the size of a farm is –2 hectares. In some cases feasible ranges will be determined by answers the respondent gave to other questions: for example, it is unlikely that someone both is attending primary school and is 88 years old.

Every survey has built-in skip patterns—if the respondent answers no, the next few questions are skipped. Supervisors in the field should have made sure that these skip patterns were adhered to—in other words, if the respondent said she did no farming, there should not be answers to questions about how much rice she planted. We also check these skip patterns prior to analysis.

Surveys should have a number of consistency checks built in. For example, a respondent may be asked in an agricultural survey what crops were planted, harvested, and sold. If a crop was reported as planted and sold but not harvested, this is probably an error. Ideally these inconsistencies are checked and corrected in the field, but they should also be checked during the data-cleaning process.

When we find errors in the data, we can either code a particular response as missing or fill in what we think the real response was. We should be very confident that we are right before we fill in data, but there are cases in which this is valid. For example, it may be clear that a farmer reported she farmed 2 hectares rather than –2 hectares (especially if the amount of seed the farmer reports using is consistent with a 2-hectare plot). If there is a lot of detail about the farming practices of the household, we may be justified in changing the answer to the question "Does this family participate in farming?" from "No" to "Yes."

We have to be careful not to "overclean" our data—in other words, not to force the data to conform to what we think makes sense. Just because we live in a household of four people does not mean that it is a mistake when someone reports that they live in a household of 38.

Checking for outliers We should make sure that we are aware of outliers before we conduct our analysis. For example, we want to know if there are people with very high incomes or very high test scores in our data. We may later want to see whether our results are sensitive to whether these observations are included or excluded from our analyses. Usually we do not drop these outliers from the data a priori.

Checking attrition rates Next we will want to calculate our attrition rate and our compliance rate. If our attrition rate is poor (high), we may want to go back to the field and collect more data. If that is not possible, a high attrition rate will tell us that we will need to undertake some analysis to give us an indication of how sensitive our results are to different assumptions about what happened to those for whom we do not have data. Examining our compliance rate will also suggest how we should proceed with the analysis. (We discuss ways to adjust for compliance in Module 8.2.)

Plotting and describing the data Finally, it is always good practice to understand our data before we start analysis. This can be done by plotting our data or examining the mean, median, variance, maximum, and minimum for each variable. Stata, for example, has a `summarize` command that provides summary statistics on a variable and has many different ways to plot data. Plotting data can help identify outliers and tell us whether outcomes are concentrated around certain values. A good plot can also illustrate program impact more compellingly than a regression. We provide an example of using a plot to illustrate impact later in this module.

The ITT estimate

The most basic analysis we can perform at the end of a randomized evaluation is to calculate the ITT estimate of average treatment effects. This compares the mean outcomes of those who were randomized to receive the program with those of people randomized to the comparison group.

Imagine a program in Ghana that provides scholarships to eligible students to attend secondary school.[2] Students who score well on the entrance exam but do not have plans to attend secondary school (possibly because they cannot afford to attend) are randomized into treatment and comparison groups. Those in the treatment group are offered scholarships to attend a secondary school of their choice. After 5 and 10 years the students are resurveyed and asked a number of questions about their employment and marriage status, their earnings, and their social attitudes. We are primarily interested in the economic effects of the program, so we want to know whether the average earnings of those who were offered scholarships are greater than the average earnings of those who were not offered scholarships and by how much.

What is the ITT effect?

The ITT estimates the mean of the outcome variables of all those assigned to the treatment (in this case, those offered the scholarship) and compares it to the mean of the outcome variables for those who were assigned to the comparison group (not offered the scholarship).

---

2. This example is inspired by a study by Esther Duflo, Pascaline Dupas, and Michael Kremer, which is summarized as Evaluation 3 in the appendix.

Imagine that the average income in the past month of those assigned to treatment was $45 and the average income of those assigned to comparison was $30. The ITT impact of the program is the difference between the two: $15 per month. By calculating the variance of income between the treatment group and the comparison group we can run a t-test to tell us whether the difference between the two is statistically significant. Most statistical packages will calculate a t-test for us. For example, if we have our data loaded into Stata and have a variable called `income`, which is income earned in the past week, and `treatment`, which takes the value one for those offered a scholarship and zero for those not offered a scholarship, we can ask for a comparison of means for treatment versus comparison by entering

```
ttest income, by (treatment).[3]
```

A different way of making the same comparison is to use a regression framework:

$$Y_i = c + \beta T_i + \varepsilon_i,$$

where Y_i is the income of student i, c is a constant that in this case gives us the value of earnings for the comparison group, T_i is the treatment dummy (described above), and ε_i is an error term. The coefficient on the treatment dummy (β) will give us the difference in means between the treatment and comparison groups, the estimated impact of the program. In Stata we would enter

```
regress income treatment.
```

The regression output will report the result of a t-test that shows whether the coefficient is statistically different from zero, and it is identical to the t-test comparison of means described above.

What does the ITT measure?

The ITT estimates what happens to the average person given access to the program. In our example from Ghana, it measures the impact of

---

3. All the Stata commands included in this and other modules are based on Stata 11. Because Stata commands sometimes change as the program is updated, we strongly advise those undertaking analyses to refer to the Stata manual or help function (both of which are very well written) before conducting analysis and using any of the code suggested here.

offering scholarships for those who pass the entrance exam for secondary school but who are not yet enrolled in school. It does not measure the impact of actually going to secondary school, because not all of those who are offered the scholarship take it. The ITT estimate, however, is often relevant to policy. In the Ghana case, the ITT estimate will give us an estimate of how much a policy of eliminating secondary school fees for those who pass the end-of-primary-school exam would increase earnings among the group of students who would otherwise probably not go to secondary school. It may be that in our experiment not all those who are offered the scholarship are able to take it up: maybe they need to be earning money for their family, or maybe they don't want to stay in school. But these same factors will reduce the impact of a government policy that abolishes secondary school fees for qualified students. Abolishing fees does not mean that everyone will stay in school. So a relevant question to ask is "What is the average effect of offering scholarships on those who are eligible to stay in school?"

It is also useful to think about another example: our evaluation of school-based deworming, in which children in primary schools in areas with high rates of worm infection are mass treated for parasitic worms. Here the ITT estimate tells us what happens to the average child who is eligible for treatment in the program population. It does not answer the question "What is the effect of taking a deworming drug?" Instead it estimates the impact of a real-life deworming program, in which some people in the treatment group may not have received a pill because they were not at school on the deworming day and some people would have taken deworming pills even in the absence of the program. This may well be the most relevant estimate of impact for policy purposes. Even if we decide that we want to use other estimation techniques that tell us the impact of the program on those who take it up, the ITT estimate should always be reported.

Including covariates

Covariates are any variables that are defined before the beginning of an experiment, such as gender or ethnicity, and thus cannot have been changed by the program. The start of the experiment is defined as when randomization takes place. Usually we measure covariates before the program starts, but occasionally when we do not have a baseline we use data collected after the start of the program on variables like gender that we know have not changed.

Including covariates, or control variables, in the estimating regression can give us a more precise estimate of the impact of a program. We do not need to add covariates when we analyze the results of a simple individual-level randomized evaluation because the comparison of the means in the treatment and comparison groups is valid.

As we discuss in Module 6.2, including covariates that help predict the outcome variable reduces unexplained variance. By reducing the magnitude of the "error" term we reduce the uncertainty related to our estimated effect and make our estimate more precise. The intuition for this is explained in Module 6.2.

Accounting for covariates in practice

We control for covariates by adding them to the regression. We estimate an equation as follows:

$$Y_i = c + \beta T_i + \gamma X_i + \varepsilon_i,$$

where Y_i is our outcome variable, T_i is our treatment dummy, and X_i is the set of characteristics that we want to control for. In our Ghana example, if we are controlling for gender, years of parental education, and test scores on the end-of-primary-school exam we will estimate

$$Y_i = c + \beta T_i + \gamma_1 x1_i + \gamma_2 x2_i + \gamma_3 x3_i + \varepsilon_i,$$

where $x1$ is a dummy for gender, $x2$ is a variable for years of parental education, and $x3$ is the test score on the end-of-primary-school exam. In Stata we would estimate

```
regress income treatment gender yrs_parent-
education primary_testscore.
```

It is common practice to report the estimated program impact (β) both with and without covariates to show whether the estimated impact is sensitive to slightly different approaches. If we have chosen the covariates appropriately, the precision (and possibly the statistical significance) of the estimated impact will increase with the inclusion of covariates. In most cases, however, the magnitude of the estimated effect will not change very much when we add covariates.

Which covariates to include

We may have collected a very large number of variables in our baseline. We do not, however, want to include all of them as controls in our estimating regression. With a limited sample we can accurately estimate only a limited number of coefficients, and the coefficient we are most interested in is that on the treatment dummy, which tells us the impact of the program. In the extreme, we cannot have as many covariates as we have data points in our data set. But long before we hit this binding constraint, adding additional covariates is likely to reduce rather than increase the precision of our estimate. Adding covariates increases the precision of our estimate as long as they help explain quite a lot of the unexplained variance in the outcome measures. But as we add more and more covariates, less and less of the variance is unexplained. The remaining variation may well be idiosyncratic and not be highly correlated with any observable characteristics.

Often covariates are highly correlated with each other (for example, parental education, income, and occupation are likely to be highly correlated). Adding many covariates that are highly correlated with each other adds little and may well harm our precision. Instead we want to add a few covariates that together explain much of variation in the outcome variable. Usually the baseline level of the outcome measure is the most useful covariate to include. In Module 8.3 we discuss the benefits of deciding which covariates to include before we start the analysis.

If subgroups are relevant

The effects of the program may be different for different subgroups in a population. When this happens we say that there are *heterogeneous treatment effects*. For example, providing additional textbooks may be effective only for those children whose level of reading is sufficiently advanced that they can understand the textbooks clearly. A remedial education program may be particularly helpful to those students who were falling behind the regular curriculum at the start of the program. Testing the effectiveness of a program on different subgroups can help us understand how to effectively target the program in the future. It can also help us understand the mechanism through which the program worked. For example, finding that the provision of textbooks in rural Kenya helped only the more advanced students was important evidence that the curriculum was not at an appropriate level for much of the class.[4]

---

4. Paul Glewwe, Michael Kremer, and Sylvie Moulin, "Many Children Left Behind? Textbooks and Test Scores in Kenya," *American Economic Journal: Applied Economics* 1 (2009): 112–135.

A *subgroup* is any group of individuals in a sample with at least one common characteristic, such as women or children under age 5. The group must share an observable characteristic that was determined before the start of the program.

Estimating subgroups

We estimate the impact of the program on a subgroup by dropping all the individuals who do not belong to the subgroup and then running the same estimation procedure we do for the full sample. For example, if we are interested in the impact of the Ghana scholarship program on girls, we drop all the boys from our data set and estimate the ITT as we did for the full sample. As long as the subgroup is defined using characteristics like gender that were determined before the start of the program, we are not introducing selection bias.

Low power in subgroup analysis

Because we are estimating the effect of the program in a subgroup of the whole sample, we do not have as many data points and so may not have as much power as when we estimate the average effect on the whole sample. This means that the minimum program effect we can distinguish from zero will be larger in the subsample than if we were using the full sample.

This lack of power is particularly acute when we try to compare relative effect sizes in different subgroups, and usually we will need very large samples to do this effectively. When the estimated effect sizes in both subgroups are imprecisely measured, we have very little power to determine if they are different from each other. Even if we find that a program effect is significantly different from zero in one group and not significantly different from zero in another subgroup, that does not mean that we know the program is more effective in one group than in the other. Let's look at an example.

Imagine that we are interested in understanding whether the scholarship program in Ghana is more effective in increasing wages for girls than for boys. We find that the coefficient on the treatment dummy for girls is $15, while the estimate for boys is $10. Imagine that the confidence interval around the effect on girls is ±$9 and the confidence interval around the estimate for boys is ±$10. In other words, our standard errors tell us that there is a 95 percent chance that the range between $6 and $24 contains the true impact on girls, while there is a 95 percent chance that the range between $0 and $20 contains the true impact on boys. Even though the estimated impact is significantly different from zero for girls but not boys, there is a lot of overlap between the two confidence intervals, which should give us pause before we conclude anything definite about the relative impact of the program on the two groups.

Formally, if we want to test whether the effect of a program is the same for two different subgroups, we do a t-test for the equality of the coefficients in the two treatment groups. In Stata we would create a treatment dummy for girls (T_girls) and a treatment dummy for boys (T_boys). We would also need to include a dummy for girls in general. Then we would estimate the effect of the two treatment groups and ask if the two coefficients are statistically different from each other (this is a form of interaction estimation that we discuss more below). In our Ghana example,

```
reg income T_girls T_boys girls
```

and

```
test T_girls = T_boys.
```

If we are analyzing a group-level randomization with data collected at the individual level and our subgroups are defined at the individual level, we may not lose as much power when we estimate subgroups as in the case of an individual-level randomization. This is because the main determinant of power is usually the number of groups. For example, if we randomize by community and we want to examine the effect of a program on girls (compared to boys), as long as there are some girls in all our communities we will still have as many communities in our subgroup analysis as in our main analysis. Our power for the subgroup analysis may be lower than that for the main analysis but not necessarily by much.

Interaction terms

Interaction terms provide another way to test whether our program had a different effect on different types of participants. Subgroup analysis is useful when the different types of people we want to test fall into clear categories, such as males versus females. But not all variables are of this kind. Some, such as income, test scores, or age, are continuous. From continuous variables we create categories, such as rich and poor, old or young. Sometimes that is appropriate. For example, in our remedial education case, only those falling below a certain threshold were sent to the remedial tutor, so a continuous variable (test scores) was used to create categories, and thus testing in categories makes sense. But in other cases we may think the program effect may change gradually in line with the continuous variable. Maybe the benefits of a savings program will decline with age as younger people will be able to benefit from the program for longer. There is no one cutoff below which the program starts to be more useful to the young.

We test such a hypothesis by including an interaction term in our estimation equation as follows:

$$Y_i = c + \beta_1 T_i + \beta_2 AT_i + \beta_3 A_i + \varepsilon_i,$$

where A_i is a variable that is equal to the age of individual i when the program started, Y_i is our outcome measure (savings at the time of retirement), T_i is our treatment dummy, AT_i is an interaction term created by multiplying A_i and T_i, and ε_i is our error term. The constant c gives us the mean of our comparison group. Note that whenever we include an interaction term we must always include the components of the interaction. In other words, if we want to include the combination of T_i and A_i, we also need to include T_i and A_i separately.[5]

The coefficient on the interaction term (β_2) tells us, in this case, whether the treatment increases, decreases, or is constant with age. If $\beta_2 = 0$, the program has the same impact on people whatever their age when they started the program; if β_2 is greater than zero, the program impact increases with age at the start of the program; if it is less than zero, the program has less impact as age increases.

We have to be careful when including interaction terms in the interpretation of the average impact of a program because the overall impact is spread across β_1 and β_2. To calculate the average impact of the program we take the estimating equation, plug in the coefficients we have estimated, and calculate what the difference in Y_i would be if $T_i = 1$ is compared to $T_i = 0$. A number of the elements in the equation are the same in either case and can be ignored, so we are left with two terms: $\beta_1 T_i$ and $\beta_2 AT_i$. Therefore, if we want to find the average impact

---

5. For a good discussion of using dummies and interaction terms in regressions, see Peter Kennedy, *A Guide to Econometrics* (Cambridge, MA: MIT Press, 2008).

of the program on a person of the average age, we calculate the average age at the start of the program, multiply it by β_2, and add this to β_1.

Multiple observations

It is possible to analyze the results of a randomized evaluation simply by comparing outcomes at the end of a program for the treatment and comparison groups. Often, however, we have collected baseline data as well as endline data and therefore have two observations for each unit in our analysis—one from before the program started and one from after it started. This opens up additional ways to analyze our data. One option is to include baseline values of our outcome variable as a control in our regression (as we discuss above). Another option is to calculate the change in our outcome variable by taking the difference between the outcome at endline and at baseline; we can then use the change variable as our outcome. When we do this we are imposing a structure on our regression, in other words, assuming a certain relationship between the outcome at baseline and at endline. It makes sense to do this only if we have a strong reason to think this structure does in fact hold.

In some cases we have many observations for each unit in our analysis, including several observations before the program was introduced and several observations after. This allows us to check whether the treatment and comparison groups were following similar trends before the program and judge whether the impact persists or dies out over time.

An evaluation of the impact of the Vietnam draft on earnings collected eight years' worth of data on federal Social Security taxes for those randomly chosen to be eligible for the draft and those not eligible. Because these taxes are mandated under the Federal Insurance Contributions Act (FICA), they are a particularly reliable indicator of earnings and are referred to as FICA earnings. The evaluation divides the sample into white males and nonwhite males and examines earnings subject to FICA. The sample is further divided into three cohorts, each of which was randomized for draft eligibility at different times. By plotting the earnings data over time for each subgroup it is possible to show that the earnings of draft-eligible and draft-ineligible males were at similar levels and following similar trajectories prior to the draft lottery. For white males, FICA earnings diverged immediately after the lottery (Figure 8.1). The evaluation also estimates the impact of the draft lottery on earnings for different cohorts using a

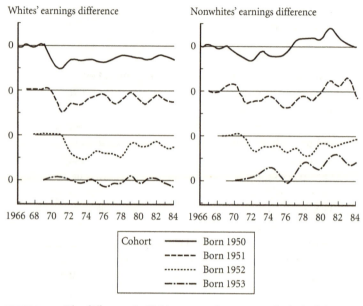

Whites' earnings difference

Nonwhites' earnings difference

1966 68 70 72 74 76 78 80 82 84   1966 68 70 72 74 76 78 80 82 84

Cohort	————	Born 1950
	– – – –	Born 1951
	··········	Born 1952
	—·—·—	Born 1953

FIGURE 8.1 The difference in FICA earnings by Vietnam draft eligibility status

Source: Joshua D. Angrist, "Lifetime Earnings and the Vietnam Era Draft Lottery: Evidence from Social Security Administrative Records," *American Economic Review* 80 (1990): 313–336.

Notes: The figure plots the difference in Federal Insurance Contributions Act (FICA) taxable earnings by draft eligibility status for the four cohorts born between 1950 and 1953. Each tick on the vertical axis represents 500 real (1978) dollars.

regression framework, but the plot of the data demonstrates the impact (on whites' earnings) in a stark and convincing way.

Having multiple observations taken after the introduction of the program allows us to see whether the impact of the program persists over time, decays, or strengthens. Again there are a couple of different ways we can structure this analysis. We could run our basic ITT average treatment effect analysis as discussed above for each different time period separately, see which time periods have treatment effects that are statistically different from zero, and run a *t*-test to see if the treatment effects for different time periods are different from each other. If we have only two post-treatment time periods, this might be the most appropriate approach. If we have many post-treatment observations and we want to test whether the effects of the program decay, we might want to run our data in panel form, with an outcome indexed both by individual (i) and by year since treatment (a), so that we will have multiple observations for the same household or individual (Y_{ia}).[6] Imagine, for example, that we have panel data on income and healthcare expenditures for households for three years and our treatment was provided in the first year. Our data would be structured in the following way:

Household (HH)	Year	Years since treatment	Income ($)	Health expenditure ($)
HH1	2004	0	21,510	551
	2005	1	22,341	782
	2006	2	22,514	321
HH2	2004	0	16,221	364
	2005	1	14,964	1,894
	2006	2	15,492	236

Our treatment dummy (T_i) is the same whatever year we are looking at. A_{ia} is a years-since-treatment variable, and AT_{ai} is an interaction term that is created by multiplying A_i and T_i. Note that this is similar to but not exactly the same as the set-up discussed under interactions. The difference is that in this case we are dealing with a panel and we have multiple values of A for each individual (one for each year) whereas above we had just one value of A_i (age at the start of the program). We estimate the following equation:

$$Y_i = c + \beta_1 T_i + \beta_2 AT_{ai} + A_i + \varepsilon_i.$$

We can then test whether the coefficient on β_2 is less than zero (in which case the treatment effect decays over time) or is greater than zero (in which case it grows over time) using a t-test.

Multiple treatments

Until now we have assumed that we have one treatment group and one comparison group, but in many cases we have multiple treatment

6. For a good discussion of the econometrics of panel data, see Jeffrey M. Wooldridge, *Econometric Analysis of Cross Section and Panel Data* (Cambridge, MA: MIT Press, 2001).

groups. The basic analysis of multiple treatments closely follows that for single treatments.

In an evaluation of a program designed to empower adolescent girls in Bangladesh there were three main treatments: an afterschool girls' club with a curriculum designed to teach health education, promote staying in school, and in some cases teach financial literacy; an incentive (cooking oil) to delay marriage until the age of 18; and a combination of the girls' club and the incentive to delay marriage.[7]

The basic regression for analyzing the program was similar to the standard ITT analysis except that instead of one treatment dummy there were three. A number of basic covariates were also included in the regression:

$$Y_i = c + \beta_1 T1_i + \beta_2 T2_i + \beta_3 T3_i + \gamma_1 x1_i + \gamma_2 x2_i + \gamma_3 x3_i + \varepsilon_i.$$

This gives an estimate of the impact of each treatment compared to the comparison group. The results might be presented as in Table 8.1.

We see that the girls' clubs had no statistical effect on either the highest class passed or whether a girl was married. The incentive increased the average number of grades successfully completed from 8.1 to 8.3, while the club plus the incentive increased this outcome from 8.05 to 8.37. The incentive decreased the percentage of girls over the age of 19 who were married at midline by 7 percentage points.

We might be tempted, when looking at these results, to conclude that the incentive-plus-girls'-club treatment had a greater impact on education than the incentive alone and that the incentive was more effective in reducing the proportion of girls who married than the incentive-plus-girls'-club treatment. However, we have to be careful when comparing the effects of different treatments (just as we had to be careful in comparing effects on subgroups). Although the coefficient for the incentive treatment on grades successfully completed is smaller than the coefficient for the incentive-plus-girls'-club treatment, the two are not statistically different from each other (as confirmed by a t-test). And even though the coefficient on marriage for the incentive treatment is significant and the coefficient for the incen-

---

7. In fact, the original design included two alternative versions of the girls' club treatment but because neither of them had any impact the two were combined into one treatment for the analysis. This ongoing study by Field and Glennerster is summarized as Evaluation 7 in the appendix.

TABLE 8.1 Coefficients from multiple treatments in a study of girls' empowerment in Bangladesh

Outcome	Comparisons mean	T1: Girls' club	T2: Incentive	T3: Club + incentive
Highest grade completed	8.05	0.079 (0.141)	0.270 (0.161)	0.318* (0.175)
Whether married	0.65	−0.006 (0.027)	−0.070** (0.031)	−0.020 (0.032)

Notes: Under each estimated coefficient is the standard error of the estimate. The asterisks indicate statistical significance (one asterisk indicates significance at the 10 percent level, and two asterisks indicate significance at the 5 percent level). T1, T2, and T3 are the three treatment groups.

tive-plus-girls'-club treatment is not significantly different from zero, the two are again not significantly different from each other.

It is always important to test whether coefficients on different treatment dummies are significantly different from each other before making statements about the comparative effectiveness of different treatments. We test whether coefficients on treatment dummies are significant from each other by using a t-test in the same way that we test whether a coefficient is statistically different from zero. We cannot, therefore, on the basis of these results, say that the combination of incentive and empowerment program is more effective in increasing education than the incentive on its own.

Beyond average effects

Until now we have discussed only comparing means in the treatment and comparison groups. However, we might be interested in other kinds of effects. For example, if we introduce a new variety of rice we may find that it increases average rice yields, but we should also check to see whether it increases the variance of rice yields. A rice variety that increases average yields but has a higher chance of producing zero harvest may not be considered an improvement by farmers. Similarly, providing people with health insurance might reduce people's average out-of-pocket health expenditures, but this may not be the primary purpose of the program. A key benefit of health insurance that we will want to test for is whether it reduces the number of cases of very high out-of-pocket payments.

We do not attempt here to go through all the different ways in which it is possible to analyze the results of randomized evaluations that do not rely on a comparison of average treatment effects. These analytical techniques are covered well in standard econometric textbooks.[8] We do, however, provide some examples of how these results have been applied to randomized evaluations.

An evaluation of a school voucher program in Colombia examined the impact of being randomly assigned to receive a voucher to pay tuition at a private school on scores on a nationwide university entrance exam.[9] (Identification numbers of lottery winners and losers were matched to the identification numbers of those taking the test.) The problem was that not all participants in the study took the exam, and more lottery winners took the exam than did lottery losers (because winning the lottery, going to a private school, and having future school fee payments conditioned on good grades led to higher school completion rates). As we discuss in Module 7.2, this type of differential attrition bias (when the program ensures that more of the weaker students will be around to take the test) means that we are likely to underestimate the true effect of the program if we simply compare the means of the treatment and comparison groups.

Instead the authors used a quantile regression approach. They compared the outcomes of those at the 70th, 75th, 85th, and 95th percentiles among lottery winners and losers, finding the strongest effects on males at the lower end of the percentiles tested (i.e., the lower end of those who were still taking the college entrance exam).

The advantage of the quantile regression approach is that it allows us to look at the effect of a program not just on mean outcomes but also on the whole distribution of outcomes and test whether the program changes the distribution of outcomes at the top, at the bottom, or throughout the distribution.

MODULE 8.2 Catalog of Corrections

Although the basic analysis of a simple, individual-level randomization is straightforward, there are a number of adjustments that either have to

---

8. See, for example, Joshua D. Angrist and Jörn-Steffen Pischke, *Mostly Harmless Econometrics: An Empiricist's Companion* (Princeton, NJ: Princeton University Press, 2008).

9. This study by Joshua Angrist, Eric Bettinger, and Michael Kremer is summarized as Evaluation 10 in the appendix.

or can be made to correct for how the randomization was carried out and for threats that may have arisen to the integrity of the experiment, including noncompliance, attrition, spillovers, and group-level randomization. This module discusses those adjustments.

If there is partial compliance

Partial compliance occurs when some people in the treatment group do not take up a program or some people in the comparison group do take it up. In our Ghana secondary school example, some of those who are offered a scholarship may not end up going to secondary school. Some of those not offered a scholarship may manage to scrape together the funds, either this year or in future years, to pay the school fees. The ITT estimate will tell us the impact of offering students scholarships, but it will not tell us the impact of going to secondary school because of this partial compliance.

In the Ghana example we might hope to have full compliance when we start the study. There is a chance that all those offered the scholarship will go to secondary school and none of the comparison group will. In other cases, we design the experiment knowing from the start that there will be substantial noncompliance. This is the case with encouragement designs. We randomize the encouragement to take up the program rather than access to the program itself (Module 4.3). We hope that take-up will be higher in the treatment group than in the comparison group, but we can be pretty certain that there will be less than 100 percent take-up in the treatment group and more than zero percent take-up in the comparison group. In this sense, noncompliance is an integral part of encouragement designs.

Analysis of the average effect on compliers

Although understanding what happens to the average person targeted by the program (whether or not he takes it up) is useful, we may also be interested in the effect on those who actually took up the program. What was the impact of the deworming drug on the children who took the medicine as part of the deworming program? What is the impact on earnings of going to secondary school in Ghana? This is what the average effect on compliers tells us. (If no one in the comparison group takes up the program, the average effect on compliers is called the effect of the treatment on the treated.) This term is often used interchangeably with the average effect on compliers, but the two terms are not the same if there is take-up in the comparison group. Thus here we talk about the average effect on compliers—that is, the effect on those who take up the program as a result of our intervention.

Calculating the Wald estimator

Using the Wald estimator is the most basic way of calculating the effect on compliers, and to calculate it we need to make an assumption. We have to assume that the entire difference in outcomes between the treatment and comparison groups can be attributed to the additional people who take up the program in the treatment group. If this assumption holds, all we have to do to turn the ITT estimate into an estimate of the impact on compliers is to divide by the difference between the take-up rates of the treatment and comparison groups:

$$\text{Estimate of impact on compliers} = \frac{\text{ITT estimate}}{(\text{Take-up in treatment} - \text{take-up in comparison})}$$

or

$$\text{Estimate of impact on compliers} = \frac{(\text{Mean in treatment} - \text{mean in comparison})}{(\text{Take-up in treatment} - \text{take-up in comparison})}.$$

A simple example makes the point. Imagine that in our Ghana example, of the 500 students who were offered scholarships, 250 took them up and completed secondary school, while none of the 500 students in the comparison group managed to raise the money to go to secondary school. The difference in the take-up rate was 250/500, 50 percent, or one-half. Imagine, too, that the average monthly income of those who were offered scholarships was $45, while the mean income of those in the comparison group was $30 a month. The difference in mean income between these groups was $15 per person (the ITT estimate) or $7,500 in total income between the two groups.

The Wald assumption says that those in the treatment group who did not take up the program got no increase in income from the fact that they were offered the program but did not take it up. In other words, the entire difference in income between the two groups was due to the 250 students—half of the total treatment group—who took up the program. If an average difference of $15 per person was driven by half the group, the program must have increased the monthly income of the 250 compliers by $30 a month. Put another way, the total income in the treatment group was $22,500 and the income in the comparison group was $15,000, with a difference of $7,500 between the two groups. If we assume that this entire difference came from the 250 students who took up the scholarship, we can divide $7,500 by 250 and get a program impact of $30 a month for those who took up the program.

Now let us look at a slightly more complicated example. If we found that take-up among those offered the scholarship was 80 percent and the take-up in the comparison group was 5 percent (because some of the comparison group managed to raise the money to go to secondary school in subsequent years despite not being given the scholarship), the difference in the take-up rate would have been 75 percent, or three-fourths. If we found a difference in income between the treatment and comparison groups of $15 per month, we would scale this ITT estimate up by four-thirds and again get an estimate of the treatment on compliers of $20 a month.

Impact on compliers and subgroup analysis

If the take-up rate is much higher in some subgroups of the population than in others, we can use this to help us make our estimated effect on compliers more precise. For example, if we find that the rate of take-up of our scholarships is very low among those children whose parents have no education or who live a long way from the nearest secondary school, we may want to drop these children from our sample. We are not introducing a bias into our estimation because we are dropping children based on a characteristic that was established before we started the experiment and we are using the same criteria to drop people in both treatment and comparison groups. It is as if we had decided even before we started the experiment not to assess the impact on these types of children. Once we have selected the subgroup on which we want to estimate the impact on compliers, we calculate the relevant ITT and related Wald estimator in the usual way.

Subgroups and defiers

In Module 7.1 we discussed the problem of defiers. Defiers are people who not only fail to comply with their treatment status but act in the opposite way to expectations. They are less likely to take up the program because they are in the treatment group or more likely to take up the program because they are in the comparison group. It is possible to deal with defiers in the analysis only if they fall into an identifiable subgroup. In this case we calculate the impact of the program on the defiers separately and can then calculate an average treatment effect between those who comply and those who defy.

Instrumental variables estimation of impact on compliers

The other way to estimate the impact on compliers is to calculate it in an instrumental variables regression framework (the instrumental variables methodology is discussed in Module 2.2). In other words, we use whether someone was randomly assigned to be offered the program as an instrument to predict whether or not she actually took up the program. Our random assignment is a valid instrument if the only way the random assignment affects the outcome is through the increased take-up. In other words, it is valid only if being assigned to treatment but not taking it up has no impact on the outcome (we discuss cases in which this assumption may not hold below). This is the same assumption that we needed for the Wald estimator.

To estimate the impact on compliers using instrumental variables, we estimate a first-stage regression in which we predict take-up from the random assignment. For our Ghana example,

$$\text{sec\_ed}_i = \alpha_1 + \gamma T_i + \varepsilon_i,$$

where sec_ed is a dummy that takes the value one if the adolescent completed secondary school and zero otherwise.[10] T_i is a dummy that takes the value one if person i is allocated to the treatment group. We then regress our outcome variable (in the Ghana case, income) on our predicted take-up variable (in this case, predicted secondary education or $\widehat{\text{sec\_ed}}_i$, that is, the level of secondary education that we predict when we run the first regression):

$$Y_i = \alpha + \beta \, \widehat{\text{sec\_ed}}_i + \varepsilon_i$$

Both stages of the estimation process can be done in Stata with the following command:

```
ivregress 2sls income (sec_ed = T).
```

10. There are many ways to define our outcome variable: years of secondary school, a dummy for any years of secondary school, or a dummy for completing secondary school, for example. Here we use a dummy variable for secondary school completion to simplify exposition.

The main advantage of estimating the impact on compliers in the instrumental variables regression framework is that we can include control variables that may help us predict who takes up the program among the treatment group. For example, children who are offered a scholarship but live a long way from a secondary school may be less likely to take up the scholarship than those who live near a secondary school. In general, living near a secondary school may be correlated with going to secondary school, but usually we cannot use that to estimate the effect on earnings of going to secondary school. Those who live near a secondary school may be different in many ways (other than educational attainment) from those who live farther away. They are likely, for example, to live in larger communities with more job opportunities. But by combining what we know about the relationship between distance and education and our randomized treatment dummy, we have the opportunity to improve the precision of our estimate of the impact of secondary education on income. We do this by including as a control in our first equation a variable for distance to the nearest secondary school and an interaction term (which takes the value zero for those in the comparison group and takes the value of the distance to the nearest secondary school for the treatment group). This allows us to compare those close to a secondary school who do and do not get a scholarship. Therefore,

$$\text{sec\_ed}_i = \alpha_1 + \gamma_1 T_i + \gamma_2 (T \times \text{distance})_i + \gamma_3 \text{distance}_i + \varepsilon_i$$

and

$$\text{Income}_i = \alpha_2 + \beta \, \widehat{\text{sec\_ed}}_i + \text{distance}_i + \varepsilon_i,$$

where distance_i is a variable measuring the distance to the nearest secondary school of person i and $(T \times \text{distance})_i$ is the interaction of the treatment dummy with the distance variable. It is important that any nonrandomized controls (in this case, distance to the nearest secondary school) be added to both equations. Only the treatment dummy was randomized, so only the dummy and the interaction term (of dummy and distance) are valid instruments; these are the only right-hand-side variables that should be included in the first equation and not in the second. This approach can be employed in Stata using the `ivreg2` command in the following way:

```
ivreg2 2sls income (sec_ed =
                  T Tinteractdistance) distance,
```

where `Tinteractdistance` is the name for our interaction variable $T \times$ distance.

When is the estimate on compliers useful?

If we want to know the impact of introducing a program on the population, we want to look at the ITT estimate. We know that when we scale up the program we are unlikely to get 100 percent take-up. Imperfect take-up is an inherent part of the program, and we don't want to pretend that it does not exist.

But in other cases the estimate of the program's impact on compliers is useful. For example, if we find a moderate ITT impact of a program, this could be the result of two very different scenarios, and distinguishing between them is useful. Under the first scenario there was low take-up of the program but large impacts on those who took it up. The other scenario is that there was widespread take-up but moderate impacts on those who took it up. The ITT estimate is the same under both scenarios, but the estimate of the program's impact on compliers is different because this estimate asks, "What is the impact of the program on those who take it up as a result of our intervention?"

Perhaps the most important use for the estimate of the program's impact on compliers is for evaluations that use an encouragement design. In these designs we are less interested in the impact of the encouragement than in the impact of the program whose take-up the encouragement is designed to increase. For example, if we provide encouragement to sign up for a bank account, we might be more interested in the impact of having a bank account on savings rather than in the impact of a program that provides coupons to sign up for a bank account. Or if we give coupons for extension services, we might be using this as a way to test the impact of extension services rather than as a way to test a program of giving vouchers for extension services.

What to consider when estimating the impact on compliers

We should never, ever, drop noncompliers from a study. Dropping noncompliers from the sample reintroduces selection bias, defeating all the careful work we did to achieve internal validity. People who fail to comply are systematically different from those who do comply. For example, children who are less healthy are more likely to miss school and not receive deworming medicine when the others at their school are treated. When we randomized, we made the treatment and comparison groups equivalent in the proportion of these children included. If we drop these children from the sample being analyzed, the treatment group we end up with is no longer comparable to the comparison group because it now has a higher proportion of children with better outcomes. Likewise, those in the comparison group who find their own way to access treatment are not representative of our comparison group, and dropping them also reintroduces selection bias.[11]

We should never change anyone's randomly assigned treatment status based on actual treatment. We might be tempted to change the treatment status of noncompliers to reflect what actually happened during the program. Why not put all those who were treated into the treatment group and all those who were not treated into the comparison group? To do this would reintroduce selection bias.

When is it inappropriate to use estimated impact on compliers?

Our estimate of the impact of a program on compliers rests on the assumption that treating the compliers has no effect on the outcomes of the noncompliers. Using this estimation procedure when this assumption does not hold will generate biased estimates of program impact. There are two main instances in which this assumption might fail: (1) when there are positive (or negative) effects from being offered the program even if it is not taken up and (2) when there are spillovers, either positive or negative, within the treatment group. These conditions and the reasons for them are similar to those that exist when an encouragement design is not appropriate (Module 4.3).

When an offer, but not take-up, changes outcomes There may be cases in which simply being offered access to a program may have an effect even if the program is not taken up. If this is the case, estimating the

---

11. It is legitimate to drop a subgroup, defined based on a pre-program characteristic, in which take-up is low. For example, if those living more than 10 miles from a secondary school are very unlikely to take up a secondary school scholarship, we can drop from the analysis all those in the treatment and comparison groups who live more than 10 miles from a secondary school. This is very similar to controlling for distance to secondary school in the analysis described above.

program's impact on compliers is not valid because not all of the impact of the program is concentrated in those who take it up. If there are positive effects of being offered access to a program, even without take-up, using a Wald estimator or instrumental variables approach as discussed above will overestimate the impact of the program on those who do take it up.

Imagine a program that offers food for work to farmers whose crops fail. Only those whose crops fail will take up the program. However, those assigned to the treatment group know that if their crops fail they will have access to this program, and this may well influence their behavior. They may grow crops with a higher average yield but also more risk. If we assume that all the benefit of the program is concentrated among those who take part in the food-for-work program we will overestimate the impact of the program on those who take it up in this case: we will in effect be taking all the benefits experienced by those who do not take it up and assigning them all to the individuals who did take it up. Note that the ITT estimate in this case will be valid.

When there are positive spillovers within the treatment group Similarly, when there are positive spillovers, those in the treatment group benefit from the fact that they are surrounded by those who take up the program and the benefits they receive are assumed, under the Wald and instrumental variables approaches, to be experienced by those who take up the program. This overestimates the true impact on compliers. Positive spillovers within the treatment group, but no spillovers to the comparison group, are most likely to occur when we randomize at the group level.

Microfinance is an example in which there is a potential for positive spillovers within the treatment group (in this case, a community). It is possible that those women who take up microfinance will start businesses and employ their neighbors to help them or that they will share some of their increased income with their neighbors. Thus even women who do not borrow may benefit from being in a community where microfinance is offered.

When there are negative spillovers within treatment groups A similar concern arises if there are potential negative spillovers within the treatment group from those who take up the program to those who do not take it up. In this case we would underestimate the benefits to those who take up the program if we calculated impact on compliers using the Wald or instrumental variables approach.

Microfinance also provides an example in which negative spillovers are possible. For instance, women with existing businesses may be hurt by the arrival of microfinance because they will face more competition from new borrowers who start businesses that cater to the local community and offer similar products. This is a negative spillover that will mainly affect those in the treatment community, including those who do not take up microfinance.

If there is attrition

Attrition is the absence of data because the researchers cannot measure the outcomes of some of the participants who had been randomly assigned to either the treatment or the comparison group. As discussed in Module 7.2, in some cases attrition is unrelated to the program, but in others it is affected by the program, meaning that how many people and what type of people cannot be found at the endline are different in the treatment and comparison groups. Random attrition reduces statistical power, but differential attrition undermines the validity of the experiment by reintroducing selection bias. When there is differential attrition between the groups, the allocation of the treatment is no longer random vis-à-vis those who remain behind and whose outcome data are available for use in estimating the program's impact.

Attrition can invalidate a study, so the best thing is to limit attrition during design and implementation using the approaches set out in Chapters 4 and 7. Despite our best efforts, there is usually at least some attrition. We deal with it at analysis as follows:

1. *Determine the overall attrition rate.* What is the rate of attrition in the whole sample?

2. *Check for differential attrition.* Are the rates different in the treatment and comparison groups? Are the same types of people attriting in the treatment and comparison groups? Is attrition correlated with any observables?

3. *Determine the range of the estimated impact given the attrition.* What is the greatest and least impact the program could have had, given the attrition we observe?

As you can see, these steps do not really "deal with" attrition. Rather they are a way of showing that attrition is not crippling, that the impact estimates may still be valid despite the attrition, and that we can estimate the potential effect of attrition. This argument is more plausible if attrition is lower, so the first step is always to limit attrition and to document the remaining attrition.

Determine the overall rate of attrition

In our Ghana example, in the midline survey we find that 100 of the 500 children in the comparison group have migrated away looking for better opportunities and cannot be tracked; 50 of the scholarship winners also migrated to get married and to look for work. In total, data are missing for 150 of the girls, so the attrition rate is 150/1,000, or 15 percent.

Over the long term, all the remaining lottery losers are still in the area and can be tracked, but now the 50 scholarship winners with the highest baseline test scores have left the province to go to university and do not have time for the survey. In the long-term survey, data are missing for 150 + 50 = 200 of the students, and the attrition rate is 200/1,000 = 20 percent.

Check for differential attrition

Differential attrition means that the attrition rates are different between the treatment and comparison groups or between the different subgroups. In the second step, we check the patterns of attrition: Is the attrition rate different across treatment and comparison groups? Do the characteristics of the dropouts differ by assigned treatment, by subgroup, or by any observable characteristic?

In the midline follow-up there is differential attrition between the groups. The rate of attrition is higher in the comparison group than in the treatment group. When we look more closely we find that of the 100 students from the comparison group who left, 90 are boys and only 10 are girls. We find that of the 50 people from the treatment group who moved out, only 10 were boys who went to look for work, and 40 were girls who became pregnant and left to start families. In this case, there is differential attrition both within and across the groups.

In the long-term follow-up, there is no differential attrition rate between the groups. In each group, data are missing for 50 participants. But when we look at the causes of attrition, we see that they are different between the treatment and comparison groups. In the treatment group, the children with the best educational outcomes migrated (education opened up new opportunities for them), and we cannot measure their outcomes.

Determine the range of the estimated impact given attrition

In order to attempt to calculate the true impact we have to fill in the missing data by creating new data. Replacement data can never be as informative as a participant's real data. There are two approaches: (1) using model-based approaches and (2) constructing bounds. Both help to demonstrate how sensitive our results are to different scenarios of what might have happened to those people for whom we do not have data. The less attrition there is, the less sensitive our results are likely to be.

The first approach, the archetype of which is Heckman's selection model, looks at the characteristics of those who attrite and assumes that their outcomes will be equal to those of people with the same characteristics. In our Ghana example, the probability of being in the final data set is correlated with baseline test scores, and this relationship is different between treatment and comparison groups. It is therefore important for us to include baseline test scores in our model estimating the extent of attrition bias. To do this, we calculate the relationship between baseline test scores and income for the treatment group and the comparison group separately within the subset of the sample for which we have final income data. We then allocate "estimated income data" to those with missing data, based on their baseline test scores.

The problem with this approach is that it assumes that, within a group with similar baseline characteristics and treatment status, those people we cannot find are the same as those people we can find. Yet the very fact that we cannot find these people means that in at least one way they are different from the people we can find. We have no way to test whether our assumption is accurate because we do not have data on those who have dropped out.

Use models with follow-up of a subsample of attriters In Chapter 7 we discussed an approach to attrition that involves following up on a randomly chosen subsample of those who cannot (initially) be found at endline. If we succeed in finding all, or close to all, of this subgroup, we can use the model approach with more confidence. Because our subsample is randomly selected, we are more confident that the assumption behind the model approach holds, namely that on average this subsample has the same characteristics and outcomes as the others we did not find in our initial endline. We can therefore scale up the results from the subgroup to replace the missing data for the other attriters, with more confidence in our results.

For example, let's imagine that we are not able to find 100 members of the treatment group and 100 members of the comparison group at endline in our Ghana study. We randomly choose 50 percent from each group to follow up very carefully. If we manage to find all 50 of our randomly chosen treatment attriters, we can take each of the outcomes and scale it up two times to fill in the missing data from the other treatment attriters. We can do the same for the missing comparison attriters.

The drawback of this approach is that it is useful only if we can find all or virtually all of the subsample that we follow up. If we find only some of them, we cannot be confident that those in the subsample that we found have the same outcomes on average as those we did not find.

Use bounds The second approach constructs bounds on the estimate. We will look at two methods, the Manski-Horowitz bounds and the Lee bounds (or the Lee trimming method). The Manski-Horowitz upper bound is constructed by assigning the most positive outcome to all of those who drop out of the treatment group and assigning the most negative outcome to all of those who drop out of the comparison group. The lower bound is constructed using the opposite assumption: the most positive outcome to the dropouts from the comparison group and the most negative to the dropouts from the treatment group. One limitation of the Manski-Horowitz method is that it requires the true value of the outcome of interest to lie in some bounded interval: if this interval is unbounded or has very large bounds (if the outcome is income or profits of a firm, for example), the Manski-Horowitz method will yield very large (and hence not very informative) bounds on the estimate of the parameter of interest.

Constructing Lee bounds involves throwing out a fraction of the observations from the group that has less attrition. Because the objective is to test the robustness of the result, we drop those observations that most contribute to finding the result. For example, if there is 10 percent attrition in the treatment group and 15 percent attrition in the comparison group and our result without taking attrition into account suggests that the program has a positive effect, to test the robustness of that result we drop the top 5 percent of observations in the treatment group and perform our analysis again. If, in contrast, the dropout rate is 15 percent in the treatment group and 10 percent in the comparison group, we drop the bottom 5 percent of the observations in our comparison group.

In contrast to the Manski-Horowitz method, the Lee trimming method does not require the true value of the outcome of interest to lie in some bounded or small interval; however, it requires a "monotonicity" assumption that every individual surveyed in the study would also have reported an outcome had he or she been part of the other (treatment or control) group.[12] Both approaches to putting bounds on the results tend to generate wide bounds (though less wide in general in the Lee case), which make it hard to draw any definitive conclusions about the impact of a program unless attrition is very low.

Example: Testing the sensitivity of estimates to assumptions on attrition An evaluation of the long-run impacts of a program that promoted positive interactions between mothers and their children during early infancy in Jamaica faced a challenge of attrition.[13] Some of the children in the study, who were now adults in the labor force, had migrated and could not be found, leading to missing data. The level of migration was higher among those exposed to the treatment than among those in the comparison group. Because migration was mainly to the United Kingdom and the United States, where wages are typically higher than in Jamaica, it is likely that selective attrition was leading to an underestimate of the impact of the program on wages. Nevertheless, the authors wanted to assess the sensitivity of their results to different assumptions on attrition. They used two approaches. First they predicted the earnings of migrants based on their characteristics and those of their families. Then they tested whether their results were sensitive to dropping all migrants (in both treatment and

12. A very clear and detailed comparison between the Manski-Horowitz and Lee bounds can be found in David S. Lee, "Trimming for Bounds on Treatment Effects with Missing Outcomes," NBER Technical Working Paper 277, National Bureau of Economic Research, Cambridge, MA, June 2002.

13. Paul Gertler, Arianna Zanolin, Rodrigo Pinto, James Heckman, Susan Walker, Christel Vermeersch, Susan Chang, and Sally Grantham-McGregor, "Labor Market Returns to Early Childhood Stimulations: A 20-Year Follow-Up to the Jamaica Study," report, University of Chicago, https://heckman.uchicago.edu/sites/heckman.uchicago.edu/files/uploads/Gertler-etal_2012.pdf.

comparison groups) from their data. They found that the program still had statistically significant positive impacts on earnings even after these adjustments.

If spillovers occur

When the effect on those receiving treatment produces a secondary effect on those who are not treated, we say there are spillovers. We discussed spillovers within the treatment group above; here we are concerned about spillovers that may occur between the treatment group and the comparison group. In Modules 4.2 and 7.3 we discuss how to limit spillovers. If we have used a group-level randomization so that all spillovers are contained within the treatment and control groups, we need to adjust for this group-level randomization, as discussed in the next section. Other designs do not contain spillovers within groups but allow for us to measure the extent of spillovers. Here we describe how to analyze impacts and measure spillovers in these cases.

What issues arise with spillovers?

If the program affects the outcomes of the comparison group, this means that the comparison group is no longer a valid counterfactual: it does not tell us what would have happened in the absence of the program. If there are positive spillovers, our estimated impact will be an underestimate. If there are negative spillovers, our estimated impact will be an overestimate.

How do we adjust for spillovers?

It is possible to adjust for spillovers only if we can identify at least some individuals or groups that are not affected by the program. To do this we must have a theory of how the spillovers occur. Spillovers may occur downstream from the program, within a certain geographic radius, or within the social network of those in the treatment group. We now have effectively three groups: the treatment group, the spillover group (i.e., that part of the comparison group that may be affected by the program), and the nonspillover comparison group. Now we can estimate the impact on both the treatment group and the spillover group in relation to the uncontaminated comparison group.

This approach is valid only when it is randomly determined whether an individual from the comparison group ends up in the spillover group or the nonspillover group (sometimes referred to as the "control control"). This is not always the case. In particular, people who live in densely populated areas are more likely to live, say, within 1 kilometer of an individual in the treatment group than are those living in less densely populated areas. If we are using social network information to predict spillovers, someone with many social contacts is more likely to know a person in the treatment group than someone with few social contacts. We therefore have to control for any factor that may increase the chance of being in the spillover group.

Let us return to the example of the school-based deworming program. Randomization was at the level of the school to deal with the majority of spillovers. However, the researchers studying the deworming program also tested for between-school spillovers. They knew that children who lived near each other might go to different schools, and thus children in comparison schools might still benefit from deworming in nearby schools. To test this assumption, they drew circles of different radii (for example, 3 kilometers) around each school and counted how many children attending school were within these radii and how many of these children had been treated. Although the number of children attending school within a 3-kilometer radius is not random, the proportion of these children who go to treatment schools is random. Therefore, we can include in our regression a variable for how many pupils are within a 3-kilometer radius and a variable for how many pupils were treated within that 3-kilometer radius. In their analysis the researchers looked at multiple circles of different radii at the same time, but here we show the analysis for one circle of 3-kilometer radius for the sake of exposition. Those who are interested in the more detailed approach can refer to the published paper.[14]

$$Y_i = \alpha + \beta T_i + \gamma_1 N_i + \gamma_2 N^T_i + \varepsilon_i,$$

where Y_i is our outcome of interest, T_i is the treatment dummy for individual i, N_i is the number of pupils within a 3-kilometer radius of individual i's school, and N^T_i is the number of treated pupils within a 3-kilometer radius of individual i's school. The treatment effect is spread between two coefficients, β and γ_2. To calculate the impact of the program we need to multiply the coefficients by how many children benefited from the treatment and from the spillovers. First we multiply β by the number of children who were enrolled in schools

14. Edward Miguel and Michael Kremer, "Worms: Identifying Impacts," *Econometrica* 72 (2004): 159–217.

allocated to the treatment group. Then we multiply γ_2 by the average number of treated pupils within a 3-kilometer radius of a treated school.

If we randomized at the group level

Sometimes randomization is at the group level rather than the individual level. Instead of children, we randomize schools; instead of pregnant women, maternal clinics; or instead of workers, their households.

Analysis at the group level

The simplest and most conservative approach to analysis when randomization is at the group level is to analyze the data at the group level. If our data are collected at the group level (for example, if our outcome is the percentage of unoccupied beds in a hospital or the number of wells in a village), this is the only way we can analyze our data. If our data are at the individual level and we want to analyze at the group level, we will need to aggregate our data.

An evaluation of a community-driven development program in Sierra Leone collected data on the quality and quantity of public goods, participation in community decisionmaking, social capital, and collective action. Some of the outcomes were measured at the community level (such as the number of women who spoke at a community meeting) and some at the individual level (such as membership in a savings club). However, data collected at the individual level were aggregated to the community level: for example, the percentage of individuals who were members of a savings club. The analysis was then carried out at the community level.

Analysis at the individual level when randomization is at the group level: Why we need a correction

When randomization is at the group level and all our outcome data are at the individual level, we can still collapse all our data to group aggregates and analyze it at the group level. However, when there are many clusters, it is more common to analyze at the individual level but correct for the fact that randomization was at the group level.

Outcomes tend to be correlated within groups. Two people who live in the same town tend to be more similar than two people drawn at random from across the country. This is for two reasons: (1) people tend to live near, work with, or join social groups with people like themselves, and (2) individuals in groups can be affected by the same shocks, as when a tidal wave hits a village or a good principal leaves a school.

Our statistical tests assume, unless we indicate otherwise, that each data point we have is independent. In other words, our approach assumes that we have randomly allocated individuals into our treatment and comparison groups from one long list. But in a group randomization we first randomly draw groups and then collect data on a random sample of individuals from each group. Everyone in a particular group will be assigned either to the treatment group or to the comparison group. This group structure reduces our statistical power (as discussed in Module 6.1) and the precision with which we can estimate our effect size. This is a particular problem when there is a high degree of correlation in outcome measures within groups. If we don't take into account group randomization and within-group correlation, we will underestimate the magnitude of our standard errors: we might conclude that our estimated coefficient was significantly different from zero, while in fact, with appropriate standard errors, our estimate would be insignificantly different from zero.

Take a hypothetical example of a program that provides additional textbooks to schools. Treatment is randomized at the level of the school. Imagine that one of our treatment schools happens to start a school meals program that sharply increases the attendance of both children and teachers at the school. Another treatment school happens to have a new principal who takes extra steps to encourage teachers and children to attend more frequently. If we were looking at the data and did not realize that the evaluation was randomized at the school level, we would see a dramatic rise in attendance for hundreds of children and teachers in program schools. If the higher attendance rate improves test scores, we might even see higher test scores in the treatment schools compared to the control schools. That would appear to be strong evidence that textbooks increase attendance with a weaker effect on test scores. However, once we know that the evaluation was randomized at the school level and that the jumps in attendance and the increase in test scores were concentrated in two particular schools, this information would provide less compelling evidence regarding the overall program impact. We can conclude that the program is a success only if we see increases in attendance and test scores that are more broadly based across many schools.

Correcting for group-level randomization when analyzing at the individual level

The most common way to adjust for group-level randomization is to explicitly take into account the extent to which people in a group have correlated outcomes. This is often referred to as "clustering standard errors." When we analyze an individual-level randomization we are estimating

$$Y_i = \alpha + \beta T_i + \gamma X_i + \varepsilon_i.$$

We have one error term, ε_i. This picks up the extent to which an individual's outcome cannot be explained by the mean in the comparison group (α) or, for those in the treatment group, the treatment effect (β), or by other covariates like age and gender (included in our matrix of control terms, summarized here as X_i). As discussed in Module 6.2, in a group-level randomization we estimate two different types of errors —a group-level error and an individual error:

$$Y_{ij} = \alpha + \beta T_i + \gamma X_i + \nu_j + \omega_{ij}.$$

The group-level error (ν) has a different value for each group j and picks up the extent to which that group is different from the rest of the sample in ways that cannot be explained by treatment status. If we are adding covariates to our analysis, as discussed in the next section, the error terms are the part of the outcome that cannot be explained by the mean in the control group, the treatment effect, or by covariates (like the average age or income of the group). The individual error term (ω) picks up any difference from the rest of the sample that cannot be explained by the fact that i is a member of group j or by treatment status or covariates.

Most statistical packages have commands that allow the evaluator to estimate group errors in this way. In order to do this, however, we need a variable that specifies which group each individual in our sample belongs to. For example, if we randomize at the school level, we need to create a variable that takes a specific value for each school. If we randomize at the village level, we need to create a variable that indicates which village every individual belongs to. In Stata, estimating a group-level randomization is very similar to estimating an individual-level randomization except that we add `cluster (group_ID)` as an option at the end of the regression, where `group_ID` is the variable that indicates which group an individual belongs to (e.g., `village_10`).Thus in our Ghana scholarship example, if we had randomized access to scholarships by the primary school that children attended, we would run

```
regress income treatment, cluster(school_ID),
```

where `school_ID` is a variable that has a value associated with each particular school in our sample and is the same for all children who attended that school.

Clustering must always be done at the level at which randomization was carried out. Outcomes are correlated within all sorts of groups. Children of the same age may have similar test scores and may face correlated shocks, for example. But we don't need to adjust for all these possible groups. To the extent that some members of the group are in treatment and some are in the comparison group, these correlated shocks will wash out. We do not have to worry that children whose parents have less education are likely to do less well in secondary school. Their test scores are correlated with each other, but there are equal numbers of children from this group in the treatment and comparison groups. Nor do we need to cluster at a level lower than the one at which we randomize. For example, if we randomize at the level of the school, there is no need to cluster at the class level and the school level. The clustering at the school level will encompass clustering at the class level.

When we allocate an entire group to either the treatment or the control, as we do when we randomize at a group level, we have no control for any shocks experienced by that particular group or community. Fortunately (if we have done our sample size calculations correctly), we have many treatment communities and many comparison communities. On average we can expect that the community-level shocks in treatment communities will be the same as the community-level shocks in control communities. But although we may interview 20 people in a community, we have only one village-level shock. We don't have 20 independent draws from which we can estimate the extent of village shocks; we have 1 draw that is repeated 20 times. If we fail to cluster at the level at which we randomize, we are assuming that there are no community-level shocks and that those in a community or a school are no more similar to each other than they are to others in the sample.

Adjusting for group randomization with very small samples

The clustering approach discussed above provides an accurate adjustment for standard errors with group randomization in large samples. As samples get smaller, the adjustment becomes less accurate. When we have very small samples, therefore, we have to use another approach, although even this does not entirely solve the problem. There is no single definition of what counts as small because there is no single cutoff point at which the estimated standard errors become invalid. Instead there is a continuous decline in reliability as samples get smaller.

Randomization inference is an alternative approach that can be used when samples are small. Under this approach, we directly calculate whether the difference between the treatment and the comparison groups that we find is in the 5 percent tail of all the possible differences between randomly chosen groups. Specifically, we take all our outcome data and generate all the different combinations in which we can split the sample into two groups of equal size. For each grouping we calculate the difference in means between the groups. This generates a frequency curve of all the possible "effect sizes" that would be generated by combinations of outcomes that could have come about by chance. We then determine if the difference we observe is in the top 5 percent of all the differences we have generated.

For example, imagine a program in which the management of health services in a district is contracted out to an NGO.[15] There are four districts of which half were randomly chosen to be contracted out. There are six different ways to put these four districts into the treatment and comparison groups. In fact, districts 1 and 4 were randomly put into the treatment group and districts 2 and 3 into the comparison group. Imagine that the outcome of interest was the percentage of children immunized in the district and the results for each district are as follows:

15. This example is inspired by Erik Bloom, Indu Bhushan, David Clingingsmith, Rathavuth Hong, Elizabeth King, Michael Kremer, Benjamin Loevinsohn, and J. Brad Schwartz, "Contracting for Health: Evidence from Cambodia," Brookings Institution, Washington, DC, http://www.brookings.edu/views/papers/kremer/20060720cambodia .pdf. In this case 8 districts out of 12 were randomized for contracting out, and randomization inference was used for the analysis.

District	Percentage immunized
1	50
2	20
3	70
4	100

For each combination we calculated the difference in the mean immunization rate between the constructed treatment and the constructed comparison groups. So if 1 and 2 are assumed to be in the treatment group and 3 and 4 are in the comparison group, the mean outcome for treatment is 35 and the mean outcome for comparison is 85. The difference between them (i.e., the treatment effect) is –50. We calculate this difference for all the possible combinations as follows:

Treatment district	Comparison district	Difference in means
1, 2	3, 4	–50
1, 3	2, 4	0
1, 4	2, 3	30*
2, 3	1, 4	–30
2, 4	1, 3	0
3, 4	1, 2	50

*Combination chosen at random for implementation of the program.

The combination that coincides with how the program was actually randomized (districts 1 and 4 were treatment and 2 and 3 were comparison) gives a difference in means between the treatment and comparison groups of 35. This difference is the second highest out of six: in other words, it is not in the top 10 percent of possible outcomes (it is in only the top one-third of outcomes). There is a reasonably high probability that this combination came about by chance, so we do not find a statistically significant effect of the program. This approach is far from a panacea; with only 4 groups, as in the example above, we have 6 possible combinations, so we can make inferences only up to the 1/6 level. If we want to test at the 5 percent significance level, we need at least 20 combinations, or 6 groups.

If there is stratified or pairwise randomization

Our standard statistical tests are based on the assumption that each observation is drawn independently, as is the case in a simple individual-level randomization without stratification. For example, if we have 1,000 students in our Ghana scholarship program and half will receive scholarships, this assumption means that any combination of 500 students receiving the scholarship is equally likely. But if we stratify, say on gender, to ensure that exactly 500 of the students who receive the scholarship are girls, this assumption is no longer valid. There are some combinations of lottery winners that are ruled out by our stratification. For example, we are ruling out the possibility that all of the 500 who receive the scholarship are boys. It is therefore recommended that we adjust our standard errors for the constraints we put on the randomization. Some econometricians would go further and say it is required that we adjust for our stratification. To the extent that we have stratified on variables that are good predictors of the final outcome, this adjustment will help us estimate the effect of the program more precisely. In other words, in most cases we want to perform the adjustment.[16]

When we have stratified

Usually when we stratify we are doing so to impose balance—for example, making sure that an equal number of boys and girls receive a scholarship. The chance of receiving the scholarship is the same for each group and (on average) is the same as it would have been if we had not stratified. To adjust for this type of stratification we simply add a dummy variable for the different stratum. In our Ghana case we would add a dummy variable `male` that would take the value one if the student was male and zero otherwise.

If we have more than two strata, we need to add more than one variable. If in our Ghana example we had stratified by region (north and south) and by gender, we would have four groups: northern males, northern females, southern males, and southern females. In this case we can add three dummies, which take the value zero or one depend-

---

16. For a good discussion of the econometrics of stratification, see Guido Imbens, "Experimental Design for Unit and Cluster Randomized Trials," International Initiative for Impact Evaluation (3ie), Washington, DC, http://cyrussamii.com/wp-content/uploads/2011/06/Imbens_June_8_paper.pdf.

ing on whether an individual falls into a particular category (e.g., northern male). We always have one group that does not have a dummy associated with it. This is the base case against which the other groups are compared (see "collinearity" in any econometrics textbook for more explanation of this point). There may be different numbers of students in these strata—for example, there may be more eligible students in the south than in the north. As long as we choose the same proportion of students for treatment from every strata (in this case half), adding dummies is all we need to do.

When we have matched

Matching is an extreme form of stratification, and we use the same approach to adjust for it. In other words, we include dummies representing every matched pair (but one) in our analysis. In our Ghana example, if instead of stratifying by gender we had put students into pairs based on their test scores and then randomized one to be offered the scholarship and one to be in the comparison group, we would need to include 499 dummies. The first dummy would take the value one for the two students with the highest test scores, zero for the rest of the sample, and so on.

When we have imbalance

Unless we stratify, we cannot guarantee that we will have balance on all variables between different randomization cells at the start of our study. And it is usually impossible to stratify on all variables for which we have data, so we will often find that our treatment and comparison groups are statistically different on at least one variable. Should we adjust for this in our analysis?

We do not have to adjust for any variable on which we have imbalance. However, if the variable is highly correlated with our outcome variable it is good practice to show the results with this variable as one of the controls in the regression, at least as a robustness check. Indeed we may well want to include this variable as a control whether or not there is imbalance on the variable in the baseline.

When allocation fractions vary by strata

In some situations the probability of being chosen for treatment depends on the stratum to which an individual or group belongs. For example, donors may wish to give more scholarships to girls than to boys. Or they may want to give the same number of scholarships to boys and girls, but there are fewer eligible girls, and therefore the chances of receiving a scholarship are higher for girls than for boys. This means that the lottery status is not random in the overall sample, even though it is random within gender. If the effects of the program are different across strata but we make no adjustment for different allocation fractions, we can arrive at a biased estimate of the average effect of the program.

To be concrete, imagine that we have 80 scholarships for boys and 240 scholarships for girls. In total, 600 eligible boys apply and 400 eligible girls apply. The chance of getting a scholarship is 13 percent for boys and 60 percent for girls. We collect baseline and endline data on all 1,000 applicants.

If we do not adjust for the different allocation fractions, our standard estimation will weight each data point equally. There are more observations for boys than for girls, so we will end up placing a greater weight on the results for boys than for girls, even though more of the scholarships went to girls. This will not help us understand the impact of the program on those who received the scholarships (because more girls than boys got scholarships), nor will it tell us the impact if we scaled the program up to a situation in which there were equal numbers of scholarships for girls and boys.

What adjustment can be made?

We adjust for different allocation ratios by calculating the impact of the program for each of the different strata and then creating a weighted average of the different impacts. We can calculate the treatment effects by stratum by running separate regressions for each stratum, or we can run one regression with a series of dummies for the different strata. In our example we could take all the data from boys and run our estimating regression as follows:

$$Y_i = c + \beta T_i + \varepsilon_i,$$

where Y_i is income in the last month, T_i is a dummy that takes the value one if a student received a scholarship, β is the coefficient on the treatment dummy and gives us the treatment effect for boys, and ε_i is the error term. We do exactly the same thing for all the data on girls to get the treatment effect for girls.

If we want to know the average effect of the program as it was implemented, we weight the treatment effects in the same proportion that scholarships were provided in the program. In our example, we give three times the weight to the treatment effect for girls that we give to the treatment effect for boys because three times as many girls received scholarships as did boys (see Table 8.2 for the precise calculation). But we may be interested in knowing what the impact of the program would have been if half the scholarships had been given to boys and half to girls. In this case we take our estimated treatment effects and give each a weight of 0.5.

It is also possible to calculate the treatment effect for the different strata by running one regression with dummies for all the strata and interaction terms with the treatment dummy. In our case we have two strata, boys and girls, and thus we create a dummy M for male and F for female. We create interactions by multiplying the treatment dummy by the gender dummies. Thus instead of putting in one treatment dummy for all those who receive scholarships, we put in two dummies: MT, which is one for all boys who receive scholarships and zero for everyone else, and FT, which is one for all girls. We then run

$$Y_i = c + \beta_1 M_i + \beta_2 MT_i + \beta_3 FT_i + \varepsilon_i,$$

TABLE 8.2 Weighted average treatment effects in the case of different allocation fractions

Factor	Boys	Girls	Total
Number of scholarships (80)	240	320	560
Number of applicants	600	400	1000
Chance of winning (allocation fraction)	13%	60%	32%
Treatment effect	$15	$25	See below
Percent of total scholarships	25%	75%	100.0%
Average effect of program with 75% of scholarships going to girls	($15 × 0.25) + ($25 × 0.75) = $22.50		
Average effect of program with 50% of scholarships going to girls	($15 × 0.5) + ($25 × 0.5) = $20		

where Y_i is the income of person i, c is a constant (in this case, the average income of girls who do not receive scholarships), β_1 tells us how much more on average boys earn than girls in a month, β_2 is the treatment effect for boys, and β_3 is the treatment effect for girls.[17] From these calculations we can create the weighted average treatment effect as above. For example, if we want to weight girls and boys in proportion to their numbers in the program, we calculate

$$\text{average\_treatment\_effect} = \hat{\beta}_2 * 0.25 + \hat{\beta}_3 * 0.75.$$

We now need to calculate the confidence interval around the weighted average treatment effect, which is given in this example by

```
Average_treatment_effect ± 2*SE(treatment_effect),
```

where

$$\text{SE(treatment\_effect)} = \sqrt{var(\hat{\beta}_2) * 0.25 + var(\hat{\beta}_3) * 0.75}.$$

If there are multiple outcomes

A program may have effects on more than one outcome. For example, a deworming program may affect both the health of children as well as their education. We may also have many different indicators of the same outcome. If we want to measure whether a program leads to greater decisionmaking power for women within a household, we may be interested in many different aspects of household decision-making and the woman's role with regard to each one of them. During analysis we could check for differences between the treatment and comparison groups for all of these different indicators: we could compare decisionmaking related to whether children attend school, what food is purchased, what investments are made, and so on.

What issues may arise with multiple outcomes?

Our standard hypothesis testing assumes that we are interested in each outcome separately. But if we are testing many outcomes, the probability of a false negative (rejecting a true null hypothesis) for at

---

17. In this case we do not include the $\beta_0 T_i$ term, because we are including the interactions with both boys and girls (which make up the full sample and are mutually exclusive), so we do not need to include the treatment's main effect.

least one of these outcomes is greater than the significance level of each test. A researcher testing 10 independent hypotheses at 5 percent will reject the null hypothesis for at least one of them with a probability of 40 percent simply by chance.

If we are looking at the impact of a remedial education program on five subjects and we find that there is a significant difference in math scores but not in scores for the other subjects, can we conclude that the program worked because it increased the test scores for math? We cannot reach this conclusion unless we adjust our statistical tests for the fact that we tested for an impact in five different subjects.[18] Similarly, if we tested for an increase in women's influence along 10 different dimensions of household decisionmaking and found that in one instance women's influence was greater in the treatment group than in the comparison group at the 95 percent confidence level, we could not conclude that the program led to increased decisionmaking power for women without further analysis based on these results.

How can we adjust for multiple outcomes?

There are four main approaches to adjusting for multiple outcomes: (1) selecting one indicator in advance to be the primary outcome, (2) collapsing the information from many indicators and outcome variables into one testable hypothesis using an index, (3) collapsing many indicators into one using the mean standardized treatment effect, and (4) adjusting our confidence intervals to take into account the fact that we are testing several hypotheses. Sometimes we want to use both approaches. Whichever approach is used, it can be helpful to specify exactly how the problem will be addressed before analysis starts through the use of a pre-analysis plan. This is discussed in the next module.

Selecting one primary outcome measure Not all indicators are equally important or relevant. By specifying in advance which outcome is of primary interest, we can reduce the problem of multiple outcomes. This approach is commonly used in medical trials. Imagine a program designed to improve math education. We collect data on math test scores but also on scores in other subjects to see if there is any spill-over to learning other subjects. We specify that math scores are our

---

18. The exception would be if this were a math program and our starting hypothesis was that there would be an improvement in math and not in any other subject.

primary outcome in advance of our analysis. If we find an increase in math scores but no increase in other scores, we no longer dismiss this as happening by chance. With this approach, if we test many secondary indicators, we may still need to use some of the other approaches, discussed below, to deal with multiple outcomes.

Collapsing many indicators into one testable hypothesis using an index
Multiple indicators that address similar issues can be grouped together and tested jointly in one specification. This is particularly appropriate when we have many indicators that all attempt to capture different aspects of the same overall concept, as in our example of measures of a woman's role in household decisionmaking. No one question in our survey fully captures the concept, but together they provide a more complete picture of decisionmaking. We are not as interested in finding the effect on each individual aspect of decisionmaking as in testing one general hypothesis regarding whether the program has an impact on women's decisionmaking by drawing on all the information from all the different indicators. We can do this in a couple of different ways.

The first and simplest approach is to collapse all the indicators that are related to a single more general concept into an index. Imagine that we have a number of questions on our survey that all have the following structure:

1. Who makes most decisions about what food items to purchase?

2. Who makes most decisions about what educational expenditures to make, such as tuition, uniforms, and so on?

3. Who makes most decisions about whether to buy clothing and what clothing items to purchase?

We can assign a value of one if the woman says she makes the most decisions in a given area. We then create an index that adds the number of areas in which the woman is the main decisionmaker.

The drawback of creating an index is that it forces us to give relative weights to all our different indicators. For example, in the above example we put equal weight on the woman being the chief decisionmaker on food purchases as on her being the chief decisionmaker on education purchases. However, some form of weighting has to be applied whatever approach we use to collapse a lot of information to test one hypothesis.

Collapsing many indicators into one using the mean standardized treat-ment effect The second approach is to use the mean standardized treatment effect (sometimes called "mean effects"). Much as in the index approach, we divide our indicators into families that represent general hypotheses. In order to make our indicators within a family comparable to each other, we "demean" them. In other words, for each indicator we calculate the mean and then subtract the mean from each observation to create a new "demeaned" variable. Now all our indicators have a mean of zero. We also need to make sure that a beneficial change is measured as positive for all indicators. For example, if we are looking at whether a program increases healthy eating habits, eating more carrots is good, but eating more chocolate cake is bad. If we find a positive effect from eating carrots and a negative effect from eating chocolate cake, we don't want to take the average and find that overall we have no effect. Instead we create a new indicator, "eating less chocolate cake," for which a positive value is a success of the program.

Finally, we divide all the observations for each indicator by the standard deviation of that indicator. All the indicators then have the same unit of measurement, and we can interpret the coefficient at the end of our analysis in terms of standard deviations (as we do for minimum detectable effect sizes in power analysis).

We run the estimating regression separately for all the indicators in a family and calculate the mean of all of the effects (the average of the coefficients on our treatment dummies). The most popular approach in the literature is to calculate a simple unweighted average of all the coefficients. The standard reference for this approach is a randomized study of a program that gave people living in poor neighborhoods in the United States the chance to move to richer neighborhoods.[19]

Calculating the standard error of this average effect is not straight-forward. Fortunately, there is an add-on to Stata that calculates both the mean effect and the appropriate standard error for us.

A slightly different variant of this mean effects approach involves weighting different coefficients in the family differently using the estimation approach called seemingly unrelated regression estimation (SURE). Some questions we ask are very similar to each other, and the results are highly correlated with each other. For example, we may ask

---

19. This study by Jeffrey Kling, Jeffrey Liebman, and Lawrence Katz is summarized as Evaluation 5 in the appendix.

questions about decisionmaking on 10 different types of food purchases and only one question about whether children should go to school. If we use the standard mean effects analysis, food-purchasing decisions will have 10 times the weight in our final analysis as school-going decisions. SURE, however, would take into account that the food-purchasing indicators are highly correlated with each other and downweight them. If school-going decisionmaking is less correlated with other indicators, it is considered to have more "information content" and is given a higher weight. Although this approach has some merits, in general the profession has tended to view SURE as nontransparent because it is not clear what weights had been given to the different indicators. Most evaluators prefer the simple, equal-weight version of mean effects.

Adjusting our confidence intervals to take into account the fact that we are testing several hypotheses Another approach is to adjust the confidence intervals around our coefficients for the fact that we are testing several different hypotheses. One way to do this is to multiply the p-value (which measures the probability that an outcome is different from zero, as discussed in Module 6.1) by the number of tests we undertake. This is called the *Bonferroni adjustment,* and it suffers from being low powered. In other words, although we are less likely to reject the null hypothesis erroneously if we use the Bonferroni adjustment, we may well fail to reject the null hypothesis even if we should. An alternative adjustment is the free step-down resampling method for the family-wise error rate (FWER).[20] One of the advantages of this latter approach is that it takes into account that outcome variables may be correlated with each other.

What else should we consider in adjusting for multiple outcomes?

If we are going to make an adjustment of this kind, it is important to plan appropriately. If we don't plan, there is a risk that we will look at the data informally and run many regressions and then report only

---

20. See P. Westfall and S. Young, *Resampling Based Multiple Testing* (New York: Wiley and Sons, 1993); Michael Anderson, "Multiple Inference and Gender Differences in the Effects of Early Intervention: A Reevaluation of the Abecedarian, Perry Preschool, and Early Training Projects," *Journal of the American Statistical Association* 103 (2008): 1481–1495.

some of them in the final report or paper. We may not even keep count of how many hypotheses we tested. But if we are going to adjust for the number of hypotheses we test, we need to know how many we tried. This adjustment approach is therefore complementary to the use of pre-analysis plans, discussed below.

An evaluation of the previously mentioned community-driven development program in Sierra Leone used a combination of these approaches to adjust for multiple outcomes. The evaluation analyzed more than 300 indicators, including outcomes regarding economic activity, participation in decisionmaking, social capital, and collective action. Hypotheses of potential impacts were agreed between researchers and implementers before the program started (see Module 8.3), and outcome measures to test each hypothesis were grouped into families. The mean effect of all the outcome measures in each family were then tested as described above. In addition, the *p*-values were adjusted to take into account the fact that 12 different hypotheses were tested (Table 8.3 shows the first 6 of the 12 hypotheses tested using several adjustment approaches). Finally, the hypotheses were grouped into just two overarching families—impacts on hardware (like new public goods) and impacts on software (institutional changes)—reducing the problem of multiple outcomes.

Adjusting for the testing of multiple subgroups

Testing for effects in different subgroups raises exactly the same concerns as testing for multiple outcomes. If we divide our sample into a very large number of subgroups, the chances are that we will find at least one subgroup in which the treatment group does better than the comparison group simply by chance, even if the true effect of the program is zero. As in the case of multiple outcomes, the best way to address this concern is to limit the number of subgroups that are tested, have a clear theory as to why the subgroup might be expected to respond differently to the program, and, if possible, write down the list of subgroups to be examined before the data are examined. This idea of precommitting to how analysis will proceed is discussed in more depth in the next module. Finally, it may well be appropriate to adjust our confidence intervals for the fact that we are testing several subgroups, as described above in our multiple outcomes discussion.

TABLE 8.3 GoBifo Treatment Effects by Research Hypothesis

Hypotheses by family	(1) GoBifo mean treatment effect index	(2) Naive p-value	(3) FWER-adjusted p-value for all 12 hypotheses
Family A: Development infrastructure or "hardware" effects			
Mean effect for family A (Hypotheses 1–3; 39 unique outcomes)	0.298** (0.031)	0.000	
H1: GoBifo project implementation (7 outcomes)	0.703** (0.055)	0.000	0.000
H2: Participation in GoBifo improves the quality of local public services infrastructure (18 outcomes)	0.204** (0.039)	0.000	0.000
H3: Participation in GoBifo improves general economic welfare (15 outcomes)	0.376** (0.047)	0.000	0.000
Family B: Institutional and social change or "software" effects			
Mean effect for family B (Hypotheses 4–12; 155 unique outcomes)	0.028 (0.020)	0.155	
H4: Participation in GoBifo increases collective action and contributions to local public goods (15 outcomes)	0.012 (0.037)	0.738	0.980
H5: GoBifo increases inclusion and participation in community planning and implementation, especially for poor and vulnerable groups; GiBifo norms spill over into other types of community decisions, making them more inclusive, transparent, and accountable (47 outcomes)	0.002 (0.032)	0.944	0.980
H6: GoBifo changes local systems of authority, including the roles and public perception of traditional leaders (chiefs) versus elected local government (25 outcomes)	0.056 (0.037)	0.134	0.664

Source: Reprinted with permission from Katherine Casey, Rachel Glennerster, and Edward Miguel, "Reshaping Institutions: Evidence on Aid Impacts Using a Preanalysis Plan," *Quarterly Journal of Economics* 127 (2012): 1755–1812, Table II, 1786–1787.

Notes: GoBifo (or "Move Forward" in Krio, Sierra Leone's lingua franca) was a program that provided financial assistance (of $4,667, or roughly $100 per household) and social mobilization to village-level committees. Boldface type indicates the average estimate for a grouping of hypotheses. FWER = family-wise error rate.

MODULE 8.3 Pre-analysis Plans

In this module we discuss the rationale for and disadvantages of writing and registering a pre-analysis plan (PAP) that describes, ahead of time, how the data will be analyzed. We also discuss what should be included in such a PAP. Throughout this discussion runs a tension between the benefits of the credibility that comes from tying one's hands versus the benefit of flexibility to respond to unforeseen events and results.

The data mining problem: Why do we need a pre-analysis plan?

In clinical drug trials it has become standard to establish protocols that describe, ahead of time, how the data will be analyzed. This approach helps avoid the danger of *data mining*. As we discussed in the previous module, if two groups of people are compared on many different characteristics (height, age, weight, etc.) it is likely that on at least one characteristic there will be a statistically significant difference between the two groups, simply by chance. If we were not objective evaluators and wanted to show that a program worked, whatever the evidence said, we could compare the treatment and comparison groups on a very large number of outcome measures. We would probably be able to find one or more on which (by chance) the treatment group had better outcomes than the comparison group. We could also examine outcomes for many different subgroups within our study population (girls, boys, children over age 5, children under 5, rich people, poor people, etc.) until we found a subgroup whose outcomes were better in the treatment group than in the comparison group. Combining the two approaches and examining multiple outcomes for multiple subgroups means that we have an even higher chance of finding an outcome for a subgroup in which the treatment group performs better than the control group. This approach is called data mining—looking for the result we want in the data until we find it.

By their nature, randomized evaluations are less subject to data mining than are most other evaluation techniques. The possible outcome measures that an evaluator can use to evaluate the program are determined in advance if data are collected specifically for the evaluation. The sample and which parts of the sample are treatment and which comparison are also determined before the evaluator knows whether the treatment or the comparison group will perform better.

Nevertheless, randomized impact evaluations are not immune from the danger of data mining, nor are evaluators immune from the risk of being accused of data mining even when they had no intention of doing so. How, then, can we protect ourselves from the risk of such an accusation? One answer is to draw up a PAP or an analysis protocol that sets out how we intend to deal with the data when we get them. This plan can be submitted to a registry so that we will have an objective record of the time when the plan was written and any changes that were made over time.[21]

Another approach, discussed in the multiple outcomes section above, is to adjust our standard errors for the fact that we are testing multiple hypotheses or outcome measures. But to do this we need to have a list of all the hypotheses or outcome measures that were tested (not just all those that are reported). A PAP provides a useful and credible way of specifying how many different regressions were run, forming the basis of our adjustment calculations.

It is worth noting the distinction between registering a PAP and registering the existence of an evaluation (also common in medicine). Although a PAP and the existence of an evaluation are often registered in the same place, they perform two different functions. The registration of the existence of a trial helps address potential publication bias (in cases in which many studies testing the same question are run and only the one with a positive effect is published), whereas the registration of a PAP addresses data mining concerns within a given study. Registering the existence of a trial requires only that the evaluator submit basic information such as the location of the trial, a short description of the intervention to be tested, the main outcome measures, and usually the sample size. A PAP is a much more detailed document setting out exactly what regressions will be run when the data are available.

It has not been common practice to register either the existence of an evaluation or a PAP in the social sciences. Until recently, registries existed only for health-related trials. However, the practice is now becoming more common. In 2013 the American Economic Association launched a registry for randomized evaluations in the social sciences (www.socialscienceregistry.org). As of this writing, Experiments in Government and Politics were piloting a registry, and the Inter-

---

21. A good discussion on PAPs can be found on the website of the Berkeley Initiative for Transparency in the Social Sciences (http://cega.berkeley.edu/programs/BITSS/). The discussion in this module draws on and expands that of Casey, Glennerster, and Miguel, summarized as Evaluation 15 in the appendix.

national Initiative for Impact Evaluation were designing a registry of impact evaluations in developing countries, including nonrandomized evaluations. There is virtually no downside to registering that we are undertaking an evaluation, and there is an important public benefit, so this form of registration is strongly encouraged. There are some potential downsides to registering a PAP (especially if it is not well thought through). In the following sections, therefore, we discuss when a pre-analysis plan is particularly useful and what should be included in one.

When is a pre-analysis plan particularly useful?

Because a PAP is primarily designed to avoid cherry picking among alternative ways of calculating results, it is most useful when there is substantial flexibility as to how data can be analyzed. Three important dimensions along which there is often flexibility are the definition or choice of the primary outcome, subgroup selection, and regression specification.

When there are many alternative ways to measure outcomes

In some studies the outcome of interest is obvious and there are limited ways of measuring it. In an evaluation of a program designed to reduce teacher absenteeism, the obvious outcome indicator of interest is the number of days a teacher comes to school, with likely secondary indicators of whether the teacher is teaching when present and whether children learn more as a result of increased teacher attendance. At the other extreme, an evaluation of a community-driven development (CDD) program may seek to determine whether CDD increases trust or social capital and whether it decreases conflict. As we discuss in our section on outcome measures, attempts to capture outcomes such as social capital are likely to rely on measuring a series of concrete actions observed in the field, and the evaluators may measure many such concrete actions. Casey, Glennerster, and Miguel included over 300 outcome indicators in their evaluation of a CDD program.[22] The risk of being accused of cherry picking (or actually cherry picking, even if unwittingly) increases with the number of cherries from which we can pick.

---

22. The study of Casey, Glennerster, and Miguel is summarized as Evaluation 15 in the appendix.

Most evaluations fall somewhere between these two extremes. Let us return to our immunization evaluation example. At first glance there appears to be little wiggle room on the outcome variable. We evaluate a program designed to promote immunization by measuring immunization rates. But what is our precise definition of the immunization rate? Is it the number of vaccines delivered or the number of children fully vaccinated by the age of 2 or 5? Or should it be the number of children who have received at least one shot by the age of 2 or 5? Different definitions are used in different studies in the literature. A good study will present a range of different ways of defining the outcome and use these differences to fill in some of the details of how a program worked. In the immunization study we have been discussing in this book, the authors point out that one treatment (holding immunization camps regularly) increased the number of children who got at least one immunization, while the additional effect of the second treatment (providing incentives to attend the immunization camps) mainly worked by increasing the number of children who made it to the end of the full immunization schedule.[23] However, authors often "headline" a particular formulation of their results even when they present a wide variety of them. A pre-analysis plan allows us to specify in advance which of various formulations we consider the most important.

Most randomized evaluations do not yet include a PAP, and there is serious pressure to include one only if, as in the case of CDD, there are many indicators from which to choose or the analysis is likely to make use of subgroup analysis. But the attitude in the profession is changing, and it is likely that pressure will grow and that it will become harder over time to publish results if a PAP has not been registered.

When we want to test the effectiveness of a program on different subgroups

We may have strong theoretical reasons to think that a program will have different impacts on different types of people. We may even expect that the program will have positive effects on one type of person and

23. Abhijit Banerjee, Esther Duflo, Rachel Glennerster, and Dhruva Kothari, "Improving Immunisation Coverage in Rural India: Clustered Randomised Controlled Evaluation of Immunisation Campaigns with and without Incentives," *British Medical Journal* 2010 (2008): 340:c2220, and J-PAL Policy Briefcase, "Incentives for Immunization," Abdul Latif Jameel Poverty Action Lab, Cambridge, MA, 2011.

negative impacts on another, with an average impact of zero. However, we may worry that we will be accused of data mining if we present results showing an overall impact that is not significant but at the same time show positive effects on some subgroups and negative effects on others. This is a good reason to write a PAP. This will allow us to show that these subgroups were not picked at random from a very large number of possible ways in which we could have split the sample, that it was always our intention to cut the data a certain way.

When there are alternative ways to specify the estimating equation

In randomized evaluations there are usually only a limited number of choices to be made about how to analyze the data once we have decided how to define the main outcome variables and which subgroups we are interested in looking at. The main choices are whether to include control variables and which controls to include. Usually the results do not change very much if we do or do not include controls, and it is almost impossible to know in advance whether our results are likely to be sensitive to this particular specification change. However, there may be cases in which we know in advance that important specification decisions will need to be made. For example, if we have a small sample we will have to decide whether we want to use randomization inference to estimate our standard errors. It may be useful to commit to this approach in advance. We may also have the choice between running our analysis in levels or logs, ordinary least squares, or logit. Again, it may be worth specifying this in advance.

Drawbacks of analysis plans

Preparing a PAP has drawbacks, and some researchers strongly object to their use. Any analysis that is included in the original plan gains credibility from the fact that it was thought of in advance. But if we forget to include a subgroup or an outcome in our plan that turns out to be an important determinant of how the program is working, the fact that it was not included in the plan undermines its credibility. One response to this concern is to think carefully about our plan and make sure it is a good one. But there are also cases in which results emerge when data are analyzed that tell a coherent story but that were hard to predict in advance.

In some clinical trials, researchers commit to a very limited number of outcome measures and specifications for analyzing their data and do not even run any other specifications. Most economists would think this was a waste: if there are results that were not in our analysis plan but we think are important, most economists agree that we should include them and be transparent about the fact that they were not included in the plan.[24]

Another issue that makes the use of PAPs difficult is that the right way to perform our analysis will often be dependent on the main findings. For example, if we find that the program has strong positive effects, a good follow-up step is to examine evidence on the mechanisms through which it had an effect. If the program had negative effects, the next step might be to examine why it had negative effects. If the results are positive, the analyses might involve running different specifications and including different outcome variables than if the results were negative. It is this inability to respond to what the data say that is the main reason some researchers object to the use of PAPs.

Another example of a problem that arises when PAPs are used is that an evaluation may seek to affect a particular outcome and then test the secondary implications of that outcome. One such example is an instrumental variables approach in which the impact of a randomized evaluation is used to create a "first stage." A study in Bangladesh by Field and Glennerster is testing whether a series of different programs lead to a delay in the age of marriage of girls who are under the legal age for marriage (18). The study is designed to examine the impact of delayed marriage (using the program as an instrument) on a series of other outcomes, such as maternal and child health.[25] But whether and how the next stage of analysis is constructed depends on what is found in the first stage, that is, whether the different subprograms are successful in affecting the age of marriage.

It is possible to write an analysis plan that is conditional: if I find result X, I will proceed to the next stage of my analysis this way; if I find outcome Y, I will proceed in this alternate way. But this is hard. It is likely that we will forget one of the potential permutations of the results and therefore not define in the PAP what we would do in a particular situation.

An alternative approach is to specify in the plan that we will first look at one specific question, for example, whether the overall effect is

---

24. This is what was done by Katherine Casey, Rachel Glennerster, and Edward Miguel and summarized as Evaluation 15 in the appendix.

25. This study by Erica Field and Rachel Glennerster is summarized as Evaluation 7 in the appendix.

positive or negative or whether we have a first stage in an instrumental variables design. We can specify that, having answered this one important question, we will then stop looking at the data and write the rest of the plan about how to proceed.

At what point during an evaluation should a PAP be written?

The greatest protection against accusations of data mining comes when a PAP is written before an evaluation is started, before baseline data are collected, and before the intervention has been implemented. This timing avoids two concerns. The first is that the objectives of the program will be scaled down in response to the observed implementation and the initial objectives will never be tested for.

For example, we might be evaluating a CDD program that includes in its initial objectives a desire to reduce the incidence of conflict in the community. During implementation it becomes evident that the program is not well designed to address this issue, and it is very unlikely that any positive effect will be found along this dimension. A PAP written at the start of the project would include analysis of whether the program reduces conflict, whereas one written after project implementation might not include this objective. From a learning point of view it is useful to record that the project, which initially sought to reduce conflict, was not successful in doing so.

The second concern is that choosing outcome measures after implementation makes it possible to observe large random shocks (unrelated to the program) that affect the treatment and comparison communities differently and to adjust our outcome measures in response.

For example, imagine that high rainfall in an area leads a river to overflow its banks, flooding one community in our evaluation area that happens to be in the comparison group. The rate of crop failure is very high in this particular community as a result. Although we were not planning to look at crop failure as an outcome, we add it to our list of outcome measures and find a significant difference between the treatment and comparison groups. The PAP does not guard against this type of random shock, but writing a PAP early on limits our scope to cherry pick outcomes that have been affected by such shocks.

There are important downsides of writing a PAP early in the evaluation process. In particular, writing a PAP very early means that we have to ignore lots of information that is acquired throughout the process that could be used to improve the analysis. We may learn that the way we planned to measure an outcome is not going to yield an accurate reflection of reality—for example, because of high rates of refusal to answer certain questions in the baseline. We may want to reword questions in the endline survey or use a nonsurvey approach to calculate the main outcome measure. Observing the implementation of the intervention may make us think of other hypotheses we want to test—for example, we may become worried about a particular negative side effect of the program that we had not thought of before. Other studies may be published while our experiment is ongoing, raising important new questions that our data may be well suited to examine. All of these factors suggest that we should delay writing a PAP until later in the process.

The most common time to write a PAP is after endline data have been collected but before they have been analyzed. If there are multiple rounds of data collection, the PAP can be updated between the analyses of each round. For example, the first PAP can be written before the midline is analyzed. The plan can then be updated to set out how endline data will be analyzed, taking into account the results that have been found in the midline data.

Another alternative is to write a PAP after the endline data have been collected but to take time to look at the endline data from the comparison group before we finalize the PAP.[26] We cannot be accused of data mining because we are only looking at the endline data from the comparison group, so we cannot be looking for chance correlations in the data between outcomes and treatment status. However, we can see that certain outcome measures have very little variance, and thus there is no scope for the program to improve them. Imagine that we plan to look at whether a program increased primary school enrollment and we find in the endline that 95 percent of primary school–aged children in the comparison group are enrolled in school in the full sample, making it nearly impossible for the program to have had an impact on this outcome. We may decide to change our outcome to school attendance or secondary school enrollment.

One hybrid approach to timing the writing of a PAP is to set down a basic framework for the analysis at the start of the evaluation and fill

26. This approach was used by Amy Finkelstein, Sarah Taubman, Bill Wright, Mira Bernstein, Jonathan Gruber, Joseph P. Newhouse, Heidi Allen, Katherine Baicker, and the Oregon Health Study Group in "The Oregon Health Insurance Study: Evidence from the First Year," NBER Working Paper 17190, National Bureau of Economic Research, Cambridge, MA, 2011.

in the details as the evaluation progresses, registering a full PAP just before the final analysis.[27] By establishing the basic hypotheses that will be tested by the evaluation even before it starts, this approach avoids the first concern discussed above, namely that objectives will be scaled back as the implementation proceeds and the initial objectives will never be tested. Registering a "hypothesis" document of this kind can also be helpful for implementer–evaluator relations because it helps clarify the basic structure of the evaluation and ensures that there is no misunderstanding between the parties about what the evaluation will and will not test for.

What should we include in a PAP?

The most important components of an analysis plan are specifications of

1. the main outcome measures,
2. which outcome measures are primary and which are secondary,
3. the precise composition of any families that will be used for mean effects analysis,
4. the subgroups that will be analyzed,
5. the direction of expected impact if we want to use a one-sided test, and
6. the primary specification to be used for the analysis.

For a PAP to be useful, the definitions of the main outcome measures need to be precise. For example, instead of saying our outcome measure will be immunization rates, we might say that the primary outcome measure will be the percentage of children from birth to age 5 who have received all the immunizations under the government's recommended immunization schedule as measured by mothers' responses to the household questionnaire. We might then specify that a secondary outcome measure to be analyzed will be the average number of immunizations received by children under age 5, because we are interested not only in full immunizations but also in whether the program increased the number of immunizations. If we are going to

27. This approach is used by Katherine Casey, Rachel Glennerster, and Edward Miguel and is summarized as Evaluation 15 in the appendix.

use a mean effects approach (discussed in Module 8.2) we need to specify exactly which outcomes will be included in which families.

If we plan to test the differential effects of the program on particular subgroups, these should be precisely defined. It is also useful to include the rationale as to why the results of different subgroups will be compared. (As we discuss in Module 8.2, there should always be a clear rationale for examining the differential program impacts on particular subgroups.) If we are looking at the differential impact in several subgroups, it increases the credibility of our results if we set out the reasons why we expect that a certain group will be more positively affected by the program than another group.

If we have limited power we may want to perform a one-sided test. This involves looking only for an impact in a particular direction. For example, we think the program will increase school attendance, so we test to see only whether school attendance is higher in the treatment group than in the comparison group. As we discuss in Module 6.2, running a one-sided test requires the very strong assumption that an impact in the opposite direction (usually a negative impact) is not possible. If we want to use this approach, we should specify it in the PAP.

The detailed estimating equation that will be used should be spelled out in detail. For example, will controls be used and if so, which ones and how will they be defined? It is common to use robustness checks to test how much the results change with changes in the precise specification of the estimating equation, and these can also be set out in the PAP. However, the PAP should indicate which of the alternative specifications (for example, with or without controls) will be the primary specification and which will be the robustness checks.

Because PAPs have been used only rarely among economists and other social scientists, the profession in general will be learning by doing in the coming years. It is possible that over time a more standardized list of what should be included in these plans will emerge.

How many outcomes should we include in a pre-analysis plan?

If we write a PAP that states that we will analyze all the possible outcome measures and all the possible subgroups, we will not be much better off than if we had not written a PAP. If we then adjust our confidence intervals to take account of the fact that we have run all these different tests, we will have very little power and will find it hard to say very much about the impact of the program.

But there is no single answer to the question "How many outcome measures is too many?" As we discussed in the section on multiple outcomes (in Module 8.2), there are ways to combine multiple indicators into one outcome. But if we want to measure the different steps along the theory of change (as we said in Chapter 5 is good practice), then we may still have many different outcomes that we are measuring. This suggests another way we can guard against accusations of cherry picking outcomes. It will be helpful if we can present in our PAP a clear theory of change and show which outcome measures are designed to measure intermediate steps along the chain (i.e., secondary outcomes) and which are designed to measure the ultimate objective of the program (i.e., primary outcomes).

Imagine that we are evaluating the impact of a program that seeks to mobilize parental action to improve the quality of education in India. The final outcome of the program is the learning levels of children, and this will be our primary outcome measure. However, to understand how the program does or does not affect this outcome we will collect a number of intermediate indicators such as whether parents become more active in the local education system, whether they encourage their children to do their homework, and whether teacher absenteeism falls. All of these intermediate indicators are secondary to the main outcome of student learning (although some intermediate measures may be given higher priority than others). Prioritizing outcome measures in this way helps with the interpretation of results even when there are many outcome measures. For example, if we find that learning improves in the treatment group but all the other indicators are not statistically significant, we will interpret that result far more positively than if we find that more parents voice questions about education in the treatment group but all the other indicators are not statistically different.

Analysis plans with multiple arms

When a study includes multiple treatment arms, the number of hypotheses to be tested will inevitably be high. Imagine a case in which we are testing several different treatments against each other and against the comparison group. Each comparison of the treatment against an alternative treatment or of a treatment against the comparison group could be run as a separate experiment or written up as a separate paper. If written up as separate papers we would expect to see a few primary outcome measures and many more secondary outcomes with maybe a couple of subgroups per paper. There is no reason to have fewer total hypotheses just because we are including all the arms in one paper.

We should be guided by theory in drawing up the hypotheses to be included in the analysis plan. For example, rather than blindly testing each treatment against the others and each treatment against the comparison group (which could produce a very large number of comparisons), we might be particularly interested in comparisons of specific treatments, or we might expect certain treatments to produce greater impacts than other treatments. Any ability to structure the problem in advance and to explain why particular comparisons are being examined and what conclusions can be drawn if particular patterns of results emerge will be helpful in avoiding the accusation of data mining —even when very large numbers of hypotheses and outcome measures are included in the analysis plan.

Let us return to the example of the evaluation of the girls' empowerment programs in Bangladesh. The study was designed to assess the separate impact on women's and children's health of education, greater control over financial resources, and delayed marriage. It was also designed to test whether there was complementarity between the different approaches, that is, whether improved education had more impact if it was combined with delayed marriage. Specific interventions were included in the different arms in the following way:

1. Basic package: Included adolescent girls' clubs with the curriculum covering reproductive health, basic life skills, and homework sessions.

2. Financial literacy package: Included everything in the basic package with a financial literacy unit taught through the girls' clubs.

3. Delayed marriage incentive: Families with unmarried adolescent girls were provided cooking oil every four months as an incentive to delay their daughters' marriage.

4. Full package: Combined both the financial literacy unit and the delayed marriage incentive.

5. Comparison: Provided no treatment.

With five different treatment arms, there are potentially 10 different combinations of arms to test against each other. If there are five outcome measures we are interested in and two potential subgroups (as well as the full sample), this means that there is a total of $10 \times 5 \times 3 = 150$ main hypotheses. The objective of our analysis plan is to reduce this number to something more manageable, but it will not be a small number.

The original study objective gives us a framework for comparing the outcomes from the different arms. If we want to examine whether the empowerment program had an impact in general, we need to pool the basic and financial package groups and compare the pooled group to the comparison. But we don't need to pool every possible combination of two arms and compare them against the comparison group because most combinations don't have any special meaning in our theory. Similarly, if we want to examine the marginal impact of the financial component of the program, we will want to compare the basic package against the financial package. If we want to know the marginal impact of the incentive, we will want to compare the financial package with the financial-plus-oil package. But there is no reason to compare every pairwise combination of treatment arms against each other.

We can also use our theory to think through which subgroups will be the most interesting to examine. We know that the incentive program applies only to girls between the ages of 15 and 18, so we will want to look at that age group separately. We want to check whether the incentive program is not working through a nutritional effect, so we will want to check whether we get the same results for the incentive package among those who are and are not well nourished at baseline.

Final thoughts on pre-analysis plans

Writing PAPs in economics and related disciplines is still in its infancy, and we have a lot to learn about when they are useful, when they are constraining, and how to write them well. This module has set out some basic ideas on when they are useful as well as common components of PAPs. Before writing a PAP it is very important to carefully think through the risks and benefits. The main risk is writing a rushed and incomplete PAP, so taking the time to carefully go through the theory of change behind the evaluation being tested, and thus what should be included in the analysis, is important.

9 Drawing Policy Lessons

This chapter discusses issues that arise when we want to use the results of randomized evaluations to inform policy decisions.

MODULE 9.1: Checklist of Common Pitfalls
MODULE 9.2: Generalizability
MODULE 9.3: Comparative Cost-effectiveness Analysis
MODULE 9.4: From Research to Policy Action
MODULE 9.5: Concluding Thoughts

MODULE 9.1 Checklist of Common Pitfalls

Not all randomized evaluations are created equal. This module provides criteria for assessing whether a randomized evaluation is of sufficient quality to provide us with policy lessons. It also serves as a checklist for avoiding mistakes in our own evaluations.

One benefit of the randomized evaluation methodology is that there are some basic criteria by which to judge whether a study is valid. This (nonexhaustive) checklist provides a summary of some of the most common mistakes made and refers the reader to the relevant sections of the book that discuss each issue in greater depth. We group the mistakes into those that are made at the design, implementation, and analysis stages.

Errors in design

Ignoring spillovers

Often providing a program to one member of a community will have implications for other members of the community. If we provide information to a random sample of farmers, those farmers may easily pass the information on to their neighbors. If we have randomized at the individual level, we may well underestimate the impact of the program because our comparison group has also benefited from the program.

Designing an underpowered study

We cannot draw policy conclusions from a study in which the estimated effect size is very imprecise. For example, a study on the impact of an education program that has a confidence interval ranging from −0.2 standard deviations (SD) in test scores to +0.4SD tells us very little. This result suggests that the program could have had an impact on test scores of 0.4SD (which is a large positive effect) or it could have reduced test scores.

This type of inconclusive result usually occurs when a study is designed with too small a sample size or too many different treatment groups or when researchers fail to account for the level of randomization when calculating power (see next section).

Forgetting to cluster when calculating sample size

One of the main reasons for underpowered studies, and one of the most serious (and far too common) mistakes we see in the literature, is to calculate sample size based on the number of people surveyed without taking into account the level at which randomization is done. For example, if 1,000 people are interviewed in two districts (500 per district) and one district is randomly selected to receive the treatment while the other district is randomly picked to be the comparison group, we do not have a valid experiment despite the apparently large sample size. This is because shocks are correlated within a district. In other words, something can happen that affects all 500 people in one district and none of the people in the other district. One district may be hit by flooding, or the head of the district administration may change. If this happens, there is no way to separate the impact of the program from the impact of the flooding or change in the head of district administration. For more details about why a failure to adjust for group-level randomization is a problem, see Module 6.2.

Shortcomings in implementation

Using unreliable outcome measures

A common mistake made by impact evaluators is using an outcome measure that is unreliable. A version of this problem is seen when a study fails to recognize that a program may change what people say but not what they do. For example, an HIV education program may change how people answer questions about HIV without changing behavior. An HIV education evaluation that uses only self-reported data on sexual activity is unlikely to be a good basis for policy decision-making for this reason. For more discussion of valid outcome measures, see Chapter 5.

Collecting data differently in the treatment and comparison groups

It is extremely tempting to use program data or program staff to collect data for evaluating the program. Very often, program staff are working in treatment areas but not in comparison areas. It is not appropriate to have program staff collect outcome data in treatment areas and professional enumerators or others collect data in the comparison areas. If a study does use different approaches to collecting data in treatment and comparison areas, we won't know whether any differences we see are due to the program or to differences in the data collection process. In general, having program staff collect data is a bad idea, because staff may want to see a particular outcome or the participants may hesitate to tell the truth to the people who implemented the program.

There are many other ways this particular problem can occur. Perhaps the implementers are in a hurry to get on with the program. The evaluators want to perform a baseline survey before implementation. So why shouldn't they conduct the baseline first in the treatment areas so that implementation can start while data are being collected in the comparison areas? People may give different responses to questions in different months, so there may be systematic differences in the baseline between treatment and comparison communities. We will not know if this is because of the different timing of the survey or because there really were differences before the program. Similarly, if implementers of a program get teachers to take pictures of themselves to prove their presence, the study is not valid if they use these pictures to determine teachers' attendance for the evaluation because there are no pictures in the comparison group. For a discussion of this and other data collection issues, see Chapter 5 on outcomes and instruments.

Allowing high levels of attrition

As discussed in Module 7.2, high levels of attrition can undermine the validity of an experiment. Attrition is a particular concern if the attrition rates are different in the treatment and comparison groups or if different types of people drop out of the study in the treatment versus the comparison group. If all the high-performing students move out of comparison schools but stay in treatment schools and we collect data only in schools, it may look as though the program is effective when in fact it isn't. When we are assessing the validity of a study, it is important to check the total attrition rate, whether the treatment and comparison groups have similar attrition rates, and whether similar types of people attrite in the treatment and comparison groups. The researchers may put bounds on their estimated impact if they do have attrition.

Failing to monitor compliance and other threats

In Chapter 7 we discussed a number of threats to the validity of an experiment once it is under way, including partial compliance. One of the most common practical errors that evaluators make is not having someone on the ground monitoring the implementation as it unfolds, keeping in touch with the implementers to make sure that they are still clear on what is treatment and what is comparison, making sure that the design of the program is not changing in ways that could undermine the validity of the experiment, and observing whether spillovers appear to be a problem. Except in rare situations, it is impossible to pull off a high-quality randomized evaluation by limiting the role of the evaluator to the design, baseline, and endline phases. Usually someone from the evaluation team needs to be present at the program site throughout program implementation and data collection. It can be difficult to tell from a study write-up whether the evaluator was present on the ground throughout. However, it is important to check whether there is good documentation of adherence to the randomization and whether spillovers and noncompliance were major issues. Without this documentation it is difficult to believe the results of the study.

Mistakes and other shortcomings in the analysis

Having too many subgroups or outcome measures

A study that has 40 outcome measures for 10 different subgroups is effectively testing 400 different hypotheses. The nature of statistics suggests that there is a great chance that at least some of these tests will prove to have significant outcomes simply by chance. It is difficult to know whether to draw policy conclusions from the results when the results of only a few of many tests are significantly different from zero. Good studies will deal with this issue by grouping outcome measures (combining them into an index or grouping them into families) in a way that is intuitive. If the total population of the study is split into different subgroups and the effect tested on each, there should be a clear rationale for why each subgroup might be expected to be influenced differently by the program, and a limited number of such subgroups should be tested. In some cases, researchers may have identified in advance which subgroups they will look at, how variables will be combined, and which of the outcome variables are the most important. Module 8.3 discusses the pros and cons of these pre-analysis plans.

Dropping noncompliers

If an individual or community that is randomly chosen to take up the treatment does not take it up, it is tempting to treat that individual or community as part of the comparison group or drop the individual or community from the analysis. However, any study that does this should not be used for drawing policy lessons (unless there is a way to access the data and conduct the analysis again properly). It is not random when an individual or community fails to take up treatment, and we do not know who in the control group would not have taken up treatment if they were offered it. We can only know that two groups are the same when they are chosen randomly, so we have to stick to that allocation. The treatment group are those who were randomly picked to receive the program (whether they take it up or not). The comparison group consists of those randomly chosen not to receive the program (even if they find a way to get it). As long as we stick to this assignment in the analysis and measure how many noncompliers there are and as long as the take-up rate is higher in the treatment group than in the comparison group, the experiment is likely to be valid and we can use the results for policy analysis.[1] (However, if many people don't comply, we may have low statistical power.) For more on avoiding partial compliance, see Module 7.1, and for what to do if partial compliance arises, see Module 8.2.

Dropping matched pairs if one member of the pair does not comply

A somewhat more sophisticated version of the previous pitfall is to split the sample into pairs and randomize within each pair, with one allocated to the treatment group and one to the comparison group. Then if one member of the pair fails to comply (i.e., does not take up the program despite being allocated to treatment), both members of the pair are dropped at the analysis stage. This is not a valid way to deal with partial compliance (see Module 8.2). Although the original members of the pair may be similar on observables, as soon as one member of the pair fails to comply, this reveals additional information. We do not know which of the comparison units would have failed to comply if it had been allocated to the treatment group. The only unbiased approach is to collect data on every unit that was randomized and perform the analysis based on the original allocation to the treatment and comparison groups.

Failing to adjust for the level of randomization in analysis

Earlier in this section we said that a common mistake is failing to adjust for the level of randomization when calculating power. It is also common to see studies that fail to adjust for the level of randomization during the analysis: specifically, if data are collected at the individual level but randomization takes place at the group level, failing to cluster standard errors at the group level. An alternative, even more conservative approach, is to collapse all the data into averages at the group level and run the analysis at the level at which randomization was done. We discuss in Module 8.2 how to analyze results when randomization takes place at the group level.

Ignoring the precision of the estimate in interpreting the results

As we discussed under design errors, a study that has a wide confidence interval around its estimated effect is not very useful. But, compound-

---

1. The one exception is if we have defiers, that is, people who do not take up the treatment though they were randomized into the treatment group. We discuss this problem in Module 8.3.

ing the error of designing a poorly powered study, some evaluators fail to take into account the width of the confidence interval when drawing conclusions. For example, they may conclude that a program did not work when in fact the confidence interval is so large that we cannot rule out that the program was quite effective.

A related error is to conclude that one version of a program works better than another version when in fact the estimates of the two versions are not significantly different from each other. For example, imagine an evaluation of two approaches to improving test scores. The coefficient on the first approach is 0.3 SD, while the coefficient on the other is 0.35 SD. In both cases the confidence interval is ±0.1 SD. In this case we can say that both approaches are statistically different from zero, but we cannot say that one is better because the two coefficients are not statistically significantly different from each other. This can still be possible even if the impact of one approach is significantly different from zero and the other is not.

MODULE 9.2 Generalizability

When should we generalize the results from randomized evaluations to a new context? This module discusses how we can use both empirical testing and theory to help us decide whether and when to translate the lessons from one context to another.

Internal and external validity

Randomized evaluations test a particular program or answer a particular question in a specific geographic location with a specific implementing organization at a specific time and at a specific scale. As discussed in Chapter 2, if we conduct a randomized evaluation well, we can be reasonably confident that the impact we measure is an unbiased estimate of the true impact in this context. In other words, we have *internal validity*. But the questions most relevant to policy go beyond the specifics of one program: If the program was tested and worked well in one district of the country, will it work in other districts? If it worked in one country, will it work in another country? If it worked at one point in time, will it work at other times when conditions may have changed? If it worked at a small scale, will it work at a large scale? The extent to which we can be confident that the results found in one context will generalize to other contexts is called *external validity*.

If it were impossible to draw inferences from the impact of a program in one context to the likely impact in another context, we would have to test every program in every context and at every point in time to be able to draw any conclusions relevant to our decisions about which programs and policies we should invest in. Understanding whether and when results generalize to other contexts is critical to any attempt to draw policy lessons from randomized evaluations.

The commonality of generalizability to all forms of evaluation

The problem of generalizability (external validity) is not restricted to randomized evaluations. We have to make assumptions about the extent to which people behave similarly in different contexts if we are to draw policy lessons from any data, any impact evaluations, or any theory.

Small nonrandomized evaluations

Most nonrandomized impact evaluations also tend to be undertaken on specific programs in specific locations. So if we have results from a nonrandomized impact evaluation carried out in 240 villages in northern Ghana and a randomized impact evaluation carried out in 240 villages in northern Ghana, there is no reason to think that the results from the randomized evaluation will generalize less well to southern Ghana than the results from the nonrandomized evaluation. Indeed, if the nonrandomized evaluation has not dealt well with the potential problem of selection bias, there is less reason to think the results will generalize: if we can't be confident that the impact estimate is unbiased in the original context, there is no reason to think that it provides a good estimate of the likely impact of the program in another context. In other words, if the impact lacks internal validity, there is no reason to think it is externally valid. Internal validity is a necessary but not sufficient condition for external validity.

Large national-level or cross-country evaluations

Is a national-level or international-level nonrandomized evaluation more generalizable than a smaller-scale randomized evaluation? Finding consistent patterns or relationships that hold across very large numbers of people and across many different contexts is important and useful for understanding an issue and for policymaking. But it does not solve the problem of having to make assumptions about when and whether the results in one context generalize to other contexts. Indeed, large-scale national or cross-country studies that go beyond descriptive conclusions implicitly make the assumption that the relationship being tested is constant across contexts. Imagine that when we run a regression across all the countries of the world we find that there is no strong correlation between spending on education and learning levels. Does this mean that spending more on education has no effect on learning? It might. But it might also be the case that spending is positively correlated with learning in some cases, while in other countries more is spent on deprived neighborhoods and thus spending is negatively correlated with learning.

What if, instead of running one regression across many contexts (as in a cross-country regression), we run it in multiple contexts and find that it holds in all of them? Does this mean we can be confident that we have a generalized relationship on which we can build policy? Unfortunately this is true only if the study is designed in such a way as to distinguish correlation from causation. For example, we may find that more educated women are more likely to vaccinate their children. We may find that this correlation holds true in many different contexts and countries. But this does not mean that we can assume that if we were to increase the education of women it would *cause* vaccination rates to rise. Why? Because the women who are currently educated are different in many ways from those who are not educated—they tend to be richer and more confident. Maybe it is their wealth or their confidence that is causing the higher vaccination rates. In other words, we still have to make assumptions to draw policy conclusions from large-scale nonrandomized evaluations—they are just different assumptions. (In Module 2.2 we discuss the assumptions that are needed for internal validity for different types of nonrandomized evaluation.)

Designing randomized evaluations with an eye toward generalizability

Throughout this book we have stressed the importance of designing an evaluation with an eye to generalizability. For example, in Module 3.3 we discussed the benefits of conducting a study in a representative location and with a representative partner. We suggested testing a program that did not rely on unusual and hard-to-replicate inputs (like highly motivated staff). All of these factors make it more likely that the result will generalize. In Module 4.4 we gave an example of a randomized evaluation that built in generalizability more formally: specifically, the study was designed to be representative at the state level in Andhra Pradesh. By randomizing districts to work in and then randomizing schools to study within those districts, the authors ensured that their results were representative of, and thus could be generalized to, the entire state (with a population of 85 million).

Combining information from randomized and nonrandomized studies

We usually want to combine what we learn from randomized and nonrandomized studies when attempting to draw policy lessons, taking into account the comparative advantages of different approaches when we do this, just as we advocate using a mix of approaches to answer different research questions in Chapter 3.

For example, if we find a strong correlation between the levels of education of women around the world and vaccination rates, this may not be sufficient for us to know that more education will lead to more vaccination in, say, Tanzania. If, however, we also find that a well-conducted randomized evaluation in Ghana finds that providing scholarships to girls to go to secondary school causes increases in vaccination rates, the combination of information we now have arguably provides stronger evidence than either does individually.[2] Our confidence in the policy conclusion would be even higher if we found that the estimated impact of secondary education on vaccination in Ghana was similar in magnitude to what would have been estimated by simply comparing the vaccination rates of the children of women who went to secondary school and those of women who didn't in Ghana. In other words, the results from our randomized evaluation can suggest that in that context there was little sign of selection bias in the nonrandomized result. (This test of the amount of bias in a study that does not separate correlations from causality can be performed only when we have the results of at least one randomized evaluation.) Ways to combine randomized results with process and qualitative findings to understand generalizability are discussed further below.

Testing whether results generalize

The question of whether a particular result generalizes is an empirical one and can be tested by running evaluations of similar programs in different contexts (in different locations, with different implementers, or at different scales). We can design our original evaluation to simultaneously test the program in two different contexts: a rural site and

---

2. For the ongoing study that inspired this example, see Evaluation 16 in the appendix.

an urban site, two different cities or districts in the same country with different levels of poverty, or two different countries. If we do this, we will want to make sure that we have enough statistical power to be able to test whether the results are the same in the different contexts (see Chapter 6). An alternative is to first test a range of different approaches in one context and then test the most effective of these in other contexts.

When we test for generalizability in this way, it is useful to have an opinion about the most important differences between the two contexts and how these differences might affect how the program operates. We can then design intermediate indicators designed to describe how the program's theory of change may vary in the different contexts and how differences in context may lead to differences in impact. (In Chapter 5 we discussed the use of theory of change in more detail.)

Many programs have now been tested by randomized impact evaluations in different contexts. For example, Pratham's remedial education program was initially tested in two cities in different states of India (Mumbai in Maharashtra and Vadodara in Gujarat).[3] These different locations were chosen because of different levels of school quality in the two states. The program was then tested in a rural location (Uttar Pradesh) using a slightly different model to reflect the different needs of the new location.[4] The program is now in the early stages of being tested in Ghana.[5] The results from all these different impact evaluations in very different contexts have been similar.

Quotas for women leaders were evaluated in two different states of India (West Bengal and Rajasthan). The quotas were introduced for the leaders of local governments across India. The researchers chose to evaluate the policy in these two states because they had very different traditions of local government and because of differences in female literacy and empowerment.[6]

Even when we haven't explicitly designed an evaluation to cover two or more different contexts, we will inevitably have some differ-

3. This study by Abhijit Banerjee, Shawn Cole, Esther Duflo, and Leigh Linden is summarized as Evaluation 2 in the appendix.
4. Abhijit Banerjee, Rukmini Banerji, Esther Duflo, Rachel Glennerster, and Stuti Khemani, "Pitfalls of Participatory Programs: Evidence from a Randomized Evaluation in Education in India," *American Economic Journal: Economic Policy* 2 (2010): 1–30.
5. http://www.poverty-action.org/node/3904.
6. This study by Lori Beaman, Raghabendra Chattopadhyay, Esther Duflo, Rohini Pande, and Petia Topalova is summarized as Evaluation 12 in the appendix.

ences across communities and across individuals in our sample. Examining the extent to which we have similar or dissimilar treatment effects by type of community or individual can help us understand how a program might fare in another context. For example, we may find that a health education program was particularly effective for those who had at least finished primary school. When we think about scaling the program up, we may want to focus first on areas where primary education rates are higher while we continue to look for ways to improve health education for those with lower levels of education.

Combining testing and theory to assess generalizability

How many times do we need to test a particular program to know whether its outcomes will generalize to a new location, implementer, or scale? There is no simple answer to this question. It depends on the program, and it also depends on how similar the new context is to the one in which it was tested. In thinking through this issue, we have to be guided, at least in part, by theory. Theory can help us decide if a program is likely to be very sensitive to changes in context. It can also help us determine whether a particular context is "similar"—that is, what aspects of the context are likely to be relevant to a particular program. Theory can also help us judge whether the slight modifications in a program that always take place when it is translated to a new location or implementer are likely to be important and therefore require more testing or are superficial and unlikely to affect impact.

Take the example of deworming. Our theory of change suggests that school-based deworming leads to reductions in the number of parasitic worms in children's bodies, which in turn improves their health, which makes it easier for them to go to school, which increases their attendance at school. Some aspects of the context are so fundamental to the theory of change that there is little point in testing the program if the context is radically different. There is no point in testing the program in an area where there are no parasitic worms. But one way in which worms affect health is through anemia, and some contexts have higher underlying rates of anemia than others. The initial program was tested in an area with low rates of anemia, so we might want to see if the results are stronger in an area with higher anemia rates. Or we might want to test it in an area with a lower or higher worm load to see how the impacts vary with worm load. But in general, our theory suggests that children with worms are likely to react similarly to a deworming pill. Given that there are worms and schools, in general we would think that the impacts of a deworming program are less likely to vary by context than the impacts of other programs.[7]

In contrast, think of a program designed to improve the quality of social services by providing information on the quality of those services and encouraging local people to advocate for improvements. As discussed in Chapter 1, the effectiveness of such a program may well be highly dependent on differences in institutional context, such as how responsive government systems are to local pressure.

One important dimension of context is the implementer (NGO, private company, or government agency) running the program. Different organizations may employ very different types of staff. Some programs may be very dependent on highly trained and motivated staff, in which case the program may not generalize well to other organizations. One benefit of carrying out an evaluation with the government is that if the government is going to scale up a program, it is useful to know the program's impact as it will be scaled up. Programs that can be implemented by staff without very specific skills are likely to generalize across implementers more readily. But it is important to remember that the results of a randomized evaluation are not a black box: we can use theory and process evaluation data to unpack the mechanism by which the impact was made and thus how we might expect impacts to change if the program were implemented by a different organization. For example, we can use process data to document the quality of implementation with which a given impact measure is associated. If the program is then taken on by another implementer, we can again collect process data and see to what extent implementation differs. This will not tell us with certainty what the impact will be with a new implementer, but it will be useful to us in making a well-informed extrapolation.

In cases in which evaluations conducted in different contexts find very different results, more studies are needed to tease out the contexts in which an approach works and the details of how a successful program interacts with a particular context before we can be confident about drawing general policy lessons. We discuss an example in which this is the case in Module 1.2.

---

7. This example is inspired by a study by Edward Miguel and Michael Kremer, which is summarized as Evaluation 1 in the appendix.

MODULE 9.3 Comparative Cost-effectiveness Analysis

This module discusses how cost-effectiveness analysis can be used in comparing results from multiple randomized evaluations, the assumptions needed to make these comparisons, and how we can use sensitivity analysis of cost-effectiveness to help us decide whether a particular program is right for a given context.

Why use cost-effectiveness analysis?

Any program or policy we introduce has opportunity costs. In other words, there are alternative ways to spend our money and our time. It is not enough to know that a policy or program has a positive impact on the lives of the poor; we need to know that the policy or program is the best use of limited resources (among the set of options that are politically and logistically possible and for which we have good evidence). The differences in cost-effectiveness between programs that all have a positive impact can be very large.

Figure 9.1 shows the number of additional years of schooling that can be achieved with $100, based on the results of 11 different randomized evaluations of education programs in different countries. There are a number of caveats and assumptions behind these figures, which we will discuss in the rest of this module. But even when we change these assumptions, some programs consistently generate many more school years per $100 spent than other programs.

Cost-benefit versus cost-effectiveness analysis

Cost-effectiveness analysis shows the effect a program achieves on one outcome measure for a given cost incurred. To calculate this, all the program costs are added up, and these costs are then divided by the total impact the program had on a single outcome measure. For example, in Figure 9.1 the costs of all programs are compared according to the single outcome measure "years of schooling." *Cost-benefit analysis* translates all the different benefits and costs of programs onto one scale (usually a monetary scale). It can then be used to compare different programs or to assess whether a program is worth investing in (i.e., do the benefits exceed the costs?).

Cost-benefit analysis incorporates valuations of multiple outcomes

One advantage of cost-benefit analysis is that it makes it easier to assess a program with multiple outcomes. For example, if we have one

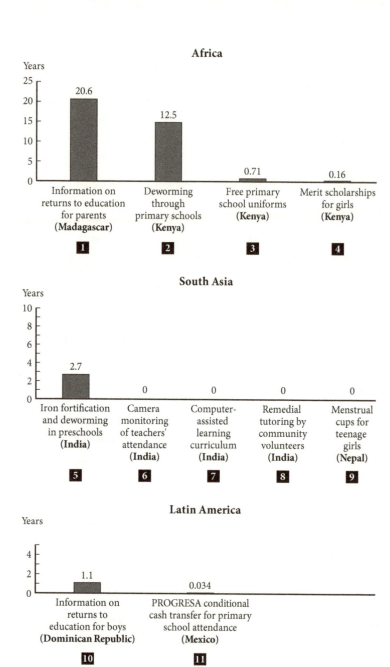

FIGURE 9.1 Cost-effectiveness: Additional years of student participation per $100 spent in Africa, south Asia, and Latin America

program that has a large impact on test scores and a small impact on health and another program that has a small impact on test scores and a large impact on health, how are we to decide which to invest in? If we place a monetary value on improvements in test scores and a monetary value on improvements in health, we can add them to each other and then compare these values to the costs of the program. The program with the lowest cost-to-benefit ratio represents the best investment (given our relative weighting on health and education).

Putting both costs and benefits on the same scale delivers not just a relative but an absolute judgment: whether a program is worth the investment. Having completed a cost-benefit analysis, we may conclude that none of the alternatives is worth investing in or that it is worth investing in several of the alternatives simultaneously. A good example of a case in which this aspect of cost-benefit analysis is useful is a program that involves an upfront investment (say, in the building of a new hospital) that will generate a stream of benefits (such as reduced maintenance costs) in the future. Another example would be a program designed to reduce government waste by increasing monitoring: a cost-benefit analysis would tell us whether the increased cost of monitoring paid for itself by reducing waste. If there is no constraint on what we can borrow and we use the cost of borrowing as our discount rate when calculating costs and benefits over time, we should implement all the programs that generate a positive cost-benefit analysis.

The downside of using cost-benefit analysis is that it requires a number of assumptions about the value of benefits on which different organizations or people may have very different views. For example, if a program reduces child mortality, we will need to put a monetary value on saving a life. We may have to put a monetary value on girls' having access to education or on reduced disability from disease, and we will be forced to make relative judgments about which of these is more valuable. Whenever we make decisions about which program or policy to invest in, we are implicitly making these comparative valuations between health and education, between the health of older people versus that of younger people. Cost-benefit analysis makes these valuations explicit and builds them into the calculations.

Cost-effectiveness analysis leaves the relative valuation
of different outcomes up to the user

Because different organizations are likely to have very different views on the relative weight to give different types of benefits, J-PAL tends to undertake cost-effectiveness rather than cost-benefit analyses. This allows those using the information we generate to impose their own relative values on different outcomes. They can decide whether achieving 13 more years of school attendance for $100 through deworming is better than achieving 490 fewer cases of diarrhea for the same cost.

Issues to consider when performing cost-effectiveness analysis
Being comprehensive and consistent about costs

Any cost-effectiveness (or cost-benefit) analysis relies on comprehensive and consistent calculation of costs across the studies included. If one study does not value the time of the volunteers who help run the program and another one does, the comparison of their respective cost-effectiveness ratios will not reflect the true difference between the programs. A key factor in being consistent is being comprehensive. We do not attempt here to replicate the detailed advice available on how to undertake cost-effectiveness studies,[8] but it is worth mentioning two key issues to consider when calculating costs.

1. *Beneficiary costs:* It is important to include not just the costs to the implementing organization but also those to the beneficiaries. If we charge beneficiaries for participation or require them to donate labor for the program, it is a real cost to the people the program is designed to help.

2. *Transfers:* Whether to include transfers (such as cash payments) to beneficiaries as costs to the program is a complex issue.[9] We can think of cash transfers as another benefit of the program, and because we don't measure other benefits (such as health benefits in education programs), why should we count cash as a benefit? On the other hand, we could think of it as a negative beneficiary cost, in which case it should be seen as both a benefit (to the beneficiary) and a cost (to the provider) so that the two net each other out. One practical approach is to show the results both with and without transfers included as a cost and

8. See, for example, Henry M. Levin and Patrick J. McEwan, *Cost-Effectiveness Analysis: Methods and Applications,* 2nd ed. (Thousand Oaks, CA: Sage, 2000), or Iqbal Dhaliwal, Esther Duflo, Rachel Glennerster, and Caitlin Tulloch, "Comparative Cost-Effectiveness Analysis to Inform Policy in Developing Countries," http://www.poverty actionlab.org/publication/cost-effectiveness.

9. This issue is discussed in detail in Dhaliwal et al., "Comparative Cost-Effectiveness Analysis."

see how sensitive the results are to different assumptions on this point.[10]

Using discount rates to compare costs and impacts across time

Some programs impose large upfront costs in the first few years but have low maintenance costs in future years. Others have low upfront costs but higher ongoing costs such as staff salaries. Some programs quickly provide large impacts; others create benefits that grow over time. To put all these programs on a similar basis, we apply a discount rate to both the costs and the impacts that will arise in the future and collapse everything into costs and impacts from the perspective of one point in time.

The main challenge is deciding the appropriate discount rate to use. We want to use a rate that reflects the trade-off over time of the different actors involved in the program—those bearing the costs and those reaping the benefits. In an economy with no distortions, the interest rate would reflect these trade-offs, but in practice, especially in developing countries, funders and poor beneficiaries are likely to have very different preferences as to the timing of benefits and costs. The poor in particular can face very high interest rates and can place a high value on benefits today versus tomorrow. The right discount rate to use may therefore depend on whether the main timing trade-offs are about costs (in which case the funder's borrowing cost is a good rate to use) or about the timing of benefits (in which case a high discount rate may be appropriate). Again, however, it is worth testing the sensitivity of our results to different discount rates.[11] In practice, most results are not very sensitive to changes in discount rates.

If programs have been implemented at different times, we also need to be careful to adjust costs for inflation.

Comparing costs across countries

If we have information on costs and impacts from programs designed to increase primary school attendance in Kenya, India, and Mexico, how can we compare those programs to help us choose the most cost-effective approach for Tanzania? Unfortunately, this is not as simple as

10 A further complication is exactly what counts as a transfer. A cash transfer is clearly a transfer and has a clear monetary value. But should we include food stamps, bed nets, free health services, or even information if it's valuable?

11. For a more detailed discussion of appropriate discount rates and some example discount rates, see Dhaliwal et al., "Comparative Cost-Effectiveness Analysis."

translating costs using market exchange rates. The problem is that the Mexican program may have been more expensive than the program tested in India because Mexico is richer and costs are higher there. These higher costs are not relevant to our decision about Tanzania. We could use *purchasing power parity* (PPP) exchange rates, which are meant to adjust for different costs in different countries, but the types of goods these exchange rates are designed to compare are not usually those that go into programs. In addition, relative costs are likely to differ between countries, so a program that relies on lots of inexpensive, educated labor in India may be much more expensive in Kenya than PPP comparisons would suggest. Ideally we would look at the components of the costs of the programs, cost them out for our particular context, and conduct a specific cost-effectiveness analysis tailored to our situation. It is important not to use PPP exchange rates to translate costs into the currency of a rich country if we want to implement a program in a poor country. This can give us a very skewed picture of the benefits we can achieve for our money. Essentially, a PPP comparison of education programs from Mexico, India, and Kenya shown in dollars tells us the cost of running these programs in the United States, which does not tell us much about what we will achieve in Tanzania. Generally, PPP comparisons can be useful for making comparisons across contexts, but it is complicated to do this carefully.[12]

Accounting for multiple impacts

Deciding which program to adopt by looking at cost-effectiveness comparisons can be complicated when a program has impacts on multiple outcomes, particularly if these outcomes affect very different aspects of people's lives. If we are comparing two programs, one of which is more cost-effective in increasing school attendance while the other is more cost-effective in increasing test scores, the comparison may be manageable. For example, we may decide that attendance is an intermediary outcome and that we care about attendance only to the extent that it increases learning. We can then ignore impacts on attendance and analyze just the relative cost-effectiveness of programs on test scores. In other cases we may be faced with multiple outcomes in very different sectors, and one may not be clearly preferable to another. For example, we may be faced with a choice between one program that is highly effective in increasing school

---

12. For more details, see Dhaliwal et al., "Comparative Cost-Effectiveness Analysis."

attendance and another that has moderate effects on both school attendance and vaccination rates. If we work for a ministry of education with a mandate to focus on education outcomes, this may not be an issue: we will prioritize the program that does the most for education. However, if we work for a foundation that is interested in improving general welfare, we may find it hard to draw comparisons across sectors in this way.

One approach to dealing with programs that have multiple outcomes is to revert to using cost-benefit analysis as discussed above. Another is to divide the program costs between the different outcomes. If there is any way to divide the costs between the different outcomes such that a hypothetical one-outcome program is highly cost-effective compared to other programs that target that outcome, the package as a whole is cost-effective. Imagine that a program improves school attendance and vaccinations and we apportion a quarter of the costs to the education component and three quarters of the costs to the vaccination component. With these costs, if the program is one of the most cost-effective programs addressing school attendance and one of the most cost-effective addressing vaccinations, we know we have a highly cost-effective package.

Sensitivity analysis of cost-effectiveness estimates

Because there are many assumptions that go into cost-effectiveness comparisons, it is useful to examine how sensitive the results are to modest changes in key assumptions. We have mentioned some types of sensitivity analysis earlier in this module. Here we discuss a number of others as well as how sensitivity analysis can be used to judge which program to introduce in a particular context—in other words, whether and when we might expect results to generalize to another context. Sensitivity analysis is possible only when we have access to the data and model behind the cost-effectiveness calculations and can modify numbers to customize the analysis for a particular context. Therefore, making the data and models used in cost-effectiveness analysis public greatly increases their usefulness to decisionmakers.

The imprecision of impact estimates

A randomized evaluation will give us not only an estimate of impact but also a confidence interval around that estimate, and some studies may estimate impacts much more precisely than others. When we make policy decisions, we need to consider not only the magnitude but also the precision of the impact estimates. We see how sensitive our cost-effectiveness estimates are to using the high and low bounds of estimated impacts shown by the confidence interval around a given estimate of impact. We may find that although one program initially appears more cost-effective than another, if we take account of the confidence bands around the estimated impacts, their cost-effectiveness is not significantly different.

For example, we can examine the 90 percent confidence intervals of cost-effectiveness for programs that increase children's time in school (Table 9.1). Some programs, such as PROGRESA in Mexico, have very precisely estimated impacts, and the 90 percent confidence interval for their cost-effectiveness is not very wide.[13] Other programs, such as information campaigns on returns to education in Madagascar, have impacts that are estimated with less precision. In this case the 90 percent confidence interval of cost-effectiveness ranges from around 1 year of schooling per $100 to almost 40 years. Despite this lack of precision in the estimate, the entire range of possible cost-effectiveness ratios for the Madagascar program is still higher than the cost-effectiveness ratio for most of the other programs in this analysis.

Sensitivity to changes in context

In the second module of this chapter we discussed when the results from a study in one context might generalize to another. Here we discuss how sensitivity analyses can help us understand which program will be most cost-effective in a new context.

We have already discussed how costs may be different in one country than another, but there are likely to be other relevant differences in context that will affect cost-effectiveness. One program may look more effective than another simply because it was conducted in an environment in which it is easier to make progress. For example, if school attendance is already above 80 percent, it is probably harder for a program to improve the numbers of children going to school than it is in a context in which school attendance is only 50 percent. For another example, if our theory of change suggests that a program is likely to affect diarrhea rates by a similar percentage whatever the rate of diarrhea, comparing the number of cases of diarrhea averted by programs in contexts with different underlying diarrhea rates will

---

13. This study by T. Paul Schultz is summarized as Evaluation 9 in the appendix.

TABLE 9.1 Confidence intervals of cost-effectiveness: Additional years of education per $100 spent

Program		Country	Time frame (years)	Lower bound	Estimate	Upper bound
1	Information session on returns to education for parents	Madagascar	1	1.1	19.5	37.9
2	Deworming through primary schools	Kenya	1	5.70	14.0	22.30
3	Free primary school uniforms	Kenya	1	0.33	0.71	1.09
4	Merit scholarships for girls	Kenya	3	0.02	0.27	0.51
5	Iron fortification and deworming in preschools	India	1	0.09	2.65	5.21
6	Camera monitoring of teachers' attendance	India	1		n.s.i.	
7	Computer-assisted learning curriculum	India	1		n.s.i.	
8	Remedial tutoring by community volunteers	India	1		n.s.i.	
9	Menstrual cups for teenage girls	Nepal	1		n.s.i.	
10	Information session on returns to education for boys	Dominican Republic	4	0.03	0.03	0.03
11	PROGRESA conditional cash transfer for primary school attendance	Mexico	4	0.08	0.24	0.41

Notes: The ranges are based on a 90 percent confidence interval of program impact. n.s.i. = no significant impact.

give undue weight to those implemented in contexts with high baseline rates. For this reason it may be better to compare percentage changes in enrollment or diarrhea across studies than to look at numbers of cases. An equivalent to this approach, and one that is perhaps easier for policymakers to interpret, is to take the percentage changes found in the studies and apply these to the diarrhea rate in our context to see the number of cases that would be averted in our context. This is what is done in Table 9.1. A final alternative is to compare studies across more similar contexts, as we do in Figure 9.1 above.

The sensitivity bands around the cost-effectiveness estimates in Figure 9.2 do not relate to the precision of the estimate in the original study. Instead, these are error bands to sensitivity to context—in this case, sensitivity to population density. Some programs are more sensitive to population density than others, and this type of sensitivity analysis can be very instructive as we think through which approach will be most useful in our context. For example, improving a water source will be much more cost-effective if many people use the same source than in a context in which the population is very dispersed and only a few families use one source.[14] The details on this sensitivity analysis are available at www.povertyactionlab.org/policy-lessons/health.

Sensitivity to changes of scale

Costs per person may fall when we bring a program up to scale if, for example, there are economies of scale in transport or training, making the program more cost-effective. If the evaluation was performed at a small scale and we plan to introduce the program at a large scale and have good estimates of the likely costs, we may want to reflect these economies of scale in our calculations. But we need to be careful that the assumptions we make about how costs change are consistent across the projects we compare and are well founded.

The magnitude of a program's impact may also change if the program is scaled up. It is quite possible that the program would be less cost-effective if it were adopted at a wider scale if monitoring were to become harder, the program were implemented less well, and impacts

14. J-PAL Policy Bulletin, "The Price Is Wrong: Charging Small Fees Dramatically Reduces Access to Important Products for the Poor," Abdul Latif Jameel Poverty Action Lab, Cambridge, MA, 2012, http://www.povertyactionlab.org/publication/the-price-is-wrong.

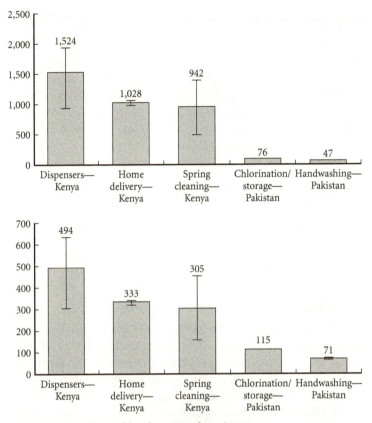

FIGURE 9.2 Incidents of diarrhea averted per $1,000 spent

Notes: Constructed using the global average number of diarrhea incidents per person per year (3.2) and the estimated averages for Kenya (2.11) and Pakistan (9.88) with confidence intervals for the population density. The marks on the bars are sensitivity bands.

declined. Without good evidence on this question, we cannot know for sure. However, we may want to see whether the results of the cost-effectiveness analysis would change if the impacts were slightly lower in an at-scale rollout.

Positive spillovers on the comparison group may disappear when a program is brought up to scale. For instance, during the randomized evaluation of a deworming program in Kenya, a proportion of the benefits accrued to children in comparison schools. These children were not treated directly, but they still experienced decreases in their worm load (and thus improvements in school attendance) because of lower transmission rates from their treated neighbors.[15] Because of the way the study was designed and analyzed, it was possible to measure the extent of the spillovers to other school-aged children as well as the benefit of the program to children in treatment schools (see Module 8.2). When the program was scaled up there was no comparison group, so in calculating likely benefits we would want to exclude benefits to children in comparison schools.

MODULE 9.4 From Research to Policy Action

The goal of conducting a randomized evaluation does not end with writing up the results and noting the impact of a particular program. When the results have important policy implications, how can the research be translated into policy change? This module discusses examples in which evaluation results have informed policy.

The multiple paths from research to policy change

There is no single path for the results of an evaluation to influence the decisionmakers who design or fund programs. How results influence debate or lead to policy change can vary by the type of policy lesson that emerges and by the kind of decisionmaker who is considering the evidence. The following examples highlight four different ways in which evidence from randomized evaluations has shaped program design or policy.

Deworming: A program evaluated with a small implementer, then replicated by larger actors

Michael Kremer and Edward Miguel worked with International Child Support Africa, a Dutch NGO working in Kenya's Western Province, to evaluate a school-based mass deworming program and found that it very cost-effectively reduced student absenteeism.[16] A quasi-experimental study found similar results from a program eliminating hookworm in the U.S. South in the early 1900s. Administration of the program on the ground was relatively straightforward, as was the

15. This study by Edward Miguel and Michael Kremer is summarized as Evaluation 1 in the appendix.

16. This study is summarized as Evaluation 1 in the appendix.

theory of change, suggesting that the results were likely to replicate to other contexts with worms.[17] As a health program delivered through schools, however, it required coordination between ministries of education and health, and this had slowed previous attempts to scale up the school-based deworming program. The evidence of the program's important education effects and its cost-effectiveness compared to alternative education programs helped break this log jam. An organization (Deworm the World) was created by a group of young global leaders from the World Economic Forum (including Michael Kremer) to help provide technical assistance to governments wanting to introduce mass school-based deworming programs, and by 2013 Deworm the World was helping support the mass government-run school-based deworming of more than 40 million children a year.

In this example, a program that ultimately was most effectively scaled up by a government was tested by an NGO. Likely factors that contributed to its scale-up were the program's low cost and high cost-effectiveness, the fact that there was evidence of effectiveness in different contexts, and the relative ease of implementation.

Free bed nets: A small-scale evaluation that helps change the larger policy debate

Jessica Cohen and Pascaline Dupas worked with a small NGO, TAMTAM, and the Government of Kenya's Ministry of Health to help generate evidence that could enlighten a policy debate that had been raging for many years: whether insecticide-treated (bed) nets (ITNs) should be given for free or sold at a subsidized price to encourage a sense of commitment from the owners to use them effectively. They found that charging even small prices significantly reduced demand and did not increase the likelihood that someone would use the nets. Several other studies found similar results for other preventive health products.[18]

The evidence was rapidly used by those advocating for free bed nets. In 2009 the British government cited the study by Cohen and Dupas in calling for the abolition of user fees for health products and services in poor countries.[19] Population Services International (PSI), a

17. Hoyt Bleakley, "Disease and Development: Evidence from Hookworm Eradication in the American South," *Quarterly Journal of Economics* 122 (2007): 73–117, doi: 10.1162/qjec.121.1.73.

18. This study is summarized as Evaluation 6 in the appendix.

19. Gordon Brown. "PM's Article on Universal Healthcare," last modified September 23, 2009, Number10.gov.uk.

leader in promoting ITNs and other health prevention technologies, moved away from their previous position that charging a small price helped ensure that products were used. PSI has increased its free distribution of ITNs to pregnant women in Kenya, including through 3,000 public antenatal clinics, while at the same time subsidizing ITNs sold commercially.[20] WHO also endorsed the free distribution of bed nets.[21]

A key component of the policy impact in this example was not whom the researchers partnered with in their initial study but that they answered a critical question in the policy debate on which there was little rigorous evidence. This example also brings out an important point about the policy impact of randomized evaluation (and evaluation in general): not only did this study contribute to understanding a particular policy question (whether a small fee should be charged for ITNs); it also contributed to a wider discussion about why we see low take-up of highly effective health prevention products. Several other studies around the same time tested the price sensitivity of other health products and found similar results, which led to a broader policy message—small charges for preventive healthcare can have large impacts on take-up. Again, the fact that this principle was tested in different contexts and related to different products with very similar results helped give the findings more credibility in the policy world.[22]

Conditional cash transfers: Evaluation of a national government program that informs a large-scale multicountry expansion

A famous, relatively early, large-scale randomized evaluation in development was that of the Mexican government's conditional cash transfer (CCT) program, PROGRESA (later Oportunidades). Senior members of the government (including the academic Santiago Levi) believed that a rigorous evaluation might help this key antipoverty program

20. Population Services International, "Malaria Prevention and Treatment," accessed May 28, 2008, http://www.psi.org/our-work/healthy-lives/malaria/about/prevention-and-treatment.

21. "Science at WHO and UNICEF: The Corrosion of Trust." *Lancet* 370 (2007): 1007, http://www.thelancet.com/journals/lancet/article/PIIS0140-6736(07)61451-2/fulltext; World Health Organization, "WHO Releases New Guidance on Insecticide-Treated Mosquito Nets," World Health Organization News Release, last modified August 16, 2007. http://www.who.int/mediacentre/news/releases/2007/pr43/en/index.html.

22. Nine studies testing the impact of price on program take-up are summarized in J-PAL Policy Bulletin, "The Price Is Wrong."

survive a change in government. The program did survive, and the evidence caught the attention of the World Bank, the Inter-American Bank, and other policymakers, who were convinced by the rigor of the evidence. A number of other countries used randomized evaluations to test their own CCT programs and found similar results to those in Mexico.

In this case, the motivation for the evaluation came from government policymakers, who were involved from the start. This meant that the evaluation was on a large scale and was conducted across different parts of Mexico. These factors likely contributed to the successful scale-up of the program, which has now been implemented in at least 30 countries.[23]

Remedial education: A large NGO's use of evidence from its own randomized evaluations to raise funds and expand programs

The Indian NGO Pratham partnered with Abhijit Banerjee, Esther Duflo, and Shawn Cole to evaluate a remedial tutoring program for children who had fallen behind academically. The original evaluation was conducted in two different states of India, and then a new evaluation of a slightly different model was carried out in rural India.[24] The evaluations provided rigorous evidence that the program improves learning outcomes, which contributed to Pratham's ability to raise funds and scale up the Read India program in 19 states of India, reaching over 33 million children in 2008–9.

In this example, the fact that the original partner had the capacity to work at a very large scale helped lead to the scale-up of the program (although Pratham was much smaller when the program was first tested than it currently is). The fact that the program was tested in different versions to suit different contexts and proved highly effective in all cases also likely contributed to its successful scale-up, as did the fact that the program was very inexpensive and did not require highly educated tutors. As we discuss below, this study also contributed to a more general policy conclusion, that a key to improving the quality of education is ensuring that teaching is aimed at the appropriate level.

---

23. Ariel Fiszbein and Norbert Schady, *Conditional Cash Transfers: Reducing Present and Future Poverty* (Washington, DC: World Bank, 2009).

24. Banerjee et al., "Pitfalls of Participatory Programs." This study is also discussed in detail in Chapter 1.

Factors to consider when translating research into policy

The examples above illustrate that there are many pathways for evidence from evaluations to inform policy. There are a number of trade-offs to consider.

Scaling up discrete packages versus applying general lessons to policy

Sometimes we evaluate a discrete program that can be replicated and scaled up as a specific package: school-based deworming and CCTs are examples of such packages. But often the most relevant policy implications emerging from a study or a group of studies are of a more general nature, such as the finding that the take-up of preventive health products falls sharply when even small prices are charged and that paying for these products does not appear to stimulate use. This type of general lesson, if confirmed in different contexts, can be used in the design of a large number of different programs.

Another example of a general lesson emerging from a combination of randomized evaluation and other research is the importance of teaching to the appropriate level for children. Descriptive work has shown that learning levels are far below curricula standards.[25] An early randomized evaluation in Kenya found that additional textbooks helped only the best-performing children, potentially because these were the only ones able to use them effectively.[26] Three studies then examined different approaches to adapting the level of teaching to that of the child: educational software that responded to how well a child answered math questions improved math scores in India, tracking incoming students by their knowledge of English (the language of instruction) improved the test scores of high- and low-performing students in Kenya, and various versions of remedial education sharply improved reading and math scores in India.[27]

---

25. For example, in India 32 percent of rural children in Standard III cannot read a simple word. ASER Centre, "Annual Status of Education Report (Rural) 2011," http://www.asercenter.org/docs/Publications/ASER%20Reports/ASER_2011/aser_2011_report_8.2.12.pdf.

26. Paul Glewwe, Michael Kremer, and Sylvie Moulin, "Many Children Left Behind? Textbooks and Test Scores in Kenya," *American Economic Journal: Applied Economics* 1 (2009): 112–135.

27. See the studies summarized as Evaluations 2, 3, and 4 in the appendix. For an overview of general policy lessons for improving educational quality, see Michael Kre-

A number of governments are now experimenting with how to incorporate this general lesson into their policy. For example, the Government of Ghana, with support from Innovations for Poverty Action, has drawn on this evidence to design, pilot, and evaluate a program that trains teaching assistants to deliver remedial education programs to help children master basic reading and numeracy skills. If found to be successful, the program may be scaled up to benefit children across Ghana.

Working with large organizations, including governments, versus small organizations

There is often a bias within organizations to listen more to evidence that is internal, and working with a government (as in the PROGRESA example above) or a large organization can ease the transition to a large scale-up because the implementer may be more likely to pay attention to evidence if it was invested in doing the evaluation. Another benefit of performing an evaluation within a large organization or a government is that the process of working on a rigorous evaluation can help increase the appreciation of rigorous evidence more generally, which can have important benefits across the organization.

However, there are also many limitations to working with large actors. It can be slow and time-consuming, and governments can change and officials move on, sometimes causing evaluations to be abandoned or radically changed midway. The high turnover in some large organizations and governments means that the hoped-for buy-in to the results of those who worked on the evaluation may not materialize.

Small or local NGOs tend to be more flexible and willing to try out innovative and unusual approaches than are governments, international agencies, or large international NGOs. This flexibility means that small implementers are often good partners for evaluations that test general questions that can have important implications across many organizations.

Bridging the gap between research and policy

The translation of evidence to action is rarely instantaneous or automatic, yet the reason we evaluate is to help improve policies in the

mer, Rachel Glennerster, and Conner Brannen, "The Challenges of Education in the Developing World," *Science*, 340 (6130) (2013): 297–300.

future. What can be done to ease the transition from evaluation results to policy change? In this section we provide some practical suggestions as to how evaluators (evidence producers) can share their results in such a way that decisionmakers can learn about them. We also provide suggestions as to where consumers of evidence can find evidence from randomized evaluations in reasonably accessible form.

Choose a policy-relevant question

If we want our research to inform policy decisions, the most important step is to conduct an evaluation that answers a relevant question that people want to learn about. Chapter 3 discusses how to do this in more depth.

Feed evidence at the right time

There are often critical times during which important policy decisions are made; for example, budget allocations tend to be established in one-, three-, or five-year cycles. Ensuring that evidence is provided at the right time can help make it more likely that the evidence will be acted on. Building a relationship of trust between researchers and policymakers is critical to this process and helps the evaluator know when it is the right time to feed the evidence.

Transfer knowledge about implementation

Often academic reports of evaluations focus on the technical details of how the impact of a program was measured and much less on the actual implementation of the program. But if other organizations or governments want to act on the evidence, they need to understand the details of what went into the program, what the implementation challenges were, and how they were overcome.

Organizations that implemented the program that was evaluated can be the best messengers of the results of the evaluation and can help those thinking about introducing a similar program. For example, when J-PAL conducted an evidence workshop in the Indian state of Bihar, the goal was to share evidence learned in other contexts with senior policymakers at the state level. For each evaluation, someone from the research team and the organization who implemented the program presented. Bihar officials were particularly interested in talking to the implementers about how they had managed the challenge of implementing the program. Similarly, when J-PAL and Innovations for Poverty Action worked with the Government of Ghana to design a new remedial education program (discussed in the previous section), they visited the Indian NGO Pratham to see some of their programs in action.

Report evaluation results in a central location

Even academics, whose full-time job is to stay on top of new literature that is being published, can find it difficult to gain an overview of the body of evidence in a sector or a region. Policymakers and practitioners can find it difficult to know where to find current evidence, and even then, results are sometimes reported in gated academic journals.

A number of organizations have made efforts to make rigorous evidence centrally available:

1. J-PAL's website has an evaluation database of more than 350 randomized evaluations conducted by J-PAL's affiliated professors. These are searchable, and the database also allows users to filter by categories such as region, sector, policy goal, and researcher name. It also produces summaries of the literature in specific sectors that cover J-PAL and non-J-PAL evaluations and draw out general lessons from the literature. The URL is www.povertyactionlab.org/evaluations.

2. The World Bank's Development Impact Evaluation (DIME) Initiative has an online database searchable by region and methodology. The URL is http://www.worldbank.org/dime.

3. The Network of Networks on Impact Evaluation (NONIE) also hosts (on the World Bank website) an evaluation database of evaluations conducted by its members. The URL is http://www.worldbank.org/ieg/nonie/database.html.

4. The Coalition for Evidence-Based Policy maintains a list of evaluations that meet its criteria for top-tier evidence. This list is focused on domestic policy related to children and young adults. The URL is http://toptierevidence.org/wordpress/.

5. The American Economic Association has a registry of all randomized evaluations (from all over the world). Over time this registry (which is still very new) will provide a comprehensive list of all ongoing randomized evaluations. It will have links to published studies and data from the evaluations. The URL is www.socialscienceregistry.org.

Disseminate results in an accessible format

Even when policymakers find evaluation results, the format of academic journal articles is not always accessible. It is therefore useful to produce a short, nontechnical summary of the results and policy implications. Many organizations, including J-PAL and the International Growth Centre, produce short policy briefs summarizing the results of randomized evaluations. It can be very useful to include the implementing organization in helping explain the results of the evaluation. In this process the evaluator needs to be careful to maintain objectivity and not suppress results that the implementer does not want the rest of the world to hear, but if the evaluation is a true collaboration, the implementer often has very useful input into interpreting the results and explaining their relevance to others.

Think hard about generalizability

As discussed in Chapter 3, if we think about generalizability at the design stage (for example, by planning to perform the evaluation in a representative location and with a representative partner), it can aid the dissemination of results. When we discuss our results, we can also explain under what conditions it might be reasonable to think the results will generalize to particular contexts.

Synthesize general lessons from multiple programs

Synthesizing general lessons that have emerged in different contexts is more valuable in sharing what works than is providing a single summary of any given evaluation. Literature reviews that summarize lessons across a sector and comparative cost-effectiveness analysis can be helpful in distilling the general lessons that emerge from a body of evidence. Module 3.1 provides a list of sources of literature reviews that cover randomized evaluations of antipoverty programs in developing countries. In reading literature reviews prepared by others it is important to consider the perspective of the writer: does the writer have a particular perspective that may influence how he summarizes the results?

MODULE 9.5 Concluding Thoughts

Running randomized evaluations is not easy or inexpensive. It requires that the evaluators understand the programs they are evaluating as well as the environments in which they are operating in great depth. Evaluators and implementers have to work hand in hand, both learning a lot about each other's work in the process. Hundreds of small but critical decisions need to be made about the evaluation design, sample size, data collection, and analysis. More often than not, problems will arise in the middle of an evaluation that threaten to drive it off course. A key government official will move on, and her successor will want to make changes that could undermine the entire study. A hurricane will lead to the resettlement of families from comparison communities into treatment communities and vice versa.

Although this work is not easy, it is important. As we have shown throughout this book, randomized evaluations have helped answer critical questions about how to improve people's lives from New York to New Delhi. But although we have learned a lot, particularly over the past 20 years—when the number of randomized evaluations has grown dramatically and the range of questions they have been used to address has broadened significantly—there is still much that we do not know. There is enormous potential to improve the effectiveness of policy if it is grounded on careful, rigorous, and relevant evaluation. But to achieve this potential we need to build a much wider and deeper evidence base on all the questions and policies that are important to people's lives.

We hope that this book will contribute to that evidence base by encouraging more people to perform randomized evaluations and will help them do so at the highest possible level of quality.

APPENDIX: RANDOMIZED EVALUATIONS REFERENCED IN THIS BOOK

The following randomized evaluations were used as illustrations of different concepts in this book. The modules in which the studies are discussed are given at the end of each summary, with boldface type indicating the module in which the discussion is most detailed. Visit www.runningrandomizedevaluations.com to find links to the academic papers from which these summaries are drawn, related policy briefs, and summaries of some of the other studies mentioned in this book.

Evaluation 1: Worms: Identifying Impacts on Education and Health in the Presence of Treatment Externalities

Authors: (1) Michael Kremer and Edward Miguel; (2) Owen Ozier; (3) Sarah Baird, Joan Hamory Hicks, Michael Kremer, and Edward Miguel[1]

Location: Budalangi and Funyula Divisions, Busia District, Western Province, Kenya

Sample: 75 primary schools with over 30,000 students

Timeline: 1997–2001

This study evaluated the Primary School Deworming Project (PSDP), which was carried out by International Child Support Africa (ICS) in cooperation with the Busia District Ministry of Health. The program randomly divided 75 schools into three equal groups, which were phased into treatment over three years.

Within each group, a baseline parasitological survey was administered to a random sample of pupils. Schools with worm prevalence over 50 percent were mass treated with deworming drugs every six months. In addition to medicine, treatment schools received regular public health lectures, wall charts on worm prevention, and training for one designated teacher. The lectures and teacher training provided information on worm prevention behaviors—including washing hands before meals, wearing shoes, and not swimming in the lake.

Deworming reduced serious worm infections by half among children in the treatment groups. Pupils in program schools reported being sick less often and had lower rates of severe anemia. Deworming increased school participation by 7.5 percentage points, which equates to a one-quarter reduction in child absenteeism. Nontreated children attending schools near treatment schools also experienced fewer worm infections and greater school attendance.

Deworming improved cognitive outcomes for infants who were not treated directly. A decade later, children who had been infants when their siblings attended schools that benefited from deworming showed cognitive gains equivalent to 0.5 to 0.8 year of schooling.

Treated students continued to benefit a decade after the program. Men who were dewormed as boys worked 3.5 hours longer per week and were more likely to hold manufacturing jobs and earn higher wages. Women who attended schools whose students were dewormed had better educational outcomes and were more likely to grow cash crops.

1. Where a summary covers more than one work, we distinguish the authors of the different works using parenthetical numbers (1), (2), (3), and so on.

Referenced in: Modules 1.1, 2.4, 3.1, 4.1, **4.6,** 5.2, 8.1, 8.2, 9.2, 9.3, 9.4

For further reading:
Baird, Sarah, Joan Hamory Hicks, Michael Kremer, and Edward Miguel. 2013. "Worms at Work: Long-Run Impacts of Child Health Gains." Working paper, Harvard University, Cambridge, MA.
J-PAL Policy Bulletin. 2012. "Deworming: A Best Buy for Development." Abdul Latif Jameel Poverty Action Lab, Cambridge, MA. http://www.poverty actionlab.org/publication/deworming-best-buy-development.
Miguel, Edward, and Michael Kremer. 2004. "Worms: Identifying Impacts on Education and Health in the Presence of Treatment Externalities." *Econometrica* 72 (1): 159–217.
Ozier, Owen. 2011. "Exploiting Externalities to Estimate the Long-Term Effects of Early Childhood Deworming." Working paper, University of California, Berkeley.

Evaluation 2: Remedying Education

Authors: Abhijit Banerjee, Shawn Cole, Esther Duflo, and Leigh Linden
Location: India
Sample: 122 primary schools in Vadodara, 77 primary schools in Mumbai
Timeline: 2001–4

Many developing countries have greatly expanded primary school access, but learning levels of those in school are often low. A 2005 survey found that 44 percent of Indian children aged 7–12 could not read a basic paragraph, and 50 percent could not do simple subtraction even though most were enrolled in school. In conjunction with Pratham, an Indian education NGO, researchers evaluated the outcome of a remedial education program in schools in Vadodara and Mumbai. A tutor (*balsakhi*), usually a young woman recruited from the local community and paid a fraction of the cost of civil service teachers (US$10–$15 per month), worked with children in grades 2–4 who were identified as falling behind their peers. The instructor met with a group of approximately 15–20 of these children in a separate class for two hours of the four-hour school day. Instruction focused on the core competencies the children should have developed in grades 1 and 2, primarily basic numeracy and literacy skills. The instructors were provided with two weeks of initial training and a standardized curriculum that was developed by Pratham.

In the 2001 school year, in Vadodara approximately half of the schools were given a tutor for grade 3 and the other half were given a tutor for grade 4, while in Mumbai approximately half of the schools received a tutor for grade 3 and the other half received a tutor for grade 2. In 2002, the tutor was provided to the previously untreated grade. In determining program impact, grade 3 students in schools that received a tutor only for grade 4 were compared to grade 3 students in schools that had tutors for grade 3, and so on.

The program had substantial positive impacts on test scores, with the greatest gains in math and among those who were originally falling behind. In both Vadodara and Mumbai, the Balsakhi program significantly improved overall test scores, by 0.14 standard deviation (SD) in the first year and 0.28 SD in the second year, with the largest gains in math. Moreover, the weakest students, who were the primary targets of the program, gained the most. The number of students in the bottom third of program classes who passed basic competency tests increased their scores by nearly 8 percentage points.

Referenced in: Modules 1.2, 4.1, **4.6**, 5.4, 6.2, 6.4, 7.2, 9.2

For further reading:

Banerjee, Abhijit, Shawn Cole, Esther Duflo, and Leigh Linden. 2007. "Remedying Education: Evidence from Two Randomized Experiments in India." *Quarterly Journal of Economics* 122 (3): 1235–1264.

J-PAL Policy Briefcase. 2006a. "Making Schools Work for Marginalized Children: Evidence from an Inexpensive and Effective Program in India." Abdul Latif Jameel Poverty Action Lab, Cambridge, MA. http://www.povertyaction lab.org/publication/making-schools-work-marginalized-children.

Evaluation 3: School Governance, Teacher Incentives, and Pupil–Teacher Ratios

Authors: Esther Duflo, Pascaline Dupas, and Michael Kremer
Location: Western Province, Kenya
Sample: 210 primary schools
Timeline: 2005–7

In 2003, Kenya eliminated school fees for primary school. This led to an almost 30 percent increase in enrollment. Many of the new pupils were first-generation students and had not attended preschool. Therefore, within the same grade, students had a wide range of initial abilities in reading, writing, and math. In collaboration with International Child Support Africa, researchers evaluated three interventions that aimed to address large class sizes and differences in initial academic achievement among students in the same grade.

Out of 210 primary schools, 140 were randomly assigned to receive the Extra Teacher Program (ETP), which provided funding to hire a local contract teacher to address classroom overcrowding. School committees were responsible for hiring the contract teachers and were free to replace or keep the original contract teacher based on performance. Contract teachers were paid approximately one quarter of the salary of regular civil service teachers but had the same educational qualifications. The remaining 70 schools served as a comparison group.

In half of the ETP schools, students were randomly assigned to the class taught by the contract teacher or the class taught by the civil service teacher. In the other half of ETP schools, students were sorted into smaller classes based on their standardized exam scores, a process called tracking. Half of all ETP schools were also randomly selected to receive school-based management (SBM) training. The training was designed to empower parents on the school committee to ensure that the recruiting process for the local contract teacher was fair and objective, as well as to monitor teachers' performance.

The ETP program increased test scores by 0.22 SD overall; however, not all students benefited equally. The impact on student test scores was much greater for students assigned to the contract teachers than for students assigned to the civil service teachers. These learning improvements were driven by changes in teacher effort. Contract teachers were 28 percentage points more likely to be teaching during a random visit than were government teachers in non-ETP schools, but the ETP program decreased effort among civil service teachers.

Combining the ETP program with SBM training increased student test scores by more than did the ETP program alone. The training enabled parents to monitor the hiring process for contract teachers more effectively and reduced the number of contract teachers who were hired simply because they were related to an existing teacher by about half.

Sorting students into classes based on their standardized test scores also improved learning. Teaching students with similar levels of academic achievement was beneficial in part because it allowed teachers to better tailor their materials to the level of their students but also because it increased teachers' attendance in the classrooms.

Referenced in: Modules 1.2, 3.3, **4.6**, 5.2, 8.1

For further reading:
Duflo, Esther, Pascaline Dupas, and Michael Kremer. 2011. "Peer Effects, Teacher Incentives, and the Impact of Tracking: Evidence from a Randomized Evaluation in Kenya." *American Economic Review* 101 (5): 1739–74.
———. 2012. "School Governance, Teacher Incentives, and Pupil–Teacher Ratios: Experimental Evidence from Kenyan Primary Schools." Working paper, Massachusetts Institute of Technology, Cambridge, MA.

Evaluation 4: Education, HIV, and Early Fertility: Experimental Evidence from Kenya

Authors: (1) Esther Duflo, Pascaline Dupas, and Michael Kremer;
(2) Pascaline Dupas
Location: Western Province, Kenya
Sample: 328 primary schools in Western Province, Kenya
Timeline: 2003–10

Early pregnancy and sexually transmitted disease are important health risks for adolescent girls in sub-Saharan Africa.

In the first of two related studies, researchers tested the impact of providing HIV education and subsidizing education on risky sexual behavior. In 2003, 328 schools in Kenya's Western Province were randomly assigned to one of four groups. In the HIV education group, three teachers per school were trained to teach the national HIV curriculum. The curriculum covers facts about the disease and encourages abstinence until marriage and faithfulness afterward. The intervention led to an increase in HIV education in schools in line with the national curricula. In the education subsidy group, students already enrolled in sixth-grade classes were given two free school uniforms over two years. The third group received both teacher training and free uniforms, and the fourth served as the comparison group.

In Kenya, 25-year-old men are far more likely to have HIV than are 16-year-old adolescent boys. Sexual relationships with older partners (often called sugar daddies) are thus particularly risky for adolescent girls. In a second study a randomly selected subset of the 328 schools also received a Relative Risk Information Campaign, in which a trained NGO worker showed 8th-grade students a short educational video on sugar daddies and led an open discussion about cross-generational sex.

Three years after the introduction of the program, data were collected on childbearing and relationships. After seven years data were collected on childbearing as well as biomarkers of sexually transmitted infections (STIs).

Providing HIV education on its own led to no change in teenage pregnancy, STIs, or schooling attainment. It did reduce the number of out-of-wedlock births by 1.4 percentage points. Subsidizing education on its own reduced primary school dropout by 5 percentage points and reduced childbearing by 3 percentage points at both the three-year and seven-year follow-ups. There was no impact on STIs. Combining the programs had rather different impacts. The school dropout rate was higher, and fertility fell less than with the education subsidy alone. STIs fell by 2.3 percentage points from a base of 11.8 percent.

Providing information about the relative risk of HIV infection by partner age reduced the incidence of childbearing by 28 percent (from 5.4 percent of girls getting pregnant within a year to 3.9 percent), suggesting that the intervention reduced the likelihood that girls engaged in unsafe sex. Specifically, the intervention seemed to have reduced unsafe cross-generational sex: the rate of childbearing with men five or more years older fell by 61 percent, with no offsetting increase in childbearing with adolescent partners. STI data are not available for this subgroup.

Referenced in: Modules 2.1, 4.1, 4.2, **4.4**, 5.1, 5.3, 5.4, 7.2

For further reading:

Duflo, Esther, Pascaline Dupas, and Michael Kremer. 2013. "Education, HIV and Early Fertility: Experimental Evidence from Kenya." Working paper, Massachusetts Institute of Technology, Cambridge, MA.

Dupas, Pascaline. 2011. "Do Teenagers Respond to HIV Risk Information? Evidence from a Field Experiment in Kenya." *American Economic Journal: Applied Economics* 3: 1–34.

J-PAL Policy Briefcase. 2007. "Cheap and Effective Ways to Change Adolescents' Sexual Behavior." Abdul Latif Jameel Poverty Action Lab, Cambridge, MA.

Evaluation 5: Moving to Opportunity?

Authors: Jeffrey Kling, Jeffrey Liebman, and Lawrence Katz

Location: Baltimore, Boston, Chicago, Los Angeles, and New York City, United States

Sample: 4,248 households

Timeline: 1994–2002

Families living in disadvantaged neighborhoods in the United States tend to have poorer health, a higher rate of unemployment, and children who perform worse in school and are more likely to get in trouble with the law than do families living in more affluent neighborhoods. It is unclear to what extent these discrepancies in health and socioeconomic outcomes are the result of living in more disadvantaged neighborhoods or the result of characteristics of individual households, such as lower education or income.

To examine the impact of living in a more affluent neighborhood on health and socioeconomic status, the authors conducted a randomized evaluation of the US Department of Housing and Urban Development's Moving to Opportunity program. Between 1994 and 1997, families living in high-poverty public housing projects in five cities were randomly assigned to one of two treatment groups or a comparison group. The first treatment group received a one-year voucher for public housing in a neighborhood with a poverty rate of less than 10 percent and mobility counseling. The second treatment group received a voucher for public housing in any neighborhood with public housing, regardless of its poverty rate. The comparison group saw no change in the public housing assistance they had been receiving before the study.

In 2002, families who were offered either voucher lived in safer neighborhoods with lower poverty rates than did the comparison group. Yet the vouchers did not affect adults' earnings, participation in welfare, or the amount of government assistance they received. Adults who were offered vouchers to live in neighborhoods with a poverty rate of less than 10 percent were significantly less likely to be obese but saw no other physical health improvements. However, receiving a voucher to live in a low-poverty area resulted in substantial improvements in adults' mental health. Female youths had better education, mental health, and physical health outcomes and reduced their engagement in risky behaviors. Male youths, in contrast, were either unaffected or negatively affected along these lines.

Referenced in: Modules 2.4, **8.2**

For further reading:
Kling, Jeffrey, Jeffrey Liebman, and Lawrence Katz. 2007. "Experimental Analysis of Neighborhood Effects." *Econometrica* 75 (1): 83–119.

Evaluation 6: Free Distribution or Cost-Sharing? Evidence from a Malaria Prevention Experiment in Kenya

Authors: Jessica Cohen and Pascaline Dupas
Location: Western Province, Kenya
Sample: 20 prenatal clinics
Timeline: 2007–8

It is often argued that cost-sharing (i.e., charging a subsidized positive price for a health product) is necessary to avoid wasting resources on those who will not use or do not need the product. Researchers explored this argument by randomizing the price at which prenatal clinics could sell long-lasting antimalarial insecticide-treated (bed) nets (ITNs) to pregnant women.

Sixteen health clinics were randomly selected to receive ITNs at a subsidized rate, with the discount varying between clinics from 90–100 percent of market price. Four comparison clinics were provided no ITN distribution program. Within a given clinic, a further discount was randomly offered to women who had already chosen to buy the nets.

No evidence was found to suggest that cost-sharing increased ITN use: women who paid subsidized prices were no more likely to use nets than those who received ITNs for free. Additionally, there is no evidence that cost-sharing put ITNs in the hands of the women who needed them most: those who paid higher prices appeared to be no sicker than those who received the nets for free (as measured by rates of anemia, an important indicator of malaria). Cost-sharing did, however, considerably dampen demand. Uptake dropped by 60 percentage points when the price of ITNs increased from zero to US$0.60.

Referenced in: Modules 2.4, 3.1, 3.2, 4.4, **5.4**, 7.2, 9.4

For further reading:

Cohen, Jessica, and Pascaline Dupas. 2010. "Free Distribution or Cost-Sharing? Evidence from a Randomized Evaluation Experiment." *Quarterly Journal of Economics* 125 (1): 1–45.

Dupas, Pascaline. 2012. "Short-Run Subsidies and Long-Run Adoption of New Health Products: Evidence from a Field Experiment." NBER Working Paper 16298.

J-PAL Policy Bulletin. 2011. "The Price Is Wrong." Abdul Latif Jameel Poverty Action Lab, Cambridge, MA. http://www.povertyactionlab.org/publication/the-price-is-wrong.

Evaluation 7: Empowering Girls in Rural Bangladesh

Authors: Erica Field and Rachel Glennerster
Location: Barisal Division, Bangladesh
Sample: 460 villages with approximately 45,000 adolescent girls
Timeline: 2007–present (ongoing)

Although secondary school enrollment rates for girls in Bangladesh are high, girls often drop out of school and are married at a young age. The Bangladesh Demographic and Household Survey found that only 19 percent of 15- and 16-year-old girls had completed secondary education and 30 percent of 15- through 19-year-olds had started childbearing. Early marriage and childbearing can harm women's health, education, income-generating potential, and status in the family. Little is known about the relative costs of these different programs and their effects on the social and economic empowerment of adolescent girls.

Researchers worked with the Bangladesh office of Save the Children USA to implement a broad range of interventions aimed at empowering adolescent girls in southern Bangladesh. The Kishoree Kontha project operated through small peer-led sessions in safe spaces (spaces in a community where adolescent girls can meet on a regular basis). Out of a sample of 460 target villages, 307 villages were randomly selected to receive one of four intervention packages. The remaining villages served as the comparison group. The four intervention packages were as follows:

1. *Basic package* Peer educators were trained to deliver a curriculum at safe spaces to girls who met several times a week for six months. The curriculum covered nutrition, reproductive health information, and negotiation skills. Groups also met for homework study sessions, while illiterate girls received literacy and numeracy training.

2. *Livelihoods package* This package complemented the basic package with additional sessions on financial livelihood readiness. Rather than providing direct vocational training, these sessions built entrepreneurial and budgeting skills.

3. *Full package* This package included all the sessions of the livelihood package but added a direct incentive to delay marriage until the legal age of 18 years. All girls in targeted villages between 15 and 17 years of age were eligible to receive approximately 16 liters of cooking oil per year, worth roughly US$15.

4. *Delayed marriage package* This package provided only the incentive to delay marriage, as described above.

Preliminary results suggest that neither the basic package nor the livelihoods package had a detectable impact on age of marriage, level of education, or measures of empowerment. The delayed marriage incentive was associated with a 7-percentage-point lower level of marriage among those aged 19 and older (most of whom were between 19 and 21) from a base of 64 percent. The full package was associated with an impact of 0.07 SD on education outcomes, mainly driven by an increase in the highest grade passed of 0.3 years and an increase in math test scores. The marriage and education results were not statistically different between the delayed marriage and full packages. The full package, however, was associated with increased levels of knowledge of contraception methods.

Referenced in: Modules 2.4, **4.6**, 7.1, 7.2, 8.1, 8.3

For further reading:
Field, Erica, and Rachel Glennerster. "Empowering Girls in Rural Bangladesh: Midline Report." Abdul Latif Jameel Poverty Action Lab, Cambridge, MA. Accessed January 3, 2013. http://www.povertyactionlab.org/evaluation/empowering-girls-rural-bangladesh.

Evaluation 8: Do Labor Market Policies Have Displacement Effects?

Authors: Bruno Crépon, Esther Duflo, Marc Gurgand, Roland Rathelot, and Philippe Zamora

Location: 10 regions throughout France

Sample: 57,000 job seekers aged 18–30

Timeline: 2007–10

Experimental studies of job placement assistance programs, though rare, tend to find positive impacts of counseling. However, an important criticism leveled against these studies is that they do not take into account potential displacement effects: job seekers who benefit from counseling may be more likely to get jobs but at the expense of other unemployed workers with whom they compete in the labor market.

Researchers evaluated the magnitude of such displacement effects of a large-scale job seeker assistance program targeted at young, educated job seekers in France. Under the program private agencies were contracted to provide intensive placement services to young graduates (with at least two-year college degrees) who had been unemployed for at least six months. The private provider was paid partially on delivery, that is, conditioned on the individual's finding a job with a contract of at least six months and remaining employed for at least six months.

After eight months eligible, unemployed youths who had been assigned to the program were 2.5 percentage points more likely to have found stable jobs than those who had not. After 12 months, however, these benefits had disappeared. In addition, there was evidence of displacement effects. Young people in areas where many young people were offered counseling but who did not benefit directly were 2.1 percentage points less likely to have long-term employment than their peers in areas where fewer young people received counseling. The displacement effects were strongest in more competitive labor markets.

Referenced in: Modules 2.4, **4.6**

For further reading:

Crépon, Bruno, Esther Duflo, Marc Gurgand, Roland Rathelot, and Philippe Zamora. 2011. "L'Accompagnement des jeunes diplômés demandeurs d'emploi par des opérateurs privés de placement." *Dares Analyses* 94: 1–14.
———. 2012. "Do Labor Market Policies Have Displacement Effects? Evidence from a Clustered Randomized Experiment." *Quarterly Journal of Economics* 128 (2): 531–580.

Evaluation 9: School Subsidies for the Poor: Evaluating the Mexican PROGRESA Antipoverty Program

Authors: (1) T. Paul Schultz; (2) Paul Gertler
Location: Mexico
Sample: 506 rural communities
Timeline: 1997–2000

Conditional cash transfer (CCT) programs have become an increasingly popular means of transferring income to low-income families and encouraging socially desirable behavior. The cash transfers are conditioned on children's attending school regularly and receiving regular health check-ups. The popularity of CCTs stems in part from Mexico's successful program, PROGRESA.

In 1998 the Mexican government implemented PROGRESA to improve children's nutrition, health, and education. Of the 50,000 communities deemed eligible for the program, 506 were randomly selected to participate in the pilot evaluation; 320 were randomly assigned to the treatment group and would receive program benefits immediately, and 186 were assigned to the comparison group and would be monitored and begin the program two years later. By the end of 1999, the program was rolled out nationally in more than 50,000 communities.

PROGRESA offered two transfers. The first was a monthly fixed stipend of 90 pesos (about US$7) conditioned on family members' obtaining preventive medical care. The second was an educational grant given to families of children starting the third grade, conditioned on children's attending school at least 85 percent of the time and not repeating a grade more than twice. The amount of the educational stipend was larger at higher grades and was also larger for girls because the government wanted to encourage older girls, in particular, to stay in school.

The results suggest that PROGRESA had a significant positive effect on enrollment, especially after primary school. For students that completed grade 6 and were eligible for junior secondary school, the enrollment rate increased by 11.1 percentage points, from 58 percent before the program to about 69 percent after. This impact was primarily driven by an increase in girls' enrollment, which increased 14.8 percentage points, while boys' enrollment increased 6.5 percentage points. PROGRESA also had a positive impact on health. Children in treatment households saw a 23 percent reduction in illness, an 18 percent reduction in anemia, and an increase in height of 1–4 percent.

Referenced in: Modules 4.2, **9.4**

For further reading:
Gertler, Paul. 2004. "Do Conditional Cash Transfers Improve Child Health? Evidence from PROGRESA's Control Randomized Experiment." *American Economic Review* 94 (2): 336–341.
Schultz, T. P. 2004. "School Subsidies for the Poor: Evaluating the Mexican Progresa Poverty Program." *Journal of Development Economics* 74: 199–250.

Evaluation 10: Are Educational Vouchers Only Redistributive?

Authors: (1) Joshua Angrist, Eric Bettinger, Erick Bloom, Elizabeth King, Michael Kremer, and Juan Saavedra; (2) Joshua Angrist, Eric Bettinger, and Michael Kremer
Location: Colombia
Sample: 1,600 applicants to a school voucher program
Timeline: 1998–2004

In the early 1990s, the Colombian government established Programa de Ampliación de Cobertura de la Educación Secundaria (PACES), which provided more than 125,000 students from poor urban neighborhoods with vouchers that covered more than half of the cost of private secondary schools in Colombia.

Because the demand for PACES vouchers exceeded the supply, eligibility was determined by a random lottery, generating a natural experiment to examine the impact of school choice on educational and other outcomes. Survey data were collected in 1998 from 1,600 previous applicants from three cohorts, primarily from Bogota, three years after they had started high school. The sample was stratified so that half those sampled were lottery winners and half were lottery losers, meaning that half of the students surveyed had been given the opportunity to attend private high schools. Surveys were conducted by telephone, and students were asked about further schooling and drop-out rates, the amount of time they spent on education, later monetary investments made toward education, and whether they had attended public or private secondary schools.

The results showed no significant differences in school enrollment between lottery winners and losers three years after application. But lottery winners were 15 percentage points more likely to have attended private schools, had completed an average 0.1 more year of schooling, and were about 10 percentage points more likely to have finished 8th grade, primarily because they were less likely to have repeated grades.

In 2005 researchers examined administrative records on registration and test scores from a government college entrance examination to analyze the long-term effects of the voucher program. Lottery winners were 7 percentage points more likely to have taken the university entrance exam, a good predictor of high school graduation because 90 percent of all high school graduates take the exam. Correcting for the greater percentage of lottery winners taking college admissions tests, the program increased test scores by 0.2 SD in the distribution of potential test scores. Boys, who have lower scores than girls in this population, showed greater test score gains, especially in math.

Referenced in: Modules **4.1**, 5.2, 8.1

For further reading:

Angrist, Joshua, Eric Bettinger, and Michael Kremer. 2006. "Long-Term Educational Consequences of Secondary School Vouchers: Evidence from Administrative Records in Colombia." *American Economic Review* 96 (3): 847–863.

Angrist, Joshua, Eric Bettinger, Erik Blook, Elizabeth King, Michael Kremer, and Juan Saavedra. 2002. "Vouchers for Private Schooling in Colombia: Evidence from a Randomized Natural Experiment." *American Economic Review* 92 (5): 135–158.

Evaluation 11: The Role of Information and Social Interactions in Retirement Plan Decisionmaking

Authors: Esther Duflo and Emmanuel Saez
Location: United States
Sample: 6,211 university staff employees
Timeline: 2000–2001

Researchers evaluated the influence of information and social networks on university employees' decisions to enroll in a voluntary tax deferred account (TDA) retirement plan. In an effort to increase TDA enrollment, the university set up a benefits fair to disseminate information about different benefit plans offered by the university. Researchers offered a $20 reward for attending the fair to a random group of employees in a subset of randomly selected university departments. Two distinct groups were studied in the experiment: employees who received the letter promising the monetary reward for attending the fair and employees in the same department as someone who received the letter but who themselves did not. These two groups were compared to employees in departments in which no one received the $20 reward offer. The study traced the reward's effects on recipients' fair attendance and TDA enrollment, as well as the social network's effects on fair attendance and TDA enrollment of non-recipients in the same department as reward recipients.

Small financial incentives successfully induced employees in treated departments (both reward recipients and nonrecipients) to attend the benefits fair. Twenty-one percent of the individuals in treated departments attended the fair compared to only 5 percent in untreated departments. After one year, the program was found to have increased TDA participation by about 1.25 percentage points for the 4,000 nonenrolled employees in treated departments relative to untreated departments. In other words, the program induced 50 extra employees to start contributing to the TDA.

Assuming that those employees who enrolled in the TDA as a result of this program contributed about $3,500 per year (the average contribution of newly enrolled employees), the extra TDA savings generated by the program would be about $175,000 per year (much greater than the inducement cost of about $12,000).

Referenced in: Modules 4.1, **4.6**

For further reading:
Duflo, Esther, and Emmanuel Saez. 2003. "The Role of Information and Social Interactions in Retirement Plan Decisions: Evidence from a Randomized Experiment." *Quarterly Journal of Economics* 118 (3): 815–842.

Evaluation 12: Powerful Women: Does Exposure Reduce Bias?

Authors: (1) Raghabendra Chattopadhyay and Esther Duflo; (2) Lori Beaman, Raghabendra Chattopadhyay, Esther Duflo, Rohini Pande, and Petia Topalova
Location: Birbhum District in West Bengal and Udaipur District in Rajasthan, India
Sample: 265 village councils
Timeline: 2000–2002

In 1993 a constitutional amendment in India called for one-third of village council leader (*pradhan*) positions to be reserved for women. The village council, which represents between 5 and 15 villages, is responsible for the provision of local infrastructure—such as public buildings, water, and roads—and for identifying government program beneficiaries.

In some states the councils on which seats were to be reserved for women leaders were chosen at random, allowing the researchers to study the policy consequences of mandated representation by determining whether there was any difference in the provision of social services between male- and female-led village councils.

Data were collected in two locations: Birbhum in West Bengal and Udaipur in Rajasthan. In Birbhum, data were collected in two stages. First, in each village council researchers conducted an interview with the *pradhan* asking about his or her family background, education, previous political experience, political ambitions, and the village council's recent activities. In the second stage, from the 5–15 villages represented by each village council, 3 villages were randomly selected to be surveyed about available public goods and existing infrastructure. The researchers also collected minutes of the village meetings and gathered data on complaints or requests that had been submitted to the village council in the past six months. Two years later, the same village-level data were collected from 100 village councils in Udaipur. However, there were no *pradhan* interviews.

The results suggest that reservation affected policy choices in ways that better reflect women's preferences. For example, in areas where women's top priorities were drinking water and roads, village councils reserved for women, on average, invested in 9 more drinking water facilities and improved road conditions by 18 percent.

In further work, the researchers investigated the impact of reservations on attitudes toward women leaders. The strength of gender occupation stereotypes were assessed using implicit association tests that assessed respondents' association of male and female names with leadership and domestic tasks. In addition, respondents were asked to evaluate the effectiveness of a hypothetical leader (with the gender of the hypothetical leader randomly assigned).

Reservations did not, in the short run, alter voters' preference for women leaders. However, repeated exposure to female leaders changed beliefs about female leaders' effectiveness and increased voters' association of women with leadership tasks. Men in villages that had been reserved twice rated the effectiveness of a hypothetical female *pradhan* above that of a male *pradhan*. The reservation policy also significantly improved women's prospects in elections open to both sexes, but only after two rounds of reservation.

Referenced in: Modules 4.1, **5.1**, 5.4, 9.2

For further reading:
Beaman, Lori, Raghabendra Chattopadhyay, Esther Duflo, Rohini Pande, and Petia Topalova. 2009. "Powerful Women: Does Exposure Reduce Bias?" *Quarterly Journal of Economics* 124 (4): 1497–1539.

Chattopadhyay, Raghabendra, and Esther Duflo. 2004. "Women as Policy Makers: Evidence from a Randomized Policy Experiment in India." *Econometrica* 72 (5): 1409–1443.

J-PAL Policy Briefcase. 2006. "Women as Policymakers." Abdul Latif Jameel Poverty Action Lab, Cambridge, MA. http://www.povertyactionlab.org/publication/women-policy-makers.

————. 2012. "Raising Female Leaders." Abdul Latif Jameel Poverty Action Lab,Cambridge,MA.http://www.povertyactionlab.org/publication/raising-female-leaders.

Evaluation 13: Microcredit in Theory and Practice: Using Randomized Credit Scoring for Impact Evaluation

Authors: Dean Karlan and Jonathan Zinman
Location: Rizal and Cavite Provinces and the National Capital Region outside of Manila, the Philippines
Sample: 1,601 marginally creditworthy applicants
Timeline: 2007–9

First Macro Bank (FMB) is a for-profit lender that operates on the outskirts of Manila. A second-generation lender, FMB offers small, short-term, uncollateralized credit with fixed repayment schedules to microentrepreneurs. Researchers with FMB used credit-scoring software to identify marginally creditworthy applicants, placing roughly equal emphasis on business capacity, personal financial resources, outside financial resources, and personal and business stability. This approach also allowed the researchers to assess the effectiveness of the credit-scoring approach. Those with scores falling in the middle made up the sample for this study, totaling 1,601 applicants, most of whom were first-time borrowers. Members of this group were randomly placed in two groups: 1,272 accepted applicants served as the treatment group, and 329 rejected applicants served as the comparison group.

Approved applicants received loans of about 5,000–25,000 pesos (US$200–$1,000), a substantial amount relative to the borrowers' incomes. The loan maturity period was 13 weeks, with weekly repayments required. Several upfront fees combined with the interest rate to produce an annual percentage rate of around 60 percent. Data were collected on borrowers' business condition, household resources, demographics, assets, household members' occupations, consumption, well-being, and political and community participation approximately one year after the application process was completed.

Being randomly assigned to receive a loan did increase borrowing: the probability of having a loan out in the month prior to the survey increased by 9.4 percentage points in the treatment group relative to the comparison group. Treated clients who owned businesses operated 0.1 fewer businesses and employed 0.27 fewer employees than those in the comparison group. Most measures of well-being were the same between the treatment and comparison groups, though men with loans exhibited higher levels of stress.

Referenced in: Modules 4.3, **4.6,** 5.4

For further reading:

Karlan, Dean, and Jonathan Zinman. 2011. "List Randomization for Sensitive Behavior: An Application for Measuring Use of Loan Proceeds." *Journal of Development Economics* 98 (1): 71–75.

———. 2011. "Microcredit in Theory and Practice: Using Randomized Credit Scoring for Impact Evaluation." *Science* 332 (6035): 1278–1284.

Evaluation 14: Teacher Performance Pay: Experimental Evidence from India

Authors: Karthik Muralidharan and Venkatesh Sundararaman
Location: Andhra Pradesh, India
Sample: 500 schools
Timeline: 2004–7

Public spending on education has increased significantly in the past decade, but there are substantial inefficiencies in the public delivery of education services. In the Indian state of Andhra Pradesh, teachers' salaries and benefits make up over 90 percent of primary education expenditures, but the rate of absenteeism among teachers is high.

Researchers used a randomized evaluation to investigate whether basing teachers' pay on students' test scores leads to improved teacher and student performance and how this impact varies with school-level versus individual incentives. Teachers in treatment schools were offered bonus payments on the basis of their students' average improvement in math and language test scores, with the average bonus around 3 percent of a typical teacher's annual salary. In group-incentive schools, all teachers received the same bonus based on average school-level improvement in test scores, while the bonus for teachers in individual-incentive schools was based on the average test score improvement of students taught by a specific teacher.

The results suggest that paying teachers based on students' performance is very effective in improving student learning. At the end of the second year of the program, students in incentive schools scored higher on math and language tests than those in comparison schools (0.28 and 0.16 SD higher, respectively). Students in incentive schools also scored higher in science and social studies, for which there were no incentives, suggesting that there were positive spillover effects. School-level group incentives and teacher-level individual incentives performed equally well in the first year of the program, but the individual-incentive schools significantly outperformed the group-incentive schools in the second year. However, there was no reduction in teacher absenteeism in incentive schools.

Referenced in: Modules 4.4, **9.2**

For further reading:

Muralidharan, Karthik, and Venkatesh Sundararaman. 2011. "Teacher Performance Pay: Experimental Evidence from India." *Journal of Political Economy* 119 (1): 39–77.

Evaluation 15: Reshaping Institutions: Evidence on Aid Impacts Using a Pre-Analysis Plan

Authors: Katherine Casey, Rachel Glennerster, and Edward Miguel
Location: Bonthe and Bombali Districts, Sierra Leone
Sample: 236 villages and 2,382 households
Timeline: 2005–9

Community-driven development (CDD) programs give grants to local communities to provide local public goods while also seeking to strengthen local systems of participation and accountability. The Government of Sierra Leone piloted such a CDD program (called GoBifo, or "Move Forward" in Krio) as a way to help rebuild infrastructure and promote the inclusion of women and youth in decisionmaking following 10 years of devastating civil war. Researchers, the World Bank, and the government's Decentralization Secretariat collaborated to evaluate this pilot.

Communities from two ethnically and politically distinct districts were randomly assigned to either the treatment or the comparison group. Villages in the treatment group received US$5,000 in grants and were regularly visited by a GoBifo facilitator who helped community members create or revamp village development committees (VDCs), set up bank accounts for the VDCs, establish transparent budgeting practices, and create village development plans that included specifics on how GoBifo grants would be used. The inclusion and participation of marginalized groups in the decisionmaking process were central to the project.

In addition to household surveys, three structured community activities (SCAs) were administered to assess levels of collective action, the participation of minorities, and elite capture. The SCAs were designed to measure how communities responded to concrete, real-world situations in three areas in which GoBifo had sought to change behavior: (1) raising funds in response to a matching grant opportunity, (2) making a community decision between two comparable alternatives, and (3) allocating and managing an asset that was provided for free.

GoBifo villages had a larger stock of higher-quality local public goods, such as a primary school or community grain-drying floor, than did comparison areas. There was also more market activity in treatment communities, including the presence of more traders and items for sale.

There is no evidence that the program led to fundamental changes in local institutions or decisionmaking. Despite the fact that many women in treatment villages participated in GoBifo decisions, they were no more likely to voice opinions in community meetings after the project ended or to play leadership roles in other areas. Nor were treatment communities more successful in raising funds in response to the matching grant opportunity.

Referenced in: Modules **5.4**, 8.3

For further reading:
Casey, Katherine, Rachel Glennerster, and Edward Miguel. 2011. "The GoBifo Project Evaluation Report: Assessing the Impacts of Community Driven Development in Sierra Leone." http://www.povertyactionlab.org/evaluation/community-driven-development-sierra-leone.
———. 2012. "Reshaping Institutions: Evidence on Aid Impacts Using a Pre-Analysis Plan." *Quarterly Journal of Economics* 127 (4): 1755–1812. doi: 10.1093/qje/qje027.

Evaluation 16: Returns to Secondary Schooling in Ghana

Authors: Esther Duflo, Pascaline Dupas, and Michael Kremer
Location: Ghana
Sample: 2,068 students
Timeline: 2006–18

With substantial increases in the proportion of children in sub-Saharan Africa completing primary school, there is pressure to increase government expenditure on and access to secondary education. Yet evidence of the economic and social returns to secondary education is sparse. In Ghana the direct costs of fees and materials (around US$350 over four years in Ghana) are a major barrier to attending secondary school.

Researchers are evaluating the long-term (10-year) impacts of scholarships on secondary school enrollment and the returns to secondary education in Ghana. Six hundred eighty-two students were selected (by lottery) to receive scholarships that covered 100 percent of the tuition and fees at local public senior high schools. The scholarships were announced during the 2008/9 academic year, and more than 75 percent of the scholarship winners enrolled in senior high schools that year, almost four times the number of the comparison group. Most of them were expected to graduate in June 2012.

Data will be collected through 2018 on labor market outcomes, health, marriage and fertility, time and risk preferences, technology adoption, and civic participation. Because follow-up data are not yet available, lessons on the impact of increased access to secondary education cannot yet be drawn.

Among scholarship winners (the treatment group), the enrollment rate was 75 percent in the school year 2008/9, almost four times that of the comparison group. Three years later, the enrollment rate was still twice as high among those who received scholarships compared to those who did not, at 73 percent overall (81 percent among boys and 64 percent among girls).

Referenced in: Modules **8.1–8.3,** 9.2

For further reading:

Innovations for Poverty Action. "Returns to Secondary Schooling in Ghana." New Haven, CT. Accessed January 3, 2013. http://www.poverty-action.org/project/0077.

Numbers in parentheses at the end of each definition are the modules in which the term is used. Boldface indicates the module(s) in which the term is discussed in most detail.

adverse selection: The increased likelihood that those with a higher risk of a bad outcome will choose to participate in a program rather than those with a low risk. Individuals know their risk, but program implementers cannot tell the risk of those individuals. (**4.3**)

allocation ratio or **fraction:** The proportion of people within a given sample randomly allocated to receive a program. (**4.3–4.5,** 6.1–6.4, 8.2)

anticipation effect: A change in behavior of a comparison group because they expect to receive access to the program later on (or in a rotation design where those in the current treatment group change their behavior because they know they are going to become the comparison group later). (4.3, **7.4**)

attrition: The absence of data because the researchers are unable to measure all or some outcomes of some of the people in the sample. (**4.2**–4.5, 5.4, 6.5, **7.2**–7.4, 8.2, 9.1)

baseline: A measurement made before the start of a program that can serve as a comparison with later measurements. (1.1, 2.2, 2.4, 4.3–4.5, **5.2,** 5.4, 6.1, 6.3–6.4, 7.2, 7.4, 8.2–8.3, 9.1, 9.3)

before/after comparison: A research approach that measures how outcomes for program participants changed from before the introduction of the program to after the program has been in operation for some time. (**2.2**)

Bonferroni adjustment: An alteration of the confidence intervals around coefficients to adjust for the fact that several different hypotheses are being tested. (**8.2**)

causal impact: Any change in outcome that is caused by a program; the difference between an outcome with the program and the outcome that would have been seen in the absence of the program. (**2.1**, 2.3, 2.4, 3.3, 9.2)

comparison group: People who are used to identify what would have happened in the absence of a program. In a randomized evaluation it consists of those randomly chosen not to receive access to a program. (1.1, **2.1**, 5.2, 9.1)

compliance: Study participants' adherence to their assigned treatment regime. (1.2, **4.2**, 6.1, 6.4, 7.1, 7.4, 8.2, 9.1)

conditional cash transfer: Cash that is offered on the condition of participants' complying with specific socially desirable behaviors. (**2.4**, 3.2, 4.1, 6.4, **9.4**)

confidence interval: A range of values around an estimated value (e.g., an estimated effect size) within which the true value is likely to fall. The confidence interval depends on the significance level chosen. (**6.1**, 8.2)

cost–benefit analysis: An approach to comparing the costs and benefits of different programs in which all the different benefits of a program are translated onto one scale (usually a monetary scale) and then compared to the costs of the program. (3.1, **9.3**)

cost-effectiveness analysis: An examination of the cost to achieve a given impact on a particular indicator that is used to compare different programs that have the same objective measured using the same indicator. (3.1, 6.3. **9.3**, 9.4)

counterfactual: A conditional statement of how the people in a program would have fared if the program had never been implemented, which is used to understand the causal impact of the program. (**2.1**, 2.3, 2.4, 3.1, 4.2, 4.3, 7.3, 8.2)

critical value: The level of an estimated measure (e.g., treatment effect) that exactly corresponds to the significance level. Anything above this is statistically significantly different from zero at the significance level (e.g., at the 95 percent level); anything below it is not. (**6.2,** 6.3)

cross-section comparison: *See* **simple difference comparison.**

data mining: Looking for the result one wants in the data until one finds it. (**8.3**)

defiers: Individuals or groups who do not take up a program because they are allocated to the treatment group or do take it up because they are allocated to the comparison group; that is, those who defy the assignment made by the evaluators. (**7.1,** 8.2)

demand effects (aka **response bias**): Participants' change in behavior in response to their perception of the evaluators' objective. (7.1, **7.4**)

descriptive survey: An examination that describes the current situation but does not attempt to answer causal questions about why the situation is as one finds it. (**3.1**)

difference-in-difference: A research approach that combines a before/after comparison with a participant/nonparticipant comparison. It measures changes in outcomes over time of the program participants relative to the changes in outcomes of nonparticipants. (**2.2,** 2.3)

dummy variable: A factor that takes the value of either zero or one; that is, a special type of binary variable. (4.5, **8.1,** 8.2)

encouragement design: A research plan in which both treatment and comparison groups have access to the program but some individuals or groups are randomly assigned to receive encouragement to take up the program. (**4.3,** 4.5, 5.2, 6.5, 8.2)

endline: Measurement at the end of a study. (1.1, 2.2, 2.4, 4.3. 4.5, 5.2, 6.1, 6.3–6.4, 8.2–8.3, 9.1)

evaluation-driven effects: Changes that occur when an evaluation itself, and the way in which it is administered or the way its outcomes are measured, affect the way people behave—for example, Hawthorne and John Henry effects. (**7.4**)

exact matching: An evaluation approach in which participants are compared to at least one nonparticipant who is identical on selected observable characteristics, that is, characteristics for which the researchers have data, such as age and occupation. Participants who have no direct match are dropped from the analysis. (**2.2**)

exclusion restriction: An assumption that must hold if any instrumental variable strategy, including an encouragement randomization strategy, is to be valid. It states that the instrument can affect the outcome only through its effect on the instrument. In other words, the instrument cannot have a direct effect on the outcome. (**4.3**)

exogenous shocks: Events that generate variation in conditions across a study area and are not correlated with any underlying condition or characteristic of the population they affect. They allow us to discern causal relationships. (**2.2, 2.4,** 6.2, 6.3)

experimental protocol: A plan that describes intentions for treatment allocation, program and evaluation implementation, and data collection logistics. (2.3, 3.3, 4.2, **7.1,** 8.3)

externalities: *See* **spillovers.**

external validity (aka **generalizability**): The acceptability of the results of an evaluation in terms of supporting the intended point or claim in contexts other than those in which the experiment was conducted. (2.4, 4.4, **9.2**)

false positive (aka **Type I error** or **alpha error**): A result that occurs when researchers find a statistically significant effect of a program even though the program did not actually have an impact, causing them to wrongly infer that the program had an effect. (**6.1**–6.2)

false zero (aka **Type II error**): An effect that occurs when researchers fail to find a significant effect even though there truly is a treatment effect, causing them to wrongly infer that the program does not work. (**6.1**–6.2)

general equilibrium effects: Changes in outcomes (such as prices and wages) that are determined by the pressure to equalize forces (usually demand and supply) derived from interactions across many people. (2.4, **4.2, 7.3**)

generalizability: *See* **external validity.**

Hawthorne effect: A change that occurs when a treatment group works harder than normal in response to being part of an evaluation; an example of an evaluation-driven effect. (**7.4**)

heterogeneous treatment effect: A change that occurs when the results of a program are different for different subgroups in a population. (**8.1**)

implicit association test: An experimental method that relies on the idea that respondents who more quickly pair two concepts in a rapid categorization task subconsciously associate those concepts more strongly. It can be used to test for prejudice. (5.1, **5.4**)

imprecise zero: An effect that results when researchers can rule out neither a large effect nor a zero effect because their confidence bands are very wide. (**3.3**, 6.1)

indicator: An observable metric used to measure outcomes. (1.2, 1.3, 4.3, 4.4, **5.1**)

institutional review board (IRB): A committee that reviews research proposals to ensure that they comply with ethical guidelines and whose permission is required before research involving people (human subjects) can proceed. (**2.4**, 4.2, 5.4)

instrument: The tool used to measure indicators. (**5.1–5.4**)

instrumental variable: A factor that does not suffer from selection bias and is correlated with the outcome variable that allows researchers to estimate the causal impact through one very specific channel. (**2.2**, 4.6, 8.2, 8.3)

internal validity: The acceptability of the results of an evaluation in terms of the causal impact of the intervention. (8.2–8.3, **9.2**)

intertemporal correlation: A measure of how correlated outcomes for individuals are over time. (**6.4**)

intracluster correlation: A measure of how much more correlated those within a cluster are compared to those in different clusters; a key component of the design effect, which is a measure of how much less precise the researchers' estimate is, for a given sample size, when they move from an individual-level randomization to a group- or cluster-level randomization. (**6.2–6.3**)

John Henry effect: A comparison group's change in behavior in response to being part of an evaluation. (**7.4**)

matched randomization: A procedure in which two units are matched on a list of important characteristics and then one of them is randomly assigned to a treatment group and the other to a comparison group. (**4.4**)

midline: A measure taken in the middle of a study. (6.4)

minimum detectable effect (MDE): The smallest change in an outcome that a given evaluation design will be able to detect with a given probability. Researchers choose their sample size so as to be able to achieve an MDE. (6.2, 6.3, **6.4**)

monotonicity assumption: The requirement that when an encouragement design is used, everyone must be affected by the encouragement in the same direction. (**4.3**)

moral hazard: Lack of incentive to avoid risky behavior when one is insured against risk. (**2.3**)

multivariate regression: A statistical approach in which the correlation between an outcome and several different factors is assessed. The relationship between the factors and the outcome can be interpreted as causal only if the variation in the factor is exogenous (in other words, caused by some random factor). (**2.2**)

needs assessment: Research that carefully collects descriptive information, both qualitative and quantitative, about problems that may exist and the needs of the population a program is designed to serve. (**3.1**)

noncompliance: Failure to follow a randomized treatment assignment; that is, those assigned to treatment end up not receiving the program or those assigned to the comparison group receive the program. (**7.1**, 9.1)

null hypothesis: An assumption that the treatment effect is zero for all subjects; it is designated H_0. (**6.1**, 6.2)

one-sided test: An examination in which one looks for either a positive impact or a negative impact of a program but not for both at the same time. (6.2, **8.3**)

outcome: The level of a variable that is used to measure the impact of a program. (**5.1**–5.4)

oversubscribed: A program that has more people interested in participation than the program has resources to serve. (**4.1**)

phase-in design: A research plan in which people are selected to enter into a program at different times. (**4.3**, 5.2, 7.2, 7.4)

power: *See* **statistical power.**

power function: An equation relating statistical power to its determinants: (1) the level of statistical significance, (2) the minimum detectable effect size that practitioners and policymakers care about, (3) the variance of the outcome of interest, (4) the proportion of units allocated to the treatment, (5) the sample size, and, if performing a group-level randomization, (6) the size of the group and (7) the intracluster correlation. (6.1, **6.3**, 6.4)

pre-analysis plan: A proposal that describes, ahead of time, how the data from a study will be analyzed to address concerns about data mining. (8.2, **8.3**)

process evaluation: Research that uses qualitative or quantitative methods to assess whether a program is being implemented as planned. There is no attempt to examine the impact of the program. (**3.1**)

proof-of-concept evaluation: A test of whether an approach *can* be effective in the best possible situation even if that is not the form in which the approach would be implemented when scaled up. (**3.3**)

purchasing power parity (PPP): The exchange rate at which we could purchase a standard basket of goods in two countries. (**9.3**)

randomization cells: The divisions into which eligible units are assigned by means of random selection. In a simple evaluation that measures the impact of a program, the list of eligible units is randomly selected into two cells: treatment and comparison. In more complicated evaluations, the units may have to be assigned to more than two cells. (**4.4**)

randomization device: The method used to randomize eligible units. This can be mechanical (a coin, die, or ball machine), a random number table, or a computer program with a random number generator. (**4.4**)

randomized assignment: Taking a pool of eligible units—persons, schools, villages, firms—and then allocating those units to treatment and comparison groups by means of a random process such as a toss of a coin, a random number generator, or a lottery. (**2.3**, 4.1, 4.3, 8.2)

random number table: A list of unique numbers that are randomly ordered. (**4.4**)

random sampling: Selection of units from a population in an unpredictable manner to create a group that is representative of the entire population. Characteristics of this group can then be measured to infer the characteristics of the entire population. (2.3)

regression discontinuity design: An evaluation approach that can be used when a program has a strict eligibility cutoff based on measurable criteria, allowing a comparison of outcomes for those just above and just below the eligibility cutoff. (**2.2**)

research hypothesis: A supposition that the effect of a program is not zero. (**6.1**)

residual variance: A divergence in measured outcomes between people (or units) that cannot be explained by the program or any control variables (e.g., gender or age) that may be used in research analysis. (**6.3**)

respondent: The person or group of people that researchers interview, test, or observe, to measure given indicators. (**5.1**)

rotation design: A research plan in which everyone needs to receive a program but resources are too limited to treat everyone at once so groups take turns receiving the program. (**4.3**)

sample size: The number of units on which data are collected in the evaluation or a research program. (**6.1**, 6.3, 6.4)

sampling frame: A list of eligible units from which participants in the study are drawn. (**4.4**, 4.6)

selection: The process by which participants in a program are determined. (**2.1**)

selection bias: The tendency for an estimated effect to be different from the true effect in a particular direction because of researchers' failure to take into account the tendency for those who receive a program to be different from those who do not receive the program. (**2.1–2.3**, 5.2)

simple difference comparison (aka **cross-section comparison**): A measure of the difference between program participants and nonparticipants after the program has been initiated. (**2.2**)

simple random assignment: Random allocation of individuals from a large pool of eligible units to different groups. (**4.4**)

social desirability bias: The tendency of study participants to give an answer to a question that is in line with social norms even if this does not accurately reflect their experience. (**5.3**)

spillovers (aka **externalities**): A program's effects on those who are not in the program. Spillovers can take many forms and can be positive or negative. (3.1, **4.1**, 4.5, 7.3)

standard deviation: A measure of dispersion from the mean in the underlying population from which subjects are sampled. (**6.1**–6.5)

standard error: A measure of the precision of the estimated size of an effect (the larger our standard error, the less precise our estimate). Formally, the standard error of a sample is equal to the standard deviation of the underlying population divided by the square root of the sample size. (**6.1**, 8.3)

statistical matching: Comparing program participants to a group of nonparticipants that is constructed by finding people whose observable characteristics (e.g., age, income, education) are similar to those of the treatment group. (**2.2**)

statistical power: The likelihood that an experiment will be able to detect a treatment effect of a specific size. For a given minimum detectable effect size and level of significance, power is a measure of how precisely the researchers will be able to measure the impact of the program. (**6.1**–6.5)

stratification or **stratified random sampling:** An assignment method in which the pool of eligible units is first divided into strata or groups based on observable characteristics and then the procedure for random assignment is followed within each stratum. (**4.4**, 4.5, 6.4)

subgroup: Any group of individuals in a sample with at least one common characteristic established prior to the start of the program. (**8.1**, 8.2)

survey effects: Any change of behavior of a treatment or comparison group caused by being surveyed. (**7.4**)

t-test: A statistical examination that determines whether two variables are statistically different from one another (often used to determine whether an estimated coefficient or effect is statistically different from zero). (4.4, 6.1, 8.1)

theory of change: A supposition made at the beginning of a program specifying the steps in the pathways through which the intervention(s) could lead to an impact. (1.2, **5.1,** 8.3, 9.2)

treatment density: The proportion of people within a unit (a school, a community, a marketplace) who receive access to a program (i.e., are included in the treatment). (4.2, **4.5,** 4.6)

treatment group: Those who were randomly chosen to receive access to a program. (**2.1,** 5.2, 9.1)

treatment lottery: A research design in which units (individuals, households, schools, etc.) are randomly assigned to the treatment and comparison groups. The treatment group is given access to the program; the comparison group is not. (**4.3**)

true difference: The dissimilarities that researchers would find (on average) if they ran the perfect experiment an infinite number of times. (**6.2**)

true positive: The situation when researchers find a statistically significant treatment effect and the program does in fact work. (**6.1**)

true zero: The situation when researchers find no statistically significant treatment effect and the program does not work. (**6.1**)

undersubscribed: A program whose take-up is low and the program is serving fewer people than it has resources to cover. (**4.1**)

variable: A numeric value of an indicator. (2.2, **5.1**)

INDEX

Page numbers for entries occurring in boxes are followed by a *b*, those for entries in figures, by an *f*, those for entries in notes, by an *n*, and those for entries in tables, by a *t*. Page numbers in *italics* refer to modules that discuss work to which the author contributed.

spillover effects on, 314, 315; statistical matching of, 35–36; take-up rates in, 47; unobservable differences with treatment groups, 28, 35, 38–39, 47. *See also* allocation fractions; evaluation effects; random assignment

compliance: defiers, 138, 300, 301–3, 306, 343–44; documenting, 305–6, 389; dropping noncompliers, 346–47, 390–91; importance of, 300–303; increasing, 296, 303–5, 389; partial, 292–93, 298–303, 341–49, 389, 390–91; by program staff, 116, 299–300, 304; randomization levels and, 116–17, 304–5; rates of, 326; statistical power and, 292–93, 296

computer-assisted interviewing, 197–98, 325

computerized randomization devices, 146, 147, 148f, 149. *See also* software

conditional cash transfer (CCT) programs, 81–82, 83, 103, 406, 407t, 412–13, 433–34

confidence intervals, 89–90, 246, 370, 391–92, 405–6

CONSORT guidelines, 160

control variables, 260, 295, 297, 329–31

cost-benefit analysis, 399–402, 405

cost-effectiveness analysis: advantages of, 399, 401–2; comparative, 399–410; cost calculations in, 402–3; cross-country comparisons, 403–4, 406–8; discount rates in, 403; examples of, 79–80, 399, 400f, 406–8, 407t, 409f; issues in, 402–5; methodologies of, 78; with multiple outcomes, 404–5; projections, 275–76; sensitivity analysis of, 77–78, 402–3, 405–10; use of, 77–78, 79, 399

counterfactuals, 24–25, 27–28. *See also* comparison groups

covariates, 329–31. *See also* control variables

credit scores, 107, 139, 165–66, 235–36, 438. *See also* microfinance

Crépon, Bruno, *161–79*, 179, 432

critical values, 256–57, 257f, 258f, 262–63, 263f

cross-country evaluations: cost-effectiveness analysis, 403–4, 406–8; generalizability of, 393–94

crosscutting questions, 86–87

cross-section comparisons, 33–34

Das, Jishnu, 232

data analysis: cleaning data, 325–27; common pitfalls in, 390–92; examples of, 18–19; plotting and describing, 327; transparency of, 51. *See also* intention-to-treat analysis; pre-analysis plans

data collection: of baseline data, 53, 198–99, 312, 335; common pitfalls in, 388–89; costs of, 53–54; enumerators of, 195–98, 212; error prevention in, 325–26; from existing sources, 54, 149–50, 190–92, 211; field testing of, 210–12, 311; limiting attrition in, 311–13; locations of, 202; methods for treatment and comparison groups, 209–10; plans for, 14–16; for process evaluations, 73; randomization methods and, 201–2; statistical power and, 294–96; terminology of, 181t; timing and frequency of, 198–202, 212, 282–84, 295, 312–13. *See also* nonsurvey instruments; surveys

data mining, danger of, 373–74, 376–77

Deaton, Angus, 96

defiers, 138, 300, 301–3, 306, 343–44, 391n

demand effects, 306, 317, 319

descriptive methodologies, 68–72

housing voucher programs, 49, 105, 369, 428–29

Humphreys, Macartan, 230

hypothesis testing: confidence levels, 249–51; critical values, 256–57, 257f, 258f, 262–63, 263f; effect sizes, 255–60, 256f; minimum detectable effect, 257–59, 259f; with multiple outcomes, 366–71; null hypothesis, 247–49; one-sided, 257, 257f; possible cases, 249–51, 250f; research hypothesis, 247, 248; treatment effects, 247–48, 251, 256–57; two-sided, 268; Type I errors, 249; Type II errors, 251; use of, 246–47, 253–55

IATs. *See* implicit association tests

ICS. *See* International Child Support

IIT. *See* intention-to-treat analysis

impact evaluations: appropriate use of, 68, 81–84; case study of, 95–96; costs of, 53–54, 94–95; field partners for, 92–94; funding of, 94–95; prioritizing questions for, 84–95; qualitative, 29–31; questions for, 81–84; registering, 374–75, 417; reporting results, 417–18. *See also* randomized evaluations

impact questions, 68

impacts: definition of, 24; measurement of, 24–28. *See also* outcomes

implicit association tests (IATs), 233–35

incentives. *See* encouragement

incognito enumerators, 217

India: castes in, 233; constitution of, 184–86, 436; doctors in, 231–32; education in, 6–7, 209–10, 233; health interventions in, 95–96, 103, 221; industrial pollution in, 214; investment in girls in, 221; police responsiveness in, 215–16; remedial education in, 104; social networks in, 239–40; standardized tests in, 230–31; teacher performance pay in, 143, 439; voter education in, 112; women as village council leaders in, 106, 184–90, 189t, 224–25, 232–33, 234–35, 396, 436–37. *See also* remedial education evaluation

indicators: case study examples of, 183–90; definition of, 181t, 182; desktop assessment of, 202–10; detectable, 204; exclusive, 206–7; exhaustive, 205–6, 206f; feasible, 204; field testing of, 210–12; indices, 368, 390; in literature, 182–83; logically valid, 181, 203; mean standardized treatment effects, 369; measurable, 203–4, 205t; observable, 204; precise, 205–6; proxy, 208–9; reliable, 207–10, 388; specification of, 180–82

individual-level randomization: statistical power and, 267–70, 269f; steps in, 109, 110f. *See also* randomization levels

Indonesia: corruption in, 217, 219; deforestation in, 223; road construction projects in, 219

inference: causal, 24–28; randomization, 360; statistical, 249–51

informed consent, 60, 61–62, 118, 215

Innovations for Poverty Action, 76, 415, 416–17

insecticide-treated (bed) nets (ITNs): distribution tasks, 73; evaluation design, 53–54, 82, 141, 429; free distribution of, 55, 227, 411–12, 429–30; target populations of, 316; user fees for, 55, 429–30

institutional review boards (IRBs), 60, 64, 118, 215

instrumental variables, 41–43, 344–45, 378

instruments: cultural contexts of, 211; definition of, 181t; field testing, 210–11, 311. *See also* surveys

intention-to-treat (ITT) analysis: with attrition, 349–54; average treatment effect estimates, 327–29; covariates in, 329–31; data preparation for, 324–27; with group randomization, 356–61, 391; interaction terms, 333–35; with multiple observations, 335–37; with multiple outcomes, 366–71, 374; with multiple treatment groups, 337–39; outcomes analyzed, 339–40; with partial compliance, 341–49; with spillovers, 354–56; with stratified randomization, 362–66; with subgroups, 331–33, 343, 371

intention-to-treat (ITT) effects, 327–29

interaction terms, 333–35

International Child Support (ICS) Africa: Extra Teacher Program of, 87–88, 162–63, 164f, 425–26; HIV education program of, 104, 114, 115; randomized evaluations of, 1–2; women's self-help groups of, 63. *See also* Primary School Deworming Project

International Growth Centre, 418

International Initiative for Impact Evaluation (3ie), 75–76, 374–75

interventions. *See* programs

intracluster correlation, 283–84

IRBs. *See* institutional review boards

iron supplementation, 116–17

ITNs. *See* insecticide-treated nets

Jamaica, early childhood studies in, 353–54

Jamison, Julian, 229

Jensen, Robert, 221

job placement assistance programs, 59, 178–79, 432

John Henry effects, 317, 318–19, 321

J-PAL (Abdul Latif Jameel Poverty Action Lab), 4, 65, 76, 401–2, 416–17, 418

justice principle, 61, 62

Karlan, Dean, *161–79*, 166, 236, 438

Katz, Lawrence, *340–72*, 428–29

Keniston, Daniel, 216

Kenya: natural springs protection in, 52; water purification program in, 201, 220, 320–21, 323. *See also* insecticide-treated nets; Primary School Deworming Project

Kenya, education in: Extra Teacher Program, 87–88, 162–63, 164f, 425–26; impact evaluations in, 1–2, 87–88, 104, 114, 150, 161–65, 312, 396, 425–26; school-based management in, 162, 163–65, 426; teacher attendance in, 200–201; textbook use in, 331, 414. *See also* HIV education

Khemani, Stuti, *3–23*

King, Elizabeth, *98–108*, 434–35

Kling, Jeffrey, *340–72*, 428–29

Kothari, Dhruva, 96

Kremer, Michael, 1, *98–108*, *140–53*, *161–79*, 165, 169, 192, 220, 226, *324–85*, 410–11, 423–24, 425–26, 427–28, 434–35, 441–42

labor. *See* employment

lawmaking, 88–89

Lee bounds, 352–53

levels of randomization. *See* randomization levels

Levi, Santiago, 412–13

Liberia, collective action in, 229–30

Liebman, Jeffrey, *340–72*, 428–29

Lind, James, 48b

Linden, Leigh, *161–79*, 170, 231, 233, 424–25

Lipeyah, Paul, 1

list randomization, 235–36
literature reviews, 73–77, 95–96
logistics, feasibility and, 119
lotteries. *See* treatment lotteries

malaria. *See* insecticide-treated nets
Malawi: conditional cash transfers in, 83; HIV testing in, 223, 227
Manski-Horowitz bounds, 352
Massachusetts Institute of Technology (MIT), 4. *See also* Abdul Latif Jameel Poverty Action Lab
matched pairs, 159–60, 363, 391
McKenzie, David, 160
MDE. *See* minimum detectable effect sizes
mean standardized treatment effects, 369
measurement: alternatives, 375–76; issues in, 89; randomization levels and, 111–12. *See also* indicators; instruments
mechanical randomization devices, 144–45
mechanical tracking devices, 221–22
Medicaid, 104, 125
medical research: clinical trials, 48b, 123, 373, 374, 377; ethical guidelines for, 64, 123
Medicare, 121
medicine: biomarkers, 220–21; diagnostic skills, 231–32. *See also* health care; HIV
Mexico: emissions test cheating in, 237; PROGRESA program, 103, 406, 407t, 412–13, 433–34
MFIs. *See* microfinance institutions
microfinance: credit score use in, 107, 139, 165–66, 235–36, 438; impact evaluations of, 50, 82, 90–91; personal use of business loans, 235–36; randomized evaluations of, 109–10; spillover effects of, 348, 349

microfinance institutions (MFIs), 103–4
Miguel, Edward, *161–79*, 169, *212–40*, 220, 410–11, 423–24, 440–41
minimum detectable effect (MDE) sizes, 257–59, 259f, 268–70, 273–77, 279, 292–93
MIT. *See* Massachusetts Institute of Technology
moral hazard, 139
Moving to Opportunity program, 49, 369, 428–29
Mullainathan, Sendhil, 216, 220
multistage experiments, 138–39
multivariate regression, 34–38
Muralidharan, Karthik, *392–98*, 439
mystery clients, 214–16

needs assessments, 68–72, 95
NERICA. *See* New Rice for Africa
network effects, 237. *See also* social networks
Network of Networks on Impact Evaluation (NONIE), 417
New Rice for Africa (NERICA), 266–67
NGOs. *See* nongovernmental organizations
nonexperimental methods: before-and-after (pre/post) comparisons, 31–33; cross-section comparisons, 33–34; difference-in-difference comparisons, 38–39; multivariate regression, 34–38; qualitative, 29–31, 70; regression discontinuity design, 39–41; statistical matching, 35–38; use of, 57
nongovernmental organizations (NGOs), 1–2, 3, 92–94, 415
NONIE. *See* Network of Networks on Impact Evaluation
nonsurvey instruments: biomarkers, 220–21; cheating checks, 236–37; direct observation, 212–19; games, 228–30; implicit association tests,

pre-analysis plans (PAPs) (*continued*)
timing of, 379–81; usefulness of,
375–77, 385
Primary School Deworming Project
(PSDP), Kenya: evaluation of,
166–69, 423–24; expansion of, 2;
need for, 70; phase-in design of,
107, 167, 168, 202; results of, 2, 56;
spillover effects of, 409–10; theory
of change in, 397–98, 410–11
prioritizing questions, 84–95
probability. *See* statistical concepts
process evaluations, 72–73
process questions, 68
Programa de Ampliación de
Cobertura de la Educación
Secundaria (PACES), 434
programs: admission cutoffs of, 107;
costs of, 119; designing, 8–10,
102–3; entitlements, 121; evolution
of, 102–4; expansion of, 85–86, 104;
implementation of, 17–18, 416–17;
maturity, 91–92; oversubscription
of, 105; phased admissions of, 107;
pilots, 12; popular, 85; procedural
variation in, 296; process evaluations of, 72–73; representative,
90–91; scaling up, 86, 398, 408–10,
411, 414–15; undersubscription of,
105–6. *See also* compliance;
spillovers; treatment groups
program staff: absenteeism of, 6,
22, 69, 72; compliance by, 116,
299–300, 304; evaluating, 72;
involvement in evaluations, 93,
196, 305, 322, 388; skills of, 86,
398
PROGRESA program, Mexico, 103,
406, 407t, 412–13, 433–34
propensity score matching, 36, 37
proxy indicators, 208–9
PSDP. *See* Primary School
Deworming Project
PSI. *See* Population Services
International

public health impact evaluations, 91.
See also Primary School
Deworming Project
purchase decisions, 226–28
p-values, 248

qualitative methods, 29–31, 70
quantile regressions, 340
questions: crosscutting, 86–87;
descriptive, 67–68; impact, 68;
for impact evaluations, 81–84;
prioritizing, 84–95; process, 68;
strategic, 67

RAND Corporation, 145
random assignment: advantages of,
44, 47; balance checks for, 149–51,
151t; distinction from random
sampling, 45b; eligible units for,
141–43, 146; ingredients of, 141;
paired, 158–60; simple, 146–49;
steps in, 45–47, 46f; stratified,
152–58, 155f, 160–61, 293–94,
362–66; to treatment groups,
44–47, 99, 120; treatment lotteries,
120–28. *See also* allocation
fractions
randomization: of access to treatment, 44–47, 99, 120; best practices
in, 160–61; of encouragement to
participate, 100–101, 101f, 105–6;
ethical considerations in, 122–23,
126–27, 135, 138; examples of,
12–13, 13t, 161–79; fairness of, 65,
116, 118–19, 125; opportunities for,
101–7, 102t; program aspects for,
98–99; re-, 152–53; of timing of
access, 99–100, 100f
randomization devices: computerized, 146, 147, 148f, 149; mechanical, 144–45; random number
tables, 145
randomization levels: attrition and,
115–16, 310–11; choosing, 108–11,
112t, 291–92; compliance and,

Topalova, Petia, *180–90*, 233, 235, 436–37
Townsend Thai Survey, 50
tracking devices, 221–22
treatment densities, 115, 178–79
treatment effects: average, 327–29, 341–43, 344–49, 364–66, 365t; on compliers, 341–43, 344–49; heterogeneous, 331–33; hypothesis testing, 247–48, 251, 256–57; mean standardized, 369; weighted, 364–66, 365t
treatment groups: balanced, 149–52, 151t, 154, 199; comparability with comparison groups, 47, 154, 301, 307–10, 321, 322; eligibility criteria for, 107, 123–28, 166; interactions with comparison groups, 113–15; number of, 143–44, 290–91, 337–39; paired matching, 159–60, 363, 391; random assignment to, 99; rotation of, 106; statistical matching of, 35–36; take-up rates in, 47; timing of access to treatment, 99–100, 100f; unobservable differences with comparison groups, 28, 35, 38–39, 47. *See also* allocation fractions; compliance; random assignment
treatment lotteries: around cutoffs, 123–28, 128f; ethical considerations in, 122–23, 126–27; use of, 120–22
Type I errors, 249
Type II errors, 251

Uganda: community accountability in, 5–6, 22; women's programs in, 229
unemployment. *See* employment
United Kingdom, tax collection in, 191–92
United States: deworming programs in, 56, 410; employment discrimination in, 216; entitlement programs in, 121; housing voucher

programs in, 49, 105, 369, 428–29; Medicaid, 104, 125; Medicare, 121; retirement savings decisionmaking in, 105–6, 170–74, 435–36; welfare reform in, 121n
US Department of Housing and Urban Development, 49, 105, 428–29
US National Commission for the Protection of Human Subjects, 60–61
units of randomization. *See* randomization levels
Uttar Pradesh (UP). *See* remedial education evaluation

validity: ensuring, 386–92; of indicators, 181–82, 203; internal, 392, 393. *See also* generalizability
variables: control, 260, 295, 297, 329–31; definition of, 181t; instrumental, 41–43, 344–45, 378; for stratified random assignment, 155–58, 160. *See also* indicators
variance: residual, 259–60, 281–82; sampling, 259–60
VDCs. *See* village development committees
VECs. *See* village education committee
Vietnam-era military draft, 106, 144, 145, 335–36, 336f
Vietnam veterans, 54
vignettes, 231–33
village development committees (VDCs), 440
village education committee (VECs), 7, 8–9, 11, 12, 14, 20

Wald estimator, 342–43
WDRs. *See* World Development Reports
weighted average treatment effects, 364–66, 365t
Weinstein, Jeremy M., 230

Western Electric Company,
Hawthorne effects, 317–18, 321,
322
WHO. *See* World Health
Organization
women, as political leaders, 106,
184–90, 189t, 224–25, 232–33,
234–35, 396, 436–37
women's empowerment programs,
Bangladesh: data analysis of,
338–39, 339f; delayed marriage
incentives in, 174–78, 378, 431;
evaluation of, 430–31; modules of,
304, 338, 384; results of, 56;
tracking participants of, 312–13
Work and Iron Status Evaluation,
116–17
World Bank: conditional cash
transfer programs and, 413;

Development Impact Evaluation
Initiative, 75, 417; World
Development Reports, 4, 75
World Bank Participation Sourcebook,
9
World Development Reports (WDRs),
4, 75
World Economic Forum, 411
World Health Organization (WHO),
167, 412
worms. *See* deworming programs;
Primary School Deworming
Project

Zambia, water projects in, 79–80
Zamora, Philippe, *161–79*, 179, 432
Zinman, Jonathan, *161–79*, 166, 236,
438
Zwane, Alix Peterson, 220

CPSIA information can be obtained
at www.ICGtesting.com
Printed in the USA
JSHW031527200323
39190JS00001B/18